# The Kosovo T

## THE HUMAN RIGHTS D

EDITORIAL TEAM

Ken Booth
*Editor*


with
Alex J. Bellamy, Ian R. Mitchell and Patricia Owens
*Assistant Editors*

---

## Related Books

**Peacebuilding and Police Reform**
Tor Tanke Holm and Espen Barth Eide (eds.)

**Peacekeeping and the UN Agencies**
Jim Whitman (ed.)

**Peacekeeping and Conflict Resolution**
Tom Woodhouse and Oliver Ramsbotham (eds.)

**Peace Operations between War and Peace**
Erwin A. Schmidl (ed.)

**Beyond the Emergency: Development within UN Missions**
Jeremy Ginifer (ed.)

# The Kosovo Tragedy

## THE HUMAN RIGHTS DIMENSIONS

*Editor*

## Ken Booth

**FRANK CASS**
LONDON • PORTLAND, OR

*First published in 2001 in Great Britain by*
FRANK CASS PUBLISHERS
Newbury House, 900 Eastern Avenue, London IG2 7HH

*and in the United States of America by*
FRANK CASS PUBLISHERS
c/o ISBS, 5824 N.E. Hassalo Street
Portland, Oregon 97213-3644

*Website* http://www.frankcass.com

British Library Cataloguing in Publication Data

The Kosovo tragedy : the human rights dimensions
1. Human rights – Serbia – Kosovo  2. Kosovo (Serbia) –
History – Civil War, 1998–
I. Booth, Ken
323'.094971

ISBN 0 7146 5085 4 (cloth)
ISBN 0 7146 8126 1 (paper)


Library of Congress Cataloging-in-Publication Data:

The Kosovo tradgey : the human rights dimensions / editor Ken Booth.
   p. cm.
   This group of studies first appeared in a special issue of the
International journal of human rights, Vol. 4, nos. 3/4 (Autumn/
Winter, 2000).
   Includes bibliographical references and index.
   ISBN 0-7146-5085-4 – ISBN 0-7146-8126-1 (pbk.)
   1. Kosovo (Serbia)–History–Civil War, 1998–    . 2. Human
rights–Yugoslavia–Kosovo (Serbia)  3. Kosovo (Serbia)–Politics and
government. I. Booth, Ken, 1943–    . II. International journal of
human rights. v. 4, nos. 3–4 (Special number)
   KZ6795.K68 K67 2001
   323.4'9'094971–dc21
                                                                00-065626

This group of studies first appeared in a special issue of the
International Journal of Human Rights [ISSN 1364-2987] Vol.4, Nos.3/4
(Autumn/Winter, 2000) published by Frank Cass and Co. Ltd.

Printed in Great Britain by Antony Rowe Ltd., Chippenham, Wiltshire

# Contents

Preface      ix

Introduction: Still Waiting for the Reckoning      *Ken Booth*    1

### PART ONE: PERSPECTIVES

1. Genocide: Knowing What It Is
   That We Want to Remember,      *Tim Dunne*
   or Forget, or Forgive      and *Daniela Kroslak*    27

2. The History and Politics of
   Ethnic Cleansing      *Carrie Booth Walling*    47

3. Rape in War: Lessons of      *Caroline Kennedy-Pipe*
   The Balkan Conflicts in the 1990s      and *Penny Stanley*    67

### PART TWO: PROLOGUE

4. Warnings from Bosnia: The Dayton
   Agreement and the Implementation of
   Human Rights      *Marianne Hanson*    87
5. Human Wrongs in Kosovo, 1974–99      *Alex J. Bellamy*    105

6. OSCE Verification Experiences in Kosovo:
   November 1998–June 1999      *William G. Walker*    127

PART THREE: WAR

7. Reflections on the Legality and Legitimacy
   of NATO's Intervention in Kosovo      *Nicholas J. Wheeler* 145

8. The Kosovo Refugee Crisis: NATO's
   Humanitarianism versus Human Rights      *Jim Whitman* 164

9. International Humanitarian Law and
   the Kosovo Crisis      *Hilaire McCoubrey* 184

10. The Kosovo Indictment of the International
    Criminal Tribunal for Yugoslavia      *Marc Weller* 207

PART FOUR: AFTERMATH

11. From Rambouillet to the Kosovo Accords:
    NATO's War against Serbia and Its Aftermath      *Eric Herring* 225

12. The Ambiguities of Elections in Kosovo:
    Democratisation versus Human Rights?      *Ian R. Mitchell* 246

13. 'Post-Conflict' Kosovo: An Anatomy Lesson
    in the Ethics/Politics of Human Rights      *Jasmina Husanovi*      263

PART FIVE: FORUM
Is Humanitarian War a Contradiction in Terms?

A Qualified Defence of the Use of Force for
'Humanitarian' Reasons      *Chris Brown* 283

Can There Be Such a Thing as a Just War?      *Melanie McDonagh* 289

The 1999 Kosovo War through a
South African Lens      *John Stremlau* 295

No Good Deed Shall Go Unpunished      *Colin S. Gray* 302
Air Power and the Liberal Politics of War      *Tarak Barkawi* 307

Ten Flaws of Just Wars      *Ken Booth* 314

'Humanitarian Wars', Realist Geopolitics and
Genocidal Practices: 'Saving the Kosovars'          *Richard Falk*  325

PART SIX: DOCUMENTS

United Nations Convention on the Prevention and Punishment
of the Crime of Genocide                                          337

Resolution 1160 (1998). Adopted by the Security Council at
its 3868th meeting, on 31 March 1998                              341

Resolution 1199 (1998). Adopted by the Security Council at
its 3930th meeting on 23 September 1998                           345

Interim Agreement for Peace and Self-Government in Kosovo,
23 February 1999                                                  349

Proposal of the Parliament of Serbia for Self-Governance in
Kosovo and Metohija, 20 March 1999                                363

Military Technical Agreement, 9 June 1999 between the
International Security Force ('KFOR') and the Governments
of the Federal Republic of Yugoslavia and the Republic of Serbia  364

Resolution 1244 (1999). Adopted by the Security Council at
its 4011th meeting, on 10 June 1999                               369


Notes on Contributors                                             376

Index                                                             379

# Preface

The conflict in, around and above Kosovo in 1999 has been described as being as significant for international politics as the pulling down of the Berlin Wall. Its significance derives from many things, including evidence of NATO's ambitions, the implications for the future of the United Nations, the role given to air power and the evident military limitations of the European Union. But at the heart of the significance of Kosovo's history in recent times – in the build-up, conduct and aftermath of the NATO bombing campaign in 1999 – has been the issue of human rights.

An international group of specialists – nine nationalities in all – discuss key and controversial aspects of the human rights dimensions of the Kosovo tragedy, including: analysis of concepts such as 'genocide' and 'ethnic cleansing'; accounts of the wrongs done to the victims in Kosovo; examination of the run-up to the war in 1999; the background of the earlier experiences in Bosnia; description of the way the war was fought; speculation about the implications for human rights of what has developed since the bombing campaign stopped; and debate about the possible lessons to be learned from what has been called – sometimes with pride, sometimes with irony – the 'first humanitarian war'.

In preparing this volume, a number of debts have been incurred. The first is to Frank Barnaby, the founder and editor of *The International Journal of Human Rights*. When I suggested to him that he might organise the journal's first Special Issue around the human rights dimensions of the war that was then controversially taking place in the Balkans, he readily agreed; and straight away volunteered me to do it. As on other occasions over the years, I have never ultimately regretted any of the experiences for which Frank has so cheerfully volunteered me. Once again I have learned a great deal, and most importantly that 'Kosovo' is not simply a Balkan or even a European matter; it is of global significance. At the start of a century that will see a further shrinking of time and space, and simultaneously the predictable overloading of all human and environmental systems, Kosovo tells us critical things about the practice of international politics, and asks us fundamental questions about global issues.

I want to thank several people at Frank Cass for entrusting me with this first Special Issue of *The International Journal of Human Rights*, especially Stewart Cass and Cathy Jennings. As desk editor of the journal, Cathy has been everything an academic editor would wish: supportive, professional, a source of good advice, sympathetic towards the inevitable glitches – and, crucially, flexible with the deadlines.

Thanks go to the *South African Journal of International Affairs* for permission to reprint the essay by John Stremlau, 'The 1999 Kosovo War through a South African Lens', originally published in Summer 2000, Vol.7, No.1, pp.131–7; to *Politikon*, for permission to borrow heavily from my 'The Kosovo Tragedy: Epilogue to Another "Low and Dishonest Decade"', originally published in Summer 2000, Vol.27, No.1, pp.5–18; and to *Civil Wars* for permission to use extracts from my 'NATO's Republic: Warnings from Kosovo', originally published in Autumn 1999, Vol.2, No.3, pp.89–95.

The task of editing this volume would have been heavier without the assistance of several present and former graduate students in the Department of International Politics at the University of Wales, Aberystwyth. In the summer of 1999, helping to get everything started, I would like to thank Lars Christoffersen, Aoibheann O'Keefe, and Fleur Van Der Schalk. Particular thanks are due to the three members of the editorial team: Alex J. Bellamy, Ian R. Mitchell and Patricia Owens. In addition to helping comment on and edit the drafts, they collected the documents, Alex and Ian wrote chapters, and Patricia compiled the index. Elaine Lowe, the Departmental Secretary, coordinated the papers as efficiently and helpfully as ever. Thanks also go to Antony Smith of the Geography and Earth Sciences department, for drawing the map of the former Yugoslavia.

Finally, I want to thank the contributors, each of whom was extremely busy with life as well as work, and in several cases suffered serious illnesses in the course of the project. One must be mentioned. It is with great sadness that I record that Hilaire McCoubrey died shortly after completing his chapter, at a terribly early age. When he told me one day that he was 'struggling' to complete his contribution I had no idea of the full import of his message. To all the contributors, but especially Hilaire McCoubrey, I want to record my debt for setting precious time aside because they shared my belief in the significance of the human rights dimensions of the Kosovo tragedy.

KEN BOOTH

The Federal Republic of Yugolsavia, 1999

# Introduction:
# Still Waiting for the Reckoning

## KEN BOOTH

The contagion of human wrongs and the need for human rights were constants in the unfolding of the tragedy of Kosovo through the 1990s. Today, a year after the fighting started – even though Milosevic lost the war, NATO triumphed and an international protectorate oversees the reconstruction – nobody believes that ethnic harmony, the rule of law and human security are imminent in the province. A comprehensive exploration of the human rights dimensions of the Kosovo tragedy therefore requires little justification.

The contributions to this volume do not present a comprehensive history of the embattled land of Kosovo. This is an important task that some have already attempted, and on which others are now working. Rather, the volume explores the central human rights aspects of the conflict that attracted world attention in 1999. In particular, it attempts to offer perspectives on some of the key (and often controversial) concepts relating to human rights, such as 'genocide', 'ethnic cleansing' and 'rape in war'; it discusses the most important human rights lessons from the recent past in Bosnia; it examines the evidence of human wrongs leading up to the outbreak of fighting between NATO and Serbia; it outlines the human rights dimensions of the war and the negotiations that took place just before and just after it; it interrogates the lawfulness and legitimacy of NATO's 'humanitarian' actions and the part played by outsiders in dealing with – and perhaps intensifying – the refugee crisis; and it looks at the problems and prospects on the ground in Kosovo in terms of the development of human rights in the months since June 1999, when Kosovo became an international protectorate. The main essays are followed by a forum in which a range of authors offer contending viewpoints about what Adam Roberts originally called 'humanitarian war': is it a contradiction in terms? Finally, there is a selection of key documents of direct relevance to the discussion of human rights in Kosovo.

Despite such wide coverage, it has not proved possible to address every dimension of human rights, or every opinion, and none of the contributors has been able to explore their subject areas to the depth they would have ideally desired. Nevertheless, the breadth of the coverage, together with the references and documentation, provides an advanced and comprehensive analysis of this complex, controversial and critical area of collective human behaviour. Furthermore, there is no party line among the contributors, save for an agreement that what happened and is happening in Kosovo is of enormous significance for the way people(s) think and act in relation to the global contagion of human wrongs and the desperate need for human rights.

## THE SIGNIFICANCE OF KOSOVO?

Almost as soon as it began, NATO's bombing campaign over Kosovo in 1999 was believed by its opponents and supporters alike to be an event of outstanding international importance. The British Foreign Secretary later described it as being of comparable significance to the dismantling of the Berlin Wall ten years earlier. What is in dispute is not its significance, but the precise character of that significance.

The recent history of Kosovo raises some of the most fundamental issues in contemporary world affairs: the responsibilities of 'outsiders' when terrible abuses of human rights are taking place within other countries; the meaning and limits of sovereignty under present conditions; the way governments think about security; the political and military constraints and practicalities when it comes to trying to intervene; the appropriateness of military force for humanitarian purposes; the implications for relations between intervening states and those which on principle and pragmatics oppose them; and the question of whether the war over Kosovo would be the first 'humanitarian war' or the last. Kosovo asks these fundamental questions: its interpreters give a range of answers.

Some of the short-term implications of the Kosovo war are readily apparent and relatively uncontroversial when compared with questions about the longer term. For example, the war had an immediate impact on the domestic politics of several countries. It was a distraction that helped President Clinton slip through 'Monicagate' less damaged than he might otherwise have been. On the other hand, it could severely damage his

Democrat successor were a disaster to occur affecting US personnel in Kosovo in the period before the November 2000 presidential election. In Russia, old fears were provoked by NATO's determination to use force against Serbia in the absence of explicit UN authorisation; this came on top of a decade of organisational expansion eastwards, and thus strengthened traditional preferences for a tough and nationalistic leader in Moscow.

In international politics, NATO's rhetoric and actions with respect to Kosovo in the spring and early summer of 1999 made it more difficult for the so-called international community to continue to stand aside (as it disgracefully had for nearly a quarter of a century) when Indonesia's control over East Timor came to crisis point in the late summer of the same year. Shortly afterwards, Russian forces pounded Grozny as part of their renewed attempt to subdue Chechnya; the leaders of the Western states were perhaps less comfortable than would otherwise have been the case in preaching about killing civilians, had they not done the same in Serbia and Kosovo not long before, albeit in different circumstances.

During the 1990s NATO had lost its Soviet empire and not yet found a role. Kosovo gave the alliance the opportunity to develop a new rationale and strengthen the confidence of its supporters. But the outcome was not entirely positive. The war – and specifically the failure to finish it off as speedily as had been predicted – spoiled the alliance's fiftieth birthday celebrations in Washington in April 1999. There were other problems. The different interests, outlooks, and material commitments of the United States and the Western European allies raised awkward questions – still unanswered – about burden-sharing. Within Western Europe itself, doubts were raised about the future ability of the EU to become a serious actor in world affairs, especially as long as its military potential remained limited. The actual military operations and the equipment used by NATO forces will continue to be minutely examined in order to learn lessons about tactics and technology; and without doubt, the campaign will have been highly profitable for defence contractors, and especially those at the most expensive high-tech end of the market. The war for some time to come will be used as a counter-argument against pressures to reduce force levels or defence budgets.

In addition to these implications for external actors in the conflict, there have obviously been direct effects on the politics and economics of south-eastern Europe. These include questions about: the continuing instability of the region while Milosevic's regime survives; the prospects for security without the cooperation of Serbia; the shift in international attention and material support from Bosnia to Kosovo; the future of Montenegro within the Federal Republic of Yugoslavia (FRY); the

degraded GNPs of the countries caught up in the war; the implications
for neighbouring territories if the Kosovar Albanian restoration results in
a new sovereign state pressing for a Greater Albania; and all the problems
of reconstruction within Kosovo itself, from disposing of the unexploded
munitions to rebuilding houses, from policing the streets to building an
effective civil society, and from varieties of dependence on external
agencies to constructing a new polity based on the rule of law.

If some short-term consequences, implications and questions thrown
up by the war are clear, the long-term significance of Kosovo for the
unfolding of world politics is a matter for intense speculation. What does
Kosovo signify for the future authority of the United Nations? For the
potential drift from a 'cold peace' to a Cold War between a NATO-led
West and the rest? For US global interventionism? For the employment
of NATO as the military arm of a benign liberal imperialism? And what
do the events of 1999 in the Balkans signify for human rights? For
regional organisations in dealing with humanitarian crises? For ideas
about the responsibilities of outsiders to the victims of sovereign power?
For the use of force as a continuation of human rights politics? For the
acceptability of inconsistency and hypocrisy in the way governments deal
with human rights emergencies? As we stretch into the future, 'Kosovo'
asks more questions than it answers.

Uncertainty certainly surrounds the future of the territory itself.
Whatever one's views about the wisdom of NATO's war against Serbia,
pessimism quickly became the prevailing mood following its cessation.
The triumphal entry of KFOR into the bomb-damaged province in June
1999 was not followed by the province's triumphant reconstruction.
Instead, the return of the ethnically cleansed Kosovar Albanian refugees
was followed by the ethnic cleansing of the Kosovar Serbs under the eyes
of KFOR; the latter's inability to create a comprehensive system of law
and order postpones the construction of an effective human rights
culture. And ultimately, there has to be some resolution of the meaning
for Kosovo of its so-far vaguely defined status: 'autonomy within the
Federal Republic of Yugoslavia'. The situation in Kosovo today, under the
dark shadow of the recent past, burdened by multi-level current problems
and facing a future of uncertainty, can be no consolation to any onlooker,
including those who predicted that a bad peace would follow from a
misjudged war.

For an unpredictable period ahead, Kosovo will remain a land of
question marks. Answers, as they emerge, will be shaped by what one
thought about the validity of the use of force by NATO in 1999.
Likewise, views about the military campaign will be retrospectively
affected by one's verdict about the success, or otherwise, of the

international protectorate in bringing about a satisfactory transformation in post-conflict Kosovo, from a place symbolising human wrongs into a land practising human rights. For the moment, expectations are low. If this continues, one wonders how long it will be before some Western politicians, journalists and intellectuals – including some of the foremost champions of militant humanitarianism in 1999 – will be writing articles calling on NATO and the UN to declare the victory over Milosevic's regime as complete, announce the completion of the task of implementing self-government in Kosovo in the context of an acceptable level of local security, and then withdraw their military contingents from Kosovo, leaving it, as in earlier periods of history, at the mercy of the balances and imbalances of local power.

## THE KOSOVO TRAGEDY

Students of human rights must believe that it is possible to recognise and learn from the warnings evident in the outbreak, course and aftermath of the Kosovo war. For this reason alone, it must never become a forgotten war. The most important warning of all may be overlooked because of the attention that is normally demanded by the fire and fury of war – in this case the clinical airborne fire on the part of NATO and the ethnic fury of Serb forces on the ground. This warning is that Kosovo was a tragedy that might have been avoided.

The main title to this volume – *The Kosovo Tragedy* – was not chosen lightly. The history of Kosovo can be conceived as a 'tragedy' in all senses, from the everyday meaning of 'terrible outcome' to the classical conception of a drama whose final mayhem is determined by the fatal flaws of the participants. In a traditional conception of 'tragedy', the war in 1999 was obviously the culmination of a dramatic and disastrous series of events, with serious moral significance. This is still clearly the case, albeit in a less newsworthy fashion. It was a drama with an unhappy but meaningful end: all were losers. The only consolation some could find is that the outcome was not as unhappy as it might have been. Like all tragedies in a classical, Shakespearian sense, the story of Kosovo was a conflict in which the protagonists were engaged in a struggle with themselves as well as others, and in which plans and hopes were always likely to be subverted by a fatal flaw. Rugova's Ghandianism, Serbian nationalism, Albanian solidarity and Western liberalism all had high ideals, in their different ways, but each had its own fatal flaw. For Shakespeare, such fatal flaws meant that a tragedy was a catastrophe destined to happen.

The fundamental political question for analysts is whether Kosovo was really a tragedy in this latter, classical, sense. Could something have been done to have changed the collision course of the contending 'flaws' of the key players? Were the flaws, in fact, 'fatal' (and so unchangeable) or simply 'well established' (and hence amenable in principle to change)? My own preference is to eschew the attribution to Kosovo of the classical definition of tragedy, with its sense of inevitability, as blighted characters move with preordained certainty to an unhappy ending. This is a conclusion about politics I want to avoid, and believe that history supports this view, though some of history's sub-plots have always done their best to try and suggest otherwise. Kosovo is best understood not in the classical (deterministic) definition of a tragedy, but in the ordinary sense of a disastrous series of events whose outcome is of serious moral significance. From this latter perspective, things could have been done to change the course of the story; instead, governments, speaking the words of old scripts, took fatefully wrong decisions at key moments through the 1990s and earlier. Different political scripts would have produced different decisions. Getting governments to learn new scripts is often difficult, but history shows that it is not impossible – particularly, sadly, following catastrophes.

The moral significance of the Kosovo tragedy will be particularly distressing if nothing is learned from the recent past; that is, if all the suffering comes to nothing in terms of the security of the people(s) of the Balkans. It will be equally distressing if the key players interpret the tragedy in the classical sense, and draw the conclusion that what will be will be. Historical fatalism – the idea that the region is necessarily dominated by ancient enmities, bound to continue for ever – would be the worst outcome. Such a mixture of realist conservatism and human nature pessimism will be self-fulfilling.

The politics and international politics of the Balkans have been prone to the handing down of old scripts, but new ones exist and can be learned. This goes for those outside the region, as well as those within. I do not wish to hide or minimise the personal and political responsibility of any of the local perpetrators of human wrongs in the story of the disintegration of Yugoslavia, and this is especially the case with those elites and leaders who manufactured this human tragedy of historic proportions. Nevertheless, we should also recognise the responsibilities of the Western powers over time in helping to create the context in which it took place. This is another dimension of the tragedy. People and governments, sometimes for good reasons, sometimes for bad, involved themselves and made things worse.

The unhelpful role of extra-regional states – today euphemistically called the 'international community', in the past more truthfully labelled and capitalised as the 'Great Powers' – is the theme of Misha Glenny's book *The Balkans 1804–1999: Nationalism, War and the Great Powers.*[1] The book explains that a great deal of the suffering in the Balkans since the start of the nineteenth century, though obviously not all of it, has been the result of the interference and ambitions of outside powers – acting individually or collectively. A pattern of meddling in and withdrawal from Balkan politics developed; the nations of the region were used and then abandoned. This book, like other lengthy studies,[2] shows that explanations of the history of the region in terms of factors such as 'ancient hatreds' is too simple, though bloodletting and historical myths cannot be ignored. Who was killing whom, and why, is a very complex matter and resists crude headlines. Why the people(s) of the region for long periods were able to live together is as interesting as why sometimes they did not; but peace gets paragraphs whereas conflict is the stuff of chapters.

The problem remains the meaning given to history, and here unscrupulous politicians and others, as ever, manipulate the past for their own purposes. Ethnic hatreds and 'eternal enemies' do not have to be historically true, to be real; they only have to be politically believable. And it is not difficult in conflicts, as Glenny's book underlines, to believe that the current enemy is the eternal enemy.

Part of the tragic story of the Balkans, therefore, must focus on the players that have entered from the wings – literally so in 1999. The long history of external intervention in the Balkans has been one of Machiavellianism and miscalculation, of indifference and intervention. What happened in 1999 and since is no different. In the decade or so leading up to the ethnic cleansing of the Kosovar Albanians by the Milosevic regime, the international community – in the shape of the Western powers – played a role in both the disintegration of Yugoslavia and in the unfolding of the Kosovo crisis. Both these histories are long and complicated, and tell us much about the prevalence of human wrongs and the difficulties facing human rights. In the case of the disintegration of Yugoslavia, one lesson is the importance of the way economic factors can shape the context of human rights, and in the case of Kosovo's tragedy, another points to how easily opportunities can be missed. Putting these two together, we can see once more the historic pattern of liberal Great Power capitalist politics: a deadly dialectic of indifference and intervention.

For the purposes of this Introduction, there is a twenty-year, a ten-year and a five-year history of Yugoslavia/Kosovo to consider. The twenty-year history consists of the West's changing relationship with Yugoslavia, from that of the Cold War to the more complex one following Gorbachev's accession to power in 1985. As the most prominent member of the 'awkward squad' among eastern Europe's socialist countries, Yugoslavia long enjoyed a special position in Western Cold War thinking. With the collapse of the Soviet experiment, Yugoslavia lost the geopolitical status it had developed in a bi-polar world, and with it went its economic privileges. In addition to losing its advantages in attracting Western credits, Yugoslavia became exposed to intense competition and IMF conditionality, like other struggling states in the new era of neo-liberal domination. The changes in the structures and ideology of global power coincided with the worsening of long-predicted nationalist stresses and strains. In Tito's Yugoslavia of 'Brotherhood and Unity', the land of the southern Slavs was a carefully balanced polity; it survived, even flourished, despite the problems within (such as the domination of Serbia) and the attractions without (such as the desire of some to join the 'normal' states of the European community). Over the twenty-year period, Western interest in Yugoslavia during the Cold War was quickly followed by Western indifference. Then, in 1999, this part of the continent was re-discovered, and variously described by Western leaders as Europe's 'doorstep' or 'heart'.

The ten-year history of Kosovo is one of missed opportunities on the part of the West to try to steer it away from the denouement threatened by the rehearsing of old scripts. As Milosevic's oppression of the Albanian Kosovars intensified after 1989, specialists on the region tried to draw attention to the dangers, but Western governments had other pre-occupations, both globally and in relation to the increasingly violent politics of the disintegrating state of Yugoslavia. In these circumstances, what was happening in Belgrade was much more important for them than what was happening in Pristina. What was happening in Kosovo was the construction of an apartheid state. In response, a posture of non-violence was adopted by the Albanian Kosovars under the leadership of Ibrahim Rugova. The Western powers were more concerned with the regime in Belgrade than the Albanians in Kosovo, where Serb oppression continued to grow, leading to the rise of a 'terrorist' challenge on the part of some Kosovar Albanians. In 1996 the first Serbs were killed by the *Ushtria Climitare e Kosoves* (UCK)/Kosovo Liberation Army (KLA); the stage was now set for the biggest escalation in violence yet.

The five-year recent history of Kosovo/Yugoslavia was opened by the Dayton Peace Agreement. As the situation in Kosovo deteriorated, the West learned the wrong lessons about the use of air power in Bosnia, guilt deepened about the massacre of Muslims at Srebrenica, the implementation of Dayton on the ground in Bosnia did not proceed as well as had been hoped and the urge to do something strengthened. This urge became part of the politics and psychology of the two most prominent leaders of the Western alliance. For the beleaguered and anti-Vietnam War President of the United States, Bill Clinton, the opportunities to cut a dash in history were running out, while for the new Prime Minister of the United Kingdom, Tony Blair, Kosovo was an opportunity to demonstrate what an ethical foreign policy might look like, both for Britain and the 'international community'. The deadly dialectic was working again, as the Western powers shifted from indifference to interventionism.

We cannot know whether different Western policies in recent years could have helped to construct a multi-ethnic Kosovo, with human rights and democracy, and security and the rule of law. At least in the short run, such a benign result now looks very unlikely. What can be said about the post-June 1999 situation is that state/Belgrade/Serb violence against the Albanians has stopped, and so the majority (virtually mono-ethnic) population has now some hope of living in reasonable security for as long as the protectors remain. When they are gone, Kosovo will have to face the threat of Serb forces on its borders looking for revenge, unless by that point the politics of Belgrade have been radically transformed by progressive civil society. This (temporary) security of the Albanian Kosovars is the result of the withdrawal from the battlefield of Serb forces in the face of massive NATO power, and then the flight of the Kosovar Serb minority in the face of the vengeance of the liberated Albanian majority.

Force often seems to have the last word in international affairs, but at the most it can do only so much. NATO's air power, backed by the threat of a ground invasion, helped stop some human wrongs in Kosovo; but it cannot vindicate human rights in the sense of creating a polity there in which all its inhabitants (pre-March 1999) can live together in peace, and flourish. The latter requires a Yugoslav or Kosovo state, part of a Balkan-wide security community, in which all the traditional ethnic groups in the province can become so confident in the embedding of Europe-wide standards of governance, security and human rights that all the refugees would want to return. It would be a polity with a common belief in a predictably peaceful future, based on a culture of democracy that was not a creature of ethnic politics. This is not an impossible scenario, but today it seems like a dream; it is not one likely to result from the policies of today's power brokers in the region.

Looking back over the events of the last quarter of a century from the present vantage point, there is a strong temptation to interpret the unfolding events of the Kosovo tragedy with a sense of inevitability. But was it really a classical tragedy – a catastrophe destined to happen – or was it a familiar sort of tragedy in international politics – a catastrophe that could have been avoided? We know how it ended, and this pulls us towards the view that what happened had to happen. But hindsight also helps us to see potential turning-points – turning-points indeed that some wise heads pointed out at the time. We know the old scripts which led some leaders and groups to particular outlooks and decisions. But we also know there were other scripts and other choices. To reject an open-ended view of history is to replicate a political fatalism that flies in the face of experience. It constitutes historical denial. If key players in the politics and international politics of south-eastern Europe think in fatalistic ways, then the Kosovo tragedy, in one form or another, will be replayed.

Encouragement that the history of the region is not pre-destined, forever doomed to cycles of bloodletting, can be taken from the realisation that positive change can take place in international politics. What once seemed to be a situation of inevitable conflict can within a short (historical) time be consigned to the past. In 1940 a war-free Western Europe based on democracy and economic integration was not an impossible scenario, but it was a dream. When we think of the radical change in the relationship between France and Germany between 1940 and 1950, or between the white supremacists and the black majority in South Africa between 1985 and 1995, or between Protestants and Catholics in Northern Ireland during the 1990s, we might reject the conclusion that the identity politics of the Balkans are bound indefinitely to be characterised by violence.

## HUMAN RIGHTS DIMENSIONS

Readers will note a range of opinions among the contributors below in their interpretation of events and ideas, and about what could have and should have been done in Kosovo in 1999, and in previous (and subsequent) years. The contributions have been organised into six parts, in a broadly chronological framework, though there is inevitably overlap between the sections. Pasts, presents and futures do not come in neat packages; sometimes in the Balkans, as elsewhere, there is nothing so future-oriented as an argument about the past.

The aim of Part One, Perspectives, is to open up discussion about several highly charged issues: genocide, ethnic cleansing and rape in warfare. The attitudes and behaviour that these words label has deformed human history. Their manifestations have by no means been unique to the twentieth century, though the recent past has witnessed some of their most terrifying outbreaks – including the Balkans. More positively, it has only been since the Second World War that such behaviour has been named and criminalised by what passes for international society. This is no consolation to past victims, but it does represent some sort of progress in the development of what has been called a 'human rights culture',[3] and may limit the number of victims in future. Although the concepts discussed in Part One became part of everyday political language in the 1990s, the three essays here attempt to uncover some of their theoretical and historical complexities. In this part Kosovo is used as an illustration rather than the focus for definitive judgement about these deforming practices, though the authors do not always eschew judgement.

The first contribution addresses the act – genocide – that more than any in history shocked humanity's conscience into recognising the need to put human rights at the centre of the international arena. The 1948 Genocide Convention made genocide a crime, and sought to prevent and punish it. In practice, the record of enforcement by the international society of states has failed to match the aspiration of those who, in the aftermath of the Nazi Holocaust, cried 'Never again'. Tim Dunne and Daniela Kroslak discuss the debates surrounding the meaning and interpretation of the Convention, with particular reference to its silences and ambiguities, and to the differences between those they call the 'restrictionists' and those they call the 'expansivists' in terms of its application. These perspectives are discussed with relation to Kosovo, and the authors conclude that it is problematic to label as 'genocide' the violent conduct of the Milosevic regime towards the ethnic Albanians. This verdict is not meant to minimise the terrifying behaviour of Milosevic's forces and paramilitaries in Kosovo; rather it is a judgment on the meaning of the Convention. An important conclusion of the authors is that the concept of genocide will continue to be stretched, unhelpfully, until international law recognises ethnic cleansing for the particular crime it is.

Ethnic cleansing is the subject of the contribution by Carrie Booth Walling. She shows that territorial dispossession on the basis of ethnic characteristics has had a long history, and is not uniquely related to the 1990s and the Balkans. 'Cleansings' of one sort or another have taken place since antiquity, and though they have not always been on an ethnic basis, they have always been associated with extreme brutality. The essay shows that the 1990s were marked not only by the prominence given to ethnic cleansing in the world's news headlines, but also by a normative shift against such conduct. The latter represents a historic landmark. The essay argues that ethnic cleansing has been closely tied not only to elite power politics in different countries, but also to the rise of the ideal of the nation-state and associated principles relating to national self-determination and sovereignty (including security). While all these motivations persist, the satisfactory development of relevant international law will be limited. The latter will also be complicated by the close and ambiguous relationship between the concepts of ethnic cleansing and genocide. All genocides involve ethnic cleansing, but not all ethnic cleansings involve genocide: ethnic cleansing is the use of ethnic terror to bring about territorial dispossession, not the attempt to eliminate an ethnic group as a collective – though obviously terror will involve some elimination, and here we have to consider the ambiguous terrain of 'genocidal acts'. The essay argues that ethnic cleansing, for the present, remains a term of politics, not law. It is a practice that involves a range of criminal offences relating to the spreading of ethnic terror, but there is not a specific crime called 'ethnic cleansing'.

One practice that creates and spreads terror, and has through history, is the gendered terror of rape in war. Caroline Kennedy-Pipe and Penny Stanley argue that rape has been one of the traditional realities of war, but one which for the most part has been shrouded in silence. It was only as a result of the media representation of mass rape in the Balkan conflicts in the 1990s that its extent and true horror began to be revealed – though much inevitably remains in dispute. Rape is the most personal of crimes, and the subject of much controversy in the context of domestic law. It is unsurprising, therefore, that the circumstances of war complicate even more than usual the vexed questions surrounding rape, relating to motivation, accurate reporting, the identification of perpetrators and ultimately the carrying out of due process and conviction. The authors point to some positive developments: consciousness of the phenomenon has been widely raised, it is now on the international agenda for discussion and action, and alleged perpetrators have been brought to justice. However, they think that we are far from the time when rape in war is likely to disappear; nor has international society reached that stage of development in which all or even most of those who commit it are likely to suffer appropriate punishment.

Part Two, Prologue, sharpens the focus of the volume onto the Balkans, and examines important human rights dimensions in the period leading up to the start of NATO bombing in March 1999. Together, the contributions here help us think about the ostensible lessons of the recent past, and the dynamics leading up to the war. Marianne Hanson examines what has happened in Bosnia, and in particular in the period since the Dayton Peace Accords in 1995, as a way of offering warnings about the difficulties that are and will be faced in implementing human rights in Kosovo. The overall picture she presents is not encouraging, because the extent of the progress with respect to the implementation of human rights in Bosnia has been disappointing. It is true that the fighting has stopped, and that freedom of movement has been a notable achievement, but ethnic integration has not been forged, minority returns have been limited, ethnic violence continues, and democratic elections have reinforced ethnic divisions. Against the background of the recent past, and everybody's inexperience of dealing with such situations, it would have been unwise to have expected an easy ride. The need for reform is readily apparent in several areas. While recognising the relevance of the situation in Bosnia to today's situation in Kosovo, the essay emphasises that, as ever, it is unwise simply to attempt to draw across from one case to another. There are differences as well as similarities between the two conflicts, the chief one being that those responsible for running the international protectorate in Kosovo today can learn from the experiences of Bosnia. The essay ends with the admonition that the international protectors in Kosovo cannot now use the excuse of lack of experience, as did their counterparts who moved into Bosnia after Dayton.

It is the scale and character of the human rights abuses in Kosovo over several decades that is the subject of the contribution by Alex J. Bellamy. In 1999 the world's headlines for a period were dominated by what was happening in Kosovo, and most people seemed unaware that this was a tragedy whose dynamics had been accelerating for a decade, and developing for a generation. The essay traces these dynamics back to the major turning point of the 1974 Yugoslav Constitution. The situation in Kosovo started to deteriorate as Serb chauvinists began a systematic campaign against the Kosovar Albanians. It started in the form of propaganda, which included efforts to dehumanise the Albanians; it proceeded through the removal of their political, social and economic rights; and then culminated in direct physical violence. For a period in the early 1990s, the Kosovar Albanians attempted to cope with their deteriorating situation by a strategy of non-violence. Through this period, the international community ignored Kosovo, and specifically the worsening plight of the Kosovar Albanians. Faced with brutality from Belgrade and marginalisation by the international community, the ethnic Albanian population turned to violence themselves. This formed the immediate background to the conflagration in 1999.

The rapidly deteriorating situation on the ground was the background to the focus of the contribution from Ambassador William G. Walker, the head of the OSCE Kosovo Verification Mission (KVM), who gives his personal views on the mission that went into the province in November 1998 to monitor the human rights crisis. He examines the establishment of the mission, its (not explicit) human rights mandate, the difficulties it faced, and then what it did 'in exile' following its withdrawal after 19 March 1999. Among its initial problems were the difficulties involved in finding trained human rights verifiers, and then the difficulty of maintaining a position of neutrality once its work had begun. Although the Ambassador accepts that the Mission ultimately ended in failure, he argues that it did make a difference for several months with respect to monitoring a wide range of human rights abuses, together with its 'aggressive' pursuit of factual human rights reporting in Kosovo. These activities were obviously not likely to make the KVM appear neutral in the minds of the regime in Belgrade. The latter was the key; it was the extent of Milosevic's ambitions in Kosovo that was the root of the KVM's ultimate failure. Although the Mission failed, the author concludes that it helped to reveal the centrality of human rights abuses in the continuing crises in Kosovo, achieved some positive results in the short term, and learned some valuable lessons with respect to human rights verification.

Part Three turns to War, and addresses four sets of issues relating to the fighting in 1999, though each predated the bombing and has important implications for international relations in general. These issues are: the legality and legitimacy of NATO's bombing campaign, the rights of refugees and the responsibilities of outsiders, the laws-of-war aspects of NATO's military strategy, and the significance of the indictments by international tribunals for individual war crimes.

Nicholas J. Wheeler discusses issues of legitimacy and legality with respect to NATO's intervention in Kosovo – issues that are crucial in relation to the debate about the justification, or lack of it, for NATO's use of military force on a massive scale on behalf of human rights. The issues are crucial not only in relation to this case but in relation to the precedents set for other regional organisations when faced by similar problems. The discussion is based on the distinction between 'solidarism' and 'pluralism' in international society – between those wanting to promote a more collectivist international society and those wanting to leave authority and norms based firmly in the hands of separate sovereign states. A policy of humanitarian intervention clearly fits more comfortably within the norms of the former than within those of the latter. During the Cold War, pluralist norms dominated. Humanitarian interventions took place, controversially, in particular human rights crises, with some opinion thinking them legitimate, though not legal. In the period since the end of the Cold War more solidarist practices and attitudes have emerged, and the essay discusses in particular whether Kosovo represents a watershed in terms of the norm of humanitarian intervention in international society. It is argued that NATO's case for military intervention was stronger in terms of legitimacy than legality, but that nevertheless Kosovo does represent something of a landmark in terms of international law, though not the undisputed precedent some have argued. As a precedent for future international action on behalf of human rights, the author concludes that Kosovo's significance relates to NATO's future action in relation to Europe only, and not beyond, though it may be significant for other regional organisations in other continents.

These issues of legality and legitimacy surrounding NATO's military campaign in 1999 were themselves provoked by a human rights emergency focused primarily on refugees. In his contribution, Jim Whitman addresses the rights of refugees and the responsibilities of outsiders in the Kosovo crisis. His central argument is hostile to the claims of Western leaders about their motivations, for he attempts to show that there was a blurring of the strategic and humanitarian boundaries on the part of NATO to a much greater extent than the official position would allow, or even recognise. The essay begins by identifying the rights of refugees in general, and also in relation to the situation in Kosovo. It then sets the refugee crisis there in the wider context of the sensitivity in Western Europe – a growing 'Fortress Europe' – to asylum-seekers and refugees. The author argues that the prospect for the rights of refugees generally and for the peoples of the Balkans in particular has been worsened by NATO's use of armed force in 1999; the outcome is not seen as a victory for human rights, but rather for NATO's 'humanitarianism', which should be conceived as a functionally separate category of action. This 'humanitarianism' is said to be part of a wider policy based on strategic and political interests, which included a concern to keep the refugees within the region. The consequences of separating humanitarianism and human rights are far-reaching. They include: driving post-war Kosovo towards a mono-ethnic entity, undermining the international protection regime for refugees, refiguring rather than reducing ethnic tension in the Balkans, sidelining the UNHCR, and weakening the UN and the law-based order on which human rights ultimately depend. In a world in which the problem of refugees (including internally-displaced persons) is growing in scale and complexity, NATO showed in 1999 that human rights are at best only a secondary consideration in the policy making of its leaders.

Examining the application of international humanitarian law in the Kosovo conflict, Hilaire McCoubrey argues that in this crisis, as in so many others over the years, international humanitarian law is a standard of behaviour whose application in particular situations leaves plenty to be desired; this is not only because of the chosen behaviour of the participants, acting under all the pressures of violent circumstances, but also because of the inherent difficulties, dilemmas and ambiguities of law in the context of war. The crisis began with fighting within the state of Yugoslavia, between the Kosovo Liberation Army (KLA) and the Federal (Serbian) forces. Such struggles invariably degenerate into very dirty wars, and this was no exception. As ever, when insurgency violence is met by the brute force of state power, the obstacles to the application of humanitarian norms are fully exposed. The issues clarified somewhat once the conflict took on the form of a more traditional war (though it could not be declared as such) between the NATO alliance on the one side and the sovereign state of the FRY on the other. Traditional questions were raised, for example, about discrimination in the laws of war as a result of the strategy NATO adopted – high-level aerial bombardment and long-distance cruise missile attack. The contribution discusses some of the controversial incidents that arose from this: the ostensible 'mistakes', the 'collateral damage' and the 'accidents'. Finally, the essay looks at the implications of the war for the future of international humanitarian law in the light of the revival of Just War thinking, and warns of the dangers of states in the twenty-first century being pushed along by Just War rhetoric, rather than being restrained.

The possible role of international legal instruments, and especially the issue of individual complicity in human rights abuses, is the focus of Marc Weller's contribution. He explores the strategic use of international criminal jurisdiction, and in particular the Kosovo Indictment of the International Criminal Tribunal for Yugoslavia. It is argued that this Indictment, issued against the highest political and military leaders in Milosevic's regime, represents a very significant stage in the emergence of an international constitution; international humanitarian law has been developing since 1945 and the Tribunals created for the conflict in Yugoslavia and then Rwanda represent major steps in the process. The significance of the Yugoslav Tribunal derives from its origins (a Chapter VII Security Council resolution), its genuine supranational authority and what is argued has been its profound political impact on the Kosovo conflict. The latter is evident in the way the Tribunal has effectively denied the Milosevic regime the hope of achieving its main aims in relation to Kosovo. As a result, the Yugoslav Tribunal has been a more important contributor to the emerging international constitutional order than the recently established International Criminal Court, which was set up as its more permanent and comprehensive successor. The significance of the Tribunal in a wider strategic sense results from its insistence on the application of humanitarian law in 'internal' or 'mixed' armed conflicts, and its contribution to clarifying and perhaps advancing the issue of military and political command responsibility in cases of 'systematic and unlawful' campaigns of violence. The Tribunal, especially in relation to its work focusing on Kosovo, is another development leading to the further shrinking of areas of exclusive state jurisdiction. This development in international criminal law can therefore legitimately be regarded as a milestone in the promotion of human rights globally.

Part Four, Aftermath, examines various dimensions of the human rights situation in Kosovo since June 1999, when Milosevic withdrew Federal troops from the province. Many questions have to be asked, and many issues remain unresolved, as the next act in Kosovo's embattled history unfolds before our eyes. Will a Just War be followed by a just peace, as the supporters of NATO's military campaign had hoped, or is it more likely, as NATO's critics feared, that air-delivered humanitarianism will be followed by a human rights disappointment on the ground?

Every set of diplomatic exchanges between the so-called international community and Belgrade through the 1990s had an important human-rights dimension, by omission or commission. Eric Herring compares the framework of possibilities for human rights in today's Kosovo in the light of two sets of negotiations – those which were demanded by NATO and rejected by Belgrade at Rambouillet in February 1999, and those eventually demanded by NATO and accepted by Belgrade which brought an end to the military campaign in June 1999. He explores the meanings of the two sets of proposals at the time and afterwards, arguing that the terms put forward at Rambouillet were unworkable and should lead us to question the 'humanitarian' aims and justifications offered by NATO. The war that then resulted from the unworkable terms was brought to an end by the Kosovo Accords, which in turn have only made matters worse. Employing the traditional formula that a better peace is the only justification for war, the author concludes that by this test, and using human rights as the measure, the Kosovo campaign failed. At the heart of the failure is a flawed humanitarianism: NATO must radically change its own attitudes and behaviour with respect to humanitarianism, he believes, before it attempts violently to alter that of others.

One of the prevailing assumptions of Western globalism in recent decades has been that a direct relationship exists between democracy and human rights. In his contribution Ian R. Mitchell shows that the relationship is more complex than this easy and comfortable assumption suggests. The argument reveals a paradox at the very core of NATO's intervention in 1999. The war arose out of human rights abuses and was fought by NATO ostensibly for human rights; it delivered to Kosovo for the first time the possibility of democracy and democratic elections; yet the result of that victory looks likely to deliver the sort of outcome the war was fought to prevent, namely a mono-ethnic Kosovo, with independence not autonomy a political priority. Mitchell's contribution does not abandon the idea of a democratic Kosovo, but seeks to clarify the debates, ambiguities and implications of delivering on the democratisation agenda with respect to human rights. Elections are seen as the key test of that agenda, and one that needs to succeed, but he thinks this an unlikely result first time. All the signs point to the top-down imposition of elections resulting in the institutionalisation (as in Bosnia) of ethnicism. This will then underline one of the themes of the essay, namely the tension between the aims of those charged by the international community with responsibility for the development of self-government in Kosovo, and the wishes of the *de facto* local authorities in Kosovo today. The latter's ambitions inevitably raise controversial questions regarding long-term sovereignty over Kosovo.

The final contribution in this section, by Jasmina Husanović, discusses the current security situation in Kosovo from a bottom-up perspective. She shares Mitchell's view that mechanical democracy-building and election procedures cannot in themselves deliver a better situation; indeed they may simply perpetuate the ethno-nationalist matrix. In this regard, as in others, the way the international community has handled the situation has done little to eradicate insecurity on the ground. With this in mind, the essay examines some of the reasons behind the failure of the 'new' ethics and politics of human rights; in particular, it is argued that external attitudes have been dominated by ideas of victimisation and ethno-nationalism which only perpetuate communities of fear in Kosovo. The propagation of human rights requires a different approach to the one that has characterised the period since the end of the bombing and the return of the Albanian Kosovar refugees. This must involve a more effective and emancipatory promise. To date, a gap has been revealed between the sound-bite ethics and politics of humanitarian intervention by the international community and what has happened at the grass-roots level. The current human rights/security situation in Kosovo seems to be pointing to a complete failure, characterised as it is by violence, ethnic radicalisation, disenchantment, and incompetence. In such circumstances, human rights and security need to be rethought in a manner that is more sensitive to the grass-roots realities of highly divided and destabilised peoples. Husanovic looks forward to the growth of a politics of responsibility at the grass-roots level, free from regressive myths and exclusionary practices, and instead embracing the ethics/politics of human rights embodied in the multi-ethnic Kosovar NGO which calls itself the 'Post-Pessimists'.

Part 5 consists of a Forum on the disputed notion of 'humanitarian war': a war ostensibly fought not for traditional purposes of 'national interest' but essentially to defend human rights. The 1990s saw a number of 'humanitarian interventions' – notably Somalia, Bosnia, Haiti – but NATO's campaign against Serbia was the first purely humanitarian war in the sense that military force was used against a state because of massive human rights abuses by the government against a section of its population. The other cases had been situations of state collapse or civil strife.

Chris Brown begins by offering a 'qualified defence' of NATO's campaign, setting the use of military force in the context of careful theoretical distinctions and complex practical alternatives. He concludes that in the circumstances NATO leaders found themselves, the use of force to prevent and then redress a great wrong was 'the right – and humanitarian – response to a difficult situation'. Melanie McDonagh agrees that the cause was just and the response appropriate, though warns about confusions caused by absolutist notions. From many visits to the former state of Yugoslavia she has no doubts that the ethnic terror had to be stopped, on pragmatic as well as moral grounds. What is at issue for her is not whether the campaign was a Just War, but whether a just peace can be created. 'Bombing for human rights?' is a question John Stremlau also answers in the affirmative, and sees the intervention as a 'hinge point' in European history. He argues that the effort to redress human rights abuses in Kosovo was primarily a 'regional experiment' but argues that the origins, course and outcome of the conflict provides sharp reminders to other regions, such as southern Africa, about the dangers of ethnic factionalism and the need to give priority to human rights.

The Forum then moves to a set of more critical perspectives, beginning with Colin Gray's critique of NATO's military action from the perspective of 'neo-classical realism'. His argument is concerned with the political consequences of actions, and the need for state leaders to have sensible guidelines for policy. He sees 'hope and good intentions', though inherently attractive and praiseworthy, as failing those tests of usefulness. Indeed, he believes that those who engage in *Moralpolitik* are likely to do more harm than good. Tarak Barkawi's critique develops a similar theme, but focuses on society rather than strategy. He discusses the relationship between the contemporary character of Western society and the use of air power from a safe height. On both pragmatic and ethical grounds he sees NATO's Kosovo campaign as another example of the flawed 'liberal politics of war'. It is the flaws of the doctrine of Just War (the ancient but direct ancestor of the contemporary notion of humanitarian war) that are addressed in the next essay. In it I argue that gross human wrongs do not necessarily require a military response from outsiders, while the tradition of investing war with ethical legitimacy feeds mindsets that help perpetuate one of the most pervasive and destructive human wrongs of all: war itself. Finally, Richard Falk looks into the cockpit of Kosovo and the interplay between 'genocidal practices', 'humanitarian wars' and 'realist geopolitics'; he concludes that a 'complex mixed message' emerges. Stripped to its essentials, the theme of his essay is that, at this stage in world politics, any genuine humanitarian moves by states are likely to be 'underfunded and insufficient'. In contrast, interventions backed by the requisite will and resources are likely to be strategic in motivation, and humanitarian only in rationalisation; such interventionary violence will be 'illegal and anti-humanitarian'. This, in his opinion, is the meaning of Kosovo.

## THE MEANINGS OF 'KOSOVO'?

The future will decide on the symbolic meaning or meanings of 'Kosovo'. The history of international politics through the twentieth century was marked by conflicts that came to be invested with particular historical meaning, and policy followed what became mental signposts: Sarajevo, Munich and Vietnam were only the most prominent. The names alone of certain cities, countries and years became enough to conjure up a complex of memories, lessons and warnings. Some became 'syndromes'; their invocation ended arguments and sometimes guided policy. Will 'Kosovo' take on such powerful symbolic significance? If so, what will it mean? Where would a Kosovo syndrome lead?

'The memory of the past is a prize worth struggling for' is one of the important themes Tina Rosenberg develops in her account of the changes in Eastern Europe from one orthodoxy to another[4] following the eruptions of 1989. In this vein she approvingly quotes George Orwell's remark that 'Whoever controls the past controls the future.' The past has always been a struggle in the Balkans, as it has in other lands overburdened by history and torn by ethnic conflict, from Israel/Palestine to Ireland/Ulster. History in these lands is never simply the study of the past; to an important degree it is a re-creation of the present and as such is part of a struggle for the political future. The contestation for power which characterises all politics involves a power-struggle over memory. The future can belong to those who can make a particular constellation of power appear to be a 'natural' extension of the past.

Earlier in this Introduction, I suggested that reinterpreting the past was one way of helping the reinvention of a more progressive future. But the past is more often used for other purposes, namely to manipulate politics in the present for purposes of ambition. Memory matters, and nowhere more so than in the troubled lands of south-eastern Europe. If all this is true, then whoever controls the history of the Kosovo tragedy as it developed through the 1990s and beyond will define the future political meaning of Kosovo, and hence the direction it signposts.

The meanings given to the past, especially by the powerful, will help shape the future. Historically, such meanings have often been regressive, constructed by human nature pessimism and deterministic formulae equating 'what was' to what 'will be'. Political common sense, fuelled by high-octane historical myths, attempts to replicate the future in its own image. But different accounts of history can shape alternative futures. Part of reinventing the future lies in reinterpreting the past – a past which for students of International Politics has for so long been in the thrall of realist international historians. A more emancipatory future requires a history that that can show that the past was more open than it usually appears, dominated as our thinking is by the knowledge of the end of a story. By re-reading the past in a more open fashion it is possible to rethink future possibilities – forecasting the cross-roads that will appear, but re-imagining the reasons for taking different routes than the ones taken with the old road maps of the past. If we believe that the Kosovo tragedy need not have happened as it did, and better understand what went wrong, when and how, we will have better resources for doing it different next time – whoever the 'we' is. History often is painted in the darkest colours, but it is also a resource for rational hope. The recent battlegrounds of the Balkans are of nothing compared with the centuries of princely/dynastic/ethnic/national/state rivalries in Western Europe. But this historic cockpit of realist international relations has become an extended community in which interstate war has now become unthinkable. Is there any reason in principle why the peoples of the Balkans cannot also achieve a plateau of stable peace? If enough people want it to be, it can be.

We are still very close to the events that led to the war in 1999, and of course the jury has to remain out on the work of the international protectorate, now attempting to construct a better post-war situation. Critical distance is a luxury, because policies have to be made immediately, and so the construction of meaning has to be equally instantaneous. This encourages closure of discussion. But historical accuracy and rational policy-making over the longer-term require that discussion be kept going, lest it become dominated by clichés, false memories, political spin, and legend. All these are encouraged in a world of instant communications and instant history. In a period when the fog of war has been dispersed by a snowstorm of spin, I am not alone in thinking that the more I accessed the Kosovo war through press briefings, 'correspondents', official spokesmen and their political leaders, the more

I felt the real story was somewhere else. More than usual with governments, I believed that I was not being fed 'information', but being told what to think. Such cynicism was fully justified, because, in the months since the war, we have become accustomed to hearing new revelations: about the damage done by NATO air power to Yugoslav forces' equipment in Kosovo, the allegations about the destruction of the Chinese Embassy in Belgrade, the numbers of civilians killed (by both the Serb ethnic cleansers and NATO bombers), the numbers of women raped, the differences of opinion among the NATO political and military leaders, the readiness and capability of the international forces that went into Kosovo, the presence of US military Psyops personnel working as interns in CNN headquarters during the war, and on and on.

The meanings and significance given to Kosovo will, of course, be in part the plaything of contemporary politics. As a result, the embattled province has already largely dropped from the front pages of Western newspapers. This is not inconvenient to Western leaders, especially those who would rather have the high hopes they deliberately generated in March 1999 not remembered too well. The political agenda has moved on, and Kosovo has not kept up. If Kosovo does not now look like the undisputed triumph of the just, then Western politicians will just keep away. Those governments once so prominent in the fighting no longer seem keen to send their political leaders for shirt-sleeved photo-opportunities. But to a degree NATO has put itself, politically, in a no-lose situation. It can claim to have won the war against Milosevic (despite the UN) and it has a plausible post-withdrawal defence (pass the problem on to the UN). Consequently, it may not be long in the future before the Western leaders decide to withdraw, declaring that they and their forces have done their job, and any failure to turn their humanitarian mission into a just peace is the fault of others: local ethnic hatreds and the ineffective UN. If – when? – this happens, we will see again, in the early years of the twenty-first century, the replaying of the old story of the previous two. Once more, the Western powers will have swung between destructive involvement in the Balkans, and destructive withdrawal.

One meaning of Kosovo is surely incontrovertible, and this makes it of more than merely regional significance. Kosovo offers a global warning that ethnic harmony is not guaranteed, that local tyrants might exploit ethnic issues for their own interests, and that ruthless regimes will not desist from inflicting gross human rights abuses. Consequently, the dilemmas of intervention/non-intervention (and every case of the latter is also a version of the former) will confront outsiders, be they governments, alliances, civil society or individuals. Governments in democracies in particular will have to take positions on brutalities beyond borders in order to lead or respond to electorates who, to a greater or lesser extent, are sure to have views.

In the future politics of humanitarianism, 'Kosovo' will surely be one of those mental signposts mentioned earlier. When it comes to war, it is a moot point whether it is worse to remember badly, and learn the wrong lessons, or to forget, and learn nothing. Kosovo risks both outcomes, depending on who is doing the remembering, and who the forgetting. This is why the struggle over memory and history is so important now, before a syndrome is concretised. When – if? – Kosovo becomes a comfortable consensus, it will help shape, for better or worse, the international politics of humanitarianism and the lives of the countless victims of human rights in global politics. Consequently, those who believe passionately in the significance of Kosovo must play their part now in ensuring that complexity and openness is not lost, as we still wait for the reckoning.

## NOTES

1. Misha Glenny, *The Balkans 1804–1999. Nationalism, War and the Great Powers* (London: Granta, 1999)
2. See especially Noel Malcolm, *Kosovo: A Short History* (London: Macmillan, 1998) and Tim Judah, *Kosovo: War and Revenge* (New Haven, CT: Yale University Press, 2000).
3. The phrase was coined by Eduardo Rabossi: it is quoted and discussed in Richard Rorty, 'Human Rights, Rationality and Sentimentality', in Stephen Shute and Susan Hurley (eds), *On Human Rights. The Oxford Amnesty Lectures 1993* (New York: Basic Books, 1993), pp.115–6.
4. Tina Rosenberg, *The Haunted Land: Facing Europe's Ghosts after Communism* (London: Vintage, 1995), p.xviii.

# PART ONE:

# Perspectives

# 1
# Genocide:
# Knowing What It Is That We Want to Remember, or Forget, or Forgive

## TIM DUNNE and DANIELA KROSLAK

'The Holocaust was born and executed in our modern rational society.' This view, expressed by Zygmunt Bauman, has become influential in sociological accounts of the barbarism committed by the Nazis against Jews and other groups.[1] Bauman's argument steers us away from the conceit that the Holocaust was a freak accident, one that Western civilisation would never repeat. Given the genocidal violence we have witnessed in the 1990s, his critique of liberal narratives of historical progress is an important one. But his book *Modernity and the Holocaust* is problematic for the reason that acts of systematic slaughter against collectivities (including Jews in Europe) pre-date modernity; moreover, it is precisely *modern* ideas of responsibility that have given us a moral vocabulary – and an institutional context – for trying to remove the worst kind of crime from the landscape of international politics. The main focus of this essay will be the meaning given to genocide by lawyers, activists and intellectuals. In this sense, the complex causes of genocide remain outside the scope of our argument. Looking at the meaning and interpretation of genocide necessarily involves examining the controversy that has raged for the last half century between 'restrictionists', who want to maintain a narrow interpretation of the Genocide Convention, and writers we refer to as 'expansivists', who believe that the category must be adapted to conform to new patterns of violence directed at collectivities.

In contrast to Bauman's view of genocide being a peculiarly modern phenomenon, the jurist who invented the term – Raphael Lemkin – argued that it had been part of human history since antiquity. But until the moment of its inclusion in the indictment of German leaders at

Nuremberg in 1945, it had been an evil practice without a name.[2] Part 1 of this contribution will consider the evolution of the Genocide Convention of 1948 and the term *genocide*. In particular it focuses upon the various debates that ensued regarding the referent group (who is to be included), the psychological state of the perpetrators (their intentions or motives), and the extent of the violence (what counts as 'in whole or in part').

Part 2 will show, through a discussion of the case of Kosovo, what is at stake in this debate. Prior to and during the NATO bombing of the Federal Republic of Yugoslavia (FRY), many Western journalists and state leaders accused President Milosevic's government of committing genocide. Yet a substantial body of opinion believed that although massive human rights abuses took place in Kosovo, they should not be have been labelled 'genocide'. This dispute prompts us to question the adequacy of our moral and legal vocabulary for describing large-scale killings of groups.

Most activists and writers working in the area of 'genocide studies' consider the Convention on the Prevention and Punishment of the Crime of Genocide to be inadequate but recognise that a contested convention is preferable to none at all. Towards the end of the essay, we consider the various ways in which the Convention is being re-interpreted. One important site for renewed legal interpretation concerns the war crimes tribunals set up to consider accusations of genocidal crimes in relation to Rwanda and the wars in Bosnia and Kosovo. These and other legal innovations are considered in Part 3; notably the International Court of Justice's consideration of genocide in relation to alleged war crimes committed by the Federal Republic of Yugoslavia during the Bosnia conflict. We will end with an evaluation of how far the world has moved towards overcoming some of the weaknesses evident in the founding document.

## THE GENOCIDE CONVENTION AND DILEMMAS OF INTERPRETATION

Raphael Lemkin, a Polish born Jew (1900–59), devoted his life to the singular cause of taking a stand against genocide.[3] With the outbreak of the Second World War, he joined the Polish underground, escaping to the United States in 1941. It was in his 1944 study of Nazism that he invented the word *genocide* from the Greek *genos* (race or tribe) and the Latin *cide* (killing).[4] He defined the neologism as 'a co-ordinated plan of different actions aiming at the destruction of essential foundations of the life of national groups, with the aim of annihilating the groups themselves'.[5]

Lemkin's lobbying helped to galvanise the UN General Assembly to pass a resolution that both recognised genocide as a crime, and charged the Economic and Social Council of the UN (ECOSOC) with responsibility for drawing up a draft convention. The text of the 1946 Resolution included the following statement:

> Genocide is a denial of the right of existence of entire human groups, as homicide is the denial of the right to live of individual human beings; such denial of the right of existence shocks the conscience of mankind, results in great losses to humanity in the form of cultural and other contributions represented by these groups, and is contrary to moral law and to the spirit and aims of the United Nations. Many instances of such crimes of genocide have occurred, when racial, political and other groups have been destroyed, entirely or in part. The punishment of the crime of genocide is a matter of international concern.[6]

The two years that elapsed between the Resolution and the Convention provide a good example of how difficult it is to translate a general principle into a legal covenant that gives effect to it. In addition to the inherent problems, to complicate matters further, outside ECOSOC relations between the great powers were deteriorating significantly.

The question of the inclusion of the category of 'political groups' was hotly debated within ECOSOC. The Soviet Union strongly opposed deviating from the highly restrictionist view that genocide was intimately connected with fascism. One obvious reason why their representative took this line was to avoid any accusation that Stalin's slaughter of 6,500,000 'kulaks'[7] between 1930 and 1937 constituted genocide. France, on the other hand, put forward the view that while in the past, genocide had been committed against racial or religious groups, in the future it was likely to be carried out against political targets.

The omission of political groups neglects the fact that genocide against a racial or religious group is usually the result of political conflict. This point was made strongly by the Haitian representative, who argued that a government responsible for genocide 'would always be able to allege that the extermination of any group had been dictated by political considerations, such as the necessity for quelling an insurrection or maintaining public order'.[8] The proposal to include political groups in the Convention was eventually ruled out because of the widespread fear that this might lead to intervention in the domestic affairs of states. The example of Vietnam's intervention in Cambodia in 1979 to halt the genocide, and the widespread criticism this action received, adds weight to the view that a political conception of genocidal violence would erode the non-intervention principle.[9] This sentiment prompted Leo Kuper, much later, to draw the bitter conclusion that 'many nations were unwilling to renounce the right to commit political genocide against their own nationals'.[10]

After lengthy debates on this and other issues,[11] the Convention was approved by the General Assembly of the United Nations on 9 December 1948. The main articles to note for present purposes are I, II and III:[12]

*Article I*
The Contracting Parties confirm that genocide, whether committed in time of peace or in time of war, is a crime under international law which they undertake to prevent and to punish.

*Article II*
In the present Convention genocide means any of the following acts committed with intent to destroy, in whole or in part, a national, ethnical, racial or religious group, as such:
(a) Killing members of the group;
(b) Causing serious bodily or mental harm to members of the group;
(c) Deliberately inflicting on the group conditions of life calculated to bring about its physical destruction in whole or in part;
(d) Imposing measures intended to prevent births with the group;
(e) Forcibly transferring children of the group to another group.

*Article III*
The following acts shall be punishable:
(a) Genocide;
(b) Conspiracy to commit genocide;
(c) Direct and public incitement to commit genocide;
(d) Attempt to commit genocide;
(e) Complicity in genocide.

In 1998 the Convention celebrated its fiftieth anniversary. Peoples around the world are aware of its existence, and at the last count, 130 governments had ratified the treaty.[13] Despite the existence of a widespread consensus regarding the declaratory importance of the Convention, the genocide in Rwanda in 1994 underscored the gap that exists between the normative aspiration, that the practice must be prevented, and the cold reality of its persistence. Given the scope of this essay, it is not possible to address all the issues raised by this yawning gap between the standard and the practice; this would require an analysis of the causes of genocide as well as the adequacy of the instruments for dealing with it once an outbreak has started. Instead, we will examine how far the conceptual weaknesses in the Convention have contributed to international society's inability to respond effectively to targeted violence against collectives. Our analysis finds fault with both the restrictionists, who maintain that only Armenia, the Holocaust and Rwanda are legitimate examples of genocide, and expansivists, who attach the label to a wide range of human tragedies and even environmental disasters. We begin by discussing three of the chief difficulties in theorising genocide, and hence in devising counter-strategies: the problem of scale, referent and intent.

## The Problem of Scale

The Convention is very vague regarding the scale of atrocity necessary for a crime to be called genocide. The intent to destroy 'in whole or in part' opens up a number of definitional ambiguities. Is there not a significant difference between Hitler's extermination of six million Jews between 1939 and 1945 and the murder of between tens of thousands of Sudeten Germans by Czechs after the war? Similarly, is not Australia's extermination of large sections of Aborigine societies in the nineteenth century a greater crime than the premature deaths of indigenous peoples caused by disease and neglect? Jean-Paul Sartre famously argued that colonisation is inherently an act of genocide since colonisation cannot be pursued without a systematic destruction of all native features of society.[14] But was the attempt by Lord Milner to anglicise (i.e., colonise) the South African education system genocidal in the same sense that Pol Pot exterminated millions of Cambodians?

Israel Charny is one writer working in the area of genocide studies who is content to work with a 'generic definition' that does not exclude any case of mass murder irrespective of racial, national, ethnic, cultural, religious or political categories. In his words, 'whenever large numbers of unarmed human beings are put to death at the hands of their fellow human beings, we are talking about *genocide*'.[15] He claims that it is 'a moral absurdity and an insult to the value of human life to exclude from full historical recognition any instance of mass killing as if it were undeserving of inclusion in the record'.[16] He fails to see, however, that it is not a question of 'undeserving' in the sense of being included in the record but of attempting to identify a *particular* kind of atrocity. A useful analogy can be found in domestic law. In cases of homicide we rightly consider the crime of the serial killer to be more repugnant than manslaughter. The important point here is that comparability is not the same thing as equivalence, and the challenge is to find adequate means to express the 'gradations of genocide'.[17]

Charny's expansivist understanding of genocide even goes as far as claiming that massive deaths resulting from the meltdown of a nuclear reactor would count as genocide. Just such an incident happened in Chernobyl, Ukraine, in 1986. Hundreds lost their lives and many thousands were irradiated. This was a tragic consequence that followed from human error, but it was not genocide. The line of argument pursued by Charny leads to the flattening out of history. Acknowledged masters of this practice are the Holocaust deniers such as Ernst Nolte who equate what Germans did at Auschwitz with what Americans did at My Lai in Vietnam. Colin Tatz refers to this danger as 'comparative trivialisation'. If we allow this to happen, he argues, 'then we acquiesce in the demise of genocide and its meaning'.[18]

Other writers in this field concur with this dismissal of the expansivist position. Helen Fein, for example, rejects a wide application of the label genocide: 'If we aggregated all cases of mass death – from war, genocide, migrations, and slavery – together, we would probably reach rather banal and very general conclusions. And it would reduce recognition that the causes of the genocides occurring during two world wars in this century … were distinct from war deaths'.[19] She dismisses the trend to attach the label to various political struggles, citing as examples speeches by anti-abortion and anti-nuclear activists as well as partisans of both sides in the Israeli-Palestinian conflict.'[20] Fein is convinced that 'labelling them with a super blanket of generalised compassion as certified victims of "genocide"'[21] does not help the victims of any of these violations.

The view expressed by Chalk and Jonassohn is representative of most scholarly work on genocide. They argue that it is important to delimit genocide from other forms of gross human rights abuses since 'neither our understanding of them nor our exploration of possible means of prediction and prevention will be facilitated by lumping them all together'.[22] One way of overcoming this problem would be to maintain some kind of victim threshold, rather in the way that the definition of war is sometimes associated with a minimum casualty level of 1,000 battle deaths.[23] Leo Kuper insists that the qualification for genocide be set at a minimum of 'substantial' or an 'appreciable' number of victims'.[24] While not going as far as expansivists like Charny, Barbara Harff challenges the argument that numbers matter. In her words, 'As long as one can identify victims as members of a deliberately targeted group whose existence or survival is at stake, numbers of victims are irrelevant'.[25]

*Identifying a Victim-Group*

Following her rejection of the blurring of genocide with other kinds of mass atrocity, Fein emphasises that the differences between the victims of state terror and genocide is their selection, a process that is crucial in defining genocide. While victims of terror are selected because they are accused of committing 'subversive' acts, or even simply chosen arbitrarily, victims of genocide are chosen because they are members of a certain group.[26] Here she dismisses Leo Kuper's argument that the bombs dropped on Hiroshima and Dresden constituted genocide because the intent was to destroy the German and Japanese inhabitants.[27] Where Kuper emphasises the intent as the overriding element Fein argues, following her analysis and emphasis on group definition and selection, that Germans and Japanese were considered the enemy and not killed because they were German or Japanese *per se*.

In order to clarify the different kinds of victim group, Barbara Harff and Ted Gurr distinguish between politically and socially or racially motivated killings, genocide and politicide: 'genocides and politicides are the promotion and execution of policies by a state or its agent that result in the deaths of a substantial portion of a group'.[28] In cases of genocide the focus is on the communal characteristics of the victim group, whereas in politicide it is on the victim group's political opposition to the regime and to the dominant group. The problem here is that it is sometimes hard to distinguish between politicides and genocides; the Nazis had no difficulty in including political opponents in the Holocaust. A variation on this argument points to the fact that politicides often *become* genocides. In Bosnia, the ethnicity of 'Bosnian Muslims' was in part constructed by Bosnian Serb aggression.[29]

The most expansivist argument in regard to the victim group is provided by Frank Chalk and Kurt Jonassohn who define genocide as 'a form of one-sided mass killing in which a state or other authority intends to destroy a group, as that group and membership in it are defined by the perpetrator'.[30] The main difference between the Genocide Convention and this definition is that there is no restriction on the identity of the victimised group. Chalk and Jonassohn maintain that by accepting the UN definition, their research would necessarily continue the 'silence' in the genocide literature regarding 'the assault on certain victimised social groups of the past'.[31] Although Chalk and Jonassohn rightly point out the limitations of the Genocide Convention's definition – particular the erasing of the category of 'political group' discussed earlier on – their definition of the victimised group is too broad. Furthermore this definition of the group ultimately buys into the reasoning of the perpetrator, which can be a dangerous enterprise since it accepts the singling out of a certain group, reducing complex human experiences to essential ethnic, political or religious characteristics.

*The Problem of Intent*

The question is how to assess the intentions of a genocidal agent is notoriously problematic in the social sciences. Max Weber overcame the problem by assuming that instrumental rationality pervaded social action in the modern world; likewise, political economists believe that agents are motivated by the desire to maximise utility, thereby circumventing the need to inquire into the origins of their preferences. Evaluating the intentions of corporate actors like states is even more problematic. Apart from the case of the Nazis, there is no historical example where a plan to commit genocide has been so co-ordinated and well documented.

The discussion concerning intent is wide-reaching in the field of genocide studies. Leo Kuper emphasises that the *intent* to destroy is a crucial element. Destruction alone is not sufficient: 'The "inadvertent" wiping out of a group,' he argues, 'is not genocide.'[32] This means that the wholesale destruction of the Aztec civilisation following the arrival of the Spanish conquistadores in the late fifteenth century would not count as an act of genocide, since the majority of deaths were caused by disease and the ill-effects of slave labour.[33] There have been two innovative suggestions about how to overcome the dilemma of intentionality. First, the idea of developing a legal definition of genocide that follows the custom of classifying homicides by degree (first degree and second degree murder/genocide).[34] Second, it has been argued that it is possible to separate intentions from motives. According to Hurst Hannum and David Hawk, the '"intent" clause of Article II of the Genocide Convention requires only that the various destructive acts – killings, causing mental and physical harm, deliberately inflicted conditions of life, etc. – have a purposeful or deliberate character as opposed to an accidental or unintentional character.'[35] This effectively shifts the focus from a legal language of guilt to a more sociological assessment of the causes of genocidal conflicts.[36]

This last issue of 'intent' is probably the least problematic aspect of the Convention. Even where the destruction of 'a national, ethnical, racial or religious group' has been least organised, as was the case with the genocide against the Aborigines in Australia, it is relatively easy to find evidence of official complicity. While there was no 'Hitler' in London plotting their destruction, there were plenty of colonial government employees justifying the attacks on their culture and civilisation with reference to arguments about racial inferiority. And there were many more policemen out in the bush obeying the order of 'dispersal', the euphemism for shooting on sight when a group of Aboriginal men gathered together.[37] In short, it is hard to resist the conclusion of Chalk and Jonassohn that 'it is not plausible that a group of some considerable size is victimised by man-made means without anyone meaning to do it!'[38]

The related issues of the identity of the target group, and the scale of the destruction, are less easily resolved. By leaving out the destruction of political classes, such as intellectuals (1970s Cambodia) or kulaks (1930s Soviet Union), the Convention is too restrictive.[39] But in terms of scale, the Convention is arguably too broad. There is no mention of a minimum threshold, thereby enabling those wishing to take an expansivist view to argue that countless dictators have sought to destroy 'in part' the form of life of particular religious or national groups within their states.

The ambiguities evident in the text itself lead genocide scholars to draw sharply diverging conclusions about its adequacy. The most adamant defender of the Genocide Convention definition is Leo Kuper. In his extensive writings on the subject he maintains, contrary to many of his colleagues: 'I do not think it helpful to create new definitions of genocide, when there is an internationally recognised definition and a Genocide Convention which might become the basis for some effective action, *however limited the underlying conception*'.[40] Contrary to Kuper and Fein, Chalk and Jonassohn conclude that 'although it marked a milestone in international law, the UN definition is of little use to scholars'.[41] The position taken in this essay is that the chasm opening up between legal and academic definitions of genocide needs to be bridged. Academic thinking needs to be sensitive to the uniqueness of genocide as a crime under international law and the international legal regime must find ways of identifying (and punishing) gross human rights violations that fall short of genocide.

## KOSOVO AND THE NEW DEBATE ON GENOCIDE

From the beginning of 1999, some Western journalists, intellectuals,[42] and state leaders increasingly applied the term genocide to describe the actions of the Milosevic regime in Kosovo. As the British Defence Secretary, George Robertson, put it: 'These air strikes have one purpose only: to stop the genocidal violence.'[43] How should we interpret this claim, in the light of the Convention and the scholarly debates discussed above? Is it an example of a further widening – hence trivialising – of the concept? Or does Kosovo comply with what we have called an expansive reading of the Convention?

There is no doubt that politicians and the media engaged in absurd parallels between the herding of Jews onto trains leading to forced labour and/or the gas chambers, and the forced transportation of Kosovars to refugee camps in Albania and Macedonia.[44] Robin Cook argued that 'the appalling mass deportations we saw from Pristina, particularly the use of the railways, is evocative of what happened under Hitler and again under Stalin'.[45] There is no question that this kind of argument conforms to what Tatz referred to as 'comparative trivialisation'. Other world leaders were more guarded in their assessments. The UN Secretary-General said that the actions of the FRY were in violation of humanitarian law (not explicitly the Genocide Convention). His preferred description for the barbarous acts was 'ethnic cleansing'.[46] The differentiation between *genocide* and *ethnic cleansing* is important here since it shows that the interchangeable use of the two concepts has added to the debate about the prevention and punishment of genocide. We would like to argue that the confusion between genocide ethnic cleansing has led to a widening perception of genocide in international law. Although both concepts describe large-scale killings of groups, and genocide can be seen as a particular – the ultimate – form of ethnic cleansing, a legal differentiation is necessary to avoid misinterpretation under international law. Both terms have often been used in similar contexts, and wrongly so; however, unless ethnic cleansing is recognised in international law, the expansion of the concept of genocide will continue.

People who argue that genocide was committed in Kosovo insist on the ambiguity of the 'whole or in part' clause of the Convention. They maintain that a part of the population was targeted to be exterminated. However, although orders may have been given to massacre certain elements of the Kosovo Albanian population – such as occurred in the village of Racak – the intent was not to exterminate the group as a whole. Torture and mass killings were a systematic pattern of state terror, especially in the first five months of 1999; however, these were used as methods of intimidation and not as part of a more general policy 'aimed at the destruction of a target group'.[47]

What then distinguishes ethnic cleansing from genocide? It is not a matter of scale, since this is not an explicit element of the Convention. The key difference is that ethnic cleansing implies the forced removal of a victim group from a territory; it is a matter of *dispossession* and not *destruction*. The element of destroying a particular culture or nation means that none of the victim's family, race, ethnic or other group will be left to carry on its tradition, pass on its folklore and religious beliefs. This is the main difference between genocide and other massacres since in cases where genocide 'succeeds' no members of the victim group are left to take the side of the victim. Other victims of massacres might still have the hope that their children or like-minded survivors will be able to continue the cultural traditions in another country, with the possibility of returning to their homeland at some future date.

In short, we believe that those who seek to describe the conduct of the Milosevic regime in Kosovo in genocidal terms are wrong because the aim was not to destroy Kosovar Albanians as a group. Ever since the mid-1980s, and especially since 1989, Kosovars had been subjected to a campaign of terror which included arbitrary arrests, rape, state terror and violent clashes between demonstrators and security forces. The Albanian language was banned in the media, ethnic Albanian students were refused further education, political activists were imprisoned for their actions (prisoners of conscience), and unlawful deaths occurred in custody as a result of torture and other kinds of ill treatment.[48] From 1996 onwards the Belgrade Government justified its human rights violations in terms of the need to respond to 'terrorist' activities by the KLA. In 1998 the level of violence escalated even further with extrajudicial and other killings and the beginnings of forced displacement.[49] This campaign of violent exclusion sought primarily to suppress calls by ethnic Albanian leaders for independence rather than attempt to eradicate Kosovar Albanians as a group.

This interpretation appears to find favour with Amnesty International. In a recent analysis, published in 1998, it argues that 'the authorities' unstated policy appears to be to encourage their departure'.[50] One victim of continuous ill-treatment at the hands of police asserts that the various visits by police were intended to intimidate his family into leaving: 'They even said to me once, "What are you doing here, go to Switzerland or we'll kill you. You're either stupid or crazy to remain in Kosovo."'[51] This supports the argument that although subjected to state terror and ethnic cleansing the Albanians of Kosovo were not denied their right to life, even though forceful deportation and violent intimidation denied them the possibility of continuing their culture in what they regarded as their home. In cases of genocide the targeted group are not given the chance to practice their tradition elsewhere.

## MODIFICATIONS TO THE ANTI-GENOCIDE REGIME, FIFTY YEARS ON

Kosovo has not been the only event that has triggered a heightened sense of self-reflection among leaders of states and international public opinion. Guilt about the failure to do anything substantive to stop the genocide in Rwanda continues to stalk the committee rooms of the United Nations[52] and national governments.[53] In a highly charged appearance in Rwanda in March 1998, President Clinton acknowledged that he and other world leaders should have intervened to prevent

Africa's contemporary holocaust. As he put it, 'we did not act quickly enough after the killing began. We did not immediately call these crimes by their rightful name: genocide.'[54] At the end of the same year, the General Assembly reaffirmed 'the significance of the 1948 Convention on the Prevention and Punishment of the Crime of Genocide, by adopting a resolution on the fiftieth anniversary of that treaty',[55] a text which was fittingly introduced by Armenia, one of the first victims of genocide in the twentieth century. The discussion in the UN General Assembly in 1998 on the prevention, detection and punishment of genocide marked a significant moment of international reflection fifty years after the establishment of the Genocide Convention.

The contours of the debate were familiar; restrictionists and expansivist positions were both in evidence. Alamgir Babar, representative of Pakistan, expressed his support for 'the extension of the Tribunal's jurisdiction over the crimes committed in Kosovo'.[56] His broad view of genocide was to some extent supported by Volodymyr Yel'chenko of Ukraine who insisted that 'the definition of genocide should be expanded to include all groups targeted by policies which led to the destruction or any delineation of humanity. ... Chemical, biological or radiological warfare could also be regarded as innately genocidal.'[57]

The Austrian representative Ernst Sucharipa weighed in with the counter-restrictionist argument that genocide is 'a crime on a different scale than all other crimes against humanity'.[58] Thus, the extension of the concept was a counter-productive enterprise. The representative of Israel, Dore Gold warned of the 'politicisation' of the International Criminal Court by including as war crimes actions that had no connection whatsoever with the history of genocide. This simply abused the Genocide Convention and insulted the memory of the millions who died in Nazi-occupied Europe'.[59] Nevertheless, what was interesting about the Israeli statement was the willingness to contemplate ways in which the Convention could be strengthened by including 'groups that had so far resisted classification'.[60] Even restrictionists were taking seriously the question of broadening the treaty.

Equally, the establishment of the two international tribunals for Rwanda and the former Yugoslavia have added new impetus to the international fight against crimes against humanity and war crimes. On 2 September 1998, Jean-Paul Akayesu was found guilty of the crime of genocide by an international court. And it was Jean Kambanda, Rwandan prime minister during the genocide, who on 1 May 1998 was the first person to accept culpability for genocide before an international court. In addition to their slow but deliberative judicial function, the War Crimes Tribunals are also playing a part in widening the definition to include such practices as rape (in contravention of Article 2b). The representative of Tanzania heralded this as 'a groundbreaking interpretation that would have far-reaching significance in cases elsewhere'.[61] On the fiftieth anniversary of the Genocide Convention, the debate served to affirm the presence of old cleavages as well as a willingness to contemplate new approaches to the concept of genocide.

In legal terms the application of the concept of genocide in the International Criminal Courts for Rwanda and Yugoslavia seems to have enabled a clarification of many of its ambiguities. Especially in the case of the break-up of the former Yugoslavia, divisions remain as to whether or not the 'crimes against humanity' that have been identified constitute genocide or not. The Tribunal seems to have taken several approaches in order to try those responsible for the atrocities. First, there is a focus on *acts* of genocide; in other words, the court does not differentiate between genocidal acts and genocide, which means that there is a focus on 'acts' of genocide and not a policy of destruction as a whole. Restrictionist approaches would emphasise the 'intent to destroy' clause of the Genocide Convention, whereas expansivists would underline 'acts of genocide' and the different acts concerned. Since the Tribunal does not make such a distinction and focuses its interpretation of the Genocide Convention on the acts committed, several indictments became possible even though there are good reasons for believing that some of these crimes should have been tried not as genocide but as ethnic cleansing, were it a legal term. Thus, former Bosnian Serb President Radovan Karadzic and General Ratko Mladic (commander of the army during the war), were both indicted on charges of genocide, crimes against humanity and violation of the laws or customs of war. The interpretation of the Tribunal focuses on the acts that can be separated from a policy as a whole, i.e., what was formerly considered genocide. Hence, Mladic and Karadzic could be indicted for the massacre that occurred in Srebrenica in July 1995.

In the case of Kosovo, Slobodan Milosevic's indictment asserts that 'between 1 January 1999 and late May 1999, the military forces and some police units of FRY, the police force of Serbia and associated paramilitary units jointly engaged in a widespread and systematic series of offensives against many towns and villages predominantly inhabited by Albanian in the Province of Kosovo'.[62] Charges are made on the basis of individual criminal responsibility and superior criminal responsibility in connection with the violation of the laws or customs of war and crimes against humanity (Article 5 of the Statute[63]). What is crucial here concerning the argument made above is that Milosevic has not been indicted on charges of genocide. Hence, even with a broadened approach of genocide put forward by the Tribunal, the actions of Milosevic have, until now, been considered to fall outside of this category of international crime.

If there were to be a change in Milosevic's indictment, and consequently a judgment, concerning the atrocities in Kosovo under the charge of genocide, this would mean that there had been a clear shift away from the original definition of genocide, and its founding spirit which referred to a specific crime. As argued above, this crime ultimately seeks the extermination of a group. However, since ethnic cleansing does not constitute a crime under international law, those atrocities that can be summarised under this label will be tried under international law as a form of genocide. This of course dilutes the concept that was established by Raphael Lemkin in order to describe a very specific kind of atrocity.

Words evolve and meanings change. If *genocide* has become a more broadly defined term than restrictionists would interpret it, due to its application in the International Criminal Tribunal for Rwanda and Yugoslavia, then one has to accept such changes. It is through the Tribunal's work that the concept of genocide has become clearer, even if broader. The inclusion and acceptance of rape as a genocidal practice and especially the punishment of genocide as an established procedure reflects these changes. A more clearly defined concept of genocide might also give more prospect to the prevention of this crime, where the UN Convention on the *Prevention* and Punishment has evidently failed.

## CONCLUSION

'It was a complete delusion to suppose that the adoption of a convention of the type proposed, even if generally adhered to, would give people a greater sense of security or would diminish existing dangers of persecution on racial, religious or national grounds.'[64] These realist intimations were uttered by Sir Hartley Shawcross, the British delegate to the committee that formulated the text of the Convention. Fifty years later, we need to ask he was right? What *difference* has the Genocide Convention made? Has it all been 'a complete delusion'?

It is easy to point to the failures of the Convention. To get a sense of these, we only need to dwell for a moment on two words in the title; 'prevention' and 'punishment'. It would be hard to provide conclusive evidence that the treaty has prevented potential genocides, and it took fifty years before convicted perpetrators were punished by an international body. Yet the case in defence of the Convention is not so easily dismissed. To begin with, it sets a normative standard that has achieved near universal acceptance in international society, unlike other aspects of the human rights regime that remain contested.[65] The illegitimacy of genocide is something that no state challenges.

Many of the reasons for the failure to develop an effective anti-genocide capability lie beyond the scope of this essay; to address these, one would need to reflect on the origins of such violence, as well as the structural and institutional constraints militating against the collective enforcement of agreed norms. Our ambition in this essay has been more modest. By focusing on the Convention and the work of leading theorists working in this area, we have sought to clarify what genocide is and how it has been interpreted. In this aim, we have been guided by Colin Tatz's thought that 'it is essential that we know what it is we want to remember, or to forget, or to forgive'.[66]

Our discussion of the debates surrounding the meaning of genocide (the 'what it is') reveal the following key arguments. First, that the consensus supporting the Genocide Convention masks important disputes around issues of intent, scale, and identity of victim-group. For instance, by excluding the category of 'political' from the list of referents, many states have been able to attempt to destroy their political opponents without being legally responsible according to the terms of the Convention. Second, we showed that Kosovo is a good example of the dispute between those who want to define genocide very broadly (expansivists) and those who want a narrower definition (restrictionists). Widely labelled a genocide by politicians, journalists, and some genocide studies scholars, the judgment of these expansivists is called into question because Kosovar Albanians were in the main expelled from Serbia rather than liquidated. Here we drew a distinction between a policy of dispossession (ethnic cleansing) and destruction (genocide). But until the term ethnic cleansing is recognised in international law, genocide will continue to be stretched, fuelling the fears of restrictionists of 'comparative trivialisation' across cases.

Kosovo is part of a new debate about genocide, in which we sketched the contributions of the various war crimes tribunals to the development of new interpretations of genocide. Once again, this provided evidence that state leaders and legal practitioners are becoming increasingly aware of the need to differentiate within the category in order to avoid the perils of either restrictionism or expansivism. What is missing from this new thinking on genocide is an effective means of including the victims' understandings of what *it* is, and whether meaningful distinctions can be made between dispossession and destruction.

The starting point for critical thinking about international relations requires that victims of world politics be put at the centre of our inquiry into who gets what, when and how, on a global scale.[67] 'To remember' –

following Tatz – means remembering *all* the victims of genocide. It means remembering too the fates of non-Jewish Germans, Romani (Gypsies) and homosexuals at the hands of Nazis. In the case of America, where Holocaust studies is a respected part of the curriculum, it means remembering the destruction of the indigenous cultures of the Americas as well as the horrors of Auschwitz or Treblinka. It means remembering that the destruction of ethnic groups has a history stretching to the earliest recorded history, such as the Athenian assault on the islanders of Melos. It means remembering the haunting words by George Santayana at the entrance to Dachau museum: 'Those who forget the past are doomed to repeat it.' Finally, by remembering past genocides, we might all become more human, more caring, and therefore less likely to walk away when called upon to risk lives and commit resources to protect strangers in danger.

We cannot forget the past, but we might want to forget – or unlearn – certain kinds of behaviour that contributed towards the production of genocidal massacres. We need to forget the idea that genocide is exceptional, forget that governments are normally benign institutions to provide for our welfare and security. Few have made this argument with as much force as the political scientist R.J. Rummel: 'In total, during the first 88 years of this century, almost 170 million men, women, and children were shot, beaten, tortured, knifed, burned, starved, frozen, crushed, or worked to death, buried alive, drowned, hanged, bombed, or killed in any other of the myriad ways governments have inflicted death on unarmed, helpless citizens and foreigners.'[68] The discipline of International Relations needs to forget its habit of selectively describing and explain the past. Instead of taking 'family snaps' of human history,[69] we must not forget the blood and immorality. Having spent years researching the worst atrocities of the twentieth century, Rummel expressed his amazement at the Political Science and International Relations literature; it just did not explain, he said, 'the existence of a Hell-State like Pol Pot's Cambodia, a Gulag-State like Stalin's Soviet Union, or a Genocide-State like Hitler's Germany'.[70]

The grip of realism on foreign policy has led to moral indifference on the part of statist elites to the fate of those beyond their jurisdiction. We should not forget that the allies in the Second World War were indifferent to the victims of the Final Solution; that American companies traded with and profited from German businesses in the 1930s; or that world leaders were complicit in the Indonesia genocide in East Timor in 1975. The role of so-called external bystanders is not a neutral one. As the Holocaust survivor Elie Wiesel put it, 'The opposite of love, I have learned, is not hate, but indifference.' But what of the indifference shown by internal bystanders, those living in fear of their lives and those of their families? At the end of *The Drowned and the Saved*, Primo Levi recounts the correspondence he engaged in with German citizens who had read his *Survival in Auschwitz*. One woman wrote:

> I was born in 1922, grew up in Upper Silesia, not far from Auschwitz, but at the same time, in truth, I knew nothing (please do not consider this statement as a convenient excuse, but as a fact) of the atrocious things that were being committed, actually a few kilometres away from us. And yet, at least until the outbreak of the war, I happened to meet here and there people with the Jewish star and I did not welcome them into my home nor did I offer them hospitality as I would have done with others, but did not intervene on their behalf. That is my crime. I can come to terms with this terrible levity of mine, cowardice and selfishness only by relying on Christian forgiveness.[71]

Situations can make rescuers or perpetrators of us all. Perhaps the opposite of hatred is not love, but forgiveness.

ACKNOWLEDGEMENTS

The subtitle of this essay has been adapted from a phrase used by Colin Tatz in his essay 'Genocide and the Politics of Memory' in Colin Tatz (ed.), *Genocide Perspectives: Essays in Comparative Genocide* (Sydney: Centre for Comparative Genocide Studies, Macquarie University, 1997), p.313. The authors would like to thank Alex J. Bellamy and Paul Williams for their comments on an earlier draft, and Ken Booth's judicious advice as the draft neared completion. In addition, Daniela Kroslak would like to thank Rémy Ourdan for raising some thought-provoking issues.

NOTES

1. Zygmunt Bauman, *Modernity and the Holocaust* (Ithaca, NY: Cornell University Press, 1989), p.x.
2. Leo Kuper, *Genocide. Its Political Use in the Twentieth Century* (London: Penguin, 1981), p.22. The generic phrase 'crime against humanity' predates the term genocide; it was used by France, Great Britain and Russia in a 'joint declaration' (24 May 1915) denouncing the massacres of Armenians by the Ottoman Government.
3. As early as 1933, Lemkin submitted to the International Conference for Unification of Criminal Law a proposal to declare the destruction of racial, religious, or social collectivities a crime (of barbarity) under the law of nations'. Quoted in Leo Kuper, *Genocide* (note 3), p.22.
4. Raphael Lemkin, *Axis Rule in Occupied Europe: Laws of Occupation, Analysis of Government, Proposals for Redress* (Washington, DC: Carnegie Endowment for International Peace, 1944).
5. In Saul Mendlovitz and John Fousek, 'Enforcing the Law on Genocide', *Alternatives*, Vol.21, No.2 (1996), p.243.
6. United Nations General Assembly Resolution 96-I, 11 December 1946.
7. Defined by R.J. Rummel as 'the better-off peasants and those resisting collectivisation

[in the Soviet Union]'. For this description, and the estimate of the number killed, see his entry 'Soviet Union, Genocide In' in Israel W. Charny (ed.), *Encyclopedia of Genocide Vol II* (Oxford: ABC-CLIO, 1999), pp.520–1.
8. Quoted in Kuper, *Genocide* (note 3), pp.28–9.
9. For a detailed consideration of this case in a comparative framework, see Nicholas J. Wheeler, *Saving Strangers: Humanitarian Intervention in International Society* (Oxford: Oxford University Press, 2000).
10. Kuper, *Genocide* (note 3), p.29.
11. For a comprehensive discussion of these debates, see Kuper, *Genocide* (note 3), Chapter 2, 'The Genocide Convention'.
12. Quoted in Kuper, *Genocide* (note 3), p.210.
13. As of 16 November 1999. See www.un.org/Depts/treaty/final/ts2/newfiles/part_boo/iv_l.html.
14. Jean-Paul Sartre, 'On Genocide' in *Ramparts*, Vol.6, No.7 (1968).
15. Israel W. Charny, 'Toward a Generic Definition of Genocide' in George J. Andreopoulos, *Genocide: Conceptual and Historical Dimensions* (Philadelphia, PA: University of Pennsylvania Press, 1994), p.74. His generic definition in full is: 'Genocide in the generic sense is that mass killing of a substantial numbers of human beings, when not in the course of military action against the military forces of an avowed enemy, under conditions of the essential defencelessness and helplessness of the victims'. Ibid, p.75. Notice here that even Charny's expansivist notion rules out the mass killing of American Indians and many other bands of indigenous warriors.
16. Charny, 'Toward a Generic Definition' (note 16), p.91.
17. Tatz 'Genocide and the Politics of Memory' (note 1), p.311.
18. Ibid., p.313.
19. Helen Fein, *Genocide: A Sociological Perspective* (London: Sage, 1993), p.xi.
20. Ibid., p.5.
21. Helen Fein, 'Genocide, Terror, Life Integrity, and War Crimes: The Case of Discrimination' in Andreopoulos, *Genocide* (note 16), p.105.
22. Frank Chalk and Kurt Jonassohn, *The History and Sociology of Genocide. Analyses and Case Studies* (New Haven, CT: Yale University Press, 1990) p.4.
23. This is the operational definition employed by J. David Singer in his Correlates of War Project. See, J.David Singer and Melvin Small, *The Wages of War, 1816–1965: A Statistical Handbook* (New York: Wiley, 1972).
24. Kuper, *Genocide* (note 3), p.32. In another essay, he argues that the criterion 'in part' should mean an 'appreciable part': Leo Kuper, 'Theoretical Issues Relating to Genocide: Uses and Abuses' in Andreopoulos, *Genocide* (note 16), p.32.
25. Barbara Harff, 'Recognising Genocides and Politicides' in Helen Fein (ed.), *Genocide Watch* (New Haven, CT: Yale University Press, 1992) p.30.
26. Fein, 'Genocide, Terror, Life Integrity, and War Crimes' (note 22), p.98.
27. Kuper, 'Theoretical Issues' (note 25), p.33.
28. Harff, 'Recognising Genocides and Politicides' (note 26), p.27–8.
29. David Campbell, *National Deconstruction: Violence, Identity, and Justice in Bosnia* (Minneapolis, MN: University of Minnesota Press, 1998). Leo Kuper seems to recognise this point in the following passage: 'Policies which have the effect of collectivising the members of the society into polarised sections increase the potentiality for genocide.' Kuper, *Genocide* (note 3), p.55
30. Chalk and Jonassohn, *The History and Sociology of Genocide* (note 23), p.23.
31. Frank Chalk, 'Redefining Genocide' in Andreopoulos, *Genocide* (note 16), p.50.
32. Kuper, *Genocide* (note 3), p.32.
33. See Tzetvan Todorov, *The Conquest of America* (New York: HarperCollins, 1984). p.133.
34. This is Ward Churchill's classification in Fein, *Genocide* (note 20), p.15.
35. Quoted in Fein, *Genocide* (note 20), p.20.
36. Ibid., p.20.
37. Although not formally sanctioned, 'these shootings were tacitly approved by senior

South Australian police officials. See Richard Kimber, 'Genocide or Not? The Situation in Central Australia, 1860-1895', in Tatz, *Genocide Perspectives* (note 1), pp.33–65.
38. Kurt Jonassohn, 'What Is Genocide?' in Fein, *Genocide Watch* (note 26), p.21.
39. Moreover, there is a danger that the very text can produce the kind of collectivist thinking about identity that informs the thoughtways of the perpetrators. David Campbell develops the logic of this argument. Because Bosnia was a multi-cultural entity, it was difficult – in the absence of partition – to invoke the Convention in order to protect citizens in danger. In Campbell's words: 'In the guide of a "civic" conception – the national group – we find the convention depends on "ethnic formulations"'. Campbell, *National Deconstruction* (note 30), p.108.
40. Kuper, *Genocide*, p.39 (note 3); emphasis added.
41. Chalk and Jonassohn, *The History and Sociology of Genocide* (note 23), p.10.
42. The genocide studies scholars Israel W. Charny and Steven L.Jacobs refer to the 'genocide perpetrated against the Albanian Kosovars' in Charny, *Encyclopedia* (note 8), p.645.
43. Quoted in Stephen Bates, Ian Black and James Meek, 'Bombers Target Troops', *The Guardian*, 29 March 1999. p.1. Susan Sontag is one example of a public intellectual who labelled the war 'genocide'. See her 'An Evil that Makes the Balkan War Just', *The Observer*, 16 May 1999, p.15.
44. Ken Booth, 'The Kosovo Tragedy – Epilogue to Another "Low and Dishonest Decade"?', Keynote address given at the South Africa Political Science Biannual Congress, Saldanha, South Africa 29 June 1999.
45. Quoted in Stephen Castle, 'Milosevic may be charged with Genocide', *The Independent*, 19 June 1999, p.4.
46. Quoted in Martin Kettle, 'UN Head Voices Deep Rage', *The Guardian*, 1 April 1999, p.3.
47. Barbara Harff, *Genocide and Human Rights: International Legal and Political Issues* (Denver, CO: Monograph Series in World Affairs, 1984) p.12.
48. Amnesty International, *Kosovo: The Evidence* (London: Amnesty International, 1998), pp.33–46.
49. Ibid., p.18.
50. Ibid.
51. Quoted in ibid., p.48.
52. United Nations, *Report of the Independent Inquiry into the Actions of the United Nations during the 1994 Genocide in Rwanda*, 15 December 1999.
53. See also the reports by the French Assembly and the Belgium Senate: Assemblée Nationale, Mission d'Information commune, *Enquête sur la tragédie rwandaise (1990–1994)* (Paris: Assemblée Nationale, Dian-55/98) and Sénat de Belgique, *Commission d'enquête parlementaire concernant les événements du Rwanda, Rapport* (Bruxelles, 6 décembre 1997).
54. President Bill Clinton, quoted in Charny, *Encyclopedia of Genocide* (note 8), p.13.
55. UN Press Release GA/9523, 2 December 1998.
56. UN Press Release GA/9652, 8 November 1999.
57. UN Press Release GA/9523, 2 December 1998.
58. UN Press Release GA/9523, 2 December 1998.
59. UN Press Release GA/9523, 2 December 1998.
60. UN Press Release GA/9523, 2 December 1998.
61. UN Press Release GA/9652, 8 November 1999.
62. Indictment Information Sheet, Milosevic & others Case (IT-99-37-I), http://www.un.org/icty/glance/milosevic.htm
63. Article 5 of the Statute of the International Tribunal entitled 'Crimes against humanity' states: 'The International Tribunal shall have the power to prosecute persons responsible for the following crimes when committed in armed conflict, whether international or internal in character, and directed against any civilian population: a) murder; b) extermination; c) enslavement; d) deportation; e) imprisonment; f) torture; g) rape; h) persecutions on political, racial and religious grounds; other inhumane acts.

64. Sir Hartley Shawcross, representative of the United Kingdom, in the debate on the Genocide Convention quoted in Kuper, *Genocide* (note 3), p.19.
65. Tim Dunne and Nicholas J. Wheeler (eds), *Human Rights in Global Politics* (Cambridge: Cambridge University Press, 1998). See especially the contributions by Ken Booth, Chris Brown and Bhikhu Parekh.
66. Tatz 'Genocide and the Politics of Memory' (note 1), p.313.
67. There is a burgeoning literature that begins with this critical commitment. See especially, among his many contributions, Ken Booth, 'Security and Emancipation', *Review of International Studies*, Vol.17, No.4, pp.313–26. For an excellent monograph that brings critical theoretical insights into the study of security, see Richard Wyn Jones, *Security, Strategy, and Critical Theory* (Boulder, CO: Lynne Reinner, 1999).
68. R.J. Rummel, 'The New Concept of Democide', in quoted in Israel W. Charny (ed.), *Encyclopedia of Genocide: Volume 1* (Oxford: ABC-CLIO, 1999), p.28.
69. This is Ken Booth's metaphor. See this argument developed further in his 'Human Wrongs and International Relations', *International Affairs*, Vol.71, No.1 (1995), pp.103–26.
70. Rummel, 'The New Concept of Democide' (note 69), p.34.
71. The identity of the letter-writer is not disclosed by Levi, referring to her simply as 'a librarian in Westphalia'. See Primo Levi, *The Drowned and the Saved* (New York: Vintage, 1989) translated by Raymond Rosenthal, p.181.

# 2
# The History and Politics of Ethnic Cleansing

## CARRIE BOOTH WALLING

It was the second week of April, when the paramilitary Serb forces drove us out and told us to move in the direction of Albania. The grief was unimaginable, the leaving of houses and everything we possessed. I remember the name of the Serb police[man] who entered my house. His name is Xubisha. I will remember always the hatred in his face.

– Aishe from Rahoveci, Kosovo[1]

In Kosovo, as in other countries such as Bosnia, Burundi and East Timor, survivors of extreme ethnic oppression recount stories of horror and brutality similar to that told by Aishe. Indeed, ethnic cleansing, in practice and in discourse, has become a common feature of international politics. The prevalence of ethnic cleansing at the end of the twentieth century is frequently understood to derive from 'ancient hatreds', which had previously been suppressed by Cold War structures. Contrary to this perspective however, ethnic cleansing can be seen as a the result of the exploitation of insecurity and the manipulation of national history by power-seeking political elites. Whatever its immediate causes in the 1990s, the roots of ethnic cleansing extend back to early centuries and are well-documented. The historical record strongly suggests that contemporary ethnic cleansing may be intricately linked to the political ideal of the homogenous sovereign state and the principle of national self-determination. Furthermore, ethnic cleansing seems to operate in the gap between conflicting international rules and norms, which makes it difficult for supporters of the principles of international law to prevent and respond to its political use.

## THE CONCEPT OF 'ETHNIC CLEANSING'

It is not known who first introduced the phrase 'ethnic cleansing'; indeed its origins are highly contested. 'Forced population transfer' is a general synonym, but ethnic cleansing is a distinctive type and indeed represents an escalation of the idea of population transfer entirely based on ethnic criteria. The Greek word *andrapodismos,* used to describe the conquering of Thebes by Alexander the Great in 335 BC, is an antecedent of the term ethnic cleansing because it combines notions of deportation and enslavement.[2] It differs, however, in that it lacks an ethnic connotation. In practice, 'ethnic cleansing' is most closely related to the German word *Judenrien* (meaning literally, clean of Jews) which was used by the Nazis to describe the areas from which Jews had been deported or expelled during World War Two.[3] Ethnic cleansing is similarly linked to the Russian words, *chistka* and *etnicheskoye chishcheniye*. The former, which combines the notions of purging and cleaning, was used to describe Stalin's ideological cleansing of the Soviet Union. Soviet officials used the latter phrase, literally translated as 'ethnic cleansing', during the 1980s to describe the ethnic-based expulsions which took place between Armenians and Azerbaijanis in Nagorno-Karabakh.[4]

'Ethnic cleansing', however, did not enter the popular language of politics until the break-up of the former Yugoslavia in the early 1990s. Popularised by Western journalists, 'ethnic cleansing' is a literal translation of the Serbo-Croatian/Bosnian phrase *etnicko ciscenje*. The phrase is believed to have been part of the Yugoslav National Army's (JNA) military vocabulary to describe its policy of expelling Muslims and Croats from the territories conquered by the Serb-dominated rump Yugoslavia.[5] Initially the term did not have the negative connotations that it now carries. In fact, it was used openly by then Serbian President, Slobodan Milosevic, and the regime's nationalist supporters. 'Cleansing' was used specifically for its positive connotations of cleanliness and purification that masked the 'dirty truth' of its implementation: forced deportation, murder, and rape.

Although the removal of populations by states, government elites and rival ethnic groups can be traced to antiquity, distinctive differences exist between contemporary ethnic cleansing and its early antecedents – forced population transfer and removal. These methods are a part of a wider continuum ranging from genocide at one extreme to emigration under pressure at the other.[6] As defined by the United Nations Commission of Experts in a 1993 report to the Security Council, 'ethnic cleansing is the planned deliberate removal from a specific territory, persons of a particular ethnic group, by force or intimidation, in order to render that area ethnically homogenous'.[7] The term 'ethnic' refers to a group of people that share a distinct racial, national, religious, linguistic or cultural heritage, including shared history and perceptions, group identity and shared memory of past glories and traumas. Because 'ethnic cleansing' is exclusively based on ethnic criteria, it is distinct from other forms of large-scale population removal, which can include religious cleansing, ideological cleansing (based on class or directed at political adversaries), strategic (applied to politically unreliable populations in sensitive military areas), economic and gender cleansings.[8] State-directed movements of ethnic groups are designed to consolidate state power over a specific territory. This can be accomplished by moving members of the dominant or favoured ethnic group into the contested territory or an enemy group out of the territory; however, they often occur in conjunction.[9]

Ethnic cleansing entails actions of various types and degrees, committed by one ethnic group (usually supported and directed by a state or powerful political elites) against another to compel flight. In some instances, however, measures are taken to aggressively assimilate the targeted population into the culture of the predominant ethnic group through either coerced or biological assimilation.[10] These practices can include the prohibition of ethnic association; the banning of minority language and/or religion; forcibly changing distinctive family names; and restrictive marriage and birth control laws intended to prevent the ethnic group from reproducing itself. Most frequently, however, the aim of ethnic cleansing is to expel the despised ethnic group through either indirect coercion or direct force, and to ensure that return is impossible. Terror is the fundamental method used to achieve this end.[11]

Methods of indirect coercion can include: introducing repressive laws and discriminatory measures designed to make minority life difficult; the deliberate failure to prevent mob violence against ethnic minorities; using surrogates to inflict violence; the destruction of the physical infrastructure upon which minority life depends; the imprisonment of male members of the ethnic group; threats to rape female members, and threats to kill.[12] If ineffective, these indirect methods are often escalated to coerced emigration, where the removal of the ethnic group from the territory is pressured by physical force. This typically includes physical harassment and the expropriation of property. Deportation is an escalated form of direct coercion in that the forcible removal of 'undesirables' from the state's territory is organised, directed and carried out by state agents. The most serious of the direct methods, excluding genocide, is murderous cleansing, which entails the brutal and often public murder of some few in order to compel flight of the remaining group members.[13] Unlike during genocide, when murder is intended to be total and an end in itself, murderous cleansing is used as a tool towards the larger aim of expelling survivors from the territory. The process can be made complete by revoking the citizenship of those who emigrate or flee.

It is important – politically and legally – to distinguish between genocide and ethnic cleansing. The goal of the former is extermination: the complete annihilation of an ethnic, national or racial group. It contains both a physical element (acts such as murder) and a mental element (those acts are undertaken to destroy, in whole or in part, the said group).[14] Ethnic cleansing involves population expulsions, sometimes accompanied by murder, but its aim is consolidation of power over territory, not the destruction of a complete people. These two processes, although similar, are not the same. All genocide involves ethnic cleansing, because the physical elimination of a people by definition means physical displacement. However, the reverse is not true: ethnic cleansing does not equate with genocide, although it may be its precursor, and it may involve 'genocidal acts'.

## ETHNIC CLEANSING: A BRUTAL BRIEF HISTORY

The political meaning given to the territorial dispossession of ethnic groups has changed radically over the centuries. In the earliest times it was virtually part of the natural order of state-building. From the 1920s to the 1940s it was viewed positively as a tool of international peace and security. By the end of the twentieth century it was widely, although not universally, seen as evil and destructive. Throughout history, though, population transfer and ethnic cleansing have been closely associated with the process of state building.

In early centuries, population cleansing was used as a political tool to ensure control over alien or recently conquered territories. Often the victims of cleansing were enslaved or vanquished from the conquered territory. Population removals were inter- and intra-civilisational and were driven by strong economic motivation. The Assyrians, who are credited with initiating forced population movements as a state policy, resettled up to 4.5 million people during the years 883–59BC and 669–27 BC.[15] Economic and political factors were most salient in population cleansings during these periods, but occasionally these movements were motivated by ethnic factors.

Throughout the Middle Ages, economic cleansing became less prevalent and instead population cleansing took on a largely religious character. With the spread of Christianity and Islam throughout much of the world, population cleansing become organised around the notion of collective religious identity, and hostility was directed at religious minorities rather than conquered populations. Religious cleansing entails the removal of a well-defined population from a specific territory based on the characteristics and traits that made it undesirable – namely an alien religion.[16] Some ethnic enmity occurred within the religious blocs; ethnicity played a secondary role in medieval cleansing.

The religious motivation of population removals, so prominent in the Middle Ages, lost much of its salience early in the modern period. Nonetheless, between 1530 and 1730 ethnic enmity remained couched in religious terms. For example, at the end of the sixteenth century, Spanish persecution of Protestants in the Low Countries sent more than 175,000 Protestants into flight. Another example seen in the beginning of the seventeenth century was the mass expulsions of Irish Catholics from Ulster.[17] After 1730, forms of population cleansing began to proliferate, including ideological, strategic and ethnic justifications for cleansing. Population movements of this time lost their partial, incomplete character and acquired one of totality.

Between 1755 and 1900, most population cleansing was intimately related to colonialism and European imperialism. Population expulsions of this period sometimes had an ethnic character, but they served a primarily strategic purpose. Examples include the cleansing of francophone Acadians in Canada, the Native Indians by Americans, Aborigines in Australia, and the Maori by the British in New Zealand. After 1900, despised populations were cleansed based on markers such as ethnicity, language, and culture. During this period, ethnic cleansing emerged as a planned and deliberate policy and gained some of the brutality we are familiar with today.[18] The expulsions in Ottoman Turkey serve as an example.

One of the often-cited ethnic cleansings of the twentieth century was that of the ethnic Armenians at the hands of the Ottoman Turks. As an Orthodox Christian population with deep sympathies for co-ethnics in Russia, the Armenian population of Turkey was viewed by state leaders as a highly suspect fifth column. As Turkish ties to Europe increased, and the ethnic Armenian population became restless, Turkish government leaders inflamed ethnic enmity between the ethnic Armenians and other national groups, and incited violence against the former. Once a multiethnic and tolerant society, Turkey adopted ethnic cleansing during its transition from a multiethnic state to a national state. In the process, what began as ethnic cleansing developed into genocide. During the ensuing wars (1894–96 and 1915–16), over ninety per cent of ethnic Armenian territory was cleansed of its inhabitants through deportation, death marches and murder. Because Turkish policy was aimed at the complete physical and cultural annihilation of the Armenian ethnic group, it is more accurately classified as genocide and not ethnic cleansing.[19] For this reason, the case of Armenia, along with other genocides including the Holocaust, Pol Pot's Cambodia and Rwanda are not central to the present discussion.

Arguably, the defining historical moment for contemporary ethnic cleansing was the 1919 territorial settlement between the Allied and Associated Powers and Germany, which officially endorsed population transfers in accordance with the doctrine of national self-determination. In fact, population transfer was viewed as a legitimate means of creating a better fit between 'national boundaries' and the peoples living within their territory.[20] In effect, citizen rights became intrinsically linked to ethnicity. In theory, population movements would ease the tensions both within and between states by diminishing the threat of secessionist claims and wars over territory. In practice, states were assigned to dominant ethnic groups –'nations' – and although the treaty guaranteed minority rights, there was little international enforcement or oversight. Movement of minorities was often coerced – encouraged by local violence and state seizure of properties. Population flight among minorities increased significantly after the treaty's signing, and by 1926 there were nearly ten million refugees in Europe.[21] In total, between the years of 1919 to 1938, 'population movements' affected nearly 21,260,000 individuals of varying European nationalities.[22]

The principle of compulsory population transfer gained increasing international acceptance during the inter-war period. The Treaty of Lausanne, which involved the exchange of almost two million Orthodox and Muslim minorities between Greece and Turkey in 1923, was approved and supervised by the League of Nations.[23] Lord Curzon, who had been British Foreign Minister (1919–24) and a participant at the Lausanne conference, however, argued strongly against the transfer, which he described as 'a vicious solution for which the world will pay a heavy penalty for a hundred years to come'.[24]

Before 1939, the Nazi Party expelled Jews from German and occupied territories through fear and the mechanisms of ethnic cleansing described above. Physical extermination – indeed, genocide – began seriously after 1941. Ethnic cleansing by the Nazis, however, always had genocidal possibilities due to the extreme racist attitudes of its perpetrators. Ethnic cleansing, and later genocide, was intricately connected to the creation of the German Master *Volk*/state. In *Mein Kampf,* Hitler described his theory of *Lebensraum*: 'The foreign policy of the Volkist state must safeguard the existence on this planet of the race embodied in the state, by creating a healthy, viable natural relation between the nation's population and growth on the one hand and the quantity and quality of its soil on the other.'[25]

During World War Two, Adolf Hitler took population removal to its deadliest extreme: the Holocaust. In the quest for a 'pure' national state, Hitler transplanted millions of ethnic Germans in conquered territories and deported millions of Jews and other populations deemed threatening to the German *Volk* including Poles, Gypsies, homosexuals, and the physically and mentally handicapped. 'Pure cleansing' evolved into genocide as he tried to carve out *Lebensraum* (which describes an imperialist drive for natural resources, exploitable markets and power over vast territories) in an effort to ensure national/racial survival, and the elimination of European Jewry.[26]

Following the end of World War Two, the allied powers were once again faced with daunting decisions regarding future international stability. Yet instead of marking a shift from the earlier endorsement of population transfer, and despite Article 49 of the Fourth Geneva Convention (which prohibited the forced transfer of populations) and Article 6 of the Nuremberg Charter (which identified population transfer as a crime), the transfer of ethnic Germans from throughout Europe to what remained of Germany was authorised by Article XIII of the Potsdam Protocols.[27] Winston Churchill and Franklin D. Roosevelt endorsed and authorised population transfer as a necessary means to ensuring future peace and stability in Europe. Both leaders believed that the temporary discomfort and dislocation of the displaced civilians was a small price to pay for long-term security in central and eastern Europe. In a speech before the House of Commons on 5 December 1944 Churchill had remarked:

> A clean sweep will be made. I am not alarmed by the prospect of the disentanglement of populations, nor even by these large transferences, which are more possible in modern conditions than they ever were before.[28]

In the light of the failure of League of Nations' minority system, and with the memory of the inter-war problems resulting from minorities in Europe fresh in the minds of European leaders, forced population transfer was viewed as a means of permanently eliminating Europe's 'minority problem'. The transfer went forward with explicit instructions for an orderly and humane transfer. More than 14 million Germans were expelled under conditions of starvation and terror. Over two million Germans died in the process.[29]

During this same time period, Joseph Stalin orchestrated mass deportations of national and ethnic groups deemed threatening to the state, and those he sought to punish for cooperation with the occupying Germans. For example, ethnic Germans, Greeks and Bulgarians of Ukraine and the Crimea were deported *en masse* because they were viewed as unreliable, and even dangerous. The Kalmyks and Karachai were entirely ethnically cleansed in 1943. Later deportations included targeted groups from the North Caucasus to the Balkans.[30] During his grip on power, Stalin ethnically cleansed millions of Soviet citizens.

Although not labelled as ethnic cleansing at the time, hundreds of thousands of Arabs were forcibly expelled from Palestine by Israeli Jews in 1948. Nearly 400 Arab villages were depopulated and subsequently razed to the ground to prevent the almost 700,000 Palestinians who were made refugees that year from returning to their homeland. The largest expulsions occurred out of the towns of Lydda and Ramle in July, when over 50,000 people were forcibly removed. Atrocities included massacres, such as the one at Deir Yassin, and random killings. Palestinian Arabs also directed atrocities at Israeli Jews, yet there were far fewer by comparison. During the war of 1948, Arab forces conquered and depopulated fewer than 12 Jewish settlements.[31]

The 1990s further bear witness to the prevalence and cruelty of ethnic cleansing. Examples include ethnic conflict in Bosnia; mass rape in Bosnia and Rwanda; Iraqi attempts to annihilate Kurds; systematic attacks on Kurds in Turkey; murderous cleansing in East Timor; the occupation and destruction of Palestinian settlements by Israel; and ethnic oppression and terror in Kosovo. These ethnic cleansings were historically unique in that developments in mass media communications brought ethnic cleansing into living rooms around the world. International inaction evoked widespread moral outrage, and many domestic constituencies tried to shame their governments for failing to intervene. The response of Western governments was cautious; that of others even more so. Finally, well after ethnic conflict engulfed the Balkans, ethnic cleansing was recognised as a potential source of international instability. In an act of restitution, the United Nations Security Council voted unanimously to approve *The Statute of the Yugoslav War Crimes Tribunal*, marking a strong normative shift against accepting cleansing as a solution to minority/ethnic problems.[32] The massacres and mass rape campaigns of the Rwandan genocide were virtually ignored while they were happening, despite the ostensible universal condemnation of ethnic cleansing and genocide. Although ethnic cleansing is no longer viewed as a possible answer to some of the problems of international peace and security as it was during the inter-war and early post-World War Two periods, a clear and unambiguous policy to halt its use has yet to be developed.

The brief history just recounted has demonstrated that ethnic cleansing is not a new phenomenon, even if the term itself is recent, nor unique to a particular group of people or confined to a geographic area. The forcible removal of a population from a particular territory has been used by the state to consolidate power and enforce order over territory under its control since state-building began. In varying forms and degrees, ethnic cleansing has been evident on every continent.[33] The historical record suggests that population removal has been an instrument of nation-state creation, and that contemporary ethnic cleansing is fundamentally linked to the homogenous sovereign state as the model form of political organisation.[34] Indeed a culture of population removal has been perpetuated over time providing a precedent for the lethal ethnic cleansings prevalent at the end of the twentieth century, which has been described as one of 'ethnic engineering'.[35]

## ETHNIC CLEANSING: ITS CAUSES AND SYMPTOMS

The causes of ethnic cleansing are highly contested. Arguments range from linking ethnic cleansing to totalitarian regimes at one end of the spectrum to linking it with democracies on the other, and from understanding the phenomenon as unleashed by ethnic hatreds to understanding it as the result of elite power politics. The argument here is that ethnic cleansing can be seen as the result of the exploitation of insecurity and the manipulation of national history by power-seeking political elites. Furthermore, ethnic cleansing may be intricately linked to the political ideal of the homogenous sovereign state and the principle of self-determination. In effect, ethnic cleansing seems to operate in the gap between two core principles of international law: the inviolability of borders enshrined in the United Nations Charter and the principle of self-determination. The result is that states and intergovernmental organisations are often ill-equipped to respond to ethnic cleansing precisely for this reason, and because the protection of state rights can conflict with the human rights guaranteed by the Universal Declaration of Human Rights. One argument is that ethnic cleansing is an instrument of nation-state creation; however, considerable debate exists within this perspective regarding the relationship between ethnic cleansing and particular forms of political organisation. R.J. Rummel argues that it is primarily the tool of authoritarian and totalitarian states, and that the more authoritarian a state is the more likely it is to commit crimes such as ethnic cleansing. Echoing the 'democratic peace' thesis, Rummel argues that in general democracies do not engage in population cleansings, whereas 'totalitarian regimes slaughter their own people by tens of millions'.[36] Rummel identifies the assertion of absolute power as the ultimate cause. He argues that within totalitarian regimes, power is unchecked; but in democratic societies power is restrained by the participation of the lower and middle classes in selecting its holders. Rummel admits that democracies are responsible for some forms of democide – *government mass murder* – but argues that nearly all cases occurred within the context of war, were carried out in an undemocratic fashion, and were directed against enemy civilians.[37] Government mass murder may contain ethnic hatred, but has not been part of a policy of ethnic homogeneity as defined earlier.

Far from exempting democracy from the horrors of ethnic cleansing, Michael Mann argues that democracy and ethnic cleansing are intrinsically connected; ethnic cleansing is 'democracy's dark side'. Mann argues that the dominant Western system of democracy generates a sense of alien 'other' through its majoritarian governing principles. The citizen body is seen as sharing distinctive virtuous characteristics that distinguish it from other groups. The notion of 'We the People' results in a division between 'we' and 'other'. Democracies are able to physically exclude the 'other' through the right of territorial sovereignty. In such ways, ethnic cleansing becomes the most undesirable consequence of vesting political legitimacy in the people because it is always justified in their name.[38] Mann takes the argument even further by pointing out that many democratic states are themselves born of conflict – the result of ethnic cleansing.[39] He argues that once the nation removes 'others' it requires little further violence to sustain its position. He writes, 'impeccably liberal nation-states can bloom above the mass graves of the cleansed – in the US, in Australia, in Germany – and eventually perhaps in Serbia'.[40] To encourage democracy world-wide means accepting the conflict out of which it arises.[41] This is an uncomfortable argument for proponents of liberal democracy, but it is one that must be confronted.

Democracies are not innocent of population cleansing, but ethnic cleansing and genocide have also been associated with authoritarian and totalitarian regimes such as Nazi Germany, the former Soviet Union, Iraq or Serbia. Nor can it be denied that Western democracies have intervened to halt ethnic cleansing in many cases at the end of the twentieth century. This is not to say that democracies do not participate in ethnic cleansing. Despite the slowly emerging norm against ethnic cleansing, democratic states inconsistently respond to and sometimes support particular instances of ethnic cleansing, creating an uneasy relationship between the two. Yet, democracy in and of itself is not the cause of ethnic cleansing. Perhaps democratic, authoritarian and totalitarian states perpetuate and even exacerbate ethnic cleansing due to their very organisational logic –

the homogenous, sovereign state as the ideal form of political organisation. The actual cause of ethnic cleansing, however, seems to be rooted deeper than the state system that may perpetuate its practice.

At its heart, ethnic cleansing seems to stem from fear, hatred, and insecurity – derived from ethnic mistrust. Yet there are competing models for understanding how this insecurity becomes manifest and why it leads to ethnic cleansing. The fear model of ethnic conflict, outlined by David Lake and Donald Rothchild, is 'bottom up' – ethnic insecurity spreads within a territory or community and leads to violence. They argue that ethnic conflict results from the collective fears of the future (often lived through the shared memories of the past) by groups that feel unprotected by the state.[42] The failure of the state to inspire confidence, ensure fair representation, and genuinely consider the needs of any minority population, combined with perceived ethnic threats and personal vulnerability, forces people to rely on the informal networks of the ethnic community to which they belong.[43] Distrust, information failures, problems of credible commitment and incentives to use pre-emptive force exacerbate fear and lead to state failure. Ethnic nationalism is born of the belief that the ethnic group will provide security and protection against 'the enemy', which the state in which they live fails to provide. Ethnic groups that fear for their safety easily lock into difficult strategic dilemmas with rival groups that can escalate to the level of ethnic cleansing.

An argument very similar to the Lake and Rothchild model can be made using the state as referent. The very act of regrouping by ethnicity may threaten the territorial integrity of the state and can also become a motivating factor for population cleansing. Motivated by fears of minority irredentism, the governments and dominant ethnic groups of many states utilise ethnic cleansing as a way to deal with their 'minority problem(s)'. Not infrequently, insecurity within states may be blamed upon a minority ethnic group. Growing insecurity on the part of the majority group may become heightened, and spark ethnic cleansing. These fears include: losing demographic control over state territory due to high minority birth-rates; the crippling of the economy and international sanctions as a result of the poor treatment of minorities; fear of international conspiracy to create an ethnic supra-state with state minorities being a fifth column; and the collapse of law and order due to the terrorist activities of the minority.

V.P. Gagnon offers a rival explanation to the fear model of ethnic cleansing. Gagnon argues that ethnic violence is not caused by ethnic sentiment or external security concerns. Instead, he contends that ethnic-based violence results from the dynamics of within-group conflict. Fear and grievances are frequently manipulated and capitalised upon by politicians and nationalist elites who seek to increase their own power, as well as that of the state. The power model is 'top down'. By exploiting insecurities derived from ethnic mistrust and manipulating national histories, politically threatened elites may provoke violence along ethnic cleavages in an effort to construct a political context in which ethnicity becomes the primary –and only politically relevant—identity.[44] In this way, elites at the same time can shift the political agenda away from issues on which they are threatened by domestic challengers to one in which ethnic grievances become the focus of debate.[45] According to this argument, ethnic cleansing is ultimately the result of a particular type of power politics that capitalises upon latent ethnic mistrust more than a particular type of regime, and is an often used tool in state-creation based on ethnic nationalist ideals.

The case of Kosovo supports Gagnon's argument. In the quote at the beginning of this article, Aishe describes the hatred in the face of the Serb policeman that forces her from her home. In Kosovo, this hatred did not become manifest prior to Slobodan Milosevic's bid for political power, nor did it prompt ethnic cleansing until under his direction, despite existent antagonisms between Serbs and ethnic Albanians. The other wars in the former Yugoslavia also support this perspective. For example, prior to Yugoslavia's break-up, intermarriage rates and tolerance levels were very high in the same ethnically mixed regions that experienced some of the most brutal violence.[46] This is not to say that fear and insecurity cannot develop along the ethnic cleavages described by Lake and Rothchild. Rather, the argument is that it is the exploitation of those latent insecurities that led to ethnic cleansing.

Ethnic cleansing, however, may be exacerbated and perpetuated by the political ideal of the homogenous sovereign state and the principle of national self-determination. In 1919, the great powers had adjusted state boundaries in an effort to create a better fit between the territory of the state and the nationality of the people living within it. In this same tradition, nation-states with 'minority problems' can physically eliminate national minorities either by removing people to fit existing boundaries or by revising boundaries to match demographics.[47] Changes have been typically justified on the basis of ethnic composition of adjacent territories, are sanctioned by the principle of state sovereignty, and are supported by historical precedent. Ethnic cleansing has been justified by states as a sovereign right to maintain law and order within their borders and to preserve their territorial integrity. The inviolability of borders is enshrined in the United Nations Charter.[48]

Ethnic cleansing is ultimately a choice and other options exist; but the norms of statism have traditionally advanced few alternatives to the movement of populations. Indeed, peaceful change remains an underdeveloped practice in international relations.[49] The revision of frontiers to match the distribution of populations contradicts the notion of territorial sovereignty when revision equates with the loss of control over a particular portion of territory. Altering the basis of the state so that it is recognised as a multi-nation state is a viable option, yet often means the lessening of power for those that hold it. The organising ideals of the nation-state system do not cause ethnic cleansing but they may support the desire of the dominant ethnic group within a multi-ethnic/national state to cleanse the state territory in the interest of its own stability and security. As a result, states may attempt to compel assimilation of the minority through repressive policies or coerce flight.

At the same time, the organising principles of the nation-state system may push ethnicities towards independence. When states attempt to strengthen control over minority populations, they sometimes promote the very action they seek to prevent. Ethnicities made fearful by repressive state measures may struggle more ardently for statehood. Statehood is idealised to the degree that an ethnic group without a state is viewed as politically incomplete and vulnerable because it lacks the protective power that the state provides. In the current international system, where the United Nations is unable to guarantee the security of minority or vulnerable ethnic groups within the territorial boundaries of the sovereign state, statehood may become seen as necessary to ethnic group survival. Threatened collectivities will strive for independence as long as repression against them continues and the ideals of freedom, self-determination, representative government, and the homogenous sovereign state are held as sacred in the international system.[50]

Ethnic cleansing thereby operates in the gap between conflicting international rules and norms: the inviolability of borders and the principle of self-determination. It may be, in fact, impossible to enforce both principles simultaneously in the same place. For example, in Kosovo, supporters of the principles of international law cannot simultaneously defend Yugoslavia's sovereignty and the Kosovar Albanians' right to national self-determination. Specifically, the United Nations Charter bans force that violates state sovereignty. At the same time, the Universal Declaration of Human Rights guarantees the rights of individuals against oppressive states. The absence of a clear policy on how to deal with this contradiction makes it easier for states to engage in ethnic cleansing. The United Nations and its member-states cannot guarantee self-determination for repressed populations, nor can they in good faith impose barriers to that independence in the name of territorial integrity. This international ambivalence emboldens those governments and political elites that would abuse their power over peoples within their territory.[51] Ethnic cleansing in Kosovo illustrates this point.

## THE POLITICS OF ETHNIC CLEANSING IN KOSOVO

In Kosovo, ethnic apartheid exacerbated ethnic mistrust and heightened the insecurity of the Kosovars. The manipulation of Serbian national history by Milosevic and Serbian nationalist elites incited virulent ethnic nationalism, evoked hatred, and made possible the terror tactics that were directed at ethnic Albanians like Aishe from Rahoveci. Ethnic cleansing in Kosovo highlights the tension between the pursuit of homogenous state sovereignty and the struggle for national self-determination, and operates in the space between them, posing a formidable challenge to supporters of the principles of international law. International ambiguity in both the definition of and response to ethnic cleansing further complicated intervention efforts. In fact, the rhetorical power of the term 'ethnic cleansing' and the politics over its use with respect to the province helped to create the context in which intervention may have perpetuated the ethnic politics of the region.

In April of 1999, Kofi Annan, Secretary-General of the United Nations, condemned 'the vicious and systematic campaign of ethnic cleansing' conducted by Serbian authorities against ethnic Albanians in Kosovo.[52] Yet ethnic apartheid had been evident in Kosovo for nearly a decade, and ethnic cleansing was widely believed to be its logical conclusion. But because ethnic cleansing operates in a gap between international norms, the United Nations and its member-states were ill-prepared to respond, creating the context in which the rhetorical power of the term 'ethnic cleansing' could be exploited in pursuit of varying regional and national interests.

The details of the break-up of Yugoslavia are widely known, but the revocation of Kosovo's autonomy is rarely cited as the catalyst for the secessions of Slovenia, Croatia and Bosnia-Hercegovina from the Yugoslav federation, and the subsequent ethnic cleansing campaigns. In fact, it was Milosevic's nationalist platform of taking back from the Kosovar Albanians the Serb-treasured lands of Kosovo – 'Serbia's spiritual and political heart' – that catapulted him into the Serbian presidency. Shortly thereafter, Kosovo lost its autonomy and the ethnic Albanians lost political and civil rights under organised apartheid. It is difficult to identify the exact point at which ethnic apartheid turned into ethnic cleansing. Nonetheless, the human rights abuses of the past decade described below are well documented:[53]

- *The removal of elected authorities*: Ethnic Albanians were removed from all positions of power including government, police and security forces, hospitals, schools, and the University.
- *Prohibition of ethnic association and minority language*: The University was closed, gathering in large groups was forbidden, children's soccer teams were disbanded, the Albanian language was largely prohibited, and the Albanian flag was banned.
- *Restricted access to education, housing, medicine, food and humanitarian aid*: Ethnic Albanians created parallel institutions to service the basic needs of its community members. In an effort to strengthen the ethnic markers between the Serbian and Albanian communities of Kosovo as well as to foster divisions within the ethnic Albanian community, hospitals often refused treatment to injured Albanians, universities were closed to ethnic Albanians and schools in Kosovo were segregated. Repressive legislation was enacted, some of which aimed at simultaneously increasing Serbian and decreasing Albanian birth rates in the province.
- *Confiscation of property*: Serbian soldiers occupied Albanian homes and businesses. Serb refugees from the wars in Bosnia and Croatia were resettled in Kosovar Albanian homes after owners were forcibly removed. Stores were vandalised, and houses subjected to random search. Books were stolen, and pictures burned.
- *Detainment*: Ethnic Albanian men were randomly detained and beaten. Many disappeared.
- *Terror Campaigns*: Ethnic Albanian civilians (even children) were victims of indiscriminate violence including beatings, rape and death.
- *Political Violence*: Kosovar community leaders were assassinated, detained and beaten. Peaceful protesters were shot.
- *Deportation*: Before the NATO bombing and increasingly following the outbreak of war, ethnic Albanians were forcibly removed from Kosovo. Some were loaded onto trains and buses that took them to the Albanian border. The lives of sons and husbands were ransomed, and sometimes the families could not pay the price.
- *Murderous cleansing*: War provided the cover for demonstrative acts of violence against familial clans and villages. Civilians were killed by sniper fire, burned in houses, raped, and slaughtered at the hands of paramilitary soldiers in an effort to incite fear and compel flight.

Through this system of ethnic apartheid and with the installation of Yugoslav troops and Serbian paramilitary groups, Milosevic attempted to decrease 'irredentism' in the province, tighten control of its borders, break established links with the Albanian 'homeland', diminish the perceived military threat from neighbouring Albania, inflict terror upon the Albanian population and compel flight. At the same time, Serbian resettlement, particularly using Bosnian-Serb refugees (who were themselves the victims of ethnic cleansing), was undertaken to consolidate Serbian control of the province and its resources, alter the demographic balance between ethnic Albanians and Serbs, intimidate local groups, and monitor ethnic Albanian activity for the state.[54] Ethnic Albanian solidarity increased with the intensity of human rights abuses against them. In response to severe ethnic apartheid, a decade-long non-violent struggle for independence began. The Kosova Liberation Army (KLA) emerged shortly after the distinctly non-violent Kosovar Albanians were denied participation in the 1995 Dayton Accords. The inability of the non-violent movement to garner international support, combined with increasing ethnic oppression, heightened polarisation between the Serbs and Albanians in Kosovo. The KLA launched a guerrilla campaign against Serbian authorities, which locked the two sides into a spiralling cycle of ethnic violence and reprisal.[55] Ethnic cleansing directed against the ethnic Albanians ensued.

The use of the term 'ethnic cleansing' to describe state-directed assaults against minority or vulnerable ethnic groups is a powerful political tool; it denotes abuses to be condemned and perhaps directly opposed by those who use the phrase. The use of the terms 'population transfer' and 'genocide' are similarly political. For example, the term 'population transfer' does not carry the same obligations for action as 'ethnic cleansing'. Conversely, the term 'population transfer' can be used to mask brutal acts of ethnic cleansing, and evoke images of more peaceable and humane population exchanges.[56] Similar tensions exist between the political usage of the term 'ethnic cleansing' and that of 'genocide', which explains the politics surrounding the sometimes-inappropriate usage of the terms.[57]

With regard to Kosovo, the politics of language were evident. Hesitant to enter the conflict in Kosovo as it escalated after 1995, major powers refrained early on from using the discourse of ethnic cleansing to describe the human rights abuses there. Ethnic cleansing in Kosovo only became labelled as such when the national interests of these same powers were at stake. As Robert Hayden has put it, 'The depiction of the expulsion of a population depends on the political position of the party making it'.[58] The rhetoric of ethnic cleansing and later genocide was used to lay the groundwork for, and became the political defence of, NATO bombing.

As NATO bombs fell on the Federal Republic of Yugoslavia, 'ethnic cleansing' and 'genocide' were used interchangeably by NATO powers to justify intervention. Yet 'ethnic cleansing' and 'genocide' are significantly different. The latter describes a systematic attempt to annihilate all members of a particular group; the intent is extermination. The goal of ethnic cleansing is the consolidation of power over a specific territory through population removal. In Kosovo, the language of genocide was used by NATO powers to cast collective guilt over the Serbian people, making it easier for the NATO allies to justify the deaths of Serb civilians resulting from 'bombing errors'.[59] In reality, however, Serbia's goal in Kosovo was territorial acquisition. Population cleansing was undertaken for political purposes; it was accompanied by ethnic hatred. Serbian policy was to murder *some* ethnic Albanians to serve as an example for the many. Murderous cleansing was used as a means of compelling the Albanian population into flight but was not an end in itself. Survivor stories and casualty rates suggest that in Kosovo, most of the population was permitted to abandon the territory upon occupation.

In comparison, national governments stopped short of defining gross human rights violations as 'ethnic cleansing' (or in this case the more accurate characterisation of 'genocide') in Rwanda, precisely because its usage conveyed an obligation to respond. Similarly, other cases of human rights abuses such as those against the Kurds in Turkey or the Palestinians in the occupied territories, have not been labelled ethnic cleansing although they have the same characteristics and perpetuate similar patterns of ethnic-based violence as that occurred in Kosovo.

Such manipulations of language reveal the hypocrisy of many governments and the ways in which they have been inconsistent in their definition of, and response to, ethnic cleansing. They have intervened to halt some population transfers, yet have ignored and even encouraged others. Without consistency in the rhetorical use of these terms, the naming a particular conflict 'genocide', 'ethnic cleansing', or 'population transfer', can release observers from responsibility to deal with the horror and at the same time belittle or exaggerate the brutality of events.[60] In Kosovo, by erroneously classifying the events as genocide, NATO powers misrepresented the situation on the ground and subsequently indicted the whole of the Serbian population. In the process, NATO replicated and exacerbated the ethnic politics that it intervened to halt. In the end, NATO intervention may have created the context in which reprisals against ethnic Serbs have virtually emptied the province of its minority Serb population. The case of Kosovo demonstrates that the gap between conflicting international rules and norms in which ethnic cleansing can occur, also leaves room for states to exploit the politics of ethnic cleansing in pursuit of their own nationally driven interests.

## CONCLUSIONS

The historical record suggests that population transfer and ethnic cleansing have been widely utilised as a 'security-creating' tool by governments. Ethnic cleansing is the result of the exploitation of insecurity and the manipulation of national history by power-seeking political elites. Further, ethnic cleansing is intricately linked to the political ideal of the homogenous sovereign state and the principle of national self-determination, and operates in the gap between these two international principles. The absence of a clear policy on how to address these conflicting principles creates the space in which regimes and ethnic groups emboldened by the principle of sovereignty and fearful of others can attempt to ethnically cleanse a particular ethnic group. In this same context, states may exploit the rhetorical power of the term, 'ethnic cleansing' in pursuit of their own political agendas. Ultimately, ethnic cleansing will persist as long as the nationally homogenous sovereign state is held as the ideal form of political organisation, sovereignty is legitimated on the basis of national self-determination and gaps in international law prevent the development of an unambiguous policy to halt its use.

### NOTES

1. Aishe gave testimony to Albanian field representatives of the humanitarian organisation Women for Women International (www.womenforwomen.org) after seeking refuge in an Albanian refugee camp. Her testimony was collected in cooperation with the Albanian Human Rights Group.
2. Andrew Bell-Fialkoff, *Ethnic Cleansing* (New York: St. Martin's Press, 1996), p.9. See also P. Green, *Alexander of Macedon* (Berkeley and Los Angeles, CA: University of California Press, 1991), p.45.
3. Bell-Fialkoff (note 2), pp.35–6.
4. Bell and Howell Information and Learning, 'Critical Issues Essay: Ethnic Cleansing', http://www.umi.com/hp/Support/K12/Critical 959 L/Ethnic Cleansing.html.
5. Jennifer Jackson Preece, 'Ethnic Cleansing as an Instrument of Nation-State Creation: Changing State Practices and Evolving Legal Norms', *Human Rights Quarterly*, Vol.20 (1998), p.821.
6. Bell-Fialkoff (note 2), p.4.
7. United Nations Commission of Experts Established Pursuant to Security Council Resolution 780, UN *Commission of Experts Established Pursuant to Security Council Resolution 780, (1992): Annex Summaries and Conclusions*, UN Doc.S11994/674/ Add.2, Vol.1 (1994), p.17. See also Robert M. Hayden, 'Schindler's Fate: Genocide, Ethnic Cleansing, and Population Transfer', *Slavic Review*, Vol.55, No.4 (1996), p.733.
8. Bell-Fialkoff (note 2), pp.1–4; 53–6.
9. John McGarry, 'Demographic Engineering: the State-directed Movement of Ethnic Groups as a Technique of Conflict Regulation', *Ethnic and Racial Studies*, Vol.21 No.4 (1998), p.616.
10. Michael Mann, 'The Dark Side of Democracy: The Modern Tradition of Ethnic and Political Cleansing', *New Left Review*, No.35 (1999), p.8.

11. Roger Cohen, 'Ethnic Cleansing', in Roy Gutman and David Rieff (eds) *Crimes of War: What the Public Should Know* (New York and London: W.W. Norton & Company, 1999), p.136.
12. McGarry (note 9), pp.621–22.
13. Mann (note 10), p. 22.
14. Diane F. Orentlicher, 'Genocide', in Gutman and Rieff (note 11), p.154.
15. Bell-Fialkoff (note 2), p.1
16. Ibid., pp.15, 59.
17. Ibid., pp.17–21.
18. Ibid., p.22.
19. Ibid., pp.23–4.
20. Jackson Preece (note 5), pp.822–3.
21. Mann (note 10), pp.32–4.
22. Gianluca Bocchi and Mauro Ceruti, *Solidarity of Barbarism: A Europe of Diversity against Ethnic Cleansing* (New York: Peter Lang, 1997), p.3.
23. See Alfred M. de Zayas *Nemesis at Potsdam: The Anglo-Americans and the Expulsion of the Germans* (London: Routledge and Kegan Paul, 1977).
24. Ibid., p.12.
25. Ibid., p.90.
26. Lucy S. Dawidowicz, *The War against the Jews, 1933–1945* (New York and London: Bantam Books, tenth edition, 1975), p.90.
27. Cohen (note 11), p.138.
28. de Zayas (note 23), p.11.
29. Jackson Preece (note 5), pp.828–9.
30. Bell-Fialkoff (note 2), pp.31–2.
31. Benny Morris, 'Arab-Israeli War', in Gutman and Rieff (note 11), pp.31–2.
32. 'War Crimes Court Breaks New Ground', *Washington Post*, 2 December 1999.
33. Akbar S. Ahmed, 'Ethnic Cleansing: A Metaphor of Our Time?' *Ethnic and Racial Studies*, Vol.18, No.1 (1995), p.9.
34. See also Jackson Preece (note 5)
35. Cohen (note 11), p.136.
36. R.J. Rummel, *Death by Government* (New Brunswick, NJ: Transaction Publishers, 1994), p.19.
37. Ibid., p.14–6.
38. Mann (note 10), pp.19–21.
39. Mann (note 10), p.45.
40. Ibid., p.42.
41. Ibid.
42. David Lake and Donald Rothchild, 'Containing Fear: the Origins and Management of Ethnic Conflict', *International Security*, Vol.21, No.2 (1996), pp.41–2.
43. Akbar S. Ahmed (note 33), p.18.
44. V.P. Gagnon, Jr., 'Ethnic Nationalism and International Conflict: The Case of Serbia', in Sean M. Lynn-Jones and Steven E. Miller (eds) *Global Dangers: Changing Dimensions of International Security* (Cambridge, MA: MIT Press, 1995), pp.336–7.
45. Ibid., p.337.
46. *Demogrfska statstika* (Belgrade: savezni zavod za statistiku, 1979–89), summarised by Gagnon (note 44), pp.334–5.
47. Jackson Preece (note 5), p.820.
48. Leo Kuper, *Genocide: Its Political Use in the Twentieth Century* (New Haven, CT: Yale University Press, 1982), p.161.
49. C.A. Macartney summarised by Hayden (note 7), p.35.
50. Bell-Fialkoff (note 2), p.49.
51. See also Anna Simmons, 'Making Sense of Ethnic Cleansing', *Studies in Conflict and Terrorism*, Vol.22, No.1 (1999), pp.1–20.
52. 'Kofi Annan: "No Government has the Right to Hide Behind National Sovereignty in order to Violate Human Rights"', *The Guardian*, 7 April 1999 [transcripts of the

Secretary-General of the United Nations, Kofi Annan, addressing the Commission on Human Rights].
53. The Council for the Defence of Human Rights and Freedoms (www.albanian.com); see also Noel Malcolm, *Kosovo: A Short History* (New York: New York University Press, 1998).
54. For a discussion of state-directed demographic engineering, see McGarry (note 9).
55. Malcolm (note 53), pp.334–56.
56. Carol S. Lilly, 'Amoral Realism or Immoral Obfuscation?' *Slavic Review*, Vol.55, No.4 (1996), pp.750–1
57. Giles Foden, 'Why Serbia is Not Guilty of Genocide', *The Guardian*, 12 April 1999.
58. Hayden (note 7), p.742.
59. Alexander Cockburn, 'Where's the Evidence of Genocide of Kosovar Albanians?' *Los Angeles Times*, 29 October 1999.
60. Hayden (note 7), p.734.

# 3
# Rape in War:
# Lessons of the Balkan Conflicts
# in the 1990s

CAROLINE KENNEDY-PIPE and PENNY STANLEY

Some of the most haunting images of the wars in the Balkans were of burnt out villages, ruined crops and displaced peoples living under canvas in refugee camps. One might be tempted to think: so far, so familiar. Yet this time there was a different dimension to the news coverage. Girls and women were routinely placed before the camera or the journalist to tell their stories of rape, sexual assault and shame. For the first time, rape in war became a serious topic for journalists, politcians, laywers and scholars. This contribution looks at the questions raised by rape in the Balkan conflicts in the 1990s and argues that there are a number of lessons to be drawn from the experiences of women in these wars.

## RAPE IN THE HISTORY OF WAR

Rape in war has not been a phenomenon unique to the Balkans. It has accompanied most wars, whether they be categorised as 'wars of gain, wars of fear or wars of doctrine'.[1] As General Patton, one of the most famous World War II commanders put it: during war there will 'unquestionably be some raping'.[2] A sixteenth-century commentator on political ethics, Francisco de Vitoria, suggested that rape in war might be 'necessary for the conduct of war [and] act as a spur to the courage of the troops'.[3] Nietzsche said in a well known if by now somewhat stale sentence that 'Man should be trained for war and woman for the recreation of the warrior: all else is folly'.[4] Historically, rape has appeared as an inescapable by-product of war.

Mass rape in war is a particular feature of this terrible story. A survey of the historical evidence (and here it must be noted that its quality is often bitterly disputed) confirms its prevalence and unearths similarities in the way women and girls have been sexually abused during war through human history. From the raping of the Sabine women in Roman mythology to the accounts of sexual abuse and multilation in the Balkans during the 1990s, the act of rape has been a common feature in both the representation of and perhaps the realities of war.

The Roman myth depicting the rape of the Sabine women can be interpreted as a fundamentally political act. The rapes were not merely a cluster of individual acts of sexual violence perpetrated against individual women, but part of a premeditated war plan with political ends orchestrated by the Roman king Romulus.[5] The advocacy of rape in war was prevalent throughout ancient Near East history and is evident in the Hebrew Bible: women are frequently depicted as mere objects of male possession and control. Biblical references clearly illustrate this point in relation to the treatment of women in wartime, where they were regarded as 'spoils of war'.[6]

The ancient perception or representation of women as 'spoils of war' was consistent with the legal status of women: they were regarded as property. Hence, rape was seen as an injury to the male estate, and not to the women herself. As Susan Brownmiller argues, when rape was considered a crime against the male, the rape of enemy women in war might have had a 'salutary military effect.' She maintains that as defence of women has long been a hallmark of masculine pride, 'rape by a conquering soldier can destroy the illusion of power and property for the men of defeated side'.[7] The important point here is that the political and legal standing of women has had a direct effect on the way they were treated or mistreated in war. This has had resonance for some twentieth-century military and political elites who, like some of their ancient predecessors, have perceived rape as a useful tactic in war. The rape of females can in some instances demoralise and destroy enemy communities.

Until the twentieth century there were few detailed references to the raping of women in war. This 'silence' indicates something important about the manner in which rape in war has been regarded. One historian, N. Basher, has explained the 'absence' of rape from modern studies of war because it is 'too risky, too political a subject to be dealt with comfortably by the present day male historian'.[8] Perhaps the dominance of the profession of history by men did indeed preclude the writing of a history of war that included women or it may be that rape was simply not regarded as a subject central to an understanding of war. Whatever the explanation, in several influential historical studies such as Vern Bullough's *Sex, Society and History*[9] and J. Week's *Sex, Politics and Society*[10] rape in war is absent from all discussion.

One historical account that is unusually detailed in its recording of the violation of women in war concerns the raping of Scottish highland women, during and after the Battle of Culloden in 1746.[11] Information has been collated from old tribal records scrupulously kept by the Scottish clansmen, in which they claimed that the raping of their 'clanswomen' was a deliberate act of tyranny by the English.[12] We do not know the full story of these rapes or whether the clansmen felt shame at these incidents, yet despite omissions from the story this study is exceptional. It was not until World War I that the occurrence of rape in war was more consistently documented. Even so, the First World War historiography of sexual abuse provides ambigious and somewhat contradictory evidence for those seeking to discover the extent of the raping that took place. Partly this is because some accounts of rape were embellished by those governments such as Belgium and France seeking to enlist sympathy and support for their war aims from powerful neutral states.[13] Personal accounts of rape were distorted and exaggerated by official sources and used for propaganda:[14] these accounts appeared more dramatic and sensational than the versions gleaned from the raped women themselves.[15]

Stories of rape have therefore to be treated with caution, and the context in which such tales are told is crucial. Rarely throughout history have women had any outlets to directly express their experiences in an accurate manner. There were few female politicians, academics or journalists to represent women's concerns; women's experiences of war were on the whole told by men holding official positions. History was just that – his-story.[16]

So rape, including mass rape, has been an area of silence but also an area that has been shaped by official state (and overwhelmingly male) interpretations.[17] The discourse of nationalism has often depicted the nation as female: this idea found expression in national symbols such as in 'Marianne' in France or in the Statue of Liberty in the United States. The traditional role of Serbian women is depicted by the Mother of the Jugovici, the heroine of the Battle of Kosovo in 1389. The story goes that in spite of the death of her nine sons during the battle with the Turks, she did not weep. Her self-sacrifice became at least officially an inspiration for Serbian women.[18] In some, indeed one might argue in many, societies, women are used to represent the symbolic construction of a community or group: all that is reputedly good or admirable in that group is made visible in a female ideal. This symbolism means in effect that violence committed against women may be directed or perceived against the community as a whole.[19] The rape of women of a certain nation or ethnic group can be a symbolic rape of the body of that community. As states rebuild, after brutal wars, the emotional and physical scars inflicted on women are an often unwelcome legacy and as such it is a topic which is best avoided.

During the Tokyo war crimes trials following World War II, the issue of mass rape received international legal attention. Of particular horror was the Japanese occupation of Nanking, during which the city's population suffered extreme atrocities:[20] it became known as the 'rape of Nanking'.[21] The Chinese decision not to defend the city, and the subsequent withdrawal of its army, left it full of refugees, women, and children – totally defenceless.[22] The invading Japanese army met with minimal resistance.[23] Although none of the Japanese eventually accused were actually tried for rape, the prosecutors submitted evidence of mass rape in an effort to convict several defendants of crimes against humanity. No raped women were called to give evidence, but a group of missionaries from the Nanking International Relief Committee, who had elected to remain in the city throughout the invasion, were asked to testify. Words from the diary of an American missionary in Nanking, James McCallum, were entered as evidence and read: 'Such brutality. Rape! Rape! Rape! We estimate at least 1,000 cases a night, and many by day.'[24]

The case presented to the Tokyo tribunal was ultimately conclusive. General Iwane Matsui, the military commander of the Japanese forces which took Nanking, was found guilty of crimes against humanity, and sentenced to death by hanging.[25] Thus it appeared that mass rape in war was at last being recognised as a crime against humanity although it was many years later that the full horror of the rapes committed by Japanese soldiers was brought to light.[26] It should be noted however that revisionists in Japanese academic circles have subsequently denounced the reports of rape and atrocities at Nanking; they have disputed the claim that rape, let alone mass rape, occurred.[27]

Whatever the controversy over the details of Nanking, captured German documents presented at the Nuremberg War Crimes Tribunal in 1946 highlighted the routine use of rape as a weapon of terror during World War II.[28] Although in its founding statute there was no explicit reference to rape, the French prosecutor at Nuremberg produced evidence of mass rape committed in retaliation against acts carried out by the French Resistance.[29]

There were other stories of rape during World War II. Soviet soldiers involved in the liberation of Berlin allegedly saw it as their duty to re-establish national pride through retribution and the rape of German women.[30] The historian Cornelius Ryan obtained first-hand accounts from the victims of these rapes, and commented that 'hordes of Russian troops ... demanded the rights due the conquerors: the women of the conquered'.[31] A similar pattern of behaviour was recorded in other parts of Germany. In southern Baden-Württemberg for example, rapes were apparently committed on a large scale by French troops.[32] It is perhaps not surprising that as the Nuremberg Tribunal was constituted by the Allied powers, for the large part the acts of sexual violence against women carried out by their own soldiers were not scrutinised, let alone punished. The rapes by Soviet soldiers in Berlin for example went mainly unpunished as did the sexual assaults perpetrated by Moroccan mercenaries serving with the French Army in Italy during the military campaigns of 1943–44. Interestingly, though, the victims of this particular episode were awarded a pension by the Italian Government as compensation for their suffering.[33]

## RAPE IN WAR AFTER 1945

Rape and mass rape characterised many of the conflicts which took place throughout the post World War II era. During Bangladesh's nine-month war of independence,[34] it is claimed that there were 200,000 rapes perpetrated on Muslim women.[35] In part, it is argued, the rapes took place because Pakistani troops believed that they were 'true' Muslims and it was their 'official' duty to 'purify' the Hindu converts to Islam.[36] Many of those sexually abused were subsequently rejected by their menfolk and families, and ended up homeless and mired in poverty. While the Government did actually try to reestablish their social positions by designating them 'heroines' and established camps of a very basic kind to aid them, little thought was given to their future survival and nearly twenty years later some of these women were still inhabiting these camps and remained outcasts.[37] What this example vividly illustrated was the enduring effects that rape may have.

Given the prevalence of such experiences, the absence of rape from accounts of warfare through history appears odd. In most war zones, women remain not on the sidelines but rather inhabit front lines. By 1990 an estimated ninety per cent of war casualties were civilians – the majority of whom were women and children.[38] This is due in part to the character of modern warfare, in which both deliberate and systematic injury of civilian populations has become a priority target. In some wars violence is waged against specific ethnic groups. In such war, rape can be seen as a military strategy, a nationalistic policy and as an expression of ethnic group hatred.

Rape has therefore continued to be a feature of war in spite of attempts to legislate for some protection for women in war, and despite the increase in the 'rights' supposedly accorded to women internationally.[39] Part of the problem has been the huge gap between rights in theory and political, social and military practices. Human rights, including women's rights are recognised by governments widely, but they reserve the right to interpret them differently. There are therefore manifold problems in trying to enforce international law or conventions.

The promise of a new order for human rights was set by the Universal Declaration of Human Rights of 1948 and the four Geneva Conventions requiring civilised treatment for civilians, the sick and prisoners of war.[40] They were designed to establish standards and afford a degree of protection against rape. In practice however they had little impact in terms of safeguarding women. The Geneva Convention (IV in Article 27) formally outlawed rape although it was omitted from the 'grave breaches' regime of Article 147. However some scholars objected to the original phrasing of Article 27, which interpreted rape as an attack on 'honour'.[41] Catherine Niarchos argues that a linking of rape with ideas of '*honour*', a term which in some societies can be taken to mean 'chastity, purity and good name' is mistaken and culturally loaded. Specifically she argues that the presentation of honour as the interest to be protected is a grossly inadequate way to express the suffering of women raped in war. Her second objection to the use of honour in the context of rape is that the assault is described from the viewpoint of society and the notion of a raped women as disgraced or soiled is highlighted.[42] This 'disgrace' of course may carry potent social implications. During the conflict in Kosovo for example, it is argued that Serbian soldiers deliberately raped women in front of their families to 'shame' them and that some of the most horrific instances of gang rape were carried out to destroy families and communities.[43]

Whatever the shortcomings of the drafting of the Geneva Conventions in terms of their failure to recognise the cultural effects of rape, there was also the problem of how to implement or enforce the conventions. In 1972, for example, the United Nations Economic and Social Council expressed concern over escalating levels of brutality directed against women in war. Yet appeals to those engaged in combat to respect international law relating to women were largely ignored. According to Geoffrey Robertson, 'The systematic rape of an estimated 200,000 Bengali women by Pakistani soldiers in 1971 went entirely unpunished, and although the crime was widely committed by the military and by Fraph in Haiti under Cedra it was amnestied by United Nations negotiators in 1995.'[44]

## MASS RAPE IN BOSNIA

It was the Hague Tribunal set up for the Bosnian conflict that finally took the issue of rape in war seriously. The conflicts in the Balkans during the

1990s produced 'visible' evidence of the phenomenon of rape in war. However, they also showed the historic problem of providing accurate data on rape, revealed tales of rape for propaganda, and demonstrated repeatedly the difficulties of finding appropriate legal and political mechanisms for dealing with the abuse of women.

During the Bosnian conflict, atrocities were committed on all sides: the greatest number of sexual assaults were seemingly committed by Serb forces against Muslim women, although Catholic Croatian women were targeted as well. In Bosnia-Hercegovina it has been estimated by the European Union that in total some 20,000 women were subjected to sexual violence. As in so many other conflicts, though, the precise number of rapes committed is a matter of dispute. The Bosnian Ministry of the Interior for example claimed the figure for those raped was 50,000.[45] The Commission of Experts established to examine the issue of rape in the conflict refused to speculate on the exact number, but did state that sexual assault was used by the belligerents in Bosnia as a means to 'terrorise, to displace, to demoralise and to destroy'.[46]

The dispute over statistics in the case of the conflict over Bosnia underlines the problem of ascertaining the scale and character of sexual assaults which occur in any war. Exact figures for those raped may, for a variety of reasons, never be discovered. Many rapes are never reported as there can be an understandable reluctance on the part of those violated to come forward and provide public testimony. In addition to hidden rapes there were other complications in compiling reliable data on sexual assault from the Balkan wars. Some women, for example, were raped more than once and by different men: in the case of rape camps women were held over a period of many weeks and were raped repeatedly. Ignoring the frequency of attacks on an individual lowers the overall total of women raped and might alter the picture of how many women in total were actually sexually hurt.[47]

The Commission of Experts in Bosnia argued that rape fell into five different patterns. In the first, the rapes were committed before the fighting actually broke out. Individuals would target villages, terrorise the inhabitants and loot and rape. During the second pattern, rapes, some apparently opportunistic, occurred in conjunction with invasion. Women were raped either in empty houses or gang-raped in public. In a third pattern, women were raped while in detention: here gang rapes were common and many of the rapes were accompanied by torture. During the fourth pattern, attacks occurred in so-called 'rape camps'. This pattern was marked by frequent rapes with an alleged strategy by the captors to impregnate as many women as possible with 'Chetnik' babies.[48] In a fifth pattern, women were forced into makeshift 'brothels' to entertain troops and 'after they had served their purpose more often killed than released'.[49]

In January 1993 the United Nations sent a team of five people to investigate the reports of rape as a form of ethnic cleansing. In their investigations 119 pregnancies were identified as the result of rape in 1992. This issue of enforced pregnancy is one to which we will return.

These differing patterns of rape appear to suggest different types of sexual assault, with varying motivations. For present purposes the most striking has been so-called 'genocidal rape'[50] to accompany a strategy of ethnic cleansing.

In the conflict in Bosnia it is widely accepted that ethnic cleansing was the principal aim of the Serbian and Croatian forces. The mass graves of Srebrenica or the crimes at the Omarska camp contain clear reminders of Nazi activities.[51] Some scholars however have disagreed about the linkage between rape and ethnic cleansing. Did every episode of rape by Serbian forces indicate a strategy with an ethnic dimension as opposed to rape with an opportunistic sexual motive?[52]

The term 'genocidal rape' is both emotionally and politically loaded, but it does seem to accurately reflect the realities felt by some if not all raped women in the conflict. As we saw above, some raped Muslim women reported that their attackers claimed that they were intending to impregnate them to create Serbian babies, and that some women were held captive for a period of weeks to ensure that they did not abort the child they had conceived in rape.[53]

Beverly Allen is one who questions whether such behaviour, however traumatic for the women involved, constitutes 'genocide'. As she points out, the impregnation of women, even if forced, is about the propagation of Serbian offspring rather than the elimination of a group and thus is the antithesis of genocide.[54] However, Allen goes on to argue that the 'equation' of rape with genocide is a feasible one for a variety of reasons. In her opinion, genocidal rape was the policy of the Serbian military and it took three different forms. The most obvious occurred when the victim was murdered after rape. She also claims however that forced impregnation can be seen as genocide both in terms of breeding additional Serbian children and the use of rape as a terror weapon to force people away from their homes. In addition the torture of women during rape can also result in infertility and prevent births within the community.

The argument that Muslim women were impregnated simply in a bid to produce Serbian babies needs careful investigation. Although it has sometimes been claimed that throughout Balkan culture a child will always inherit the identity of the biological father,[55] this is not always the case. After all, a foetus does share the genetic material of both parents and unless the child is actually raised by the father, he or she is more likely to assimilate the culture of the mother.[56] Misha Glenny has pertinently argued that those children born as a result of rape are actually unlikely to assume the identity of their unknown father.[57]

Glenny also questions the assertions made by a number of scholars that somehow Muslim women were especially hurt or disgraced by the outbreak of rape in the Balkans. He argues the idea that after being raped Muslim women would be disregarded by their own communities is a gross generalisation based on distorted Western perceptions of responsibilites within Islam.[58]

Yet there are many instances from the wars in Bosnia and Kosovo in which Muslim women did indeed report their sense of enduring shame after being raped. One Kosovan Albanian women for example told a Western journalist that 'for us, you see, rape is the worst thing that can happen.'[59] Rape may have manifold consequences: unmarried women may no longer be married within the community or married women may be rejected by their husbands.[60] Glenny argues against the creation of a hierachy of humiliation with respect to rape, disputing the view that somehow Serb and Croat communities can and will cope better with rape then Muslim counterparts.

While not refuting the existence of rape camps, Misha Glenny has argued that the claim that rape represented a special war tactic of the Serbs should be regarded as 'arrant nonsense'. He argues that just as previous Balkan wars have recorded countless massacres similar to those in Croatia and Bosnia, 'so too have Balkan women always been subject to rape on a comparable scale during these conflicts'. In this view rape accompanies war as surely as does killing. Glenny concedes during 1992 that commanders used the act of rape to reinforce the psychology of violence associated with the campaigns and that in many areas the participation of soldiers in rape was expected. But he disputes the idea that rape was used by Serb or Croatian forces wholly as a tool of genocide.[61] Difficulties have also arisen from the fact that the issue of rape has been widely used in both Bosnia and Kosovo for the purposes of propaganda, with all sides probably exaggerating the abuses committed by their enemies.

Rape is therefore an area of contested data and propaganda. Yet it is not only a problem of data and widespread propaganda. There is also a problem when attempting to generalise about rape as an experience in war, of making sweeping claims about the cultural impact of rape or of trying to homogenise the motives of those involved. Yet, as will be seen in the next section, it is precisely the intentions of those accused of rape as well as the act of rape itself that stand at the centre of attempts to legislate against and punish rape during war.

## PROVING AND PUNISHING RAPE

In response to the atrocities in Bosnia, in 1993, the United Nations Security Council voted to set up the first international war crimes tribunal since Nuremberg.[62] The statute of this tribunal made explicit reference to rape and was encouraged to look at abuse of women and children. As Geoffrey Robertson has written 'One of the most notable achievements of the Hague Tribunal on the former Yugoslavia was to identify and stigmatise rape as a war crime rather than a 'spoil of war'. In terms of the history of rape in war this did mark a significant step forward. Rape was now designated both as a war crime and a crime against humanity when committed on a widespread basis with a pre-planned tactical purpose.[63]

Legal attention was focused on widespread and systematic rape. A distinction was made between opportunistic rapes and those resulting from political motivation to hurt, 'cleanse' or eradicate certain ethnic groups. This distinction allowed the Tribunal to deal with abuses such as the cases of Serb battalions which gang-raped Muslim women in public, apparently to terrorise local communities and to indict and accuse Serb police who participated in and permitted the abuse of female prisoners at a 'rape camp' established in the town of Foca in Bosnia and Hercegovina.[64] This was an important step as human rights groups, drawing on experiences in the Balkans, had pressed for a series of safeguards for women held in custody either in police stations or in camps. In Bosnia it was estimated that approximately eighty per cent of rapes occurred while women were in 'custody'.[65] At the end of 1998 the Tribunal also delivered an important judgement for the treatment of rape in war during the so-called 'Jokers Wild' case. In this judgement the commander of a Croatian paramilitary group, 'the Jokers', was rendered liable as a 'co-perpetrator' of torture for allowing a soldier to rape a women during an interrogation session which he had attended.[66]

Despite the recognition of rape as a crime in war there were serious problems in international law related to the treatment of women in conflict. The precedent established by the Tribunal regarding rape in Bosnia was specific about the circumstances as to what could justify indictment. It was not rape as a specific act against an individual women that counted but rather the use of rape as a tool of ethnic cleansing: it was political intent that was important. Rape as utilised by the Serbs to humiliate and disgrace the women for a political purpose was indictable under international law, but opportunistic rape was deemed crucial.[67] The point is that not all rapes were indictable and the issue of what might constitute proof of a political or a racist motive in rape is a complex one. Under this rubric some rapes, however savage, will never be prosecuted by international law.

In addition to these problems, the Tribunal has also been accused of failing to insist on proper proof to establish the motives of those accused of rape in war.[68] In fact many of the decisions relating to its treatment of rape have provoked censure. The latter has included the argument that the Tribunal was focused too much on rape. One international rights lawyer for example has argued that the Hague Tribunal was viewed as 'giving too much fashionable attention' to rape and that as war crimes go, rape is not as serious for women as for example the massacre of husbands and children.[69]

The criticism was also levelled at the Hague Tribunal that in the rush to indict for rape, it has failed to apply the rules of a fair trial and the demands of due process. The case of Dusko Tadic evoked controversy on this point. Tadic, a Serbian nationalist with a track record of both racist and violent behaviour, was recognised by a variety of witnesses from his activities at the Omarska camp. He had been responsible for a number of horrific incidents involving sexual torture. He was also identified by witnesses from the Trnopolje prison camp for women where he had engaged or oversaw a series of attacks including rape. In May 1997 Tadic was found guilty on 11 counts of crimes against humanity. He was sentenced to 20 years in prison.[70]

This was a landmark case in several respects. Two judges during the Tadic trial ruled that a man could be convicted of the offence of rape simply on the word of an anonymous accuser.[71] This waiving of due process by two of the three judges was in their view justified by the need to balance the right to a fair trial against the need to protect witnesses. The judges appeared to have taken into account the views long made by women's organisations, which argued that anonymity and protection for those who had suffered assault was justified. Yet lawyers objected as Tadic was not allowed to know the names of certain crucial witnesses.[72] It should however be noted that in subsequent cases the judges ruled that accusers must give evidence in a closed court or even on close circuit television.[73] This judgement was based on the view that courts established to deal with the abuse of human rights should not breach the rights of a fair trial, however dreadful the offence.[74]

The issue of how women should be treated by the international legal system and what degree of evidence they should be expected to provide to prove rape was and remains a controversial one. The issue of evidence remains central. Rape, even in peacetime and even within a domestic legislative framework, is often a difficult offence to prove. Even more difficult is the endeavour in war to prove an ethnic intent in a crime more usually associated with sexual rather than political motives.[75] Despite the problems just identified, there have been some successes in the treatment of rape in war. Feminist scholars and women's groups have argued, with positive effect as seen in the Tadic case, that the individual testimonies or voices of the female victims of war should be included in any account of rape,[76] and that the punishment of rapists in war should be a focus of international concern. One dimension to the trying of rape before the Hague Tribunal was the issue of future rape. It was hoped that the indictments for rape might have a deterrent effect in future conflicts and that the mass rapes which had characterised the early stages of the conflict in Bosnia would not be repeated.[77] This aim was disappointed, as the conflict in Kosovo soon demonstrated.

KOSOVO

While it is difficult, precisely because of the complexities of determining the scale and character of rape in war, to make a comprehensive comparison between the experiences of women in Bosnia and Kosovo, there were some striking similarities. This was especially true of the stories of rape which began to circulate shortly after May 1998, when Milosevic's forces began a major military offensive in western Kosovo. There appeared to be two Serbian aims: to close the border with Albania, prohibiting the movement of weapons by the insurgent UCK, but also to depopulate the villages and establish a Serb-controlled zone. By the first week in June the operations had succeeded, with an estimated 90,000 Kosovar Albanians displaced to Albania, Montenegro and within Kosovo itself.[78] Stories and reports of both rape and gang rape reminiscent of Bosnia became increasingly commonplace. By April 1999, shortly after the bombing had started, Western journalists were writing of the Serb use of rape as a tactic of war.[79] According to human rights groups and investigators from the War Crimes Tribunal at the Hague there was by this point credible evidence of a campaign of sexual abuse.[80]

It is not the purpose of this essay to examine the response of the NATO alliance to Serbian actions in Kosovo, but it should be stressed that it was the wholesale violation of human rights by Serbian forces that Western politicans used to justify their actions over Kosovo. In April 1999, the British Government placed rape squarely at the centre of the human rights agenda when it accused Serb forces of the sytematic rape of ethnic Albanians.[81] Specifically, the British Foreign Secretary alleged that young women fleeing their homes and heading with refugee conveys towards Kosovo's borders were separated from the refugee columns and forced to endure systematic rape in an army camp at Djakovica near the Albanian border.[82]

Whatever the appropriateness of strategic bombing as a means of dealing with human rights abuse (and many have argued that troops on the ground are a more effective military response to situations such as Kosovo[83]), the bombing did not initially prevent rape. According to many accounts the attacks on Albanian Kosovars became more prevalent. Serb military and paramilitary groups appeared to use the bombing as a pretext for horrific acts of revenge against women. One report from a village near Suva Reka in Kosovo tells of 'revenge' attacks by Serbs for the bombing. On 5 April, a few days after the bombing campaign started, Serbian police swept the area, looting and threatening the population. Some of the women were rounded up, imprisoned and raped.[84]

Women from this village, during a conversation with a Western journalist, voiced their fears for the future; this included alarm that their families and communities would be badly affected by the experiences of rape.[85] In this respect there were echoes of the fate of women in past wars who had found themselves either in refugee camps or perhaps abandoned or widowed by war. Historically this issue of what happens to women *after* rape in war has not been addressed in an adequate manner. It was raised in some of the newspaper reports from the Balkan wars.

Most of the rape in the Balkan Wars was inevitably what has been termed 'stranger rape' by enemy soldiers or paramilitaries; although it should be noted that some women were raped by former neighbours. In addition women were also likely to be subject to violent acts including rape by their 'own' menfolk on their return from the front line. The so-called SOS hotlines for women and children victims of violence in the former Yugoslavia reported a massive increase in calls with a large proportion concerning post-war incidents.[86] In the case studies which have been undertaken of women across different ethnic groups, the reasons given for the incidence of violence committed by soldiers returning from the fighting include frustration, fear, poverty and trauma caused by war. It is however extremely unlikely that these 'hidden' acts of violence will receive any international or domestic attention. Those groups which do provide support for the female victims of conflict after war, such as the Centre against Sexual Violence opened in Belgrade in 1993, are of significance as they do provide some form of care for the female victims of war regardless of ethnic, religious and national affiliations.[87]

Escape from the front line of war does not necessarily bestow personal security. Refugees who had fled Kosovo and were placed at the

Grize refugee camp in Albania for example reported that a small of number of women had been forced out of the camps at night to act as prostitutes. Part of the problem was that refugees were located in areas with little local infrastructure in regions largely run by gangs and local clans. According to the Organisation on Security and Cooperation in Europe (OSCE), at least three women disappeared from the Grize camp. The UN High Commissioner for Refugees and the OSCE attempted to investigate the removal of women (and in one instance a young man) from the refugee camps.[88]

The plight of such refugees and the insecurity of some of these camps raises the question of who or what can be or should be responsible for female security after war. The indictment and punishment of those who have perpetrated or incited acts of rape is but one issue that should be considered. Here the role of peacekeeping forces is one that needs greater consideration. Some of the women interviewed by Western reporters at the height of the war in Kosovo expressed optimism that peacekeeping forces would be deployed in a protective role.[89] Indeed, the responsible use of troops can create the conditions for post-war reconstruction. Yet even here there are complexities in the relationship between troops and women. Reports from Somalia of brutal behaviour by troops underlined the problem of 'peacekeepers'. There is a substantial body of work that examines the problem created by the 'masculinist' culture within most armed forces after war,[90] and 'protectors' may indeed turn out to be among the very men that women should fear.


## LESSONS

The Balkan wars and the reporting of those wars played a decisive role in bringing the issue of rape in war to prominence. The growing awareness and recognition of female human rights throughout the twentieth century were crucial factors in sensitising opinion to the issue of mass rape in war, and since the early 1990s, the issue has been discussed more openly than ever before. Not all 'human wrongs' reach the agenda of the United Nations but the recognition of rape as a war crime has moved from a realm of silence through stages of acknowledgement and recognition and finally, due to the attention given to the reports of mass rape from the Balkans, a place on the international agenda.

Needless to say, the issue is still controversial, beset by historic difficulties, and imperfectly dealt with. Rape, now, as it was during World War I, is still very much an issue with potent propaganda value; it is liable to distortion by journalists in search of a shocking story or politicians seeking *ex post facto* justifications for the exercise of power politics. The Balkan wars confirm the old lesson that discussion of rape is liable to distortion and that reliable evidence is hard to come by. The welcome attempts by the Hague Tribunal to indict and try perpetrators of rape still begs the question of why men rape and tends to homogenise all rape in war as somehow politically or racially motivated. One of the lessons, therefore, is that rape in war has multiple causes. The temptation is to treat all women as victims of a similar political crime – individual stories of abuse can in this context be marginalised or even silenced.

There is also the problem, again one identified earlier, that those tried for rape will tend to be drawn from the 'defeated' powers. While much attention has focussed on Serbian atrocities in both Bosnia and Kosovo, this should not conceal or distort the evidence that rapes were committed on all sides: ethnicity should not ensure that the crimes perpetrated by Croats, Muslims or Kosovar Albanians go either unrecognised or unpunished.

It is our belief that war has and will continue to render women victims. In this respect a particular suffering in conflict is related to gender. Some women endure what women have arguably always endured in war: rape, prostitution, gendered humiliation and forced impregnation. Perhaps the recent Balkan wars were in terms of rape little different to the conflicts which predated them. The develpment of international law in the treatment of rape does not in any way rectify the wrongs perpetrated against women in the past nor does it, as we have demonstrated, guarantee the future of women. Yet, rape is now prohibited under international law, even if its edict is still largely ignored and in global terms unenforceable. There are several reasons for this. First, in war, rape can be an effective weapon in demolishing enemy communities and morale. There are few incentive for militaries to relinquish the practice while humanitarian law in war remains weak. Second, the international legal system which deals with punishing rape in war can overlook or marginalise the experiences of individual women.[91] A third problem, and perhaps the most serious, is that those actors which might in the short term enforce international law are predominantly states or collections of states which place *interests* before the enforcement of human rights. The deaths of their own soldiers for the vindication of human rights globally is perhaps too high a price to pay to help strangers in peril halfway across the world.[92]

In spite of these caveats, which emphasise the difficulties of making progress, something has changed in the attitudes and behaviour with respect to the treatment of rape in war. As a result of the Balkan conflicts, it is no longer an area of silence.

NOTES

1. Martin Wight, cited in Hedley Bull and Carsten Holbraad (eds), *Power Politics* (Harmondsworth: Penguin, 1979), p.138.
2. General George S. Patton, *War As I Knew It* (Boston, MA: Houghton Mifflin, 1947), p.23.
3. Francisco de Vitoria, *On the Law of War*, trans. John Pawley Bate (Washington, DC: 1917), p.176; quoted in Michael Walzer, *Just and Unjust Wars: A Moral Argument with Historical Illustrations* (London: Pelican, 1977), p.134.
4. R.J. Hollingdale, *A Nietzsche Reader* (London: Penguin, 1977), p.275.
5. C.P. Jones, *Plutarch and Rome: Life of Romulus* (Oxford: Clarendon Press, 1971), pp.89–94.
6. *The Bible*, Deuteronomy 20:14 (King James Version).
7. Susan Brownmiller, *Against Our Will: Men, Women and Rape* (New York: Simon & Schuster, 1975) cited in Catherine Niarchos, 'Women, War and Rape: Challenges Facing The International Tribunal for the Former Yugoslavia' in *Human Rights*, Vol.17 (1995), p.661 and pp.668–671.
8. N. Bashar, 'Rape in England between 1550 and 1700', in London Feminist History Group, *The Sexual Dynamics of History* (London: Pluto Press, 1983) pp.28–46.
9. Vern LeRoy Bullough, *Sex, Society and History* (New York: Science History Publications, 1976).
10. J. Weeks, *Sex, Politics and Society* (New York: Longman, 1981).
11. Bashar (note 8), pp.28–46.
12. Ibid., pp.38–40.
13. James Morgan Read, *Atrocity Propaganda* (New Haven, CT: Yale University Press, 1972 – original 1941).
14. M.L. Sanders and Philip M. Taylor, *British Propaganda During the First World War* (London: Macmillan, 1982).
15. Testimony of a brigadier in the 20th Artillery Regiment, 16 October 1914, cited in R. Harris, 'The "Child of the Barbarian": Rape, Race and Nationalism in France during the First World War', *Past and Present*, No.141 (1993), p.188.
16. Niarchos (note 7), pp.649–690.
17. See, for example: Arthur Ponsonby, *False-hood in Wartime* (London: Methuen, 1928); and Harold D. Lasswell, *Propaganda Technique in the World War* (London: Knopf, 1927).
18. Wendy Bracewell, 'Women, Motherhood and Contemporary Serbian Nationalism' in *Women's Studies International Forum*, Vol.19, Nos.1/2 (1996), p.183.
19. Theresa Wobbe, 'Die Grenzen des Geschlechts Konstruktionen von Gemeinschaft und Rassismus', in *Mitteilungen des Instituts fur Sozialforschung Frankfurt* 2 (1993), pp.98–108, quoted in Ruth Seifert, 'The Second Front: The Logic of Sexual Violence in Wars', *Women's Studies International Forum*, Vol.19, Nos.1/2 (January/April 1996).
20. Peter Karsten, *Law, Soldiers and Combat* (Westport, CT: Greenwood Press, 1978), p.84.
21. C. MacDonald, 'Japan and the Nanking Massacre', Paper presented at the Department of War Studies, London (Pacific Security Seminar Series), 18 January 1996.
22. Arnold C. Brackman, *The Other Nuremberg: The Untold Story of the Tokyo War Crimes Trial* (London: Collins, 1987) p.176.
23. Ian Buruma, *Wages of Guilt: Memories of War in Germany and Japan* (London: Vintage, 1995), p.131.
24. Brownmiller (note 7), p.58.
25. The Tribunal ruled that the behaviour of the Japanese army could not be considered the acts of a military group that had temporarily 'got out of hand'; rather, rape, arson, and murder had continued to be committed on a large scale for at least six weeks after the initial invasion. Cited in Brownmiller (note 7), p.61.
26. Jeanne Vickers, *Women and War* (London: Zed Books, 1993), p.21; Hester Lacey, 'The Emperor's Forgotten Army', *The Independent on Sunday*, 25 May 1997, pp.40–1.
27. Iris Chang, 'It's History, Not a 'Lie'', *Newsweek*, 20 July 1998, p.29.

28. Trial of the Major War Criminals Before the International Military Tribunal 456 (1947), quoting V. M. Molotov, A Note by the People's Commissar for Foreign Affairs of the USSR (1942), cited in D. Aydelott, 'Mass Rape during War: Prosecuting Bosnian Rapists Under International Law', *Emory International Law Review*, Vol.7, No.2 (1993), pp.585–631.
29. Seifert (note 19).
30. For comments on the rapes by Soviet soldiers, see Norman M. Naimark, *The Russians in Germany: A History of the Soviet Zone of Occupation 1945–1949* (London: Harvard University Press, 1995), pp.69–140.
31. Cornelius Ryan, *The Last Battle* (London: Collins, 1966), p.26.
32. Walzer (note 3), p.133.
33. Ibid.
34. International Planned Parenthood figures, cited in Brownmiller (note 7), p.81.
35. Editorial, 'Mass Rape in War: Prosecute the Guilty', *Ottawa Citizen*, 17 January 1993, p.B1.
36. Ibid.
37. Seifert (note 19).
38. R.L. Sivard, *World Military and Social Expenditures* (Washington, DC: World Priorities Inc., 1991)
39. Rebecca Cook, 'Human Rights and World Public Order: The Outlawing Of Sex-Based Discrimination', *American Journal of International Law*, No.69 (1975), pp.497–533.
40. Niarchos (note 7), pp.675–6.
41. Ibid.
42. Ibid.
43. See for example 'Serbs make rape a weapon of war' in *The Times*, 6 April 1999.
44. Geoffrey Robertson, *Crimes Against Humanity The Struggle for Global Justice* (London: Allen Lane, the Penguin Press, 1999), p.285.
45. Aryeh Neier, 'Watching Rights; Rapes in Bosnia-Herzegovina', *The Nation*, 1 March 1993. p.259.
46. United Nations, General Assembly and Security Council, European Community Investigative Mission into the Treatment of Muslim Women in the Former Yugoslavia, Annex 1, 14, United Nations Doc. a/48/92. S/25240 (1993)
47. This is a point made by Niarchos (note 7), pp.656–8.
48. Todd A. Salzman, 'Rape Camps as a Means of Ethnic Cleansing: Religious, Cultural and Ethical Responses to Rape Victims in the Former Yugoslavia', *Human Rights Quarterly*, Vol.20, No.2 (1998), pp.348–78.
49. United Nations, General Assembly and Security Council, Mission into the Treatment of Muslim Women, quoted in Salzman (note 48), pp.356–7.
50. See Beverly Allen, *Rape Warfare: The Hidden Genocide in Bosnia-Herzegovina And Croatia* (University of Minnesota Press, 1996), pp.155–156, quoted in Salzman (note 48), pp.356–7.
51. See Martin Shaw, 'Review Essay' The Contemporary Mode of Warfare? Mary Kaldor's Theory of New Wars' in *Review of International Political Economy*, Vol.7, No.1 (spring 2000), pp.171–192.
52. Allen (note 50), pp.155–6.
53. For the reporting of this issue see Linda Grant, 'Anyone here been raped and speak English?' *The Guardian*, 2 August 1993, p.10. For an analysis of reporting of rape during the Bosnian War, see Penny Stanley, *Mass Rape in War, Feminist Thought and British Press Representations of the Balkan Conflict 1991–1995*, Ph.D. thesis, University College of Wales, Aberystywth, 1998.
54. Misha Glenny, *The Fall of Yugoslavia The Third Balkan War* (London; Penguin,1996), p.209.
55. Allen (note 50), pp.155–6.
56. For a critique of some of the ideas expressed by Allen, see Salzman (note 48), pp.356–7. See also Aydelott (note 28), pp.585–631.
57. Glenny (note 54), p.210.

58. Ibid., p.209.
59. Ibid.
60. See statement of Dr Stanley Ducharme, Boston University Medical Center, in *Nightline: Rape as a Weapon of War Against Bosnian Muslims* (ABC television broadcast, 14 January 1993), quoted in Aydelott (note 28), p.602.
61. Glenny (note 54), p.209.
62. *International Tribunal for the Prosecution of Persons Responsible for Serious Violations of International Humanitarian Law Committed in the Territory of the Former Yugoslavia Since 1991, Rules of Procedure and Evidence*, UN Doc. IT/32/Rev.3 (1995)
63. Robertson (note 44), p.285.
64. For an account of what happened at Foca, see 'Serbs enslaved Muslim women at rape camps', *The Guardian*, 21 March 2000
65. Salzman (note 48), p.357.
66. Ibid.
67. Robertson (note 44), p.285.
68. Ibid.
69. Ibid.
70. Ibid.
71. Ibid., p.285–6.
72. Ibid.
73. Ibid.
74. Ibid.
75. Ibid. See also Niarchos (note 7).
76. On the issue of female investigators and female representations to the Tribunal, see Aydelott (note 28), p.603.
77. Robertson (note 44), p.286.
78. William Hayden, 'The Kosovo Conflict: The Strategic Use of Displacement and the Obstacles to International Protection', *Civil Wars*, Vol.2, No.1 (Spring 1999), pp.35–69.
79. See for example, Sam Kiley, 'Serbs make rape a weapon of war', *The Times*, 6 April 1999, or Elizabeth Judge, 'Serb soldiers using rape as tactic of war', *The Times*, 14 April 1999.
80. See *The Times*, 6 April 1999.
81. For a critique of Western motivations, see Noam Chomsky, *The New Military Humanism Lessons From Kosovo* (London: Pluto, 1999).
82. *The Times*, 14 April, 1999,.
83. Shaw (note 51), p.171.
84. 'The Rape of Kosovo', *The Times*, 19 June 1999. See also 'Pattern of violent assaults revealed in in *The Guardian*, 21 March 2000.
85. Ibid.
86. Ibid. See also Birgitte Refslund Sorensen, 'Recovering from Conflict, Does Gender Make a Difference?' *UN Chronicle*, No.2 (1999), pp.26–7.
87. Donna M.Hughes and Kathleen Foster, 'War, Nationalism and Rape, Women Respond by Opening a Centre Against Sexual Violence in Belgrade, Serbia', in *Women's Studies International Forum*, Vol.19, Nos.1–2, pp.183–4.
88. 'Prostitution gangs stalk camp women', *The Times*, 4 May 1999. See also Anders B. Johnsson, 'The International Protection of Women Refugees: A Summary of Principal Problems and Issues', *International Journal of Refugee Law*, No.221 (1989), pp.225–28.
89. Stephen Farrell, 'Survivor tells of Serb rape campaign', *The Times*, 1 July 1999.
90. See for example, Betty A.Reardon, *Sexism and the War System* (New York, Teachers College Press, 1985); Jeanne Vickers, *Women and War* (London: Zed Press, 1993).
91. See Hilary Charlesworth, Christine Chinkin and Shelley Wright, 'Feminist Approaches to International Law', *American Journal of International Law*, Vol.85 (Oct. 1991), pp.621–5.
92. Michael Ignatieff, *The Warrior's Honour* (London:Vintage, 1998) p.4 .

# PART TWO:

# Prologue

# 4
# Warnings From Bosnia: The Dayton Agreement and the Implementation of Human Rights

## MARIANNE HANSON

The Dayton Peace Agreement (DPA) of 21 November 1995 was able to secure a halt to hostilities between the warring Serb, Croat and Bosniac parties in Bosnia and Hercegovina. However, the plan that emerged from the peace negotiations – to create stability, restore human rights and build enduring peace in the devastated state – might well be judged a monumentally difficult task. It is now over four years since the signing of the agreement (known formally as the General Framework Agreement for Peace in Bosnia and Hercegovina – GFAP) and while there have been some advances toward an integrated society, over a million refugees and internally displaced persons (IDPs) are yet to return home, ethnically motivated violence continues, and politically and ethnically biased officials and police forces hamper the integration process. Moreover, the international community's effort has come under criticism for the extent to which it has allowed the Office of the High Representative (OHR) to increase its powers of intervention in Bosnia, a shift in policy which, it is alleged, has restricted the civil and political rights of the Bosnian people.

As the United Nations, the European Union, the OSCE (Organization for Security and Cooperation in Europe), NATO and other international bodies strive to reconstruct Kosovo in the aftermath of NATO's 1999 air campaign in Serbia, there will be an at least implicit wish to accept the Bosnian project as successful; indeed, one would assume that the international community would hardly embark on its Kosovo efforts if there were widely-acknowledged serious doubts about the efficacy of implementation in Bosnia. Remarkably however, despite clear evidence that the Bosnian project is far from assured, the international community is again willing to commit itself to an implementation mission in the Balkans and will be looking to the DPA as a reference point for its intervention efforts. Undoubtedly, the Dayton Peace Agreement was a well-intentioned attempt by the international community to rebuild a state torn apart by ethnic conflict at a time when the international community had had no experience in coordinating a task of such magnitude and complexity. What has resulted, however, is a model that should serve as a cautionary tale to those embarking along a similar route.

### DAYTON: FROM SEPARATION TO INTEGRATION

The Dayton accords essentially encompassed two objectives, both of which were ultimately concerned with the restoration of human rights. The first was to ensure that the devastating conflict that had ravaged the region for three years, during which murder, torture, rape and the forced movement of populations had been commonplace, would end. The second objective was to encourage sustained peace and stability in the reformulated state of Bosnia and Hercegovina, effectively building institutions and practices which would enable communities to live together and participate in civil and political life. Yet the integration of sharply divided and hostile communities, a civilian function, was inevitably going to be a harder and more prolonged task than was the separation of warring communities, essentially a military function. Moreover, maintaining the ceasefire agreed a few weeks before the DPA, in October 1995 – while not without difficulties – had been simpler for two reasons. First, the team of American negotiators had the full support of the USA, with such support argued to be much less present for the implementation of civilian functions, given the marked divide between military and civilian objectives.[1] Second, the amount of territory held by the Serbs (49 per cent) and the Muslims and Croats (51 per cent) at the time of the talks had already been accepted by the warring parties as an agreed division. Each group was to control, roughly, what it had conquered in battle.

To ensure that there would not be a resumption of war, a NATO-led peacekeeping force (IFOR – the Implementation Force in Bosnia, subsequently SFOR, the Stabilisation Force) was established. IFOR's primary duty was the creation of the Inter-Entity Boundary Line (the two 'entities' being the Republika Srpska and the Muslim-Croat Federation) and the Zone of Separation between the two. In addition, IFOR was responsible for reducing the size and capacity of the armed forces of each group. These actions, which constituted the military requirements of the

Dayton Agreement, were successfully achieved and ensured that military hostilities were brought to an end. The much more difficult task of building enduring peace and stability in Bosnia has remained, sadly, incomplete.

Implementation of the civilian features of the agreement has proved to be a task that would have to overcome almost insurmountable hurdles.[2] This is not really surprising, especially when one looks at the nature of both the military and civilian features of the agreement. The duties assigned to IFOR, mentioned briefly above, were largely to secure a separation of the warring parties, whereas civilian implementation was focused on integration of those same parties. The charge has been that such a strict separation of military and civilian functions has meant that the latter has received inadequate support. While IFOR was given certain rights, or authorities, under Dayton to help secure political objectives, these did not amount to obligations; moreover, these rights have largely not been exercised to the extent deemed necessary by personnel on the ground. This is much to the dismay of those urging Bosnian compliance with the accords but who themselves have no military capabilities to enforce such compliance.

This concern over the civilian/military divide, a divide which was at the heart of the Dayton Agreement, is however, only one of a number of concerns and is noted here only in brief. It will be re-examined as part of an overall assessment of Dayton later in this work. Before doing that, however, it is necessary to take stock of the various achievements and deficiencies evident in the implementation of the accords in Bosnia and their implication for human rights.

## A BRIEF PROGRESS REPORT

Four years on, and despite the efforts of the international community – or perhaps because of them – the goal of establishing a stable, functioning unified state, able to manage its own affairs, still does not appear to be close to realisation. There have been some positive achievements which are contributing to the restoration of human rights and the rebuilding of the state, but progress has been painfully slow.

### Small Successes

Perhaps the most important advance to date has been the establishment of freedom of movement. Until the appearance of uniform vehicle licence plates in 1998, it had been all too easy for aggrieved nationalist groups to determine the ethnic identity of occupants of vehicles. Frequent attacks on motorists along ethnically divided lines have been reduced through this (stunningly simple) device of uniformity. Freedom of movement has also been assisted by the abolition of most inter-entity border controls and *ad hoc* checkpoints, the establishment of a new inter-entity bus line, developments towards ensuring a railway service, the introduction of a national currency (the KM – Convertible Mark) and a common passport.[3]

On the difficult issue of war criminals, there has also been some progress (although there are continuing problems with this process and criticism of the fact that it has remained incomplete, as will be discussed later). By early 1999, 81 war criminals had been indicted by the International Criminal Tribunal for the former Yugoslavia (ICTY), with between 29 and 36 per cent of these persons still at large.[4] There has also been some move towards media reform, with most television and radio stations restructured away from ethnically-defined control, and 80 per cent television coverage has been achieved through the Open Broadcasting Network (the first neutral source of news in the state). An indicator of success in this area is that the OSCE was able to hand over its monitoring responsibilities to an Independent Media Commission on 31 October 1998.[5]

Some judicial reform has also been conducted, with a Memorandum Of Understanding on Inter-Entity Legal Assistance signed on 20 May 1998, an Inter-Entity Legal Commission established in June 1998, and a new criminal code adopted by the Federation Parliament. Law enforcement and military stability have also been targeted for attention: the International Police Task Force (IPTF) has provided training for police (admittedly on an unbalanced scale, with 85 per cent of Federation police but only 35 per cent of Republika Srpska police receiving such training). The Entity Armed Forces, however, and in compliance with the Dayton accords, are still divided ethnically. Bosnia and Hercegovina is also deemed to be in compliance with the arms controls requirements of Dayton since October 1997.[6]

## Continuing Deficiencies

While the above may indicate heartening progress, in reality the deficiencies of Dayton appear to dominate and overwhelm these successes. The most disappointing aspect of implementation concerns the return of refugees and internally displaced persons. Minority returns in particular (that is, the return of persons to areas – usually their original homes – in which they now form part of an ethnic minority in that area) have been both extremely limited and, where they have occurred, dangerous for the returnees.[7] Between 1996 and 1999, there had been only around 15,000 minority returns, out of a total of around 475,000 persons returning to Bosnia and Hercegovina. 1998 had been designated the 'Year of Minority Returns', but these small numbers have demonstrated the gap between the aspirations of those working towards repatriation and the difficulties of minority settlement.[8] The overall issue of returns is itself disappointing: by 1999 only about a quarter of the more than two million refugees and IDPs had returned at all.[9] Between December 1995 and July 1998, a mere 1,920 non-Serbs had returned to the Republika Srpska, and there is ample evidence to indicate that Serb authorities especially have invoked discriminatory housing legislation to deter non-Serbs from re-settling in the area. In some cases, housing prepared for returnees is vandalised or destroyed just before refugees return. Federation authorities also continue to obstruct returns, despite new legislation designed to overcome this. On a sobering note, Human Rights Watch has observed that in the few years since the signing of Dayton, many more minorities have fled the capital, Sarajevo, than have returned.[10]

The difficulties of repatriating refugees and IDPs is compounded not only by the use of 'bureaucratic warfare' by nationalist officials and tactics of terror for those who do eventually return as minorities, but by other factors as well. Domestic economic conditions in all parts of the state have deteriorated in recent years, raising unemployment and aggravating existing ethnic rivalries. Turmoil in other parts of the Balkans also contributes to instability in Bosnia and Hercegovina as groups have sought to flee or resettle, creating a chain effect which hampers even the assessment of refugee numbers. International institutions too, have responded in inadequate ways.[11] Furthermore, over 19,000 people still remain unaccounted for in the state.[12]

The continuation of ethnically motivated violence is one of the most obvious and disturbing violations of human rights. This has been mostly related to the area of minority returns, resulting in the forced departure of many who had recently returned to their homes. Critically, local authorities appear to be taking inadequate measures to stop these attacks. This is hardly surprising as many Bosnians tasked with implementing law and order and many in the police themselves appear to be complicit in such attacks. To date, very few charges have been laid against the perpetrators of such violence, although there appears to be sufficient evidence of their wrong-doing.[13] So while freedom of movement has been noted above as one of the main achievements in Bosnia to date, this must be qualified by noting that, at least for many of those returning as 'minority returns', their freedom of movement and action has indeed been severely limited. Moreover, ethnically-motivated violence does not, for the moment at least, appear to be able to be addressed through the education system, with a number of reports noting continuing obstruction towards the integration of education.[14]

The holding of elections in Bosnia and Hercegovina has frequently been upheld as evidence of moves towards democratisation.[15] Yet while there has been a trend away from overtly nationalist ethnically-based parties in most of the elections held, this has not been uniform. Although nationalist parties have lost some ground, they still essentially retain influence.[16] Moreover, the international community was surprised when the Republika Srpska elected a hardline Serb nationalist, Nikola Poplasen to the Presidency of the RS in the September 1998 elections, replacing the more moderate President Plavsic. (Poplasen was subsequently dismissed by the High Representative on 5 March 1999, in line with the greater powers accorded to his office.) Additionally, in some cases the elections that have been held have been significantly marred by technical problems, interference[17] and inadequate preparation by international organisations.[18]

The question of the value of elections is a complex one. On the one hand they appear to confirm moves towards a semblance of democracy and vindicate the efforts of the international community.[19] Yet in reality, they may have reinforced the ethnic division of the Bosnian state. Voting along ethnic lines has merely entrenched the polarisation that has taken place in Bosnia since 1992, and some have argued that, in Bosnia's case at least, early elections may have been a mistake.[20] At least until an alternative electoral system is devised, one which requires voters to elect representatives from their own as well as from other ethnic groups,[21] thus making candidates accountable to a wider segment of the community than at present, it may be that the Dayton system freezes in place, rather than ameliorates, the sharply held differences between the entities and the groups within them. For the moment however, the jury is still out on the question of whether elections have benefited or hampered the rebuilding of Bosnia.

Economic development also remains problematic. A senior deputy to the High Representative claimed as late as May 1999 that not only does Bosnia have 'no independent judiciary, no rule of law', but it also has 'no economic activity to speak of'.[22] Independent mechanisms to monitor governmental financial transactions are not fully in place and the implementation of privatisation legislation has been slow, with corruption and cronyism endemic at high levels.[23] The Report of the Special Rapporteur on the situation of human rights in the former Yugoslavia noted that with regard to economic and social rights, violations are common and characterised by widespread discrimination on grounds of ethnic origin, political affiliation or opinion and gender.[24]

One of the most frequently heard criticisms of the Dayton implementation has been that some of the most notorious persons indicted as war criminals remain at large.[25] (This is despite the steady number of arrests made to date, noted above.) Radovan Karadzic and Ratko Mladic, in particular remain free. The Republika Srpska appears adamant in not complying with the requirements of the ICTY; worse, it has been argued that SFOR shows little stomach for actively seeking out those indicted and sending them for trial in The Hague. This has been at least partly due to the division between the military and civilian functions stipulated at Dayton, but more to the fact that NATO-led forces have chosen not to exercise – at least in any sustained way – the rights bestowed on them to arrest those indicted.[26] The implications of this incomplete procedure have been felt most acutely on the reconciliation process as some of those indicted continue to exert – and are seen to exert – influence at various levels of social and political life in Bosnia and Hercegovina.

Judicial reform and law enforcement are also singled out as areas of deficiency. Despite some progress, the judicial system still requires significant reform; many judges remain politically and ethnically biased, and the overall system, it is argued, lacks transparency.[27] Police forces remain largely mono-ethnic in character, and only slow progress has been made in hiring minority officers. Depressingly, existing police forces provide little or no help in facilitating minority returns; indeed a number of high-ranking officials have been complicit in torturing suspects and have been accused of ignoring minority complaints. While some have been dismissed for these and other violations, there appears to be little faith that the law-enforcement authorities will act impartially to protect the human rights of all Bosnians.

At the military level too, relations are fragile. There is a continuing relationship between the Bosnian Serb army (the VRS) and the army of the FRY, while the Bosnian Croat section of the Federation army still maintains its ties with Croatia. One of the greatest concerns is that the US 'train and equip' scheme, designed ostensibly to train Federation forces to defend themselves against a possible attack by RS forces, has tilted the balance of power against the Serbs and very much in favour of the Federation. Fears are that the Bosniacs in particular may wish to utilise the military superiority gained from the programme to open up old wounds and seek redress for past losses suffered at the hands of Bosnian Serbs. (It should also be noted that the 'train and equip' programme is almost universally disliked by European personnel in Bosnia.)[28]

All the above would indicate that there remain serious deficiencies in the implementation of the Dayton Agreement and that human rights, while undoubtedly far more secure than during the period of warfare, are not yet fully realised in Bosnia and Hercegovina. Significantly, even some of the most fundamental of human rights continue to be violated; attacks and even murder motivated by ethnic polarisation are not uncommon and far too few Bosnians have been able to be returned to Bosnia for the Dayton Agreement to be deemed a success. The High Commissioner for Human Rights concluded in 1998 that she did 'not see evidence to support the conclusion that the right to freedom from discrimination based on national or ethnic origin, that the prime importance of the rule of law, is fully respected anywhere in these societies'.[29]

## FLAWS IN IMPLEMENTATION

On a broader level, and especially in view of the international community's decision to embark on a second mission of reconstruction in the Balkans, there are certain strategic features of the Bosnia experience which merit examination. These centre on the problem noted above of insufficient military backing for civilian functions; the perception that the Dayton Agreements have been overwhelmed by US interests, especially the need to strengthen NATO; the problem of poor coordination by the international community; and increased intervention by the High Representative, with its implications for the process of democratisation.

### The Civil/Military Divide

As already noted, one of the main problems to come out of the Bosnian peace process has been the division between civil and military implementation. The decision by IFOR/SFOR not to exercise vigorously the right to assist with civilian implementation has significantly reduced the authority of civilian organisations to effect or enforce change. The International Crisis Group maintains that:

> in the DPA, the division between civil and military implementation was as sharp and brutal as possible. IFOR was given rights but no duties in the area of civilian implementation. At an early stage in 1996 IFOR commanders took a clear decision not to exercise those rights. Even though it rapidly became obvious that in a nation tired of war, IFOR's main task would be much easier than expected, leaving it under-employed, IFOR commanders declined to provide services in areas where, for example, impartial policing was needed, even though the UN International Police Task Force (IPTF) was having a much harder time fulfilling its own mandate.[30]

IFOR's decision can be attributed in large part to the unwillingness of the US to incur casualties in the course of monitoring the implementation of the DPA. Yet the very narrow interpretation of the agreement by IFOR has left the civilian administration without any real capacity to enforce its programme.[31] One of the end results of this is that the High Representative and others on the ground seeking to enforce compliance with civilian elements of the DPA rely principally on the leverage of aid and other financial assistance to help secure cooperation. While effective in some regions, this has not been conducive to the larger process of reconciliation and in some areas where non-compliance appears to be the norm – especially in the RS – the impoverishment of local populations continues. A second consequence of the limited effectiveness of the civilian authorities, of course, was the decision to expand the authority and powers of the High Representative.

## US Interests

The Dayton Agreements have rightly been seen as a massive commitment on the part of the US to achieving stability in the Balkans. Yet the extremely close identification of the DPA with the US is not without its problems. Susan Woodward has argued that Bosnia has become 'an American project because ... it was ... in the American interest – to preserve the NATO alliance, demonstrate US commitment to European security and reaffirm American leadership on moral principles'.[32] Woodward identifies these as the underlying aims of US foreign policy, concluding that negotiation and implementation of the DPA have served a useful purpose by, among other things, maintaining and promoting cooperation between NATO allies. The problem, however, is that this is seen to take precedence over the need to promote unity and democracy within the multiethnic state of Bosnia.

This is particularly the case if we consider recent calls to re-evaluate and, if need be, modify the original accords, calls which the US administration – conscious of the need to sell Dayton as a success to Congress – appears unwilling to heed.[33] The US has reconfirmed its determination to implement the Dayton Agreement 'exactly as it was negotiated and signed'.[34] But the refusal to consider amending the DPA is seen as intransigence; by declining to effect changes to Bosnia's constitution, to reconsider the distribution of aid and to grant greater military support for civilian functions – all of which have been requested – the conclusion drawn by critics of the implementation process as well as by indigenous Bosnians is that the US is more preoccupied with its strategic interests than with correcting the shortcomings in Bosnia evident over the past few years. This criticism may be somewhat overdrawn,[35] but there is

nevertheless no compelling reason why there should not be a formal
rethink of the contents of the DPA as well as the implementation process,
especially given the slow progress made on a number of human rights
issues. (In one sense, of course, there has been a fundamental change in the
approach taken towards implementation; this is the enhancement of the
High Representative's powers and his ability to intervene and impose
settlements on hitherto uncooperative parties. But the essential elements of
the Dayton Agreement have remained unchanged.)

## Who's the Boss?

One of the most serious flaws in the DPA was that it provided no indication
as to which organisation is the coordinating body for civilian
implementation.[36] As a result, the Office of the High Representative
(OHR), OSCE, the EU and UN have all essentially followed their own
mandates. The mission has thus suffered from a general lack of
coordination, insufficient cooperation between international organisations,
the duplication of certain tasks and an overall lack of accountability. The
competing activities of various organisations in the field have led some
observers to denounce the international community's efforts unkindly as
little more than a 'job-creation scheme' for international civil servants.[37]
The International Crisis Group has argued that 'In general, the
international "community" should be prepared to find better ways to work
together. Where a common goal is agreed, the key should be the effective
achievement of the goal, not the preservation of organisations' autonomy
within their own spheres of operation.'[38]

Those charged with providing aid have been plagued by the same
problem, with Bosnians seeking financial assistance for reconstruction
finding little in the way of focused coordination. As a result, the aid
community has been less effective than it should have been.

## From 'Helping Hand' to Iron Fist?

The Dayton model was one which purported to lend a 'helping hand' to
the people of Bosnia to rebuild their state, rather than one which
anticipated wholesale intervention in the reconstruction of social and
political life. The agreement produced a constitution for the Republic of
Bosnia and Hercegovina and called for a three-person Presidency
(Muslim, Croat and Serb). Together with other joint institutions, such as
the Parliamentary Assembly and Council of Ministers, these bodies were
given responsibility for foreign policy, foreign trade, customs, monetary
policy, immigration and a small number of other affairs. All other
matters, including civilian law enforcement, have been left to the entities
– the Republika Srpska and the Federation of Bosnia and Hercegovina.

While these bodies are as yet barely developed and severely limited in their functions, it is the issue of civilian law enforcement left to the entities which has caused most concern. Despite the continued call to Bosnian leaders to cooperate in the implementation of the civilian aspects of the DPA, this has not occurred at a sufficient level (as the brief report on implementation above has noted). In response, the High Representative has gradually increased his powers of civilian implementation, most notably with the enhancement of his mandate by the Peace Implementation Council in December 1997.

This was a controversial move. On the one hand it enabled the then High Representative, Carlos Westendorp, to dismiss obstructionist officials and impose quick solutions onto disputes that had remained unresolved for years. Indeed, it seems highly unlikely that the achievements towards establishing freedom of movement could have occurred without this approach.[39] On the other hand, increased intervention by the Office of the High Representative has drawn condemnation from observers who claim that this change in approach might further destabilise the Dayton process.

One reason for this is that increased intervention – effectively the ability to override elected or non-elected Bosnian officials – has effectively excluded Bosnians from processes designed to promote peace and democracy. Since the expansion of the OHR's powers, this exclusion has occurred at all levels, arguably making it difficult for Bosnians to look beyond their close (mono-ethnic) support networks. Chandler notes that increased intervention, by ultimately weakening the capacities of Bosnian institutions (regardless of how ineffective these might already have been), has reinforced ethnic rivalries as Bosnians have fallen back more strongly on local support networks.[40] The expanded and extended mandates of the international community have eroded what little Bosnian control was established earlier in the peace process, in turn making a mockery of earlier international attempts to build democracy through elections.[41] It also limits avenues for Bosnians to discuss, develop and decide on vital issues. The powers of the international community have grown to the extent that they significantly impact at all levels – state, entity, city and municipal. While Dayton was initially meant to bring decentralisation of political power and multi-ethnic administrations, this has obviously not occurred. The charge is that international organisations now regulate almost every aspect of Bosnian life and that Bosnians have become disempowered.[42] Moreover, there appears to be little regret on the part of the international community that this has occurred.

This view has been echoed with some concern by the International Crisis Group. While acknowledging that many officials have been obstructive and operate on the basis of protecting ethnic divisions rather than making genuine moves towards integration, it notes that some of the responsibility for the ineffective results of Dayton lies with the increasing intervention of the international community in Bosnia's political life.[43]

At a broad level, these developments raise the disturbing question of the international community itself as a violator of human rights, a charge which undoubtedly those working to rebuild Bosnia would be quick to refute. Yet there are disquieting elements to these developments which have serious consequences for any assessments of the human rights environment in Bosnia. No one would doubt that the vast majority of the actions taken by international organisations under the authority of the Dayton Agreement have been instrumental in protecting the right to life and liberty of the Bosnian people. It is also quite likely that those achievements reached through expanding the powers of the OHR to override local Bosnians – notably an increase in the freedom of movement – would simply not have been possible without such intervention. Yet given that the DPA set out to establish Bosnia as a 'democratic state, which shall operate under the rule of law',[44] it would appear that the OHR is now resigned to a far stronger model of intervention than was deemed necessary initially, a model which (out of necessity) is now less concerned with ensuring principles of democracy and which falls just short of being a 'protectorate'. The paradox is that illiberal means are increasingly being employed to achieve the liberal ends envisaged at Dayton in 1995, something not foreseen at the time of signing.

## A FORCED INTEGRATION?

The Dayton Accords assumed that the parties in Bosnia actively wished to rebuild the state of Bosnia as an integrated and multi-ethnic whole. Yet the experience of the past four years shows that this is not what the people of Bosnia desire. Whether simply out of fear for their safety or because of a clearly defined wish to live only among their own ethnic grouping and shun others, the overwhelming message implicit in the reluctance to accept the provisions of Dayton seems to be that the DPA has not succeeded because the people of Bosnia have not wished to accept its fundamental premise, i.e., that Bosnia should remain a multiethnic state.[45] The Bosnian Serbs, in particular, have been frustratingly obstructive on issues designed to bind the state together; Croats and Muslims also follow their own separatist agendas. In sum, separating the antagonists worked because that was the wish of those antagonists; similarly, integrating them is difficult because this does not appear to be the wish of the Bosnian people.[46]

While the desirability of the continuation of the mission is not under question here, given its role in preventing the conflict from re-igniting and protecting at least some of the basic human rights of Bosnia's inhabitants, arguments mount that the international community is nevertheless engaged in enforcing an unwanted arrangement, has taken over the running of Bosnia and Hercegovina at all levels and that the state's institutions have little hope of maturing or succeeding if the international community continues to overrule local wishes, however distasteful these may be to Western views. This raises disturbing questions about how far the international community ought to go in enforcing integration and multiethnicity – clearly liberal Western preferences – where this is not wanted by local populations. A fundamental reason for the low rate of minority returns is that people – out of fear, entrenched polarisation or both – simply do not wish to live in mixed communities where they constitute a minority group and perceive themselves to be at risk of further violence.

Yet for the moment at least, partition does not seem to be an option, especially as this would signal the international community's willingness to accept ethnic cleansing as a *fait accompli*. But the alternative is to continue to muddle through with a mission which while making slow moves to restoring a broad range of human rights, can claim as its best effort that it has managed to keep warring parties apart and prevent a return to the violence of the 1992–95 period. In sum, there are those who question the value of the DPA as a mechanism that so far may have only reinforced the ethnic rivalries of Bosnia and Hercegovina and which – in its present form at least – seems unable to move local parties towards genuine multiethnic institutions and practices, unless this is done at risk of violating democratic principles and imposing a protectorate over the region.[47]

## CONCLUSION

What might all this mean for the international community's decision to commence another complex and undoubtedly prolonged mission in the Balkans? The first point which can be made is the obvious but nevertheless remarkable fact that notwithstanding considerable difficulties in the implementation of the Dayton Agreement in Bosnia, the international community was willing to take on a similar human rights mission in the province of Kosovo. This in itself says something for the willingness of the international community to be actively engaged in seeking to restore human rights, at a time when its existing project proved to be far more intractable and prolonged than was ever envisaged. Dayton, as Michael Ignatieff reminds us, was going to be 'the future of

Western intervention',[48] but that future turned out to be fraught with obstruction, violence and mismanagement and demonstrated only a limited repatriation of the victims of displacement.

There are, of course, important differences between Bosnia and Kosovo that need to be noted here and which will have implications for the way in which the Kosovo mandate is carried out and human rights established.[49] The first is that the refugees returning to Kosovo will not have to encounter occupation of their property by others, as has so often been the case in Bosnia. This advantages not only the refugees but will also allow the international community to focus on reconstruction and supply in a way that has so far eluded organisations in Bosnia.

Second, those in positions of authority in Kosovo prior to the conflict (mainly Serbs) no longer occupy those positions. While this is cause for concern, in the sense that it demonstrates the exodus of the minority Serb population and presents – regrettably – yet another case of ethnic separation in the Balkans, it will make the task of civilian administration easier to establish. The international community will not be faced with obstructive authorities resistant to returnees who form minorities in the area of return, as has been the case in Bosnia.

Third, because the Serbs and Kosovar Albanians were not signatories to UN Security Council Resolution 1244, their agreement to the peace process was not sought. The advantage of this is that there are fewer chances that compromises might become part of the eventual agreement and implementation. The potential and serious disadvantage, of course, is that exclusion may lead to resentment and eventually bring with it charges of Western imperialism (regardless of whether this is done in the name of human rights or not). Bosnia provides a clear warning here: one of the chief reasons for Bosnian Serb resistance to the DPA was their exclusion from the negotiating process. Bosnian Serbs have not reconciled themselves to the Dayton process and largely because the settlement was imposed upon them, invariably baulk at major implementing measures.[50] Kosovo has been established as a protectorate in all but name, indicating that the international community has recognised that from the outset, a stronger model of intervention would be required here than was originally applied with the 'helping hand' approach in Bosnia. Yet it should not be assumed that this more interventionist model will be acceptable to Kosovars or Serbs in the long term; moreover, as in Bosnia, the international community will need to be alert to possible charges of anti-democratisation in its search to establish liberal rights in Kosovo.

Fourth, and quite distinct from the confusion which has prevailed in Bosnia, the United Nations has been tasked with heading civil implementation. There is an obvious 'chain of command' among the international organisations which should prevent at least some of the problems that have been encountered in Bosnia, where overlapping and duplicating institutions have hampered efficiency and created rivalry. There are also implications here for an improvement in the civil/military divide. Although relations between NATO and the UN remain delicate, and predictably NATO has been tasked, as in Bosnia, with implementing the military elements of the Kosovo agreement, it appears that there will be a far closer link between the two than was evident in Bosnia.

The decision to accord ultimate authority to the United Nations has the added advantage of providing a solid legal basis to the mission (especially important after the technical illegality, though probable legitimacy, of the NATO campaign against Serbia). Giving the UN this distinction also provides an opportunity for it to repair its reputation damaged in the Bosnian experience, although whether international institutions will be able to cooperate to the extent needed remains to be seen.[51]

At the time of the decision to implement the Dayton Peace Agreement, the international community can be said to have been spurred on primarily by its collective unease over its inability to bring to a speedy resolution the tragic war that had engulfed provinces of the former Yugoslavia in the years prior to 1995. A second motivating factor, however, was the sense that this was indeed a practicable mission, that there existed sufficient goodwill, resources and coordination among major states and organisations in the international system to implement it. What was lacking, of course, was any real experience of a task so demanding and complex, within a Balkan geo-strategic environment that could arguably be described as a 'worst-case scenario'. This lack of experience, together with elements of shortsightedness, intransigence and inefficiency, has meant that implementation of the DPA has been much more prolonged and arduous than was envisaged in 1995. In the case of Kosovo, there can be no similar arguments made for a lack of experience.

ACKNOWLEDGEMENT

The author wishes to acknowledge with grateful thanks the research support provided by Darina Brady.

NOTES

1. See the International Crisis Group Report 1999, 'Kosovo: Let's Learn from Bosnia: Models and Methods of International Administration', 17 May 1999, http://www.intl-crisis-group.org/.
2. This seems to have been recognised by at least some at the time: see Richard Holbrooke, the Former Assistant Secretary of State and negotiator of the Dayton Accords, 'Dayton Discord', The New Republic, Vol.217, No.9 (September 1997), pp.4–5, refuting an article critical of the Bosnia peace accords; includes author rebuttal

by Susan Ellingwood. (Online InfoTrac, *Expanded Academic ASAP*, A19696206). Holbrooke also noted that he was among the first 'to state publicly that the record on implementing Dayton was running seriously behind schedule', ibid. Various observers warned, very early in the implementation process, of the difficulties ahead. See J. Schear, 'Bosnia's Post-Dayton Traumas', *Foreign Policy*, Fall 1996, pp.86–101. (Online InfoTrac, *Expanded Academic ASAP*, A20825313); S. Woodward, 'Implementing Peace in Bosnia and Herzegovina: A Post-Dayton Primer and Memorandum of Warning', Brookings Discussion Paper, May 1996, http://www.brook.edu/fp/w-papers/daysum. html; 'Adieu, Dayton?' *The Economist*, 30 July 1996, p.44.

3. For details of these achievements, see *International Crisis Group Report 1999* (note 1); Human Rights Watch 1999, 'Bosnia and Herzegovina: Human Rights Developments', 1999, http://www.hrw.org/hrw/worldreport99/europe/bosnia.html; N. Agnihotri, 'Bosnia-Herzegovina: Unity and Progress', *Presidents and Prime Ministers*, Vol.7, No.3 (1998) (Online InfoTrac, *Expanded Academic ASAP*, A54062409); W. Clinton, 'Message to the Congress Reporting on Efforts to Achieve a Sustainable Peace in Bosnia-Herzegovina, 4 February 1999', *Weekly Compilation of Presidential Documents*, Vol.35, No.5 (1999) (Online InfoTrac, *Expanded Academic ASAP*, A54205677); *US Progress Towards Fulfillment of the Dayton Accords*, US Department of State Dispatch, June 1998, (Online InfoTrac, *Expanded Academic ASAP*, A20951919).
4. 'Message to the Congress' (note 3).
5. Ibid.
6. Ibid. See also Agnihotri (note 3).
7. See the report by the International Crisis Group, 10 August 1999, 'Preventing Minority Returns in Bosnia and Herzegovina: the Anatomy of Hate and Fear', http://www.intl-crisis-group.org/
8. International Crisis Group, 9 September 1998, 'Bosnia: Too Little Too Late', wysiwyg://report.949/http://www.intl-cr...rg/projects/bosnia/reports/bh41repa.html
9. The figures cited in this section are taken from the *Human Rights Watch Report 1999*, 'Bosnia and Herzegovina' (note 3). Note however, that the journal *Refugees* states that there has been a total of 560,000 refugee returns, including some 30,000 minority returns in 1998 alone. See R. Wilkinson, 'Rising from the Ashes? 1999 – a Year of Decision in the Balkans', *Refugees*, No.114 (1999). Nevertheless, this source, as with all sources consulted, concludes that the level of returns has been far less than originally envisaged at Dayton and that this issue constitutes one of the gravest flaws in the implementation of the DPA.
10. Human Rights Watch, 'Bosnia and Herzegovina' (note 3).
11. Wilkinson, 'Rising from the Ashes?' (note 9). Wilkinson notes, for example, that UNHCR has reduced its operating budget from $87 million in 1998 to $64 million in 1999.
12. *Amnesty International Report 1999*, 'Bosnia-Herzegovina', http://www.amnesty.org/ailib/aireport/ar99/eur63.htm
13. On this issue, see Wilkinson, 'Rising From the Ashes' (note 9); Human Rights Watch, 'Bosnia and Herzegovina' (note 3); International Crisis Group, 'Preventing Minority Returns' (note 7); Human Rights Internet, 'Bosnia and Herzegovina: Commission on Human Rights – Report of the Special Rapporteur, 1999', http://www.hri.ca/ fortherecord 1999/vol5/bosniachr.htm; *Amnesty International Report 1998*, 'Bosnia-Herzegovina', http://www.amnesty.org/ailib/aireport/ar99/eur63.htm; C. Boyd, 'Making Bosnia Work', *Foreign Affairs*, Vol.77, No.1 (1998), pp.42–55; *International Crisis Group Report 1999* (note 1); S. Woodward, 'Foreign Policy Flashpoints: Bosnia', *Brookings Review*, Vol.15, No.2 (1997) (Online InfoTrac, *Expanded Academic ASAP*, A19548340); J. Sharp, 'Bosnia: Begin Again', *The Bulletin of the Atomic Scientists*, March/April 1997, pp.17–19.
14. See, for example, *Human Rights Coordination Centre [HRCC] Human Rights Monthly Report*, August 1999.
15. See for instance the overly optimistic accounts given by President Clinton in 'Message to the Congress' (note 3) and by Bosnian Ambassador to the US Sven Alkaiaj, cited in N. Agnihotri, 'Bosnia-Herzegovina: Unity and Progress' (note 3).
16. *Human Rights Watch Report 1999*, 'Bosnia and Herzegovina' (note 3).

17. Ibid.
18. The OSCE, as the chief body responsible for overseeing elections, has been criticised for not anticipating difficulties which occurred during some of the more recent elections in Bosnia-Hercegovina.
19. On elections, Annex 3 of the Dayton Peace Agreement states the need 'to promote free, fair and democratic elections and to lay the foundation for representative government and ensure the progressive achievement of democratic goals throughout Bosnia and Herzegovina'. *The General Agreement for Peace in Bosnia and Herzegovina*, Annex 3: Agreement on Elections. http://www.ohr.int/gfa/gfa-an3htm
20. *The International Crisis Group Report* 'Kosovo: Let's Learn From Bosnia' (note 1) for example, recommends that we 'forget elections for now' for Kosovo, arguing that they have not been especially helpful in Bosnia. See also Jane Sharp, 'Bosnia: Begin Again' (note 13).
21. *The International Crisis Group Report*, 9 September 1998, 'Whither Bosnia?' offers a useful alternative electoral model. http://www.intl-crisis-group.org.
22. Principal Deputy High Representative Jacques Klein, cited in 'Bosnia: Better Luck Next Time', *The Economist*, 1 May 1999, p.43.
23. *International Crisis Group Report* 'Whither Bosnia?' (note 21).
24. *For the Record 1999: The United Nations Human Rights System*, 'Bosnia and Herzegovina: Commission on Human Rights: Report of the Special Rapporteur', http://www.hri.ca/fortherecord1999/vol5/bosniachr.htm
25. See *Human Rights Watch Report 1999* (note 3); Clinton, 'Message to the Congress' (note 3).
26. Susan Ellingwood, for instance notes that 'because the Dayton accords fudged the issue of how suspected war criminals would be arrested and brought to trial, it remains likely that the most infamous of the ... indictees ... will walk free'. See 'Dayton Discord' (note 2). See also, however, the argument by Boyd, 'Making Bosnia Work' (note 13), which suggests that the international community should scale down its efforts to pursue war criminals as it has produced a severe Bosnian-Serb backlash to the DPA.
27. See *Human Rights Watch Report 1999* (note 3); 'Message to the Congress' (note 3).
28. See the views of Boyd, 'Making Bosnia Work' (note 13).
29. Address by the High Commissioner for Human Rights to the Humanitarian Issues Working Group of the Peace Implementation Council, Geneva, 20 November 1998.
30. *International Crisis Group Report*, 'Kosovo: Let's Learn From Bosnia' (note 1).
31. W. Bass, 'The Triage of Dayton', *Foreign Affairs*, Vol.77 No.5 (1998) pp.95–108 (Online InfoTrac, *Expanded Academic ASAP*, A21115196). See also Susan Ellingwood, *Dayton Discord* (note 2); and Sharp, 'Bosnia: Begin Again' (note 13). For a US Department of State rebuttal of the view that SFOR and IFOR have not provided support for civilian implementation, see 'US Progress Towards Fulfillment of the Dayton Accords' (note 3).
32. S. Woodward, 'Avoiding Another Cyprus or Israel: A Debate About the Future of Bosnia', *The Brookings Review*, Winter 1998, p.46. Warren Bass, too, argues that the accords helped advance NATO expansion. W. Bass, 'The Triage of Dayton' (note 31).
33. See Boyd (note 13). The US State Department in 1999 reiterated its unwillingness to modify the Dayton process: 'There is, and will be, no alternative,' noted James Foley, Deputy Spokesman, *US Committed to Full Implementation of Dayton Accords* (note 3). Woodward argues, in 'Foreign Policy Flashpoints' (note 13) that a 'failure to act on the lessons learned ... in 1996 and on the choices needed in 1997 would be another in a long series of tragic missed opportunities in Bosnia'.
34. Press Statement, *US Committed to Full Implementation of Dayton Accords* (note 3); See also Clinton, 'Message to the Congress' (note 3).
35. The US President has argued that 'we tend to underestimate how much progress has been made in Bosnia since Dayton'. (Transcript of remarks by President Clinton in a roundtable discussion, *US Newswire*, 2 August 1999.
36. The division of tasks was decided as follows: the OSCE is responsible for electoral support, monitoring human rights and securing the arms control requirements of the DPA; the United Nations Mission in Bosnia and Herzegovina (UNIMBH) oversees the

operation and restructuring of the civil police; the UN's High Commissioner for Refugees is responsible for providing humanitarian relief and the repatriation of refugees and IDPs; and the EU and World Bank coordinate economic reconstruction programmes. Over all these is the Office of the High Representative, which was designed to oversee the civilian implementation of the DPA, although how the OHR was to do this vis-à-vis other organisations remained problematic.

37. *International Crisis Group Report*, 'Kosovo: Let's Learn From Bosnia' (note 1).
38. Ibid.
39. See C. Bennett, 'Bosnia: New Opportunities', *Security Dialogue*, Vol.30, No.3 (1999), pp.291–2; and *Human Rights Watch*, 'Bosnia and Herzegovina' (note 3) which notes that several dramatic improvements resulted from the High Representative's new exercise of powers.
40. David Chandler has been one of the most outspoken critics of the OHR's new powers, arguing that this effectively reduces Bosnia to a protectorate, something not envisaged in 1995. 'The Bosnian Protectorate and the Implications for Kosovo', *New Left Review*, No.235 (May/June 1999), pp.124–34. For a view which challenges the legality of *any* intervention in matters belonging to the local jurisdiction of a sovereign state (and published before the increase in the international community's powers in Bosnia) see A. Rubin, 'Dayton, Bosnia and the Limits of Law', *The National Interest*, Winter 1996, (Online InfoTrac, *Expanded Academic ASAP*, A19130146).
41. Bennett (note 39), p.291.
42. Chandler, 'The Bosnian Protectorate' (note 40).
43. *International Crisis Group Report*, 'Whither Bosnia?' (note 21).
44. *General Framework Agreement*, Annex 4, 'Constitution of Bosnia and Herzegovina', Article I, para.2. http://www.ohr.int/gfa/gfa-an4.htm. It is also worth noting Deputy Secretary of State Strobe Talbott's comments in late 1999: he reiterated that 'a state should let its people choose their leaders through elections, it should derive strength and cohesion from the diversity of its population ... a state should be a liberal democracy', *The Balkan Question and the European Answer*, Address at the Aspen Institute, 24 August 1999, p.1.
45. From the outset, the goal of a unified state was made clear: Warren Christopher in 1996 reiterated that 'the heart of the Dayton Agreement is the effective functioning of joint institutions for a unified state'. W. Christopher, *Charting the Course for Future Civilian Implementation Efforts in Bosnia*, US Department of State Dispatch, 18 November 1996. Strobe Talbott (note 43) recently reinforced the aim of the Dayton process: 'In Bosnia and Herzegovina, our goal is to give all citizens reason to feel that they belong to a single state,' p.2.
46. On this point, see Boyd 'Making Bosnia Work' (note 13); and J. Hooper, 'Is a Continued Stay of US Troops in Bosnia in the National Interest?', *Washington Times*, Insight on the News, 11 January 1999 (Online InfoTrac, *Expanded Academic ASAP*, A 53552693), who reminds us that 85 per cent of Bosnians recently polled still say that they will not vote for a candidate from another ethnic group.
47. See for instance S. Woodward, 'Avoiding Another Cyprus' (note 32); W. Bass 'The Triage of Dayton' (note 31); J. R. Hooper, 'Is a Continued Stay of US Troops in Bosnia in the National Interest?' (note 46); Boyd, 'Making Bosnia Work' (note 12); Chandler, 'The Bosnian Protectorate' (note 40).
48. M. Ignatieff, 'From Dayton to Kosovo', *Time International*, 1 February 1999 (Online InfoTrac, *Expanded Academic ASAP*, A54042873).
49. For detailed examinations of the two models, see *International Crisis Group Report*, 20 June 1999 'The New Kosovo Protectorate', http://www.intl-cris-group.org/; and the *International Crisis Group Report 1999*, 'Kosovo: Let's Learn From Bosnia' (note 1).
50. Bass, 'The Triage of Dayton' (note 31).
51. Under the Rambouillet accords, it was the OSCE, rather than the UN, which was to manage civilian aspects of the agreement, with the UN confined to the task of returning refugees to the province. *International Crisis Group Report 1999*, 'The New Kosovo Protectorate' (note 49).

# 5

# Human Wrongs in Kosovo: 1974–99

## ALEX J. BELLAMY

On 25 September 1998, Fernando del Mundo, a worker for the Office of the United Nations High Commissioner for Refugees (UNHCR) in Kosovo, made a startling observation. Writing in his diary, he noted that this day was one of particularly intense fighting in the province. His white jeep passed a convoy of Yugoslav government trucks adorned with signs announcing that they contained 'Social Humanitarian Aid of Kosovo and Metohija'. As they passed, the wind blew up the tarpaulin on one of trucks, revealing blue uniformed special police units of the Serbian Ministry of Interior (MUP).[1] How was it that these perpetrators of numerous crimes throughout Kosovo came to travel under the banner of humanitarianism? According to Human Rights Watch, these policeman, along with the Yugoslav Army (VJ), 'have attacked a string of towns and villages' and what is more, 'the majority of those killed and injured have been civilians'.[2]

Before and during NATO's Operation Allied Force, VJ, MUP and local Serbian militia forces committed horrendous crimes against the Kosovar Albanian population. Although commentators and Western politicians have been criticised for using the word 'genocide' to refer to what happened, under the terms of the 1948 Genocide Convention, I believe that it is valid to describe what happened in Kosovo between March and June as genocide.[3] After NATO's operation, extremist elements claiming to be members of the Kosovo Liberation Army (UCK) wreaked a terrible vengeance on the Serbian population of Kosovo. Following the deployment of the multinational KFOR force, a series of well-publicised incidents of murder and beatings forced around 170,000 Serbs to flee Kosovo for Serbia and Montenegro.[4] All these examples raise the central question of this essay: what is the value of life in Kosovo? This essay investigates a trajectory of decline in the value of human life from the 1970s to the conflict of 1999.

## THE 1974 CONSTITUTION: A SOLUTION FOR KOSOVO?

Histories of Serb-Albanian relations in Kosovo tend to portray that historical record as a series of bloody encounters. The first of these came during the first Balkan War of 1912–13, during which the Serbs conquered Kosovo from the Ottoman Turks. Following their military victory, the Serbs embarked on a campaign of mass murder and ethnic cleansing in Kosovo, not unlike the campaign embarked upon in 1999. One observer covering events for a Ukrainian newspaper, Leon Trotsky, reported that 'The Serbs in old Serbia, in their national endeavour to correct data in the ethnographical statistics that are not quite favourable to them, are engaged quite simply in the systematic extermination of the Muslim population'.[5] It is estimated that 25,000 Kosovar Albanians were killed at this time.[6] A revenge of sorts was exacted on the Serbs as they retreated *en masse* from the advancing Austrians during the First World War. Although there were relatively few cases of Kosovar Albanians actually attacking the retreating Serbs, most Kosovar Albanians did nothing the help the thousands of Serbs who perished while exposed to the harsh Kosovan winter. The tide turned again, however, with the formation of the Kingdom of Serbs, Croats and Slovenes, which in many respects was a manifestation of the Greater Serbia idea. Albanians were subjected to colonial rule by Belgrade, thousands were killed and imprisoned and still more were deported to Turkey. Despite this, the Second World War in Kosovo did not see the scale of blood-letting that occurred in the rest of Yugoslavia, though in the immediate aftermath of war the Communist Party cracked down severely on what it saw as irredentist Albanian nationalism. In particular, Aleksander Rankovic, the head of the Yugoslav secret police (UDBa), pursued his own vision of a united Serbia by perpetrating harsh repression in Kosovo before being deposed by Tito in 1963.[7]

The 1974 Constitution attempted to resolve the Yugoslav 'national question' and end this cycle of violence. The new constitution, an enormous tome, provided each republic and province in Yugoslavia with theoretical statehood. This effectively created a semi-confederal system in which decision-making at the centre would be dependent on a consensus of the political leaders in the republics and provinces.[8] Under this constitution, members of the different national communities in Kosovo were entitled to freely express 'their national specificities',[9] which included the right to fly their national flag.[10] The Albanian language was given an equal footing with Serbo-Croat and all school pupils were entitled to receive an education in 'the mother language', be it Albanian, Serbo-Croat or Turkish.[11] Kosovo was awarded economic autonomy through the establishment of a national bank on a level footing with the banks of the republics, and the province was granted a degree of political autonomy virtually identical to that of the republics. Most significantly, the Kosovan Communist Party would be represented in all the central organs of Yugoslavia and had voting rights identical to those of the republics: After the death of Tito, this meant that decisions could not be reached by the central government without the consent of the Party in Kosovo.[12]

According to Gazmed Zajmi, the 1974 Constitution had a calming effect on Serb-Albanian relations by producing equilibrium between the demands of the two groups.[13] By keeping Kosovo within Serbia, but granting it a significant degree of autonomy which substantively amounted to the granting of republican status in all but name, Zajmi argues that Tito was able to chart a third way through the competing demands of the national groups. An alternative perspective viewed the 1974 Constitution as an ambiguous compromise, which while trying the halt atavistic nationalisms, fuelled them by locating political power at the level of the national groupings, thus promoting the further ethnification of Yugoslav politics.[14] While providing a greater voice for Kosovar Albanian communists, the new order did not ease the suppression of those outside the Party who were advocating change. In 1976, Adem Demaci (who eventually served a total of 28 years in prison) and 18 other Kosovar Albanians were sentenced to prison for allegedly 'distributing hostile propaganda'.[15] The accusations concerned leaflets criticising the central Party, which were distributed around the University at Pristina. Because none of the accused had advocated violence, Amnesty International labelled Demaci and his 'co-conspirators' as 'prisoners of conscience' in 1985.[16]

The decentralising elements of the 1974 Constitution provoked insecurity among the Serbian community in Kosovo, who feared that a surrogate Albanian state was being formed there.[17] The establishment of an Albanian University in Pristina and the relaxation of restrictions on communication and travel between Kosovo and Albania were indicative of the Albanisation of Kosovo, for the Serbs. The Serbs argued that they had been subjected to discrimination and Albanisation in three fields: informal, institutional and ideological. Thus, the provisions of the 1974 Constitution were perceived as a threat to their economic and social status and rendered them a minority in their own homeland.[18] In 1977, a working commission of the Serbian League of Communists prepared what became known as the 'blue book', which sought to return control of the judiciary, police force and economic policy to Belgrade.[19] Furthermore, the Constitution did nothing to alleviate Kosovo's economic problems. The unemployment rate was the highest in all Yugoslavia: 27 per cent, compared to a mere 2 per cent in Slovenia, the richest republic. The per capita income had declined from 48 per cent of the Yugoslav average in 1954 to 33 per cent by 1975, and 27 per cent by 1980.[20] It is true that the reforms ushered in a period of unprecedented freedom and power for the Kosovar Albanians, and that this encouraged their political leaders to make further demands. The Serbian Community believed that they were being discriminated against as more Kosovar Albanians entered the Party, the police and the judiciary. In reality, though, they remained financially better off (every major state enterprise in Kosovo was run by a Serb) and proportionally better represented than their Albanian neighbours.[21] Fred Singleton, for example, observed that the structure of the Kosovan economy resembled that of many newly independent Third World states, with the minority group (Serbs) holding a high proportion of senior positions within the economy.[22]

The 1974 Constitution granted the Albanians the same rights as the other nations of Yugoslavia and provided for equality between the different national communities in Kosovo. It provided mechanisms for national disputes to be settled through institutional non-violent means for the first time in the twentieth century, and as such it represents the zenith of the value of life in recent Kosovan history. However, this theoretical equality served to create insecurity among the Serbian community, for they never recognised the separateness of Serbia and Kosovo. Furthermore, the Constitution failed to address any of the economic problems facing the province, unemployment continued to rise and the perceived economic differentiation between Serbs and Albanians remained a crucial issue of contention. While for many Albanian leaders 1974 represented a step on the road to a republic, for the Serbs it amounted to nothing less than a betrayal by Tito.[23]

BROTHERHOOD AND DISUNITY:
POLICE VIOLENCE IN AILING YUGOSLAVIA

By 1981 it had become clear that the 1974 compromise for Kosovo had failed, and that the value of life in the province had already begun to decline. Political and cultural freedoms for Kosovar Albanians had failed to improve the standard of living for either themselves or the Kosovar Serbs. 1981 also saw in Kosovo a return to the internal policing tactics of

Aleksander Rankovic. This was in stark contrast to what was happening in the rest of Yugoslavia, which continued along a liberalising and decentralising path. Unemployment in Kosovo remained high, a problem enhanced by the high birth rate among Kosovar Albanians that meant that an unusually large proportion of the population was under 21 years of age. One of the tactics employed to alleviate this was to recruit huge numbers of young Albanians into the recently founded the University of Pristina. Partly as a result of this, conditions in the University deteriorated and in April 1981 students took to the streets to protest at having to share dormitory beds and at the poor quality of cafeteria food.[24] Protests swept through six towns in Kosovo, and Kosovar Albanians gave voice to an array of demands. For the majority, the rallying call was 'Kosovo – Republic!' Some demanded the release of Demaci, and others insisted that the province be allowed to form a union with Albania.[25] Although evidence suggests that the protests were spontaneous and disorganised, the authorities in Belgrade insisted that they were the result of anti-Yugoslav secessionist movements that were in league with Enver Hoxha's Albania. The Party newspaper in Croatia proclaimed that the demonstrations were a manifestation of the 'organised work of internal and external enemies'.[26] Julie Mertus has identified several conspiracy theories that were aired in the Party press throughout Yugoslavia. Although most writers are agreed that the number of Kosovar Albanians demanding union with Albania was relatively small (the 1974 Constitution allowed Albanians in Kosovo to travel freely to Albania, teaching those who took up the opportunity that their own living conditions were far better than those in Albania), the Communist press insisted that the unrest was planned by Tirana and executed by fanatical Albanian nationalists.[27] The Albanian government gave verbal support to the protesters, but Mertus found no evidence to support the claim that Albania had orchestrated the demonstrations.[28]

In the immediate aftermath of the demonstrations, the Yugoslav League of Communists (LCY) singled out two particular institutions for blame. The Kosovan League of Communists was denounced for being 'permeated with counterrevolutionaries and irredentists'[29] by the state news agency *Tanjug*. The University of Pristina was found to be a hotbed of nationalist fervour, and the Belgrade newspaper *Borba* launched a campaign against the University, claiming that Kosovo was not wealthy enough to support such a large number of students.[30] The most significant immediate effect of the protests was the response of the security forces. Although the military had taken to the streets in Zagreb to support the purges of 1971, there was little actual violence and so the military had not been used against the people since 1948, when it was used to forcibly disarm Kosovar Albanians. The immediate response to the protests was large-scale and heavy-handed policing. Several protesters interviewed by Julie Mertus reported that after the marches had been violently broken up, the police broke into houses and physically attacked those suspected of participating.[31] According to Pajazit Nushi, a professor at Pristina University, the consequence of the police response to the protests in 1981 was that '120 Albanians were killed by firearms and died as a result of physical and psychic tortures of the army and police'.[32] The Yugoslav authorities admitted that as many as eleven may have died in the fighting, but Amnesty International reported that the number of dead in Kosovo was as high as three hundred.[33] 1981 therefore stands out as a significant date in the unravelling of Yugoslavia. Only a year after the death of Tito, the army and police forces were being used to suppress a popular movement. The usual Titoite response would have been a mixture of judicial purges and appeasing reform.

The police clampdown in Kosovo continued throughout the 1980s. By 1983 the proportion of those convicted on political charges in Yugoslavia that were Kosovar Albanians had reached 41.8 per cent. Between 1981 and 1983 alone, 688 Kosovar Albanians were convicted for writing 'hostile slogans'. As Christine von Kohl and Wolfgang Libal point out, what was particularly interesting about the numerous show trials of Kosovar Albanians that were held in this period was that: 'none of the "hostile groups" had actually committed an act of violence. At the most, they had simply planned actions. No stores of weapons were ever discovered. Despite this, there was talk of "plots to threaten the security of Yugoslavia".'[34] The sentences passed down were severe. Writing the slogan 'Kosovo – Republic', earned five years in prison.[35] In 1982, Amnesty International's list of prisoners of conscience included 14 new names of young Kosovar Albanians, including a school pupil.[36] The fact that those prosecuted were so young aroused consternation among human rights activists in Kosovo, and prompted many Serbs to suggest that the authorities had deliberately avoided prosecuting the ring-leaders, for political reasons.[37]

Along with police violence and the political use of the judiciary, the value of life in Kosovo was also reduced by the propagation of extensive anti-Albanian propaganda in Serbian newspapers. This served to dehumanise the Kosovar Albanians. The propaganda reflected and fuelled the growing insecurities felt by the Kosovar Serbs. The latter was markedly more prominent after the 'Serbian cultural revolution' of 1986 that lent a nationalist focus to Milosevic's 'anti-bureaucratic revolution', which began in 1987.[38] The most common charges of irredentism and terrorism were supplanted with charges of mass rape against Serb women and inhuman or uncivilised behaviour. In 1984, the Orthodox Archimandrite, Atanasije Jevtic, publicly complained about 'the rape of girls and old women in villages and nunneries' committed by Kosovar Albanians. According to one Albanian writer the impression given in many Serb publications was 'that Albanians rape anyone they can get hold of, old women, children, married women, teenagers, and that they rape them in the houses, in public places, in the street'.[39] Noel Malcolm goes on to point out that in a detailed study on the incidence of rape carried out in Belgrade in 1989, not only did Kosovo have the lowest incidence of rape in Yugoslavia, but that of the rapes committed in Kosovo, 71 per cent were same-nationality rapes.[40]

One case in particular gripped popular imagination in Serbia, prompting comparisons between Kosovar Albanian practices and methods of torture deployed by the Ottoman Turks.[41] In May 1985, Djordje Martinovic, a Kosovan Serb farmer, was rushed to hospital to have a beer-bottle removed from his anus. Martinovic claimed that he had been attacked by two Albanians who wanted to drive him from his home, though an investigation in Pristina found no evidence of an attack and doctors at Pristina hospital concluded that the wound was probably 'self-inflicted'. Whatever the truth of the incident the 'Martinovic case' came to dominate political discourse in Serbia. Most often, the case was likened to the practice of impalement carried out by the Ottoman Turks and located as an attack by all Albanians on all Serbs. One comment that was widely circulated in the Belgrade media was that 'Martinovic was a Jasenovac for one man'.[42] This claim suggested that the Martinovic case was a manifestation of genocide against the Serbian population in Kosovo, akin to that committed by the Croats in the Second World War. According to Vuk Draskovic, the voice of the Serbian national renewal in 1986:

> Can we remove the knowledge that one whole nation, the Serbian nation in Kosovo and Metohija, are being subjected to a campaign of organised terror by their Albanian neighbours and the government in that area, which is now only formally considered part of Serbia? Can we remove the knowledge of the soothing words and the promises of consolation that have been offered to Kosovo Serbs so that we can tolerate *the most brutal and most primitive outpouring of hatred and fascism?*[43]

This view was echoed in the now infamous draft memorandum written by the Serbian Academy of Arts and Sciences (SANU), which proclaimed that the Serbs were the victims of 'neo-fascist aggression in Kosovo'.[44]

It is possible to see an acceleration of the trajectory of decline in the value of a human life in the mid-1980s. In response to the 1981 protests, the security forces had used significant violence for the first time since 1948 and came increasingly to be seen as the agents of Serbian oppression in Kosovo. On the other hand, by not being seen to be pursuing the 'perpetrators' of the attack on Martinovic, the police had done little to alleviate the fears of the Serbian community. This insecurity was heightened by nationalist propaganda emanating principally from Belgrade, which characterised Albanians as an uncivilised nation of rapists who were the last bastion of the Ottoman Empire. Furthermore, Serbian insecurity and Albanian opposition continued to be heightened by the worsening economy. Despite receiving significant amounts of development investment from Belgrade, the economy remained reliant on primary rather than value-added industry and failed to generate profits for further investment. Also, Yugoslav development aid was generally awarded to projects that were politically rewarding and often contributed little to the Kosovan economy. Consequently, the black and grey economies began to grow and flourish.[45] However, there was still the facade of due process in the judiciary (though there were many political trials), Albanians and Serbs continued to enjoy extensive cultural rights, education in Kosovo was still relatively well funded and the province maintained a high degree of political autonomy.

## THE MILOSEVIC ERA 1: REMOVAL OF POLITICAL RIGHTS

The importance of the ostensible plight of the Kosovar Serbs to the rise of Slobodan Milosevic and his reliance on them to consolidate his dominance over Serbian politics in the 1990s has been well covered in works covering the collapse of Yugoslavia. By breaking with the communist mantra of 'brotherhood and unity' and the idea that compromise could be charted through the competing demands of different national groups, Milosevic was able to oust his political patron, Ivan Stambolic, and assume control of the Party in Serbia. For most commentators, it was the rise of Milosevic, some three years *before* the election of the Croatian President Franjo Tudjman and Bosnian President Alija Izetbegovic, that provoked the eventual dissolution of Yugoslavia. Although it is generally thought that, unlike Tudjman, Milosevic has not himself been a believer of nationalist rhetoric, Robert Thomas believes that he 'understood the habits and thought patterns of that creed'.[46] In this way Milosevic was cleverly able to disguise the consolidation of his own power through the rhetoric of chauvinistic Serb nationalism.

After rising to power, Milosevic moved swiftly to consolidate it. This he did by deposing the leaderships in Montenegro, Kosovo and Vojvodina, thus giving himself four votes in the federal decision-making organs. While the coups were relatively swift and easy in Vojvodina and Montenegro, given that the majority of the population there were Serbs who supported Milosevic's 'anti-bureaucratic revolution', the coup in Kosovo was only secured as a result of a huge military clampdown against Kosovar Albanian opposition and the removal of all political and cultural rights from them. This initiated two decades of intense conflict and a rapid decline in the value of life.

In the first few months of 1989, Milosevic acted to depose the leadership of the Party in Kosovo. Azem Vllasi, the Party leader in Kosovo, was arrested on the charge of 'counterrevolutionary endangering of the social order', an offence that carried the death penalty. On 23 March, the Kosovo Assembly, born in the Constitution of 1974, voted itself out of existence by accepting the new constitution proclaimed in Serbia.[47] That decision was made against a backdrop of 'hundreds' of political arrests and the stationing of tanks and armoured cars throughout the streets of Pristina, including the entrance to the assembly. According to Stanley Hoffmann, it was not NATO in 1999 that violated the sovereignty of Yugoslavia, rather 'it was Milosevic who violated [it], by abolishing it [the 1974 Constitution].[48] The essence of the constitutional change was that 'the authority of the state in all its forms and at both local and provincial levels was overthrown and handed over to Serbia'.[49]

The constitutional changes included six key elements that drastically altered life in Kosovo without the consent of the people of that province. These changes were: the subordination of provincial to republican authorities in the state administration, meaning that government in Pristina was completely subordinate to government in Belgrade.[50] The Executive Council of the Province of Kosovo was entirely subordinated to Serbia.[51] Serbia took upon itself sole responsibility for administration, the judiciary and 'self-management bodies', loosely translated as the state, the judiciary and the economy.[52] The authority of all the state bodies of the Socialist Autonomous Province of Kosovo was suspended.[53] All elected bodies and communal authorities in Kosovo were also suspended.[54] Unlimited powers were granted to enterprise managers, giving them the opportunity to dismiss Kosovar Albanians *en masse* from their jobs ostensibly on the premise of their political convictions.[55] Although the removal of political rights and autonomy from Kosovo has been widely acknowledged, what has not been appreciated is the scope of that removal. Almost overnight Kosovo was transformed from a self-governing entity into one that was entirely controlled by Belgrade. Owing to the sweeping and general nature of the reforms, Kosovar Albanians were reduced to the status of non-citizen, excluded from the decision-making processes. Their response was to demand independence and set up their own parallel state organisations.[56] Ibrahim Rugova, the unofficially elected President of Kosovo, argued that Gandhian non-violent resistance would attract international support for the Kosovar Albanian cause, and that 'we will continue this strategy because to do otherwise would have disastrous consequences for our people'.[57]

## THE MILOSEVIC ERA 2: SERBIANISATION OF KOSOVO

The Serbianisation of Kosovo occurred in several guises during the 1990s. Milosevic's regime acted to exclude Albanians from education, banned the official use of the Albanian language, severely restricted the use of Albanian symbols and attempted to redress the demographic imbalances between Serbs and Albanians. In August 1990, the Serbian administration demanded that Albanian schools teach according to a Serbian curriculum, in the Serbian language. To accompany this measure, hundreds of Albanian head-teachers were replaced with Serbs, and thousands of Albanian teachers who were deemed to be incompetent in the Serbian language were removed from their posts.[58] The official justification for these measures was that education institutions in Kosovo were bastions of counterrevolution and resistance, and that Kosovar Albanian pupils were being indoctrinated by their teachers.[59] Furthermore, it seemed only logical that a unitary Serbian state should have a unitary Serbian school curriculum. These reforms came on top of an earlier reform amounting to educational apartheid as it segregated Albanians and Serbs in schools, providing finance, teachers and facilities for the Serbian pupils while providing Albanian pupils with very little.[60] Not surprisingly, most Albanians refused to cooperate with these reforms and were forcibly barred from attending school by riot police and the armed forces – some schools were even surrounded by tanks to prevent the pupils from attending.[61] Similar reforms were initiated at the University in Pristina. Lecturers who were not dismissed were instructed to lecture only in Serbian and the numbers of Kosovar Albanians at the University were drastically reduced to only a token level by the end of 1991. Kosovar Albanian protests led only to further reprisals and dismissals, and thus in the winter of 1991 a parallel education system was formed in which dismissed teachers made use of private homes to deliver classes.[62]

A second way in which life in Kosovo was forcibly Serbianised in the 1990s was through a discriminatory language policy. Unlike the Slavic languages of the former Yugoslav nations, Cyrillic Serbian and Kosovar Albanian (very similar to the language of northern Albanian Ghegs) languages are very different. In 1991 the Serbian regime began a campaign of Serbianising all public discourse in Kosovo, rendering public signs and processes utterly alien to many Kosovar Albanians. As Pristina journalist Behlull Beqaj describes:

> The law on the official use of the language and names (27 July 1991) practically cancels the use of language. ... Resolutions concerning names of streets, boulevards, schools and other social and cultural institutions have the same intent. Based upon these resolutions, the former names were changed and the new names from the history, culture and mythology of the Serbs were introduced. All the names ... are officially written in the Serbian language and Cyrillic alphabet.[63]

The Serbianisation of public life extended to the media. Television was directly controlled from Belgrade and became a crucial propaganda tool for Milosevic. The most widely distributed newspapers were brought under *de facto* state control. In 1990, *Rilindja*, the only Albanian-language daily newspaper in Yugoslavia, was closed down with the loss of 1,300 jobs.[64] Those independent newspapers that were allowed to continue publication became subject to intense state pressure. On 2 March 1998, for example, Veton Surroi, the editor-in-chief of the free thinking Pristina-based newspaper *Koha Ditore*, was beaten by the Serbian police.[65]

For Serbian nationalists, Serbianisation ultimately meant resettling Serbs in Kosovo and depriving the Kosovar Albanians of their demographic advantage. The writings of Vasa Cubrilovic, a renowned Serbian nationalist author, became very popular in Serbia in the 1990s, particularly inasmuch as he outlined a programme for Serbianising Kosovo. Cubrilovic had written in 1937 that 'the gradual displacement of Albanians through our colonisation is ineffective ... we have only one course to follow ... that of their mass resettlement'.[66] Although the decrees of the Serbian government have been somewhat subtler than Cubrilovic's programme, the essence is the same: to dissuade Albanians from breeding and living in Kosovo, while persuading (or forcing) Serbs to migrate to Kosovo. On 11 January 1995, the Serbian Parliament passed the 'Decree for Colonisation of Kosovo of the Federal Republic of Yugoslavia'. For those Serbs wishing to move to Kosovo the state offered loans to erect houses and buy apartments, and offered plots of land free of charge.[67] The dire, and worsening, economic and political situation in Kosovo meant that very few Serbs from Serbia took up the government's offer to return to the 'cradle of Serbian civilisation' (as Kosovo is often referred to). Colonisation thus became a forcible issue. Many Serbian refugees from Croatia were forcibly resettled in Kosovo in 1995, and although many of these left soon afterwards, those that stayed – radicalised as they were by war – created greater tension and risk of violence.[68] The second way to change the demographic balance was, as Cubrilovic put it, to ensure that 'the law is enforced to the letter so as to make staying intolerable for the Albanians'.[69] Thus, the government made it illegal for Serbs to sell property to Albanians; imposed hefty sentences on any Kosovar Albanian who avoided national armed service in Croatia or Bosnia-Hercegovina; made it very difficult for Kosovar Albanians abroad to return to Kosovo; and penalised Albanian families that had more than one child, while rewarding Kosovar Serbs for having large families.[70]

## THE MILOSEVIC ERA 3: ECONOMIC APARTHEID

It was noted earlier that the constitutional changes imposed upon Kosovo by Milosevic provided ample scope for Serbian enterprise owners to remove Albanians from the official economy. According to an Amnesty International report in 1998, 'following large-scale dismissals from state enterprises, most Albanians are dependent on income from small businesses, or, often, money from relatives working abroad'.[71] The authorities often cut off this form of income however, because 'people bringing foreign currency from abroad are often the targets of police road checks, frequently leading to the confiscation of the money and ill-treatment'.[72] As a result of the mass dismissals, it was estimated that by the beginning of 1998 unemployment in the Kosovar Albanian community was higher than 70 per cent. Whatever work was available was most often in the service sector, small commerce and the more lucrative international organisation sector and the black market. According to the Pristina Economic Institute in 1996, money earned by Kosovar Albanians through regular paid work amounted to just ten per cent of total earnings, while the black economy accounted for up to 60 per cent of total economic activity.[73] The economic apartheid imposed by Belgrade was directly aimed at impoverishing the already poor (by Yugoslav standards) Kosovar Albanians. New factories were only built in areas predominantly inhabited by Serbs, and recruitment opportunities in new state-supported enterprises were only offered to Serbs. Elez Biberaj is right to surmise that economic apartheid was part of the Serbianisation plan discussed above. He argues that Serbian policies 'essentially amounted to a man-made famine'.[74] If this was the plan, it appeared to be working. Shortly before the completion of the Dayton negotiations, *Rilindja,* which had relocated in Tirana, reported that between 1991 and

1995 more than 300,000 Albanians had fled from Kosovo to flee Serbian oppression and to find work abroad to pay for basic necessities.[75] Economic apartheid also extended to the healthcare system. The seeds of distrust were sown in March and April 1990, when thousands of schoolchildren were taken to hospital suffering from stomach pains, headaches and nausea. Although the Serbian medical authorities claimed that the children were suffering from mass delusion caused by Albanian irredentist propaganda, a UN toxicology report five years later showed that blood samples contained traces of chemicals used by the Yugoslav Peoples Army (JNA) for the production of Sarin.[76] Whatever the truth of the matter this case was enough to produce mass mistrust of the Serbian healthcare system and provided a pretext for the dismissal of Kosovar Albanian doctors, producing an 'ethnically pure' healthcare system in which prescriptions could only be written in the Cyrillic script.[77] The result was that between 1992 and 1996 the incidence of preventable disease increased dramatically among the Kosovar Albanian community. In this period there were over 5,000 cases each of measles and tuberculosis.[78] In 1996 it was left to the United Nations Children's Fund (UNICEF), the World Health Organization and a Kosovar humanitarian organisation, 'Mother Teresa', to provide vaccinations against polio for Albanian children – a vaccination offered to Serbs free by the state.[79] In response, the Kosovar Albanians created a parallel healthcare system, but this lacked both funds and facilities.

## THE MILOSEVIC ERA 4: STATE VIOLENCE

By the mid-1990s, institutionalised human rights abuses had significantly devalued the value of life in Kosovo. The state itself was institutionalising violence and murder. In 1994, the head of the highest court in Kosovo bluntly stated that 'when an Albanian is accused of violating the territorial integrity of Yugoslavia, we can beat them and even kill them'.[80] State violence against the Kosovar Albanian community increased dramatically after the Dayton agreement at the end of 1995, as the Serbian government was able to pour more coercive resources into Kosovo and paramilitary leaders made notorious by their exploits in Bosnia-Hercegovina began switching their interests ιυ Kosovo. However, even prior to Dayton and the descent into violence in Kosovo, Amnesty International reported in 1994 that the police used violence on a daily basis and with impunity. The report continued by stating that 'thousands of ethnic Albanians have witnessed police violence or experienced it at first hand'. This violence usually consisted of 'brutal beatings with truncheons, punching and kicking ...[and] electric shocks are sometimes used'. Finally, according to Amnesty International, 'police officers express their ethnic hatred towards their victims. A particularly savage instance involved a police officer slashing a Serbian symbol on the chest of an 18-year old ethnic Albanian'.[81] Other incidents detailed in the report was the murder of a six-year-old boy by police and the severe beating of a 90-year-old man in one of their daily raids on Kosovar Albanian homes. At the same time as this report was released, the Helsinki Human Rights Watch also produced a report which described Kosovo as a 'police state' run by 'brute force and intimidation'.[82]

State violence in Kosovo was also legitimised through the judiciary. Not only were the perpetrators of violence identified by Amnesty International and Helsinki Human Rights Watch not brought to justice by the Serbian authorities, the judiciary acted to provide a rationale for the brutality and intimidation. In a study on the role of the judiciary in Kosovo, Human Rights Watch revealed a great discrepancy between the Constitution and Penal Code of the Federal Republic of Yugoslavia (FRY) and their implementation in Kosovo. According to Article 25 of the FRY Constitution: 'Any violence against a person deprived of liberty or whose liberty has been restricted, as well as any extortion of a confession or statement, shall be forbidden and punishable. *No one may be subjected to torture, degrading treatment or punishment*'.[83] Despite this, the report found that 'in addition to the use of torture to extract confessions, defendants are often denied access to a lawyer, not allowed to view court documentation, or refused permission to present witnesses on their behalf'. The report continues, 'the government exerts a direct influence on the outcome of most trials'.[84] It goes on to give details of hundreds of cases in which Kosovar Albanians were subjected to systematic torture in custody, a system supported and perpetuated by the judiciary in flagrant breach of Yugoslav law. In five cases during the summer of 1998, police torture resulted in the death of the victim. The report stated that 'all these cases involved young, healthy men who were seen being taken away by the police, and then were returned to their families dead'.[85]

When asked about the role of the police in Kosovo, Milosevic claimed that 'the police are not aggressive in Kosovo. They are protecting citizens, not [just] Serbs – Albanians and Gypsies – from terrorists'.[86] This explanation, given in 1998, is wholly unsatisfactory given that the terrorists referred to by Milosevic (the UCK) did not begin their clandestine activities until 1996, a full two years *after* the two reports mentioned at the beginning of this section.

## THE KOSOVAR ALBANIANS FIGHT BACK

Ibrahim Rugova justified the Gandhian policy of pacific resistance in terms of the military weakness of the Kosovar Albanians, compared with the might of the VJ and MUP. He stated: 'We would have no chance of successfully resisting the army. In fact, the Serbs only wait for a pretext to attack the Albanian population and wipe it out. We believe that it is better to do nothing than to be massacred'.[87] The crux of Rugova's strategy depended upon the international community acting to secure Kosovan independence. In 1992, he met international mediators such as David Owen and Theodore Stoltenberg and dispatched a case for independence to the Badinter Arbitration Commission but the case was not even considered. Rugova's failure was completed when the Dayton peace agreement mentioned Kosovo only once, in relation to the lifting of the 'outer wall' of sanctions against FRY.[88] The lesson learnt by many Kosovar Albanians was that passive resistance was not working. It had failed to stop Albanian exclusion from all forms of public life. It had failed to prevent economic apartheid, their impoverishment and systematic police violence and intimidation. While most Kosovar Albanians continued to support Rugova, the popular belief after Dayton was that his methods had achieved nothing.[89] The effects of the resultant radicalisation of Kosovar Albanian strategy were evidenced almost immediately. On the nights of 14 and 15 February 1996 a series of well-coordinated bomb attacks launched against Serbian target announced the explosion of the *Ushtria Clirimtare e Kosoves* (Liberation Army of Kosovo – UCK) onto the political scene.[90]

After this baptism of fire, the UCK was involved in combating the VJ and MUP forces, but was also involved in intimidating and kidnapping non-Albanian civilians as well as Kosovar Albanian moderates who continued to support Rugova's strategy. According to Amnesty International in 1998, 'the KLA [UCK] has been held responsible for a number of abductions. The dead bodies of those abducted have been found left lying in roadsides'.[91] Despite protestations from the UCK that 'we don't deal with civilians, the prisoners of war that we find we give them back', Amnesty found that while many abductees were returned there were many more who were still unaccounted for.[92] Furthermore, in a report to the House of Commons, Tim Youngs found that once open conflict between VJ/MUP forces and the UCK had broken out in 1998, 'KLA [UCK] fighters are also reported to have carried out summary executions and taken civilians hostage'.[93] A similar picture was painted by Human Rights Watch, which estimated that in 1998 138 people were abducted by the UCK.[94] Although many of the claims of atrocities committed by the UCK cannot be verified – for instance, government claims are often supported by testimony from Kosovar Albanians exposed to systematic torture in police custody – there is much independent evidence that the UCK frequently engaged in the killing and beating of captives, though this was not on a systematic basis.[95] For instance, on 19 July 1998 the UCK captured 85 Serbs. Although 35 were subsequently released, the rest are still unaccounted for.[96]

## DESCENT INTO WAR

By the beginning of 1998, eleven years of rule by Slobodan Milosevic had significantly reduced the value of life in Kosovo. Kosovar Albanians had been dehumanised, stripped of their basic human rights and subjected to an apartheid system in which they were systematically intimidated, beaten and often killed. The failure of the international community to respond to the problems in Kosovo prevented Rugova achieving the political aspirations of his constituents, leading many to take up arms against the 'Serbian oppressors'. The dehumanisation of each group by the other meant that when open violent conflict took place in 1998 and 1999 the consequences were horrific. This is not to claim a moral equivalence to both sides. In the last two years, VJ/MUP and Serb paramilitary groups committed atrocities on a massive and systematic scale, killing at least 20,000 Kosovar Albanians and maybe as many as 50,000. In many cases regional UCK units were comprised of moderates hoping to simply defend their homes and families, and the drive for an 'ethnically pure' Kosovo in 1999 must be seen in the context of a traumatised population subjected to almost complete ethnic cleansing and acts of genocide.

The tactics deployed by Serbian forces in 1998 have been widely documented by human rights associations such as Amnesty International, Human Rights Watch and Spotlight.[97] Indicative of these tactics was the attack on Donji Prekaz on 5 March 1998. According to the MUP, the incident amounted to a shoot-out between local gangs. However Human Rights Watch has put together a convincing case that in an ostensible attempt to apprehend a single member of the UCK, Adem Jashari, MUP forces murdered over 40 people. According to witnesses interviewed by both Human Rights Watch and Amnesty, the attempt to 'arrest Adem Jashari' consisted of an attack on the Jashari family compound which included armoured personnel carriers, artillery shelling and special police forces. One witness told interviewers:

> The soldiers shouted for us to out one by one or they would kill us. When my cousin Qazim (47) came out with his hands up, they killed him on the

steps. I was in the middle of the yard when it happened. We ran and had just got through the first cordon when the soldiers caught my cousin Nazim (27) who was helping his mother Bahtije along. They grabbed him, tore off the women's dress we had given him to wear, ordered him to lie down on the round and then to get up. He had to do this many times. They fired into the back of his head and back and I saw his body jerking from the bullets.[98]

A forensic pathologist who examined a photograph of the body of Nazim Jashari for Amnesty International concluded that the injuries were 'broadly consistent with the accounts of him being extrajudicially executed', and supported this evidence.[99] The Council for the Defense of Human rights and Freedoms later compiled a list of those killed in Donji Prekaz between 5 and 7 March 1998; they included six people over 65 years old, eleven teenagers, all under 18 and two children under eight years old.[100]

Throughout the summer of 1998, VJ and MUP forces conducted similar operations while the UCK combined open fighting with the kidnappings and executions outlined above. Between February and October, 2,000 (mostly civilian) Kosovar Albanians were killed and more than 300,000 were forced from their homes.[101] The temporary peace found during the winter was broken on 15 January 1999 when in retaliation for the murder of two MUP officers by the UCK, special police units massacred 45 Kosovar Albanian civilians in the village of Racak.[102]

After the collapse of the Rambouillet process in March 1999, the Serbs put 'Operation Horseshoe' into effect. This operation was designed to rid the FRY of the UCK by ridding Kosovo of its Albanian population, in ways more brutal than that envisaged by Cubrilovic 62 years earlier.[103] By 5 May 1999, the UNHCR estimated that 1,500,000 Kosovar Albanians had been forcibly displaced; over 600 settlements had been partially destroyed, including 300 villages completely razed; furthermore, summary executions were reported in over 70 towns, and as many as 50,000 Kosovar Albanians were still unaccounted for; there was widespread evidence of mass rape, and of the existence of 'rape camps', in which Kosovar Albanian women and girls were systematically raped by Serbian soldiers.[104] After June 1999, when NATO had successfully ensured that the majority of Kosovar Albanian refugees were able to return to their homes, many exacted a terrible revenge on the Serbian population. As many as 200 may have been killed, and the majority of Serbs in Kosovo have been forced to flee by a combination of unaffiliated gangsters, elements of the UCK, and angry/traumatised Kosovar Albanian mobs.[105]

## CONCLUSION

So, we return to where we began. Through this essay we have considered a trajectory of decline in the value of human life in Kosovo between 1974 and 1999. Set against a history peppered with brutality, this trajectory in recent times began after the 1974 Constitution, when the Kosovar Albanians were widely portrayed as being inhuman savages, a gang of terrorists and rapists hell-bent on irredentism and genocide. Once these views began to inform the rulers in Belgrade, the Serbian leadership acted accordingly by stripping a whole community of its citizenship and political existence within a state. This paved the way for the exclusion of the Kosovar Albanians from all forms of public life. Cultural, economic and political apartheid acted as the driving force for the creation of parallel state institutions by Ibrahim Rugova and his party, the Democratic Party of Kosovo (LDK). Between 1991 and 1995, Rugova refused to dehumanise the Serbs, reserving seats for them in the underground parliament and offering them full minority rights in an 'independent and sovereign' Kosovo. When Rugova met Lord Owen and presented his vision of an independent and neutral Kosovo 'open to both Albania and Serbia', he was greeted only with consternation.[106] Through his shortsightedness and ignorance about Kosovo, Owen directly precipitated the marginalisation of Rugova and the rise of radicalism and the UCK. Owen later described Rugova as a 'nationalist leader', giving him moral equivalence with Milosevic, and wrote: 'Rugova himself was softly spoken and *apparently reasonable* but at no time did he give me the impression that he would settle for autonomy'.[107] Had Owen bothered to look at Rugova's proposals, had he cared to look at any of the reports mentioned here, he may have seen that Rugova offered the best future for all the communities in Kosovo, based as it was on the principle of the humanity of all.

A crucial opportunity was lost. As a result, tens of thousands were killed and entire populations were forced from their homes. The dehumanising practices of the Serbs and the failure of the international community to redress them led to the dehumanisation of the Serbs themselves, and the rise to predominance of the UCK. The United Nations now faces a massive task in Kosovo. It may be decades before a human life in Kosovo is worth what it was under Tito's iron hand in 1974.

ACKNOWLEDGEMENTS

I would like to thank Ken Booth, Rob Dixon, Ian R. Mitchell and Paul Williams for their help and useful comments.

NOTES

1. See Fernando del Mundo, 'Kosovo Diary', *Refugees Magazine*, No.114 (1999).
2. These findings were in relation to the fighting in the summer and autumn of 1998. See Human Rights Watch, *Humanitarian Law Violations in Kosovo* (London: Human Rights Watch, 1999), p.5.
3. According to the international lawyer, Hilaire McCoubrey, 'Serbia would appear to have a clear case to answer in relation to genocide'. Hilaire McCoubrey, 'Kosovo, Nato and International Law', *International Relations*, Vol.14, No.5 (1999), p.42.
4. See Fernando del Mundo and Ray Wilkinson, 'A Race Against Time', *Refugees Magazine*, No.116 (1999).
5. Trotsky is cited by Noel Malcolm, *Kosovo: A Short History* (London: Papermac, 1999), p.253.
6. Ibid.
7. Ibid., pp.324–6.
8. See Lenard J. Cohen, *Broken Bonds: Yugoslavia's Disintegration and Balkan Politics in Transition* 2nd edition (Oxford: Westview, 1995), p.33.
9. Article 4 of the Constitution of the Socialist Autonomous Province of Kosovo, 1974. See Marc Weller, *The Crisis in Kosovo 1989–1999: From the Dissolution of Yugoslavia to Rambouillet and the Outbreak of Hostilities* (Cambridge: International Documents and Analysis, 1999), p.58.
10. Article 6 of the Kosovo Constitution, 1974.
11. Article 217 of the Kosovo Constitution, 1974.
12. Provisions for economic autonomy can be found in Article 292 of the Kosovo Constitution, 1974. The political status of Kosovo is principally prescribed in Articles 300, 301 and 339.
13. Gazmend Zajmi, 'Kosova's Constitutional Position in the Former Yugoslavia', in Ger Duijzings, Dusan Janjic, and Shkelzen Maliqi (eds), *Kosovo/Kosova: Confrontation or Coexistence* (Nijmegen: Peace Research Centre of the University of Nijmegen, 1996), p.98.
14. See Mihailo Crnobrnja, *The Yugoslav Drama*, 2nd ed. (London: I.B. Tauris, 1994), pp.75–6 and p.225. Crnobrnja was formerly Ambassador of Yugoslavia to the European Communities.
15. Miranda Vickers, *Between Serb and Albanian* (London: Hurst & Co., 1998), p.181.
16. See Amnesty International, *Yugoslavia: Prisoners of Conscience* (London: Amnesty International, 1985), p.6.
17. Vickers (note 15), p.182.
18. See Ivanka Nedeva, 'Kosovo/a: Different Perspectives', in Thanos Veremis and Evangelos Kofos (eds), *Kosovo: Avoiding Another Balkan War* (Athens: Hellenic Foundation for European and Foreign Policy, 1998), p.104.
19. Branka Magas, 'Yugoslavia: The Spectre of Balkanization', *New Left Review*, No.174.
20. Dennison Rusinow, *Yugoslavia: A Fractured Federalism* (Washington, DC: Wilson Centre Press, 1988), p.70.
21. Ivanka Nedeva (note 18), p.104.
22. Fred Singleton, *A Short History of the Yugoslav Peoples* (Cambridge: Cambridge University Press, 1985), p.273.
23. See Julie A. Mertus, *Kosovo: How Myths and Truths Started a War* (London: University of California Press, 1999), p.19.
24. For a detailed analysis on the student unrest in 1981 see Mertus (note 23), pp.17–95.
25. Malcolm (note 5), p.335.
26. *Vjesnik* (Zagreb), 16 April 1981.
27. Mertus (note 23), p.33.
28. Ibid., p.33.
29. *Tanjug* cited by Vickers (note 15), p.201.
30. Vickers (note 15), p.198.
31. See Mertus (note 23), pp.56–91.

32. Pajazit Nushi, 'The Phenomenon of Military-Police Violence in Kosova in the Years 1981–1992', in Jusuf Bajraktari, Lefter Nasi, Kristaq Prifti, Fatmir Sejdiu, Edi Shukriu and Pellumb Xhufi (eds), *The Kosova Issue – A Historic and Current Problem* (Tirana: Institute of History – Pristina and Institute of History – Tirana, 1996), p.150.
33. Amnesty International, *Yugoslavia: Prisoners of Conscience* (note 16), p.12.
34. Christine von Kohl and Wolfgang Libal, 'Kosovo: The Gordian Knot of the Balkans', in Robert Elsie (ed.), *Kosovo: In the Heart of the Powderkeg* (Boulder, CO: East European Monographs, 1997), p.75.
35. Mertus (note 23), p.43.
36. Oskar Gruenwald, 'Yugoslavia's Gulag Archipelago and Human Rights', in Oskar Gruenwald and Karen Rosenblum-Cale (eds), *Human Rights in Yugoslavia* (New York: Irvington Publishers, 1986), p.19
37. See Julie Mertus (note 23), p.43.
38. See Mark Thompson, *Forging War: The Media in Serbia, Croatia and Bosnia-Hercegovina*, revised ed. (Luton: University of Luton Press and Article 19, 1999), pp.52–7.
39. Malcolm (note 5), p.339.
40. Ibid., p.339.
41. Mertus (note 23), p.107. A favoured Ottoman method of execution was to impale the victim of a stake driven through the anus, up the back and out again at the neck. The victim would be impaled in public and would die a slow and painful death. Most Serbs are very familiar with the horrors of impalement thanks to the graphic description of such an execution in Ivo Andric, *The Bridge of the Drina* (London: The Harvill Press, 1995).
42. Mertus (note 23), p.110. Jasenovac was the location of the most notorious Ustashe (Croatian fascist) death camp in the Second World War, where as many as 80,000 Serbs may have been killed. While the number of dead is a hotly contested subject, there can be no doubting the symbolic importance of the word 'Jasenovac' for both Serbs and Croats. See Marcus Tanner, *Croatia: A Nation Forged in War* (London: Yale University Press, 1997), p.152 and, John R. Lampe, *Yugoslavia as History: Twice there was a Country* (Cambridge: Cambridge University Press, 1996), p.207.
43. Speech by Vuk Draskovic, 7 April 1986. Cited by Robert Thomas, *Serbia Under Milosevic: Politics in the 1990s* (London: Hurst and Co., 1999), p.39.
44. Cited in ibid., p.41.
45. See Gramoz Pashko, 'Kosovo: Facing Dramatic Crisis', in Veremis and Kofos (note 18), p.341. Also see Vladimir Gligorov, 'Yugoslavia: Facing the Dilemmas', *The Vienna Institute for Comparative Economic Studies*, Vol.5, No.4 (1995).
46. Thomas (note 43), p.47.
47. Noel Malcolm (note 5), p.344–5.
48. Stanley Hoffmann, 'What is to be done?', *The New York Review of Books*, 20 May 1999, p.17.
49. Esat Stavileci, 'Constitutional Changes and the Abolition of Autonomy', in Bajraktari (note 32), p.155.
50. See Law on the Constitutional Changes and the Law on the State Administration, *Official Gazette of the Socialist Republic of Serbia*, No.24/90.
51. Law on Changes and Additions to the Law on the Executive Council of the Assembly of the Socialist Republic of Serbia, *Official Gazette of the Socialist Republic of Serbia*, No.30/90.
52. Law on the Measures of Republican Bodies Under Special Circumstances, *Official Gazette of the Socialist Republic of Serbia*, No.30/90.
53. Decision of the Enforcement of Special Measures in the Socialist Autonomous Province of Kosovo, *Official Gazette of the Republic of Serbia*, No.33/90.
54. Ibid.
55. Law on Labour Relations under Special Circumstances, *Official Gazette of the Socialist Republic of Serbia*, No.40/90.
56. On the extent of the parallel state see: Richard Caplan, 'International Diplomacy and the Crisis in Kosovo', *International Affairs*, Vol.74, No.2, p.451.

57. *The Guardian*, 26 July 1994. For more on Rugova's political platform see: Ibrahim Rugova, *La Question du Kosovo* (Paris: Fayard, 1994).
58. von Kohl and Libal (note 34), p.93.
59. Ibid.
60. See International Crisis Group, *Kosovo Briefing*, 17 February 1998, p.5.
61. von Kohl and Libal, 'Kosovo', p.93.
62. Ibid., p.94.
63. Behlull Beqaj cited by International Crisis Group, *Kosovo Spring* part 1, 20 March 1998.
64. Elez Biberaj, 'Kosova: The Balkan Powder Keg', *Conflict Studies*, No.258 (Feb. 1993), p.7.
65. Human Rights Watch, *Humanitarian Law Violations in Kosovo* (note 2), p.66.
66. Vasa Cubrilovic, 'The Expulsion of the Albanians', *Kosova Historical Review*, No.4 (1994), p.40.
67. International Crisis Group, *Kosovo Spring*, p.8.
68. Vickers (note 15), p.284.
69. Cubrilovic (note 56), p.39.
70. See International Crisis Group, *Kosovo Spring*, p.9.
71. Amnesty International, *Kosovo: The Evidence* (London: Amnesty International, 1998), p.29.
72. Ibid.
73. These observations and figures are cited in International Crisis Group, *Kosovo Briefing*, p.16–17.
74. Biberaj (note 64), p.7.
75. *Rilindja*, 12 November, 1995.
76. Malcolm (note 5), p.345.
77. International Crisis Group, *Kosovo Briefing*, p.6.
78. International Crisis Group, *Kosovo Spring*, p.34.
79. Ibid.
80. *International Herald Tribune*, 20 January 1994.
81. *The Guardian*, 19 September 1994.
82. Ibid.
83. Article 25 of the Constitution of the Federal Republic of Yugoslavia. Emphasis added.
84. Human Rights Watch, *Detentions and Abuse in Kosovo*, FRY, Vol.10, No.10, (December 1998), p.3.
85. Ibid., p.9.
86. *Newsweek*, 21 December 1998.
87. Ibrahim Rugova, *Impact International*, 10 Apr. – 7 May 1992, p.10.
88. Shinasi A. Rama, 'The Serb-Albanian War and the Miscalculations of the International Community', *International Journal of Albanian Studies* Vol.2, No.1 (1998), p.9.
89. Ibid.
90. Fehim Rexhepi, 'What is the Liberation Army of Kosovo?', *AIM* (Pristina), 4 February 1999.
91. Amnesty, *Kosovo: The Evidence*, p.71.
92. Ibid., p.72.
93. Tim Youngs, 'Kosovo: The Diplomatic and Military Options', House of Commons Research Paper 98/93, 27 Oct. 1998, p.10.
94. Human Rights Watch, *Humanitarian Law Violations in Kosovo* (note 2), p.75.
95. Ibid., p.77.
96. Ibid., p.79.
97. See Humanitarian Law Centre, *Spotlight on Kosovo: Human Rights in Times of Armed Conflict* (Belgrade: Humanitarian Law Centre, 1998).
98. Human Rights Watch, *Humanitarian Law Violations in Kosovo* (note 2), pp.26–30.
99. Amnesty International, *A Human Rights Crisis in Kosovo Province, Document Series A: Violence in Drenica* (London: Amnesty International, 1998).
100. Physicians for Human Rights Press Release, 28 April 1998.

101. *True Stories: The Valley*, Channel 4 television documentary, 18 February 1999.
102. *International Herald Tribune*, 29 January 1999.
103. *The Observer*, 18 July 1999.
104. United States Department of State, *Erasing History: Ethnic Cleansing in Kosovo* (Washington, DC: US Department of State, 5 May 1999).
105. Rob Dixon, 'Notes on Dennis MacNamara's (head of the UNHCR in Kosovo) evidence to the House of Commons Committee on International Development', House of Commons, 9 Nov. 1999. I am very grateful to Rob Dixon for this.
106. Vickers (note 15), p.282.
107. David Owen, *Balkan Odyssey*, (London: Indigo, 1996), p.80.

# 6
# OSCE Verification Experiences in Kosovo: November 1998–June 1999

## WILLIAM G. WALKER

On 13 October 1998, Ambassador Richard Holbrooke, considered to be the pre-eminent US negotiator of agreements to halt ethnic conflict and bloodshed in the Balkans, emerged from a marathon session with the president of the Federal Republic of Yugoslavia (FRY), Slobodan Milosevic. The two were old sparring partners from the 1995 peace talks on Bosnia that resulted in the Dayton Accords. Holbrooke's announcement to the waiting media was a welcome one; he stated that he had convinced President Milosevic to accept the presence of an international civilian peacekeeping force in the troubled province of Kosovo. Holbrooke had apparently overcome the Serb leader's long-held opposition to such a foreign presence; Milosevic's steadfast assertion throughout the 1990s that whatever happened in Kosovo was a strictly internal affair that neither required, nor permitted external intervention.

In his Belgrade press conference Ambassador Holbrooke described the outline of what was, at that point, an oral agreement. An international operation on the ground in Kosovo would be mounted by the Organisation for Security and Cooperation in Europe (OSCE). The force, to be called the 'Kosovo Verification Mission', or KVM, would consist of up to two thousand internationals, drawn from personnel seconded by the 54 member states of the OSCE.[1] The verifiers[2] would be civilians and unarmed. Their principal task would be verification that all sides to the conflict were in compliance with United Nations Security Council resolutions calling for the cessation of violence and repression in Kosovo, as well as with the terms of subsequent formal agreements the FRY would commit to with the OSCE and the North Atlantic Treaty Organisation (NATO).

Milosevic also had accepted, Holbrooke announced, that NATO would conduct a parallel verification programme from overhead platforms, i.e., aircraft and satellites. The combination of OSCE ground and NATO air observation, he declared, would give a comprehensive picture of FRY and KLA compliance with the terms of the international community's demands.

Thus the world first heard of the OSCE's lead role in a peacekeeping mission to Kosovo. Surprisingly, the Holbrooke press conference was also the first time the OSCE was informed that it had been selected as the international community's instrument to bring an element of peace and stability to this badly troubled corner of Europe. An undertaking of this magnitude – 2,000 international verifiers and presumably an equal number of local staff – was unheard of in OSCE terms. If the KVM were to reach its announced goal of 2,000, it would be almost ten times the size of the next biggest OSCE mission, one deployed the previous January in Croatia with a planned ceiling of 250. The KVM complement would be almost four times the strength of all other OSCE field operations combined!

In response to such an unanticipated challenge, the OSCE – the secretariat in Vienna and the Chairman-in-Office, at the time the Polish foreign minister Geremek in Warsaw – moved immediately to implementation. First Geremek flew to Belgrade and initialled a written agreement with the FRY foreign minister. This put into carefully selected words the terms of the Holbrooke-Milosevic oral accord. In a similar vein, NATO Generals Clark and Neumann flew in and signed an agreement with the FRY defence minister covering the technical terms of NATO's participation. The OSCE Permanent Council in Vienna quickly adopted a mission mandate, with delegate after delegate addressing the obvious, that this was an undertaking of paramount importance, both to peace in the Balkans and the credibility of the OSCE as a viable peacekeeping institution. With its mandate in place, the KVM was ready to get under way. I was selected by the Chairman-in-Office as the head of mission on 26 October, a nomination later confirmed by the Permanent Council. A KVM advance party entered Pristina to begin infrastructural build-up within days of the Permanent Council's decision on the mandate. The determination was there to do a credible job; as was awareness of the magnitude of the challenges and risks ahead.

What was the ultimate goal of this KVM undertaking? Hopefully, if both sides cooperated and a cessation of hostilities was obtained, the resultant stability, however forced and tenuous, would (1) avert the humanitarian disaster predicted for those tens of thousands of Kosovars[3] who had fled the violence of the preceding summer/autumn and taken to the hills, without provision for the harsh winter months ahead; and (2) create a climate of less violence and greater stability, which would be more propitious for a successful conclusion of the negotiation process brokered by the European Union and the United States. That effort to reach a definitive political settlement, specifically a degree of autonomy for a Kosovo remaining within the FRY, had been under way for some time under the guidance of ambassadors Hill (US) and Petritsch (EU), when the outbreak of violence during the summer and autumn threatened to dash all hope of peaceful resolution.

## THE KVM HUMAN RIGHTS MANDATE

Prior to my planned 4 November arrival in Kosovo, I first visited Warsaw for consultations with the Chairman-in-Office and to attend the conference, sponsored by the OSCE's Office for Democratic Institutions and Human Rights (ODIHR), on the human dimension of OSCE missions. I also attended a meeting of the OSCE Troika[4] in Oslo before entry on duty. In both venues, the human rights mandate of the forthcoming KVM mission was the number one topic for discussion.

In Warsaw, the message was clear and, except for the interventions of the Russian delegate, unambiguous. I was told by many of the OSCE attendees, and in stronger terms by those representing the international human rights NGO community, that (1) the crisis in Kosovo was largely based on egregious violations of human rights by both parties to the conflict; (2) the KVM must be proactive in its approach to this aspect of its work; (3) it must be so 'from day one' or risk losing all credibility with the local population; and (4) to do a proper job, the KVM must recruit staff with extensive experience in the field of human rights, rather than perform on-the-job conversion of whatever personnel were contributed haphazardly by member states. The latter was important advice given that a sizable percentage of persons nominated by member states in the first call-ups had a decidedly military background.[5]

The Russian representative intervened to say that nowhere in the OSCE/KVM mandate were the words 'human rights' mentioned. He insisted that the mission could not exceed, nor unilaterally pursue an issue beyond the terms of the Permanent Council mandate. This was not the last time I would hear such words from a Russian delegate at an OSCE table. Representatives of Belarus and the Ukraine voiced similar adherence to a strict interpretation of the KVM mandate.

My words to the ODIHR assembly were a promise that I understood the importance of human rights to the credibility of the mission, that I would see to it that the subject received all appropriate attention, that I would solicit as many experienced staff as necessary, and that I would provide them with the resources and independence needed for professional human rights investigation and reporting. I was less forthcoming in response to a request from the NGOs that I share all KVM human rights reports with them on a timely basis. To this I had to say that OSCE's reporting procedures were unfamiliar to me, and that in any case modifications could only come from the secretariat in Vienna.[6]

The following six weeks were consumed with the problems, some minor, others serious, of establishing the mission. In my initial talk with Milosevic, on my way into Pristina, he promised one hundred per cent cooperation with the KVM, as called for in the agreement. After I explained what little I knew of the situation on the ground, and what my approach would be to such tasks as preparation for elections, creating a new civilian police force – all to happen as soon as the Hill-Petritsch accord was signed – Milosevic repeated his promise of total support: 'Walker, I guarantee that my government will live up one hundred per cent, no, 150 per cent, to every word as written in the agreements.' Unfortunately, Milosevic had his own interpretation – the narrowest possible – of virtually every word. These were often at variance with the interpretations of the international community I represented. As I was not present during his talks with Holbrooke, I was not in a particularly favourable position to contradict his claims as to what they had agreed to. But even allowing for differences in interpretation of this word or that, cooperation with the KVM was clearly stated as a government commitment. Neither President Milosevic nor his representatives in Kosovo were to live up to that promise.

## THE DIFFICULTIES

The KVM encountered any number of problems in pursuit of what we hoped would be perceived, accurately, as a proactive KVM human-rights posture. Some were internal to this multilateral mission, its bureaucratic structure and culture. Others were external in origin. The reality was that in the initial months of operation, the majority of those seconded to the mission were not particularly suited, either by temperament or background, for human rights verification or reporting. As noted earlier, a majority of those first sent forward by contributing member states were either military planners or civilian administrative technicians. This is hardly surprising given that the mission was established and fielded without having gone through a normal pre-planning phase, and was expected to deploy within days in a Kosovo devoid of administrative infrastructure. We also quickly learned that the international community's ability to act collectively and decisively on many issues, not the least of which was the matter of human rights, was hampered by a number of obstacles:

- Minister Geremek often said that while the KVM's mandate did not contain specific language pertaining to verification of human rights behaviour, such a provision is implicit in the mandate of every OSCE mission. While this may be true, and understood by those who pressed for robust KVM involvement, this was not the view of President Milosevic, or those in his corner.[7]

The absence of specific reference to human rights in the KVM mandate created a number of operational difficulties. While these were overcome with time, and KVM acted in conformity with the Geremek thesis that such tasks were implicit in all OSCE mandates, things would have gone smoother from day one if such wording had been explicitly included in its charter.

For starters, the lack of an explicit human rights mandate affected the initial planning and priorities given to the establishment of the KVM human rights division. The problem of job-specific recruitment is but one example. Many member states understandably were hesitant to recruit and contribute personnel with a background that did not match a specific mandated task. The Vienna personnel clearing house originally set aside the CVs of those with a human rights profile, placing at the head of the line those with more practical skills. It was not until early December that the first trained human-rights verifiers arrived in Kosovo. By the end of the Mission's presence in March 1999, of the approximately 1,350 internationals, only 80 had been processed in and assigned full time human-rights duties.

The exclusion of explicit language in the mandate, and the uniqueness of fielding a human rights operation in the midst of armed conflict, provided mission leadership little if any policy guidance on what was expected in the area of human rights. Vienna was essentially cautious, if not silent on the issue. So we devised our own approach, and integrated human rights verification into all operations. Thus the Pristina headquarters, the five regional centres and two dozen field offices throughout the province each had a human rights unit which reported to the mission human rights director, who in turn answered directly to me as the head-of-mission. As time went on, KVM became the *de facto* human rights protection mechanism in Kosovo. It was a task the vast majority of the verifiers took to heart, even those who had arrived with other attitudes and little or no human rights experience.

- Another series of problems was caused by the Milosevic regime's hardline position that outsiders had no business interfering in what it considered a strictly internal affair. While a continual irritant in all areas of KVM endeavour, this was nowhere more so then on human rights issues. Combined with the Milosevic conviction that he had committed his regime only to those matters specifically written in the OSCE-FRY agreement, he allowed nothing brought up that referred to the harsh or illegal treatment of those he accused of being 'Albanian criminal terrorists', and those who supported them. Milosevic insisted that his police were simply performing 'normal police functions', permitted under the agreement, in pursuit of lawbreakers.

  Up until October 1998 representatives of the FRY government had repeatedly and energetically rejected pleas from members of the European community to discuss the root causes of the Kosovo conflict and government prosecution of its anti-KLA campaign. At a meeting of the Peace Implementation Council (PIC) on Bosnia, held in Bonn, Germany in December 1997, the FRY delegation stormed out when the German chair, Foreign Minister Kinkel, backed by Robin Cook and other heads of delegation, insisted that the evolving crisis in Kosovo was an appropriate subject for discussion, since it threatened peace throughout the Balkans, and stimulated a refugee outflow that was already a serious problem for many European nations.

- On-the-ground observation and reporting by representatives of individual nations, including their diplomatic missions in Belgrade, was circumscribed by Belgrade's ability to control travel to and within the province. It was not until July-August 1998 that several embassies in Belgrade were able to assemble small observation missions, called KDOMs (Kosovo Diplomatic Observation Missions), and have members accredited and deployed. There was a USKDOM (American), a UKKDOM (British), an EUKDOM (European Union), and eventually French and Russian KDOMs. A significant percentage of KDOM participants had purely military backgrounds.[8] With KDOM deployment, the first sustained analysis of what was occurring in Kosovo was under way. And the picture was not a pretty one! The original concept was that the KVM would slowly absorb the various KDOMs in a seamless progression to a single international presence, the OSCE.

- Differences and tensions within the involved multinational institutions habitually led to delays, excessive caution and lack of resolve. While there was general consensus that 'something had to be done' to avoid a humanitarian disaster if winter descended and tens of thousands of Kosovars were without shelter and food in the mountains, there was little agreement on what that 'something' should consist of. Public pronouncements reflective of this hemming and hawing gave Milosevic reason to believe he could manipulate the situation, his special talent, and get away with his murderous campaign.

- No outsider wanted to jeopardise what was being done on the diplomatic front, i.e., the Hill-Petritsch negotiation process. Some argued that speaking out about human rights abuses by the Serbian security forces could only anger Milosevic, and torpedo the talks.

Problems inherent in having all six members of the Contact Group (Germany, Italy, France, Russia, the United Kingdom and the United States); not to mention 16 plus three of NATO; and 54 member states of the OSCE – all 'democratic institutions' which reach decisions based on internal consensus – comment on what KVM could and should do was a constant source of confusion. Consensus means that a single voice, often at the least contentious level of agreement, determines the course of collective action. Consensus in open meetings was often followed by non-attributable 'suggestions' that the mission not involve itself in areas too delicate to mention openly for fear that one or another member state would object, and break consensus.

- European resentments, suspicions, and uneasiness vis-à-vis the United States were ever-present. The fear, openly stated at times, was that the United States – most often in the lead on the human-rights issue – was doing so in pursuit of its own national agenda. I was accused of insisting that atrocities and human rights abuses were to be reported solely to give NATO the excuse needed to bomb and/or invade Serbia.

## WHAT THE KVM DID ON HUMAN RIGHTS ISSUES

In the mission's first days of operation, I moved to establish – as promised – a division whose sole task was coverage of the human rights question. In the division of labour among my six deputy heads of mission, the youngest – a German foreign service officer – accepted responsibility for this among other democratisation issues. Bernd Borchard was relentless in pursuit of assembling the best human-rights-watch group possible, notwithstanding cumbersome recruitment procedures. He soon appointed an experienced female lawyer as division director, who in turn recruited and brought together a multinational team. Some came with past experience, others learned on the job. Standards were high, as was morale. The director asked for and was granted direct access to the head of mission. She insisted on complete independence of action for her unit, which was also given.

The KVM human rights division was a highly decentralised operation. Its people worked out of Pristina headquarters, the five regional offices, and down to the scattered field offices.[9] They performed any and all tasks essential to maintaining the credibility of the OSCE's presence in Kosovo. The mission monitored, reported and verified human rights violations throughout the province. Human rights reporting officers met daily with regional and local authorities – the majority of them Serbs – as well as with representatives of the Kosovo Liberation Army (KLA), to discuss, protest and intervene in specific human rights issues.

The nature of KVM interventions changed over time. During the first six weeks, when most effort went into establishing the mission, opening offices, recruiting and establishing the job requirements for human rights verifiers and so on, the emphasis was on organisation, operating procedures, verification standards and reporting criteria. The second phase, from mid-December to the KVM's withdrawal on 20 March 1999, was when the KVM, its human rights division in particular, began to 'make a difference'. Several projects were initiated to increase the capacities of domestic human-rights-watch groups. The KVM also provided human-rights continuation training to its own members on such issues as freedom of movement, trial monitoring, interviewing and reporting.

Of the more than one thousand individual human-rights complaints received during the three months preceding withdrawal, KVM verified an escalating number of human-rights abuses including: right to life, right to liberty, freedom from torture and ill treatment, and freedom of movement. These, combined with humanitarian law violations that occurred in Racak, Rogovo, Rakovina and other villages, affirmed that the Belgrade authorities were in almost total non-compliance with the spirit and letter of the October agreements.

First evident in mid-January in the wake of KVM's denunciation of crimes committed in the village of Racak[10] and the government's reaction, by mid-March it was clear that the Belgrade authorities were no longer exercising even the pretence of cooperating with the KVM. Nor were its army and special police shy about employing grossly excessive force in their operations, most often actions clearly in violation of the Holbrooke-Milosevic agreement. Every KVM request for facilitative assistance and report of a compliance breach was ignored or denied. Harassment increased, interference with the verifiers as they went about their work was increasingly in evidence. Belgrade's regime-controlled media became ever more shrill and vitriolic in their coverage of the KVM and its leadership, and government spokespersons' public statements showered abuse and threats on the KVM. The message was not lost on those in the local Serb community who harboured fears and hatreds of any who threatened the *status quo*. Verbal abuse and rude gestures soon turned to overt actions against the verifiers. Ugly scenes became common when KVM vehicles entered Serb enclaves and villages. The Norwegian Chairman-in-Office, after consultations with all interested parties, concluded that the KVM was increasingly unable to perform its mandated tasks, and every day brought greater risk that one or more of the verifiers would be badly hurt. He informed me on 19 March of his decision to withdraw the mission. The KVM left Kosovo the following day, and spent the next three months in Macedonian and Albanian exile.

## WHAT THE KVM DID WHILE IN EXILE

The pace of events in Kosovo and the surrounding countries stepped up dramatically within hours of the KVM withdrawal. Milosevic's army, police and paramilitaries immediately initiated what was to become a campaign of violence and horror on a scale not seen in Europe since the 1940s. Forty-eight hours later, NATO delivered the first air strikes in an air war that was to last two-and-a-half months. Within days, what was to quickly become an avalanche of expellees and asylum seekers – eventually numbering in the hundreds of thousands – poured across Kosovo's borders, overwhelming the meagre resources of Macedonia and Albania, and catching international relief agencies totally unprepared.

The KVM underwent a major restructuring.[11] Over time the mission was reduced from over 1,300 to approximately 300. But initially, with over a thousand internationals in Macedonia, the KVM was in a unique position to help during those first weeks of chaos and suffering. Some worked with the UNHCR, NATO troops and NGOs to set up, organise and cope with the explosion of campsites, some of which mushroomed within days into veritable cities of 20,000 or more inhabitants, but cities without plumbing, potable water, cooking facilities or the other basics of life. Other KVMers began planning for what was hoped would be a speedy KVM return to Kosovo. When Albania signalled a need for help when the river of arriving refugees became a tidal wave, a KVM contingent went in and made a significant contribution in the camps, and host family situations.

This period also saw the beginning of what was to become the mission's single most labour-intensive effort on the human rights front – an attempt to catalogue, while memories were fresh and witnesses and victims were at hand, as many first hand accounts of what had happened as possible. With a team in Macedonia, another in Albania, the KVM human rights division conducted over 2,800 intensive debriefings of those identified as either victims of or witnesses to major human-rights violations. Lengthy depositions were taken in each case. The collective story that emerged is one of extreme violence and brutality, of Albanian civilians driven from their homes by overwhelming, indiscriminate force inflicted by Serb and Yugoslav authorities. The reports of mass killings, arbitrary and extra-judicial killings and the looting and destruction of property were widespread, consistent and convincing. Refugees reported being used as 'human shields' around military installations, and stripped of all identity documents and property before forced expulsion.

Effort is under way to collate the accounts. Many witnesses to the same event were scattered in the confusion of exit. Bringing together corroborative descriptions of a single event from several sources obviously lends credence to the stories. The material gathered from this collection of witness statements, systematically processed, should reveal patterns of abuse and, hopefully, expose those responsible. Once the material is organised, the result should provide a valuable road map to those seeking the most accurate picture possible in terms of human-rights violations committed during the Kosovo conflict.

## DID THE KVM LOSE ITS NEUTRALITY?

The Kosovo crisis slowly came to world attention during the late summer months of 1998. It was – from the beginning and throughout the next twelve months – a crisis clearly involving human and civil rights abuses on a massive scale. The violations, deliberate and province-wide, were committed by a government against an ethnic minority comprising a 90 per cent majority of Kosovo's population. This in the very heart of central Europe, albeit in a corner seldom before mentioned on the evening news.

But even before anchormen and editorial writers were describing and condemning outrages committed by Federal Republic of Yugoslavia security forces in the villages and countryside of Kosovo, those paying attention to prior events in the Balkans knew what the Milosevic regime was up to, and capable of. The international community, after all, had been dealing with Slobodan Milosevic, and those who carried out his orders, for the better part of a decade. There was abundant evidence of the measures he, his army, his police and the paramilitaries he unleashed for the dirtiest jobs took to impose their will on those who dared to challenge Belgrade control. First in the break-away republics of Slovenia and Croatia, and finally in Bosnia, Milosevic's willingness to resort to any and all methods to obtain, and then retain, control and power should have been crystal clear. We knew, for example, that Slobodan Milosevic employed, deployed, then defended and protected those in his forces accused of the most horrendous of war crimes. Ethnic cleansing was the hallmark of his early approach to Bosnia, and would later be his strategic vision for Kosovo.

Despite the events of the summer of 1998 – the stand-off shelling of Albanian villages by the regular army, followed by the entry of Ministry of Interior special police (MUP) units and paramilitary gangs that looted, killed and torched – there were those who preferred to conclude that this was not the Milosevic plan for Kosovo. Among these were some who would later claim, in March–June 1999 that the NATO bombing campaign alone had triggered Belgrade's brutal and massive effort to humiliate, expel, and/or kill every Albanian its forces could get their hands on. Given that the security forces employed a pattern of attack on Albanian villages during the bombing campaign indistinguishable from these earlier examples of forced cleansing, this – to me, at least – is a difficult argument to sustain. But beyond journalists' coverage during the summer and autumn of 1998, there were few who could provide first-person testimony of the abuses beyond the victims themselves. It was thus easy for those who, for whatever reason, wanted to look the other way, to buy into the excuses put forward by Belgrade and its apologists. These claimed that such a harsh campaign was necessary to defeat the secessionist threat posed by the Kosovo Liberation Army (KLA). Belgrade would point to the 'criminal acts', the 'terrorism' and what it defined as the illegal demand for 'separation and independence' of the fledgling KLA to justify the denial of civil rights to the Albanian community and the wholesale destruction of their villages in a campaign of repression not seen in Europe since World War Two.

The Kosovo crisis was not a product of, nor did it emerge from, within the province. Rather its genesis was the deliberate design of persons and issues in Belgrade stimulated by the political vision of Slobodan Milosevic. While there were any number of ingredients and complexities which led to the 1998 summer-autumn violence – populations of differing ethnicities, languages and religions; attendant cultural clashes; and the tensions of regional politics in the aftermath of the break-up of the former Yugoslavia – what catapulted the Kosovo crisis to the front pages of the world's press was the gross abuse of individual rights inflicted on a provincial population by a repressive central government.

In October 1998, the international community – specifically the FRY's European neighbours and their North American partners – was forced to take heed that the crisis in Kosovo had the potential, if not contained, to engulf south-central Europe in further bloody ethnic conflict. At that point, Ambassador Holbrooke was off to Belgrade, the Holbrooke-Milosevic agreement was announced and the multinational intervention described above began. In what for the international human-rights NGO community was a break with tradition, many called for the first time for military intervention to stop the genocide and crimes against humanity. The KVM's unarmed intervention ended in mid-June when Milosevic capitulated and accepted the entry of NATO troops. With that entry began the search for a complete accounting of human-rights violations committed during the previous decade. At last, seasoned professionals – including a number of KVM veterans – were in a position to literally unearth the facts.

I feel certain that a thorough examination will prove, once and for all, that Kosovo was the scene of human rights abuses on a previously unimagined scale.

## LESSONS LEARNED

The KVM, at least its head of mission and those working the human-rights portfolio, learned a few simple lessons as a result of their Kosovo experience. None are exceptionally insightful or necessarily applicable for the next deployment. Each international crisis, and multinational response thereto, is a unique combination of elements and must be approached as such. The lessons learned in Bosnia cannot be applied to Kosovo, however convenient it might be to equate two Balkan crises. While there are superficial similarities, the differences are greater.

For what they may be worth to those examining the KVM experience, here are the important lessons we learned:

* *Specific Mandate Language.* I have described the difficulties KVM encountered resulting from working on the basis of an implicit human-rights mandate. Agreements based on ambiguities, implicit understanding between parties might have their place. Where both sides clearly want an agreement to work, implicit accord might provide useful flexibility and manoeuvrability and enhance the chances of successful implementation. Dealing with a Slobodan Milosevic, a proven manipulator of the truth and unreliable on promises made, the clarity of intent and language cannot be left to later interpretation. If in doubt, include human rights in the mandate.
* *Human Rights Unit Independence; Direct Access to Head of Mission.* This combination was critical to the success of the KVM human-rights effort. KVM's collection, analysis and distribution of human-rights material was an extremely sensitive and important variety of tasks.

The unit director correctly saw the necessity of having unimpeded access to the head of mission. Only this would assure the benefits of front-office awareness, cover and support, and keep to a minimum those dealing with the material. The two, head of mission and director, quickly developed the ideal partnership to move the human rights agenda in a consistent, productive direction.

• *Cooperation with the NGO Community.* Of utmost importance. The engine of human-rights monitoring and advocacy historically was in the non-governmental sector. The array of NGOs covering this topic is large, and impressive in terms of impact on public and official opinion-makers. NGOs have sources of information and distribution of material networks distinct from those of national and multinational bodies. The two streams of information must be, more or less, describing the same situation. Interaction in the field, sharing of information and cross-fertilising each other's product can only make for a more accurate assessment. KVM and its parent organisation should have and could have done more.


## CONCLUSION

Despite the Kosovo Verification Mission's good intentions, the solid performance of many of its individual members and the fact that for several months it 'made a difference' in protecting the Albanian population of Kosovo from the brutal torment of their oppressors, in the final analysis the KVM was unable to achieve its goal of establishing a stable environment in which a political settlement was achievable. I can think of two reasons for that failure.

First, as the Rambouillet peace process conclusively proved, Slobodan Milosevic never intended to sign any settlement that diminished his absolute control over Kosovo and all within it. In the parlance of psychology, and in keeping with his Communist bureaucratic past, Slobodan Milosevic is a 'control freak'. If he had intended to end the conflict through negotiation, Milosevic would have signed the Rambouillet draft – which Ambassadors Hill and Petritsch felt gave him virtually everything he said he wanted – a Kosovo that remained an integral part of the FRY, in return for a degree of local autonomy. Milosevic never intended the KVM to succeed if to do so impinged on his ability to ruthlessly repress the Albanian majority in Kosovo. In my opinion, he only agreed to the OSCE presence because he was convinced that he could manipulate and contain it, taking advantage of the stresses and strains among the 54 member states and the OSCE's policy of decision by consensus. When Racak demonstrated that the KVM represented a danger, and was not subject to his control, he turned violently hostile to our presence.

Second, the KVM's inability to create conditions propitious to a political settlement was a direct result of its successes in the field of human rights. Had the KVM verifiers been less aggressive in pursuit of factual human rights reporting, had the mission dealt with Racak and other egregious abuses with the caution most international missions employ, had the international community reacted to the news from Racak with less passion and anger than it did – we would still be watching Slobodan Milosevic and his security services slowly but surely stripping the Albanian population of their dignity, their humanity, their very existence.

Human rights were the core issue behind the KVM. And human rights was the rallying cry of those who delivered the first taste of freedom to the Albanians of Kosovo.

## NOTES

1. The OSCE has 54 active members, plus one suspended membership (the FRY). Although all member states theoretically may participate in any field mission, the OSCE has an unwritten but faithfully observed tradition that neighbouring states and other nations historically involved in the dispute are not allowed to contribute. Excluded under this policy in the KVM were Croatia, Hungary, Bulgaria, Romania and Slovenia. At the time of KVM withdrawal, some 34 OSCE member states were participants in the Kosovo mission.
2. The term 'verifier', according to Holbrooke, was a carefully selected one. I was repeatedly reminded that my staff in the field was to 'verify' compliance, rather than simply 'monitor' it. Holbrooke's explanation was that 'verification' is a more robust verb than 'monitoring', and would permit the KVM to pursue a more pro-active mandate.
3. The ethnic composition of Kosovo's population is difficult to describe, far less quantify. There had been no census count since the 1980s, and there had been significant but uncounted movements of peoples throughout the 1990s. Albanians, also called Kosovars, were thought to make up approximately 90 per cent of the two-million-plus population. Serbs were a large percentage of the remaining ten per cent. But there are also Romas (Gypsies, or 'Egyptians' locally); a few Croats; Hungarians, and others. Most villages were exclusively of one or another ethnic composition. The cities – Pristina, Pec, Prizren and so on – had far greater diversity, but the pattern in each was of ethnically pure enclaves.
4. The OSCE has a revolving chairmanship, which rotates on the first of each year. The Chairman's representative in Vienna convenes and directs the Permanent Council, which takes decisions only with full consensus. A single member state can break that consensus and effectively veto Council action. The Troika is a consultative body consisting of the Chairman-in-Office, his predecessor and successor. In 1998 the Troika was composed of the foreign ministers of Denmark, Poland and Norway. In 1999, it was Poland, Norway and Austria.
5. Not surprising, since (1) setting up the logistical requirements of such a mission, in a matter of days, could only be done using military resources and know-how; (2) those best qualified to verify the terms of a military ceasefire would be persons with military backgrounds, active or retired; (3) the OSCE recruitment process calls on member

states to second personnel, at no salary cost to the OSCE. Who were the most likely to be able to pick up and leave for Kosovo the moment their government so ordered – and have relatively modest salaries for the sending state to cover? Clearly, active duty military were the quickest to come by.

6. The question of sharing our reports with the NGO community remained an unresolved issue throughout. OSCE field reporting goes first to the Chairman-in-Office, next to the Secretariat in Vienna for final review and then, when cleared, is distributed simultaneously to member states. Distribution is by placement in member-state boxes outside the Hofberg Palace, the site of Permanent Council meetings. Only then might others have access. The NGOs argued that this was a time-consuming process; and that better coordination and timely response to human-rights abuses would flow from speedier cross-checking of information.

7. In an April 1999 ODIHR conference in Warsaw, after he left the chairmanship and the KVM had left Kosovo, Minister Geremek explained his reasoning in the following terms:

> 'Whenever the OSCE is active in the field, human rights inherently belong to (sic) its mandate, and this even though it may not be explicitly mentioned there.'

> 'When, under the Polish chairmanship of the OSCE in 1998, I negotiated the mandate of the Kosovo Verification Mission, human rights was not explicit in the agreement with Belgrade. It was, however, clear to me, to Ambassador Walker and to other parties that human rights were implicit and an integral part of the mission's mandate.'

> 'The reason why the KVM also had an implicit human rights agenda was because respect for human rights is the very core of the Kosovo problem.'

> 'Kosovo illustrates a key and fundamental OSCE principal: the human dimension and the security dimension are linked and indivisible. As Kosovo shows us, there is no security and no long-term stability without respect for human rights. Therefore, human rights should never be consigned to the margins of what we, as the OSCE, are engaged in.'

While I am in complete agreement with the minister's words, I wish this had been as clearly stated, and debated if necessary, in the Permanent Council.

8. One exception was the USKDOM, by far the largest and best resourced. In addition to its military personnel, the American unit had a number of foreign service officers literally plucked from diplomatic and consular posts worldwide for TDY deployment in Kosovo. Some arrived with only a toothbrush and a vague idea of their responsibilities. They served well.

9. From the outset the KVM was highly decentralised. Early on we discovered that where the verifiers were, where the orange painted OSCE vehicles were seen, bad things tended to happen less often. On arrival, most reports of conflict and abuse came from the western half of the province. Our first offices were therefore placed there. Soon we began hearing of problems in the east, sometimes in areas that had known little trouble before. Moving to establish presence wherever there was conflict, we soon found our offices and people covering the entire province.

10. The Racak incident was decidedly a turning point, both in terms of KVM relations with Belgrade, and of the outside world's understanding of what was occurring in Kosovo. On 15 January the government announced that its security forces had encountered, engaged and demolished a KLA band in the vicinity of Racak. It reported 15 'terrorists' killed. The following morning when a KVM patrol entered the village it was told a totally different account. After shelling the village, security forces moved in, separated the men and boys from the women and children, and marched them off. Their bodies were strewn along a ravine leading out of the village. Not 15, but over 40. I and the press visited the site. The dead were mostly elderly men, all in peasant work clothes, and had died where they were discovered. The evidence of deliberate execution was overwhelming. I so described the incident in a press conference that afternoon, blamed

the security forces, and asked the government to permit the entry of investigators from the International Criminal Tribunal for the Former Yugoslavia (ICTY) in The Hague. I called on the regime to punish those responsible. The government's response was to declare me *persona non grata*. It later 'froze' me in that status.

11. Some OSCE member states, Russia leading the charge, asserted that the KVM mandate, and thus the mission, ended when it left the province. Others, the majority, supported the thesis that the mandate to report on events in Kosovo could continue to be carried out from a distance. KVM, with sources of information still in Kosovo and in contact with those in the refugee camps recently expelled, remained the single best informed and most credible source of information in the first weeks of exile. Over time this comparative advantage of sources diminished.

# PART THREE:

# War

# 7

# Reflections on the Legality and Legitimacy of NATO's Intervention in Kosovo

## NICHOLAS J. WHEELER

If, in those dark days and hours leading up to the genocide [in Rwanda], a coalition of States had been prepared to act in defence of the Tutsi population, but did not receive prompt Council authorisation, should such a coalition have stood aside and allowed the horror to unfold?[1]

This provocative challenge, issued by the UN Secretary-General to the General Assembly during its 54th session in September 1999, encapsulates the conflict between legality and legitimacy posed by NATO's military intervention in Kosovo earlier in March. On the one hand, the leading governments prosecuting the war, primarily the United States and the United Kingdom – lacked a firm basis in UN Charter law for bombing the Federal Republic of Yugoslavia (FRY). On the other, the Security Council was unanimous that the FRY was committing gross and systematic violations of human rights against the Albanian minority in Kosovo; that these constituted a threat to 'international peace and security'; and that the Security Council had demanded a cessation of the violence in three successive resolutions adopted under Chapter VII. However, owing to the threat of a Russian and Chinese veto, the Security Council was unable to authorise NATO to take military action against the FRY. Consequently, the question in the Kosovo case was not the hypothetical one posed by the Secretary-General in relation to the Rwandan genocide, since NATO in 1999 had been prepared to use force to end the atrocities in Kosovo with or without Council authorisation.

This contribution considers whether NATO's action in Kosovo represents a watershed in the development of a new norm of humanitarian intervention, and how far this is to be welcomed or feared in a society of states built on the principles of sovereignty, non-intervention and non-use of force. Does NATO's attempt at promoting justice in Kosovo signal the arrival of a doctrine of humanitarian intervention that will protect civilians who are being terrorised by their governments, or has it set a dangerous precedent that places in jeopardy the foundations of international order?

In exploring these questions, I identify three models for thinking about the legality and legitimacy of humanitarian intervention: the *posse,* the *vigilante* and the *norm entrepreneur.*[2] The idea of the posse is taken from the 'wild west' and refers to a situation where the sheriff calls upon the assistance of a group of citizens in the task of law-enforcement.[3] These individuals are given a warrant to use force from the sheriff. By analogy, the Security Council is accorded 'primary responsibility' in Article 24 of the Charter for the maintenance of 'international peace and security', and its authority under Chapter VII to authorise the use of force in defence of this purpose constitutes the Council as a posse at the global level. The response of the Security Council to the humanitarian crises in Somalia and Bosnia fits this model because the Council defined these emergencies as a threat to international security and explicitly authorised member-states under Chapter VII to use 'all necessary means' to enforce global humanitarian norms.

NATO's intervention in Kosovo does not conform to the posse model because the lack of unanimity among the permanent members led to a situation where the Alliance could not secure a warrant for military action. At this point, NATO was confronted with three possibilities. First, it could have argued that the plight of the Kosovo Albanians was so appalling as to justify intervention on moral grounds, but that it recognised that its action was an illegal one because there is no general right of humanitarian intervention under customary international law. Second, NATO governments could have defended their action on the grounds that there is a legal basis for the use of force in both treaty and customary international law. This is where the idea of an international equivalent to the vigilante comes in. The term vigilante developed in the United States in the nineteenth century and explains the actions of those private individuals who enforced the law in the absence or breakdown of officially constituted legal bodies. The key point about vigilantes is that they claim to be enforcing existing law on behalf of society; they do not advance new norms nor do they try to create new law.[4] Similarly, Alliance governments claimed (as have vigilantes in domestic societies) to be acting with the authority of the law, though no UN body authorised NATO to use military force in Kosovo,

Categorising NATO's action in Kosovo in terms of a vigilante model is at first sight appealing. The Security Council as the legally constituted law enforcement body failed to act to enforce its demands in earlier resolutions, and so NATO stepped in by claiming a legal right of humanitarian intervention. This view suited Alliance governments who wanted to argue that their action did not break international law and upheld internationally agreed standards of human rights. I argue here that this vigilante defence of NATO's action is unsustainable because there was no basis in existing law for NATO's action. The alternative interpretation of NATO's action proposed below is that members of the Alliance, notably the Blair government, were advancing a new norm of humanitarian intervention without express Security Council authorisation (I will call this 'unilateral humanitarian intervention' to distinguish it from Security Council authorised intervention).

Martha Finnemore and Kathryn Sikkink argue that the development of new norms depends crucially upon particular states acting as 'norm entrepreneurs' who attempt to convince other states to adopt the norm or norms concerned.[5] In the Kosovo case, NATO governments refused to acknowledge that they were challenging existing Charter norms concerning the prohibition on the use of force, and so they never acted as full-blown norm entrepreneurs. But the argument invoked by the British Government, in particular, in defence of NATO's bombing of the FRY, was unprecedented and raises the question of how far NATO's breach of Charter law was legitimated by other states. Finnemore and Sikkink argue that new norms emerge through a process of contestation as advocates of a new norm try to persuade a critical mass of followers that their action should not be viewed as norm-breaking behaviour. If norm entrepreneurs succeed in gaining a significant group of supporters, then a 'norm cascade' takes place as the new standard of behaviour more quickly becomes internalised. Finnemore and Sikkink consider that a fruitful area for research is to investigate how norm creation leads to new laws, and with this idea in mind, this contribution considers how far NATO's action in Kosovo sets a precedent for a new rule of customary international law supporting the legality of unilateral humanitarian intervention.

## THE CONTESTED LEGALITY OF HUMANITARIAN INTERVENTION

The contention that there already exists a legal right of humanitarian intervention rests on two foundations: first, on an interpretation of UN Charter provisions relating to the protection of human rights, and second, on customary international law. These foundations were stressed by a minority of international lawyers during the Cold War, and their proposition is that the promotion of human rights ranks alongside peace and security in the hierarchy of UN Charter principles. Here, they point to the language in the preamble to the UN Charter and Articles 1(3), 55, and 56 which impose a legal obligation on member-states to cooperate in promoting human rights.

According to Fernando Teson, the 'promotion of human rights is as important a purpose in the Charter as is the control of international conflict'.[6] Consequently he argues that the Security Council has a legal right to authorise humanitarian intervention irrespective of whether it has found a threat to 'international peace and security' under Chapter VII. Some jurists go even further and assert that if the Security Council fails to take remedial action in cases of massive human rights abuses, then individual states should act as armed vigilantes and take the enforcement of the human rights provisions of the Charter into their own hands. Michael Reisman and Myers McDougal claim that were this not the case, 'it would be suicidally destructive of the explicit purposes for which the United Nations was established'.[7] In response to the argument that unilateral humanitarian intervention violates the legal ban on the use of force in Article 2(4), they reply:

> Since a humanitarian intervention seeks neither a territorial change nor a challenge to the political independence of the state involved and is not only not inconsistent with the purposes of the United Nations but is rather in conformity with the most fundamental peremptory norms of the Charter, it is a distortion to argue that it is precluded by Article 2(4).[8]

Set against such views, the majority of international lawyers have been labelled 'restrictionists' because they restrict the legal right to use force under the Charter to the purposes of self-defence. They contend, in Rosalyn Higgins's words, 'that the Charter *could* have allowed for sanctions for gross human-rights violations, but deliberately did not do so'.[9] Consequently, restrictionists assert that there are only two legally recognised exceptions to the general ban on the use of force in Article 2(4): the right of individual and collective self-defence under Article 51 and Security Council enforcement action under Chapter VII of the Charter. The restrictionist case is buttressed by an appeal to customary international law. Article 38 of the statute of the International Court of Justice refers to this 'as evidence of a general practice accepted as law'. Customary law is different from treaty law because it is not created by written agreements between states that sets down the rules to regulate their interactions in a specific area.[10] It is not enough that states actually engage in the practice that is claimed to have the status of customary law; they must also justify the practice as being legally permitted. This subjective element is referred to by lawyers as *opinio juris* and is essential in identifying which norms of behaviour have become the customary rules that become legally binding upon states.

Restrictionists argue that state practice and *opinio juris* since 1945 does not support a legal right of unilateral humanitarian intervention. Here they point to the following: General Assembly standards on non-intervention, such as the 1965 Declaration on the Inadmissibility of Intervention that denied legal recognition to intervention 'for any reason whatever'; the 1970 Declaration on Principles of International Law concerning Friendly Relations and Cooperation that confirmed that '[n]o State or group of states has the right to intervene ... in the internal or external affairs of any other State'; and the 1987 Declaration on the Enhancement of the Effectiveness of the Principle of Refraining from the Threat or Use of Force in International Relations which stated that 'no consideration of whatever nature may be invoked to warrant resorting to the threat or use of force in violation of the Charter'.[11] The International Court of Justice in the *Nicaragua* judgment considered the question of whether there were legal exceptions to the non-intervention rule, and its judgment was that this 'would involve a fundamental modification of the customary law principle of non-intervention' for which there was no support in state practice.[12]

The concept of *jus cogens* denotes 'a norm accepted and recognized by the international community of States as a whole as a norm from which no derogation is permitted and which can be modified only by a subsequent norm of general international law having the same character'.[13] 'Counter-restrictionists' deny that the prohibition on the use of force is *jus cogens*. They claim that there is custom from the pre-Charter and post-Charter period supporting a norm of unilateral humanitarian intervention. Lawyers date its origins to the seventeenth-century Dutch international lawyer Hugo Grotius, who considered that the rights of the sovereign could be limited by principles of humanity.[14] The norm was the subject of debate among international lawyers during the eighteenth century, but it was not pressed into service by states until the early nineteenth century. The 1827 intervention by Britain, France and Russia to protect Greek Christians from the oppressive rule of Turkey set the pattern for subsequent interventions in the Ottoman Empire. In language that was little different from that used by NATO to justify its use of force against the Milosevic regime, the intervening states claimed that their action was required 'no less by sentiments of humanity, than by interests for the tranquillity of Europe'.[15]

The importance of this discussion is that if a doctrine of unilateral humanitarian intervention is part of customary international law, then we should expect to see states employing it as justification and having it validated in cases where the doctrine could be plausibly invoked. However, in the three Cold War cases where a government was carrying out the mass murder of its citizens, and where there was intervention by a neighbouring state that ended the oppression, none of the intervening states – with the partial exception of India – justified the use of force on humanitarian grounds. These cases were India's intervention in East Pakistan in 1971; Vietnam's intervention in Cambodia in 1978; and Tanzania's intervention in Uganda in 1979. The international response varied from case to case depending upon Cold War geopolitics and the particular context surrounding the use of force. Vietnam suffered the greatest condemnation and sanctioning for its overthrow of the Pol Pot regime, while Tanzania's action in removing Idi Amin was treated the most leniently, but in none of these cases was there *opinio juris* supporting a legal right of humanitarian intervention.[16]

The formation of new custom requires both state practice and *opinio juris* but it would be wrong to think that non-compliance with a rule means that it has lost its legally binding character. Rosalyn Higgins gives the example of the international prohibition on torture which continues, despite widespread non-compliance on the part of states, to be a legally binding rule of customary international law 'because *opinio juris* as to its normative status continues to exist'.[17] New custom requires states to raise novel claims that by definition cannot be contained in the existing law and this means that such claims are always open to the rejoinder that they are deviant and unlawful. On the other hand, the advocacy of new norms by a state or group of states might lead, as argued above, to a 'norm cascade'.

If we accept that there was no custom supporting a right of unilateral humanitarian intervention in Cold War international society, two questions arise. How should the reluctance of states to embrace this doctrine be explained? And how far do the reasons for this reluctance persist at the end of the Cold War?

Objections to the doctrine of humanitarian intervention usually boil down to two themes: the conflict between order and justice, and the problem of abuse. Humanitarian intervention, according to theorists of international society like Hedley Bull, exposes the conflict between order and justice at its starkest because to recognise such a legal right would 'jeopardise the rules of sovereignty and non-intervention' in a world where there is no consensus on what moral principles should govern the practice of humanitarian intervention.[18] Bull dubbed the view that order had to be prioritised over justice as the 'pluralist' conception of international society, in which states are only able to agree on a minimum ethic of coexistence. He contrasted this with the 'solidarist' conception where there is sufficient consensus on basic values to create a 'solidarity ... of the states comprising international society, with respect to the enforcement of the law'.[19] Bull argued that a solidarist society of states is one in which a right of humanitarian intervention is bestowed upon individual states who act as agents of the world common good, but maintained that the lack of solidarity on standards of justice and morality had wisely led states to eschew such solidarist ambitions. The pluralist concern is that if a right of humanitarian intervention is conceded to individual states, the door will be opened for powerful states to act on their own particular moral preferences, thereby weakening the restraints on the use of force in the society of states.

The second objection to humanitarian intervention is that such a doctrine is open to abuse. The problem of abuse only arises in a context where humanitarian justifications for the use of force have secured an important measure of collective legitimation on the part of the society of states. The concern is that by permitting a further exception to the general ban on the use of force in Article 2(4) of the UN Charter, states will be free to abuse this new legal right by claiming humanitarian justifications to cover the use of force motivated by selfish interests. The international lawyer Ian Brownlie (who represented the FRY when it tried unsuccessfully in April 1999 to persuade the International Court of Justice (ICJ) to hear its case that NATO's bombing was illegal) relates the problem of abuse specifically to the idea of vigilante action. He writes:

> Whatever special cases one can point to, a rule allowing humanitarian intervention, as opposed to a discretion in the United Nations to act through the appropriate organs, is a general license to vigilantes and opportunists to resort to hegemonial intervention.[20]

Some lawyers, who are critical of legalising humanitarian intervention because of the fear that such a rule will be abused, recognise that humanitarian intervention might be morally required in exceptional cases. Writing in 1974, Thomas Franck and Nigel Rodley argued that humanitarian intervention 'belongs in the realm not of law but of moral choice, which nations, like individuals must sometimes make'.[21] States might admit that their action is unlawful but seek to legitimate this on the grounds that it is the only means to prevent or stop genocide, mass murder and ethnic cleansing. A recent report by the Danish Institute of International Affairs on *Humanitarian Intervention: Legal and Political Aspects*, commissioned by the Danish Government, recommended adopting this policy, concluding that 'in extreme cases, humanitarian intervention may be necessary and justified on moral and political grounds even if an authorisation from the UN Security Council cannot be obtained'.[22]

Humanitarian intervention without Security Council authorisation is certainly morally preferable to the alternative of inaction in cases of extreme human rights abuses, but the Danish Institute's recommendation is unsatisfactory for two reasons. First, there is the danger that others might decide to treat the law in an equally cavalier manner in other cases, thereby fatally eroding the fabric of international law. It is an inherently flawed international legal order that expects law-abiding states to break the law in order to uphold minimum standards of humanity.[23] A second problem with the Danish Institute's position is that since it contains within it the potential to develop into a modification of existing Charter norms, why not go the whole way and argue for such a legal exception to be incorporated into international law from the outset? Surely rather than states arguing that humanitarian intervention is morally but not legally permitted, the better strategy for law-abiding states is to take the unprecedented step in post-1945 international society of invoking a new legal right of humanitarian intervention as an exception to Article 2(4) in the expectation that advocacy of a new norm will trigger a 'norm cascade', leading to a modification of customary international law. The next section asks how far the justifications employed by NATO governments for their use of force in Kosovo marked such a turning point.

## NATO'S JUSTIFICATION FOR ITS USE OF FORCE IN KOSOVO

At the request of Russia, the Security Council met on 24 March 1999 to debate NATO's action and Ambassador Lavrov opened proceedings by accusing NATO of violating the UN Charter. He argued that there was no basis in the accepted rules of international law to justify such a unilateral use of force. Russia did not defend the FRY's violations of international humanitarian law, but asserted it is only 'possible to combat violations of the law ... with clean hands and only on the solid basis of the law'.[24] Russia was supported by Belarus, Namibia and China. They pressed the point that it was only the Security Council that had the authority to sanction military enforcement action in defence of its resolutions. India, which had asked to participate in the Security Council's deliberations, supported this position, arguing that 'No country, group of countries or regional arrangement, no matter how powerful, can arrogate to itself the right to take arbitrary and unilateral military action against others'.[25]

Set against this view, NATO governments argued that their action was both legal and morally justified because it was aimed at 'averting a humanitarian catastrophe', and hence was in conformity with Security Council Resolutions 1199 and 1203, which had demanded Serbian forces to stop their violations of human rights in Kosovo. The following reveal the legal and moral arguments justifying NATO's position. The Canadian Ambassador, for example, claimed that '[h]umanitarian considerations underpin our action. We cannot simply stand by while innocents are murdered, an entire population is displaced, villages are burned.'[26] The Netherlands Ambassador acknowledged that his government would always prefer to base action on a specific Security Council resolution when taking up arms to defend human rights; but if 'due to one or two permanent members' rigid interpretation of the concept of domestic jurisdiction, such a resolution is not attainable, we cannot sit back and simply let the humanitarian catastrophe occur'. Rather, 'we will act on the legal basis we have available, and what we have available in this case is more than adequate'.[27] Unfortunately, the Netherlands Ambassador did not specify what this legal basis was.

It is to the United Kingdom Government that we have to look to find a legal defence of NATO's action. The Blair government had taken the lead in late 1998 in arguing within the alliance that there was indeed a legal basis for NATO to use force against the FRY even without explicit Security Council authorisation. This reasoning was set out in a Foreign and Commonwealth Office paper circulated to NATO capitals in October 1998. The key sections are as follows:

A UNSCR [Security Council Resolution] would give a clear legal base for NATO action, as well as being politically desirable. ... But force can also be justified on the grounds of overwhelming humanitarian necessity without a UNSCR. The following criteria would need to be applied:
(a) that there is convincing evidence, generally accepted by the international community as a whole, of extreme humanitarian distress on a large scale, requiring immediate and urgent relief.
(b) that it is objectively clear that there is no practicable alternative to the use of force if lives are to be saved.
(c) that the proposed use of force is necessary and proportionate to the aim (the relief of humanitarian need) and is strictly limited in time and scope to this aim.[28]

This paper echoes the views expressed by Anthony Aust, Legal Counsellor to the Foreign Office, when he defended the legality of the 'safe havens' in northern Iraq before the House of Commons Foreign

Affairs Select Committee in late 1992.[29] British ministers were quick to invoke this case in late 1998 as a precedent supporting the legality of NATO's threat to use force against the FRY. The government's evolving legal position was publicly set out by Baroness Symons, Minister of State at the Foreign Office, in a written answer to Lord Kennet on 16 November 1998:

> There is no general doctrine of humanitarian necessity in international law. Cases have nevertheless arisen (as in northern Iraq in 1991) when, in the light of all the circumstances, a limited use of force was justifiable in support of purposes laid down by the Security Council but without the Council's express authorisation when that was the only means to avert an immediate and overwhelming humanitarian catastrophe.[30]

At no point during the Security Council debates in March 1999 did NATO governments try to advance the argument that the bombing of the FRY was illegal but morally justified. Rather, they emphasised that their action had the backing of international law. British Foreign Secretary, Robin Cook, appearing before the House of Commons Foreign Affairs Committee in April 1999 was pressed by Diane Abbot MP on the legal grounds for NATO's action in Kosovo. He replied: '[t]he legal basis for our action is that the international community [*sic*] states do have the right to use force in the case of overwhelming humanitarian necessity'.[31] To sustain this line of legal argument, it would have to be shown that there is existing customary law supporting such a right. However, there are two main reasons for rejecting the United Kingdom Government's claim that the case of the 'safe havens' in northern Iraq establishes such a precedent.

First, the justification employed by Baroness Symons in November 1998 was not in fact the one invoked by Western governments to defend the intervention in northern Iraq. Rather, the argument in April 1991 was that Resolution 688, which had not been adopted under Chapter VII, provided sufficient legal authority by *itself* to justify the creation of the safe havens and 'no-fly' zones. In the case of Kosovo, the existing Security Council resolutions adopted under Chapter VII were not claimed to constitute express Council authorisation; rather, they were adduced as evidence that the society of states recognised an 'overwhelming humanitarian necessity' to act.

The second reason for challenging the view that northern Iraq in 1991 established a precedent is that there has been no *opinio juris* supporting it. As discussed above in relation to the judgment of the International Court of Justice in the Nicaragua case, new custom requires states to withdrawal their existing *opinio juris*. The international silence that greeted the allies' action in northern Iraq should not be interpreted as evidence that the society of states viewed these actions as permitted by international law. Acquiescence does not count as acceptance in principle of a new rule of customary international law.

Consequently, the defence of NATO's action over Kosovo in terms of the vigilante model is unsustainable because it exaggerates how far the alliance was acting in accordance with international law. Whatever Alliance governments might say to the contrary, their justifications for the use of force in Kosovo lead to the conclusion that NATO was not so much taking existing law into its own hands as establishing a normative precedent that might itself become the basis of new law.

## A NEW SOLIDARIST NORM OF HUMANITARIAN INTERVENTION?

Two days after the NATO bombing began, Russia tabled with Belarus and India a draft resolution condemning NATO's action as a breach of Articles 2(4), 24 and 53 of the Charter and demanded a cessation of hostilities. States routinely invoke Article 2(4) when they want to criticise the use of force by other states, but the claim that NATO was violating Articles 24 and 53 took the debate over the legitimate use of force into new territory. As noted earlier, Article 24 refers to the 'primary responsibility' of the Security Council 'for the maintenance of international peace and security', with UN member-states agreeing that 'in carrying out its duties under this responsibility the Security Council acts on their behalf'.[32] Under Article 53 of the Charter, the Security Council is empowered to 'utilise ... regional arrangements or agencies for enforcement action', but the Charter is explicit that this can only take place with authorisation by the Security Council. Consequently, NATO is charged with usurping the Security Council's 'primary responsibility', with the Russian Ambassador arguing that '[w]hat is in the balance now is the question of law and lawlessness. It is a question of either reaffirming the commitment of one's country and people to the basic principles and values of the United Nations Charter, or tolerating a situation in which gross force dictates realpolitik.'[33]

In response to these charges, three of the NATO states on the Security Council robustly defended 'Operation Allied Force'. The US, Netherlands and Canada rejected the charge that they were acting outside UN Charter norms, justifying their actions as being in conformity with existing Council resolutions and necessary to prevent a humanitarian catastrophe. The US argued that NATO's action was not in violation of the Charter because this did 'not sanction armed assaults upon ethnic groups, or imply that the international community should turn a blind eye to a growing humanitarian disaster'.[34] Canada stressed the international legitimacy behind NATO's actions, arguing that supporting the draft resolution would place states 'outside the international consensus, which holds that the time has come to stop the continuing violence' by the FRY against the Kosovars.[35]

When the draft resolution was put to the vote, it was defeated by 12 votes to three (Russia, China and Namibia). Speaking after the vote, the British Government argued that Security Council resolutions 1199 and 1203 determined that Milosevic's policies had 'caused the threat to peace and security in the region', and that 'military intervention is justified as an exceptional measure to prevent an overwhelming humanitarian catastrophe'.[36] This was endorsed by the French Government which argued that the 'actions decided upon respond to Belgrade's violation of its international obligations under the resolutions which the Security Council has adopted under Chapter VII of the United Nations Charter'.[37]

The legal and moral position taken by NATO governments in the Security Council debate on 26 March is not surprising, but what has to be explained is how six non-Western states came to vote with Slovenia in comprehensively defeating a Russian draft resolution condemning NATO's bombing. Nigel White argues that 'lack of condemnation by the Security Council cannot be seen as an authorisation to use force',[38] but while this is correct, the more pertinent question is whether this vote constitutes a new practice and *opinio juris* in support of a right of unilateral humanitarian intervention. The first point to make here is that of the six non-Western states on the Council which rejected the draft resolution, only three chose to make statements. The Bahrain government reiterated the standard NATO argument that the humanitarian catastrophe taking place inside Kosovo justified NATO's action, and that support for the draft resolution would encourage the Milosevic regime to continue its policy of ethnic cleansing.[39] The Malaysian Government regretted that owing to irreconcilable differences within the Security Council, it had 'been necessary for measures to be taken outside of the Council'.[40] Although this was hardly a ringing endorsement of NATO's action, the Malaysian Government is a staunch defender of the non-intervention rule, and the fact that it was prepared to publicly legitimate an action that bypassed the Security Council is highly significant. The position it took over Kosovo probably reflected the fact that NATO's intervention was in defence of Moslems. The Argentine Government was even stronger in its support for NATO's action, stating that rejection of the draft resolution was based on contributing to efforts to stop the massive violations of human rights in

Kosovo. Indeed, the Argentinean Ambassador argued that the obligation to protect human rights and fulfil 'the legal norms of international humanitarian law and human rights is a response to the universally recognised and accepted values and commitments'.[41] The implication of this was that in exceptional circumstances – such as those prevailing in Kosovo – states have a right to use force to put an end to human rights violations even without express Security Council authorisation. One important explanation for Argentina's public support of NATO's action is that its growing commitment to democratic values at home was being reflected in a commitment to defend human rights internationally. Gambia and Gabon did not participate in the debate and Brazil, which had strongly opposed any use of force by NATO without Security Council authority in earlier debates, also remained silent.

The approval given to NATO's action by the Slovenian Government was less surprising than that given by the Argentine and Malaysian Governments. The Slovenian Ambassdor, as it happened a former professor of international law, argued that while his government would have preferred direct Security Council authorisation, 'the Security Council has the primary but not exclusive responsibility for the maintenance of international peace and security'. This argument represented an imaginative response to the Russian charge that NATO was acting contrary to Article 24 of the Charter since the Slovenian Ambassador considered that 'all the Council members have to think hard about what needs to be done to ensure the Council's authority and to make its primary responsibility as real as the Charter requires'.[42] According to this view Russia and China were in breach of Article 24 because the threat of their vetoes had prevented the Security Council from exercising its 'primary responsibility for the maintenance of international peace and security'.

The various justifications for NATO's action proffered by members of the Security Council during the debate on 26 March were rejected by the sponsors of the draft resolution and their supporters. For example, the Indian representative stated that NATO 'believes itself to be above the law. We find this deeply uncomfortable.' Indeed, India challenged the international legitimacy of NATO's action by arguing that the 'international community can hardly be said to have endorsed their actions when already representatives of half of humanity have said that they do not agree with what they have done'.[43]

These arguments and counter-arguments raise the question: how many states have to validate a new practice before a 'norm cascade' takes place and a new rule of customary international law develops? The 26 March vote in the Security Council was historic because for the first time, since the founding of the Charter, seven members either legitimated or acquiesced in the use of force justified on humanitarian grounds in a context where there was no express Council authorisation. NATO's action was also endorsed beyond the Security Council by the European Union (though there was significant domestic opposition in states such as Germany, Greece and Italy), by the Organisation of Islamic states (which, like Malaysia, welcomed an action that might save Moslems), and by the Organisation of American States, which issued a statement regretting the action, but not condemning it.

NATO's justification for its use of force in Kosovo was that it expressed the collective will of the society of states as embodied in Security Council resolutions. The Security Council vote lends some support to this proposition, but it is unwise to read too much into what was effectively a 7-3 vote where only three of the seven spoke in support of NATO's action, and a variety of factors came into play, as well as the particular issues relating to Kosovo. NATO could have attempted to strengthen its claim to be acting on behalf of the 'international community' by another route, namely placing the issue before the General Assembly. Nigel White argues that the General Assembly has legal competence under the Charter to recommend military measures when the Security Council is unable to exercise its 'primary responsibility for maintaining international peace and security', and that the 1950 'Uniting for Peace' Resolution could have been invoked for this purpose. Adopted at the height of the Cold War, this Resolution was a way of bypassing the Soviet veto in the Security Council.[44]

NATO could have placed a draft resolution before the Security Council authorising it to use force against the FRY in the event that the Milosevic regime continued to fail to comply with Council resolutions. At this point, a Russian and Chinese veto would have publicly exposed these states as the ones opposing intervention to end the atrocities. Even if Russia and China had cast their vetoes, NATO would then have been able to put a procedural resolution forward requesting that the matter be transferred to the General Assembly under the 'Uniting for Peace' resolution (the right of the veto does not exist in relation to procedural resolutions). This possibility leads White to argue that had NATO 'won both a procedural vote in the Security Council and a substantive vote in the General Assembly [requiring a two-thirds majority of the Assembly], NATO then would have had a sound legal basis upon which to launch its air strikes'.[45]

NATO governments did not go down the Uniting for Peace road because they could not guarantee securing the two-thirds majority to pass a resolution recommending military action. Western governments were not even prepared to risk putting a draft resolution before the Security Council authorising the use of force, and this is a body that they can be much more confident about controlling than the General Assembly. Requiring a two-thirds majority in the General Assembly for humanitarian intervention in cases where the Security Council has found a threat to the peace but is unable to act because of the use of the veto establishes a high threshold of legitimacy, and it would certainly minimise the risks that states would abuse this right. However, the problem with this prescription is that it makes state practice the acid-test of legitimacy. Indeed, making Assembly approval a precondition for intervention poses the same question that Kofi Anan addressed to the General Assembly in September 1999: should a group of states stand aside if they cannot secure the necessary votes in the General Assembly in cases where massive and systematic abuses of human rights are taking place? If we think back to the cases of the 1970s, had India, Vietnam and Tanzania in the 1970s relied on General Assembly resolutions to legitimise their interventions, the victims of state terror in East Pakistan, Cambodia and Uganda would have been left to their fate. In the cases of East Pakistan and Cambodia, India and Vietnam's non-humanitarian reasons for intervening did not contradict a positive humanitarian outcome, but in both cases, especially the Cambodian one, the General Assembly failed to legitimate the action as a humanitarian exception to the rules of the society of states.[46]

## A HISTORICAL WATERSHED?

The experience of the 1990s suggests that the Security Council is too weak to enforce minimum standards of common humanity. In 1991, it was divided over the use of force to protect the Kurds; at the end of the decade, it was unable to issue NATO with a warrant for its use of force in Kosovo. Given the volatile domestic situation in Russia, and the heightened sensitivity of Russia and China to actions that erode the sovereignty rule, it is highly unlikely that the permanent members of the Security Council will become a humanitarian coalition of the willing in future cases of gross human rights abuses. The limited prospects of the Security Council acting as a global posse means that the enforcement of global human rights standards depends upon particular states acting on behalf of the society of states. The problem, as Brown puts it, is '[u]nder what circumstances is enforcement action to be seen as the action of "international society" and not simply the individual states who take it?'.[47]

The standard pluralist objection to humanitarian intervention, in Hedley Bull's words, is that 'states or groups of states that set themselves up as the authoritative judges of the world common good ... are in fact a menace to international order'.[48] However, as Bull also recognised, intervention which 'expresses the collective will of the society of states' may be carried out without challenging order.[49] The challenge taken up by solidarist international society theory is to find ways of making unilateral humanitarian intervention an expression of the collective will of the society of states, and not a fundamental threat to its ordering principles. In developing the norms to regulate a practice of unilateral humanitarian intervention, the moral imperative to end the mass slaughter of civilians must not be subordinated to the requirement that intervention always be authorised by the UN Security Council or General Assembly. These bodies are important in securing collective legitimation for unilateral humanitarian intervention, but they cannot be allowed a veto on whether gross violations of human rights are ended in cases like Rwanda and Kosovo.

States that decide to use force to end atrocities without express UN authorisation, either from the Security Council or the General Assembly, must justify their actions on the basis of criteria that they would applaud others invoking in similar circumstances. They should justify their actions in terms of a new legal right of humanitarian intervention in customary international law in the hope that this will trigger a 'norm cascade' in the society of states. There will be opposition to a new norm from powerful governments like Russia, China and India, but future norm entrepreneurs should seek as wide a base of legitimation as possible among domestic publics, media, other governments, human rights NGOs and wider world public opinion.

The need for legitimation is a powerful constraining force on state actions, and if governments are unable to make a plausible defence of their use of force as humanitarian, then international society and wider transnational global civil society should mobilise moral censure and economic sanctions against these states as a deterrent to others. Considerations of power and interest will clearly influence the level of sanctioning in particular cases, and if the most powerful states abused such a norm, there are clear constraints on the level of pressure that can be brought to bear on these governments. However, what is crucial is that even the most powerful governments do not want to be exposed as hypocrites. And once a state has legitimated its action as humanitarian, its subsequent actions will be constrained by the need to remain true to the humanitarian purposes that it claimed motivated its action.

What is required in the aftermath of the Kosovo intervention is that the society of states begin a genuine dialogue on the criteria that justify states using force for humanitarian purposes in cases where the Security

Council is unable to act because of the power of the veto. Governments committed to the defence of human rights should take the lead in initiating this dialogue, and what is needed is a commitment by governments to the idea that in exceptional cases the slaughter of civilians might be so appalling as to legitimate the use of force to enforce minimum standards of common humanity. It might be argued that such a modification of Charter norms is not possible in a General Assembly dominated by non-democratic regimes which are jealous of their sovereign prerogatives. One way of testing this would be for Western states to respond more urgently to the challenge raised by many southern states that the ideology of humanitarianism propounded by Western governments since the end of the Cold War masks the continuing political and economic hegemony of Western states, and the violence required to sustain it.

Creating a new norm that enables humanitarian intervention is no guarantee that it will take place when it is desperately needed, as in Rwanda in 1994.[50] The positive interpretation of NATO's action in Kosovo is that the moral claims raised in defence of Kosovo Albanians will make it very difficult for the Alliance to look on with indifference the next time genocide, mass murder or ethnic cleansing occurs in Europe or elsewhere. The problem with this argument is that it overlooks the fact that the humanitarian impulse to act in Kosovo was joined by the belief that NATO had important security interests at stake in the region, and that the credibility of the Alliance was on the line if it did not stand up to Milosevic. This combination of humanitarian emergency and hard-headed security interests is unlikely to confront the Alliance outside the Balkans, and this suggests that Kosovo does not mark the beginning of an era in which NATO will act as a global enforcer of humanitarian norms.

The Kosovo case is further limited as a legal precedent because it could only plausibly be invoked by other states in a context where the Security Council has already adopted Chapter VII resolutions identifying a government's human rights abuses as creating a threat to 'international peace and security', and where the threat or use of the veto has prevented the Council from authorising the use of force. Having watched NATO governments defend their military action in Kosovo by appealing to resolutions adopted under Chapter VII, it is likely that Russia and China will be considerably more cautious about passing such resolutions in the future.

NATO's intervention in Kosovo did secure widespread approval in the society of states, but where there is only one case in support of a new rule, states can easily nullify it by acting against the rule in future instances.[51] Consequently, given the record of state practice against a norm of unilateral humanitarian intervention in the post-1945 period, it will require additional cases where practice and *opinio juris* support this norm before a judgment can be made as to how far Kosovo marks a turning point in legitimising the practice of unilateral humanitarian intervention.

NOTES

 1. Secretary's General Annual Report to the General Assembly, Press Release SG/SM7136 GA/9596, http://srch 1.un.org:80/plweb-cgi/fastweb, 20 Sept. 1999
 2. See Nicholas J. Wheeler, 'Humanitarian Vigilantes or Legal Entrepreneurs: Enforcing Human Rights in International Society', which will appear in a special issue of *Critical Review of International Social and Political Philosophy* (forthcoming, 2000), edited by Peter Jones and Simon Caney.
 3. The idea of the posse is developed by Chris Brown in his 'The Artificial Person of International Society' (unpublished paper, supplied by the author, pp.11–12).
 4. Ibid., p.12.
 5. Martha Finnemore and Kathryn Sikkink, 'International Norm Dynamics and Political Change', *International Organization*, Vol.2, No.4 (1998), p.895.
 6. Fernando Teson, *Humanitarian Intervention: An Inquiry into Law and Morality* (Dobbs Ferry, NY: Transnational Publishers, 1988), p.131.
 7. Quoted in A.C. Arend and R.J. Beck, *International Law and the Use of Force: Beyond the UN Charter Paradigm* (London: Routledge, 1993), p.133.
 8. Quoted in Arend and Beck, *International Law and the Use of Force*, p.134.
 9. Rosalyn Higgins, *Problems and Process: International Law and How We Use It* (Oxford: Clarendon Press, 1994), p.255.
10. Arend and Beck (note 8), p.6.
11. These examples are cited by Marc Weller in 'Access to Victims: Reconceiving The Right To "Intervene"', in Wybo P. Heere, *International Law and The Hague's 750th Anniversary* (Leiden: A.W. Sijthoff, 1972), p.334.
12. Quoted in ibid., p.334. See also Michael Byers, *Custom, Power and the Power of Rules: International Relations and Customary International Law* (Cambridge: Cambridge University Press, 1999), p.184.
13. This definition from the 1969 Vienna convention on the Law and Treaties is quoted in Byers, ibid., p.183.
14. This is discussed in Francis Kofi Abiew, *The Evolution of the Doctrine and Practice of Humanitarian Intervention* (The Hague: Kluwer Law International, 1999), p.35.
15. Ibid., p.49.
16. These cases are discussed in detail in Nicholas J. Wheeler, *Saving Strangers: Humanitarian Intervention in International Society* (Oxford: Oxford University Press, 2000).
17. Higgins (note 9), p.22.
18. Hedley Bull, 'Conclusion' in Hedley Bull (ed.), *Intervention in World Politics* (Oxford: Oxford University Press, 1984), p.193.
19. Hedley Bull, 'The Grotian Conception of International Society' in Martin Wight and Herbert Butterfield (eds) *Diplomatic Investigations: Essays in the Theory of International Politics* (London: Allen and Unwin, 1966), pp.51–73.
20. Ian Brownlie, 'Thoughts on Kind-Hearted Gunmen', in Richard Lillich (ed.), *Humanitarian Intervention and the United Nations* (Charlottesville, Va.: University Press of Virginia, 1973), pp.147–8.
21. Thomas Franck and Nigel Rodley, 'After Bangladesh: The Law of Humanitarian Intervention by Force', *American Journal of International Law*, Vol.67 (1973), p.304.
22. See *Humanitarian Intervention: Legal and Political Aspects* (Danish Institute of International Affairs, 1999), p.128.

23. See Wil Verwey, 'Humanitarian Intervention in the 1990s and Beyond: an International Law Perspective' in Jan N. Pieterse (ed.), *World Orders in the Making: Humanitarian Intervention and Beyond* (London: Macmillan, 1998), p.200.
24. S/PV.3988, 24 March 1999, p.3.
25. Ibid., p.15.
26. Ibid., p.6.
27. Ibid., p.8.
28. Quoted in Adam Roberts, 'NATO's "Humanitarian War" over Kosovo', *Survival*, Vol.41, No.3 (1999), p.106.
29. See FCO text quoted in *The British Yearbook of International Law 1992* (Oxford: Clarendon Press, 1993), pp.827–8.
30. Baroness Symons of Vernham Dean, written answer to Lord Kennet, *Hansard*, 16 November, 1998, col. WA 140.
31. Robin Cook's statement is quoted in N.D. White, 'The Legality of Bombing in the Name of Humanity', paper presented at the 1999 BISA conference held at the University of Manchester, 20–2 Dec. 1999, p.7.
32. Charter of the United Nations, Article 24.
33. S/PV.3989, 26 March 1999, p.6.
34. Ibid., p.5.
35. Ibid., p.3.
36. Ibid., p.7.
37. Ibid., p.7.
38. White (note 31), p.6.
39. S/PV.3989, 26 March, 1999, p.9.
40. Ibid., p.9.
41. Ibid., p.7.
42. Ibid., p.4.
43. Ibid., p.16
44. White (note 31), pp.10–11.
45. Ibid., p.14.
46. See *Saving Strangers* (note 16), Chapters 2, 3 and 4.
47. Brown (note 3), pp.11–12.
48. Hedley Bull, *Justice in International Relations* (Hagey Lectures, University of Waterloo, 1983), p.14.
49. Bull (note 18), p.195.
50. Henry Shue, 'Let Whatever is Smouldering Erupt? Conditional Sovereignty, Reviewable Intervention and Rwanda 1994' in Albert J. Paolini, Anthony P. Jarvis and Christian Reus-Smit, *Between Sovereignty and Global Governance: the United Nations, the State and Civil Society* (London: Macmillan, 1998), p.77.
51. Byers (note 12), p.159.

# 8
# The Kosovo Refugee Crisis: NATO's Humanitarianism versus Human Rights

## JIM WHITMAN

The NATO intervention in Kosovo has been hailed in some quarters as a 'victory'; as principled action in defence of human rights; and as a triumphant defence of the rights of refugees. The argument of this essay is that the unprecedented response to the Kosovo refugee crisis was animated less by human rights principles than by a concern to contain the refugees within the region and to maintain political support for the military campaign against Serbia. NATO humanitarianism was an emergency response to an unanticipated refugee crisis of historic proportions, in which the rights of the refugees themselves and the larger issue of human rights in Kosovo did not interfere with the strategic and political concerns of Western European states. The outcome of this functional separation of humanitarianism and human rights is driving post-war Kosovo toward a mono-ethnic composition; is likely to have undermined the international protection regime for refugees; and has reconfigured rather than reduced ethnic tension in the Balkans region. I will argue that the prospect for the rights of refugees generally and for the peoples of the Balkans in particular has only been worsened by the NATO intervention.

### THE RIGHTS OF REFUGEES

A refugee is legally defined as a person who, 'owing to a well-founded fear of being persecuted for reasons of race, religion, nationality, or membership of a particular social group or political opinion, is outside the country of his nationality and is unable or, owing to such fear, is unwilling to avail himself of the protection of that country'.[1] The scale and complexity of population flight in the last decade has blurred nearly all of the clear distinctions in this field, not least in terms of the international provision of physical protection and the defence of human rights. In some cases, the only thing to distinguish the plight of refugees from the internally displaced is that the former have crossed an international border. However, while operational adaptation[2] and legal debate[3] continue apace, they do so on a foundation of established international law.

The legal rights of refugees are grounded in International Humanitarian Law (IHL), the core of which is the Geneva Conventions of 1949. Article Three of the Conventions, which is common to each of its four protocols, prohibits violence to life and person; the taking of hostages; deportations; outrages upon personal dignity; and non-judicial killing – the principal immediate causes of nearly all politically-driven refugee crises. The Fourth Protocol of the Conventions pertains not to the minimum standards of treatment for combatants and prisoners of war but to the protection of civilians. In addition, the Second Protocol pertains to every individual or category of persons not actively involved in hostilities, including civilians. The Conventions are entirely applicable to non-international armed conflicts, a point reinforced in 1977 by two additional protocols to the Conventions, the second of which deals specifically with non-international armed conflicts.

International Humanitarian Law is *jus in bello* – law in war – while Human Rights Law concerns itself with the integrity and well-being of persons at all times and in all places. Although the compass of internationally recognised human rights extends considerably beyond International Humanitarian Law, many of the provisions of IHL also find expression as negative human rights ('freedom from...') in the three documents which comprise the International Bill of Human Rights, namely, the Universal Declaration of Human Rights; the International Covenant on Economic, Social and Cultural Rights; and the International Covenant on Civil and Political Rights. Since human rights are inalienable, they apply fully to all refugees, in every instance. In addition, the Preamble to the 1951 Convention on the status of refugees provides for 'the widest possible exercise' of the fundamental rights in the UN Charter and the Universal Declaration of Human Rights. The two principal sources of international refugee law are the 1951 United Nations Convention on the status of refugees and the 1967 Protocol relating to the status of refugees. The Convention was adopted one year after the creation of UNHCR. The principal function of the High Commissioner – the protection of refugees – has remained unchanged, although the nature and scale of the current global refugee crisis[4] is all the more sobering when set against the remit of the UNHCR Statute, which was to deal with events before 1951 – essentially, the European aftermath of World War II.

Along with the surge in refugee numbers since that time, thinking about the purposes of the refugee definition established in 1951 has also evolved. According to Daniel Steinbock, the definition has three related purposes: protection against serious harm inflicted for reasons of personal status ('the persecution of difference'); protection from measures based upon the attribution of collective guilt; and the privileging of individual belief and expression.[5] In practical terms, these find expression in the essential rights of refugees: the legal obligation of states of first asylum to grant entry; *non-refoulement* (the prohibition against the forced return of refugees to a country where they are likely to face persecution); and the obligation of asylum states to provide some measure of practical support for refugees beyond the mere fact of asylum.

Since the start of the 1990s, 'humanitarian assistance' and 'humanitarian intervention' have gained considerable public resonance at the cost of conceptual and even legal precision. Although the subjects of these quite varied initiatives are frequently refugees, it should be remembered that when lawful action is taken in respect of people in flight, humanitarianism is not charity but the fulfilment of legal obligation; and the end is not humanitarianism as such, but the protection and/or restoration of human rights. The humanitarianism of emergency provision for refugees does not supplant the legal obligations of states as outlined above, any more than it ensures the human rights of refugees themselves.

However, the enactment and enforcement of international law takes place in the political realm. In the absence of a calculation of considerable political interests, the historical record strongly suggests that powerful states or coalitions will rarely act to redress gross violations of human rights or the refugee crises they routinely engender. This holds true before a refugee crisis takes place; it shapes the nature and the duration of those actions undertaken; and it largely determines the aftermath. In any particular case, the extent to which the protection and/or restoration of human rights is an objective for intervening states, rather than a constituting or immediate cause, will be a function of broader, but closely linked, political considerations. Concern for the human rights of the Kurds, for example, has hardly been a constant for the international community that intervened on their behalf less than a decade ago.

In addition to the highly conditional responsiveness of the international community to humanitarian disasters, there are also operational limitations which largely keep the human rights aspects of refugee emergencies within a crisis frame. Since the protection of refugees takes place in a 'humanitarian space' and not a living polity, emergency humanitarianism cannot address the enactment of human rights, but only the consequences of their abuse. Viewed in human rights rather than political terms, the repatriation of refugees and the return of the displaced are therefore the culmination only of crises, not the socio-political conditions that drive them.

These general conditions apply in full to the case of Kosovo, yet the nature and speed of the refugee crisis and the uniquely well-resourced and timely response have largely supplanted them as the essential context. Removed from the larger political circumstances of this case, we are left with a narrative of principled response to brutal repression, a triumph of humanitarianism and the spontaneous repatriation of some 700,000 refugees under the protection of a UN-mandated, NATO-led force.[6] Although the abstraction of operational matters from political context is essential for some purposes, the dangers of recounting the 'bare facts' of so considerable a crisis are that the scale and poignancy of the flight of Kosovar Albanians are distanced from the political interests and actions of NATO; that the issue of human rights – present and future – can all too easily be obscured by the extraordinary demands and outcomes of emergency humanitarianism; and, what follows from this, that the human rights situation in Kosovo can come to be seen as identical with the condition of the Kosovar Albanians.

## KOSOVAR ALBANIAN REFUGEES, ASYLUM AND 'FORTRESS EUROPE' PRIOR TO THE NATO INTERVENTION

In March 1997, only two years before the Kosovo refugee crisis, the Italian government had declared a state of emergency over the influx of Albanians trying to flee their own country. Under hastily legislated emergency powers, Italy set about forcibly repatriating Albanians 'deemed to be a danger to public security'.[7] In the same week, official concern in Germany over the number of asylum seekers there was expressed by the German Interior Minister as 'our boat is practically full.' A more alarming prospect – the EU directly bordering the former Yugoslavia – was raised by the arrangements for Austria to join the Schengen Agreement in October. The Chairman of the home affairs committee in the lower house of the German parliament reflected: 'All the Bosnians come here via Austria. The Albanians would come the same way. If Austria joins Schengen, that means we have no external border with Austria. It has to ensure that its southern and eastern borders hold, and that's not easy for Austria. The EU countries have no interest in porous borders.'[8]

Only six months before the start of the NATO bombing campaign, in August 1998, a mini-summit convened by the Austrian Interior Minister and attended by four of his European counterparts met to discuss a feared mass influx of Kosovar Albanians into their countries. German Interior Minister Manfred Kanther is reported to have been quite blunt: 'We do not want any more refugees from Kosovo – on no account,' asserting that Germany's refugee burden was already 'unbearable'.[9] The containment of potential refugees in their 'home regions' was not merely a possible option, but the logical extension of practices then under way, in response to the continuing human consequences of the dissolution of Yugoslavia and, more immediately, the worsening human rights situation in Kosovo.

The extent of human rights abuses and the generation of refugee flight from Kosovo throughout the 1990s is richly documented from a variety of sources.[10] In addition, the province sustained very high numbers of internally displaced persons (IDPs). Unlike refugees, IDPs do not have legal status, although non-binding Guiding Principles were established in 1998.[11] However, by that time, the legal rights even of Kosovo refugees in Western Europe were hardly assured. Germany signed a readmission agreement with Yugoslavia in 1996, clearing the way for the deportation of some 170,000 Kosovar Albanians. By the time the agreement was suspended (because of an EU ban on Yugoslav Airline flights), some 12,000 had already been deported. According to the European Council on Refugees and Exiles, in the first six months of 1998, only five per cent of Kosovars in Germany were afforded some form of protection. Elsewhere in Western Europe, the numbers were considerably lower, but the pattern was similar. For example, in the same year, Sweden deported 500 Kosovar Albanians to 'safe third countries' (in conformity with the Dublin Convention); and Austria announced that it 'would not provide temporary protected status and assistance to Kosovar Albanians, as had been granted to Bosnians, because they did not have the willingness to integrate'.[12]

By 1998, violence in Kosovo had become generalised and characterised by gross violations of human rights and humanitarian law, including murder, torture, destruction, looting and forced expulsion.[13] According to the Organization for Security and Cooperation in Europe (OSCE), the fighting between Serbian forces and the Kosovar Albanian militia, the *Ushtria Clirimtare e Kosoves* (UCK) had resulted in the internal displacement of 350,000 people in 1998 alone. This figure is believed to have been as high as 500,000 before the October 1998 agreement for the Kosovo Verification Mission (KVM) and temporary diminution of hostilities. In addition, an estimated 100,000 Kosovar

Albanians had already moved elsewhere in the region and a further 100,000 had sought asylum. The number of asylum applicants to Western Europe from the former Yugoslavia had risen 200 per cent between 1997 and 1998.

Against this background, the considerable diplomatic and political attention afforded to the deteriorating situation in Kosovo is hardly surprising. Yet behind the professed concern for the rights of Kosovar Albanians, the mini-summit of Western European Interior Ministers was able to agree that there would be no cessation in the forcible return of Kosovar Albanian asylum applicants and that no temporary stay would be granted to Kosovar Albanians.[14] In previous years, a number of initiatives had been tried and new concepts introduced in Western Europe to stem or control refugee flows. These included the introduction of 'safe areas' within a persecuting state; the concept of 'temporary protection'; the concept of a single state assuming responsibility for asylum applications;[15] and the harmonisation of visa policies.[16]

The containment of the crisis in Albania in 1997 is of a piece with these policy orientations, as was the Austrian government's 1998 offer of 5 million Austrian shillings in assistance to countries bordering Kosovo and its call for 'compensatory solidarity' from other EU states.[17]

Less than one year after the Austrian summit, on the eve of NATO's ultimatum to Yugoslavia, the European intergovernmental consultative group on asylum held one of its routine meetings. According to one commentator, the tone was 'defensive-alarmist':

> Europe had already absorbed hundreds of thousands of refugees from the previous wars in the former Yugoslavia; it could take no more. Italy – a principal destination for previous large outflows from Albania – called on UNHCR to erect a 'first line of defence' to keep Kosovo Albanians in the region, and the Italian delegation spoke of 'humanitarian containment'.[18]

There were two issues facing Western leaders and NATO planners as they contemplated a bombing campaign against Yugoslavia on behalf of the rights of Kosovar Albanians. The first is that the largest part of the violence was politically controlled and directed – something implicit both in the negotiations for the KVM and the Rambouillet discussions. In a province already occupied and terrorised, the political efficacy of a bombing campaign would need to be remarkably swift for the Kosovar Albanians not to be further imperilled. The second is that the possibility of a refugee disaster was made all the more likely by the many thousands of IDPs already dispersed throughout the province. However much faith the politicians and planners had in the notion that swift political ends could be achieved by air power, their calculations were made against two imponderables: the deployment of ground troops; and the accommodation of further Kosovar Albanian refugees in Western Europe.

## NATO INTERVENTION AND THE REFUGEE CRISIS

In terms of human rights and the political dynamics driving displacement and flight, this was a war conducted over the heads of the principal antagonists. The OSCE reported that 'summary and arbitrary killing became a generalised phenomenon throughout Kosovo with the beginning of the NATO air campaign against the federal republic of Yugoslavia on the night of 24–5 March'.[19] Yugoslavia did not capitulate immediately, and 'by March 1999, the Yugoslav military/security forces were coping with two tasks: defeating the UCK and preparing for an attack by NATO'.[20] This entailed an intensification of the destructive and repressive measures already well-recorded. Could this not have been foreseen? NATO's 'overwhelming humanitarian necessity' did not entail the dispatch of ground troops to protect innocent civilians; indeed, as the UK Ministry of Defence has made plain, the choice of means had a predictable cost. In the words of George Robertson, UK Secretary of State for Defence at the time and now Secretary-General of NATO:

> We intervened to disrupt and degrade the military machine causing the violence with the aim of bringing their [Yugoslavia's] operations to an end and preventing a humanitarian crisis. We were of course aware that violence was likely to continue until the Serbian operations could be halted.[21]

Earlier, in October 1999, Robertson had written: 'We were conscious that military action might be seized upon by Milosevic as an excuse to accelerate the offensive already under way. But while we had anticipated that the offensive could involve operations against the KLA and violent repression of the civilian population, we could not have predicted the full horror and extent of the brutality.'[22] But this should have been more than a confident prediction of consistently brutal behaviour, and certainly more than an 'excuse': NATO was now at war with Yugoslavia, with the largest part of the Kosovar population effectively caught between them – ideal conditions for the generation of a refugee disaster.

Even once the expulsions and abuses of human rights accelerated to crisis proportions, ground troops were never a serious political possibility. As a senior NATO officer remarked, 'We said from the outset that we couldn't prevent atrocities and crimes against humanity with just an air campaign. But knowing that we had to keep an alliance of 19 nations together, we knew that if we asked for ground troops, we would be asking the impossible.'[23] Clive Nettleton's observation, 'If there is going to be oppression, then you had better be near a border',[24] was never more poignant. While NATO and Yugoslavia conducted a contest of political resolve, a greatly exacerbated human rights and humanitarian catastrophe ensued, with no remission for those Kosovar Albanians unable or prevented from fleeing.

Directing NATO's war effort were officers well-versed in Clausewitz, familiar with his dictum that 'the political object, as the original motive of the War, will be the standard for determining both the aim of the military force and also the amount of effort to be made'.[25] Yet, discounting the political rhetoric which accompanied the start of the bombing, it was not until 12 April that NATO's objectives were set out in a statement issued after an Extraordinary Meeting of the North Atlantic Council.[26] By that date, some 450,000 refugees had already entered Montenegro, Albania and Macedonia.[27] One can therefore see something more considerable than casual cynicism in the remark of one NATO ambassador: 'Even if we were winning the war militarily, we would have lost the war at home if Milosevic had not started the expulsions and let us win the propaganda war.'[28] On that understanding, it seems, humanitarianism became the acceptable face of the larger war.

The combination of the scale and speed of the outflow of Kosovo Albanians into Albania, Macedonia and Montenegro was a formidable humanitarian challenge, with only the Rwanda genocide in 1994 and the Kurdish flight from Iraq in 1991 of comparable proportions. Within nine weeks of the start of the NATO bombing, some 800,000 people had fled or been expelled from Kosovo. Others put this figure as high as half of the country's two million inhabitants. On some estimates, the combination of refugees and internally displaced persons comprised more than 90 per cent of the population of Kosovo.

For NATO, the political challenge of the refugee crisis was no less daunting than the practical one. First was the matter of maintaining domestic support for the bombing campaign and the importance of being seen to be dealing with a dramatic humanitarian crisis, whose victims were NATO's intended beneficiaries. This became all the more important for NATO credibility when Yugoslavia did not capitulate quickly and the refugee flows made the question of whether ground troops should be deployed a matter of open debate. Second was the necessity of minimising refugee flows into Western Europe. Third was preventing the unexpectedly large numbers of refugees from interfering with NATO military preparedness, which had included the stationing of troops in

Albania and Macedonia. Considerable NATO resources were devoted directly to the refugee crisis in these two countries, including the construction and servicing of refugee camps in Macedonia and the dispatch of a NATO force to Albania, AFOR, with an humanitarian mandate.[29]

NATO priorities were further strengthened by its larger member states in individual and, at times, all-but-competitive initiatives. The practical participation from state and non-state actors alike, and the levels of funding made available – by August, some 2 billion dollars pledged from 60 nations and a vast array of organisations – were in many ways as extraordinary as the situation which prompted them. The measure of this is not merely that resources exceeded immediate needs, but that, for example, the 50-million-dollar expenditure on a single US Army/OFDA site, which housed a maximum of 3,500 refugees, could have funded nearly the whole of the UN's consolidated appeal for Angola.[30]

## THE REFUGEE CRISIS: 'TOO IMPORTANT TO BE LEFT TO UNHCR'?

The blurring of strategic and humanitarian boundaries – that is, the role of NATO interests as well as NATO personnel and expertise in the crisis response – meant that 'the displacement issue became an important element in the diplomacy of the war [and that for] many governments, the refugees were too important to be left exclusively to UNHCR'.[31] The overwhelming pace of the crisis in its first days brought criticism of UNHCR preparedness which, under the pressure of events, quickly established a pattern of bilateral funding and operations, marginalising the agency still further. UNHCR received only 3.5 per cent of the funds donated by the six largest EU donors; and only 20 per cent of some 250 agencies registered with UNHCR as operating partners.

Operational demands and politcal/institutional strictures frequently place UNHCR in an impossible position, one made painfully obvious by the pace and political weight of events in Kosovo. Because UNHCR must appeal to individual states to fund new emergency situations, it is subject to the political priorities of the donors. Indirectly, this frequently takes the form of 'earmarking' funds, but on clashes of principle, UNHCR has little more room to manoeuvre, since its protests to donor states concerning forced repatriations or the standards of refugee conditions can be met with threats to terminate funding. The result, as Gil Loescher recounts, is that 'in the 1990s, the United States and West European governments have continued to override UNHCR protests and disregard widespread criticism of their forcible repatriation of thousands of Hatians and Albanians'.[32]

Managerial considerations aside, UNHCR was no more surprised by events than was any other agency or any of the concerned governments. This is not only because refugee disasters on the Kosovo scale are historically rare, but also because it was thought that in the event of a serious escalation of hostilities, the Yugoslav army would seal off the Macedonian/Albanian border. The independent evaluation of UNHCR's performance noted that 'the UNHCR Special Envoy for former Yugoslavia, who from mid-1998 also covered Albania, emphasised this factor in his analysis, concluding that an escalating conflict most likely would produce more massacres and IDPs – about which UNHCR could do little – but only a few thousand refugees'.[33]

More immediately, UNHCR was quickly faced with the problem of cooperating with NATO which was a party to the conflict (acting without the authorisation of the UN Security Council) and whose interests were at least as much strategic and political as humanitarian. With the commencement of the bombing campaign, NATO was party to a war on behalf of the oppressed Kosovar Albanians and their massed flight from Kosovo was therefore politically and morally charged; and once a public debate about the deployment of NATO ground forces began, the efficient handling of refugee flows became all the more important. The UNHCR Statute stipulates that the 'work of the High Commissioner shall be of an entirely non-political character'. However, the demands and dilemmas of complex emergencies and the increasing resort to 'ethnic cleansing' as an instrument of war; donor pressures; the failure of other actors to directly and consistently engage political problems; and the perceived need for 'enterprising humanitarianism' and overseeing relief operations (despite the risks of politicisation) have served to drive a wedge between the agency's statutory purposes and the operational demands in particular cases, particularly those with a high international profile.[34]

When some 65,000 refugees attempted to enter Macedonia at the Blace crossing, UNHCR's insistence on the obligation of first asylum states met with the Macedonian counter-argument that the international community had a political responsibility for the crisis. As unprotected refugees massed in muddy fields and the situation became a focus of international media attention, Macedonia did not have to spell out a detailed argument for NATO assistance with camp-building and the transfer of refugees to third countries. On 3 April, UNHCR formally requested NATO assistance, although NATO preparations were already well under way. The refugees were cleared almost as quickly as the political impasse that had trapped them; and a 40 million dollar World Bank credit was extended to Macedonia to deal with the impact of refugees on its economy. The dilemma for UNHCR was being forced to choose between acceding to not wholly voluntary extra-regional evacuations to third countries[35] and principle – the obligations of first asylum states and *non-refoulement* – in a situation in which Macedonian intransigence, the powerful political interests of NATO states and the urgent plight of the refugees themselves combined to work against their enactment. Much as when previously faced with assisting the flight of those threatened with 'ethnic cleansing' in Bosnia, UNHCR found itself having to make choices from a short menu of dilemmas – practical, institutional and moral. Inevitably, its critics could accuse it of being either dogmatic or ineffective. In the previous year, the High Commissioner had declined an invitation from the NATO Secretary-General for joint contingency planning, emphasising the need for coordination rather than cooperation, in line with UNHCR's humanitarian, as distinct from political remit. As it happened, NATO's political embarrassment and its considerable means would almost certainly have overridden any UNHCR protest.

What remains uncertain is to what extent the Kosovo experience might jeopardise UNHCR's capacity to respond in the future, in both extreme cases of refugee flows and in those politically less significant to the larger donor states. As the independent report on UNHCR's effectiveness noted,

> As a result of [a NATO victory], adverse effects that typically follow from a blurring of the military-humanitarian distinction were limited. A longer and more inconclusive war might have produced the anticipated problems, however, by encouraging stronger 'refugee-warrior' communities in the border areas, and by further weakening the distinction between humanitarian action and the pursuit of war. In both cases, the UNHCR's status and related effectiveness as a non-political, humanitarian agency would have been eroded.[36]

After the Blace incident, the refugee crisis continued more as a matter of sheer numbers than as a political and practical challenge to humanitarian response. NATO and national contingents previously stationed in Albania and FYR Macedonia undertook humanitarian work; Italian, Greek, US, French, Spanish and Austrian forces all undertook tasks ranging from the construction of camps to logistical and other support. However, circumstance, luck and opportunism all played a part in preventing further crisis eruptions. At least two-thirds of the refugee population lived with host families or in private accommodation in Albania, some as beneficiaries of generosity; others were obliged to pay. The promised food distribution and financial assistance did not reach them by the end of June, in contrast to the priority accorded to the refugee camps, some of which were fitted and staffed to unprecedented levels.[37]

But while the world's attention was fixed on emergency humanitarianism and on the war, the plight of the displaced inside Kosovo dramatically worsened. In terms of human suffering and human rights, the plight of the internally displaced was no less critical than that of the refugees; and once the bombing commenced, they were at much greater risk from the Serbian military. There is documentation of a full range of human rights atrocities committed by Serbian forces during that period, including massacres and the deportation of Kosovo Albanians to Serbia.[38] It could be argued that by the start of 1999, the inertia of events in Kosovo was such that the international community was faced with a choice between watching the further progress of brutal repression or forcibly putting a stop to it, while minimising the human costs. On this reading, the subsequent refugee disaster serves to validate NATO's decision to act, while the relatively efficient and phenomenally well-funded response stand as a testament to principle – to human rights in general and the protection of refugees in particular.

However, against the background of a political determination to halt the influx of Kosovar Albanians into Western Europe, the humanitarianism engendered by the refugee crisis had a very practical edge – indeed, strategic necessity operated at two levels: the refugee crisis needed to be dealt with swiftly in order to progress the war; and it had to be contained, as part of the larger European effort to deal with asylum and migration numbers A political settlement conducive to the enactment and enforcement of human rights in Kosovo – and supported to the degree that both the war and the refugee crisis had been – was never likely. Once the June peace agreement was signed, the repatriation of refugees and the return of the displaced was remarkably swift: by September 1999, more than 750,000 Kosovo Albanians had returned to their homes. The way seemed open for the humanitarianism necessitated by war to find expression in the restoration of human rights in Kosovo. But although humanitarianism on a scale but rarely seen in contemporary affairs was apparently triumphant, it had been impelled and shaped by concerns that held scant regard for the human rights situation in Kosovo.

## KOSOVO SINCE JUNE 1999: REFUGEES RETURN/REFUGEES FLEE

The largest number of the refugees returned to Kosovo, spontaneously and unsupervised, within weeks of the peace agreement, despite the uncertain security situation in the country, and the lack of a well-established international support system.[39] However, this voluntary repatriation was less a conclusion to the Kosovo refugee crisis than the transition to another chapter of suffering visited by one Kosovar ethnic community upon another. With the departure of the Yugoslav military, the Serbian, Roma, Muslim, Turkish and other minorities suddenly found themselves at the mercy of the majority Albanian population. The OSCE report on Kosovo covering the immediate post-war period, June–October 1999 is stark and grim:

> One discernible leitmotif emerges from this report. Revenge. Throughout the regions, the desire for revenge has created a climate in which the vast majority of human rights violations have taken place. ...With this climate of vindictiveness a third category of victims emerged: those individuals or groups who were persecuted simply because they had not been seen to suffer before ... not only have communities been driven from their homes, but also the climate is not conducive to returns. As a result, the spiral of violence has driven a wedge between Kosovo's communities, making ever more elusive the international community's envisioned goal of ethnic co-existence.[40]

The return of Kosovar Albanian refugees sparked another refugee outflow. The arrival of KFOR troops from June 1999 has not prevented the exodus of non-Albanian Kosovars, two-thirds of whom (approximately 200,000) are estimated to have fled, mainly to Serbia. The fears of minorities in Kosovo are founded on a catalogue of murder, abduction, intimidation, property destruction and forced migration. Although the precise role of the UCK is unclear, it is plain that a culture of violence and revenge is widespread even among the civilian population. The August 1999 Human Rights Watch report noted that the response of KFOR and UNMIK to abuses against minority populations had been 'belated and uneven.'[41]

Constructing a civil administration in such circumstances requires dedicated planning, considerable resources and truly concerted effort to establish and nurture a culture of human rights[42] – a difficult enough task in the aftermath of UN peace enforcement, let alone after a war conducted by high-altitude bombing. At the start, the UN Administrator for Kosovo, Bernard Kouchner, requested 6,000 policemen, but had only 1,800 at his disposal; and by February 2000, still short of 2,750 officers for essential protection duties, he was forced to tell the world that the UN had no money to pay civil servants in Kosovo.[43] Central to the establishment and maintenance of human rights is the establishment of the rule of law, yet a pattern seen time and again, most notably in

Cambodia, is being played out once more in Kosovo: the majority of those arrested by peacekeeping troops are released because there are no courts to prosecute them. These and a host of other inadequacies indicate a lack of prior planning and, what is more important, the low priority given to the quality of the peace. The larger picture is visible in a single, pitiful example:

> UNHCR/OSCE have worked with KFOR to identify individuals or communities which require increased physical protection. In some areas KFOR has deployed a 24-hour presence. In addition, UNHCR has explored with KFOR creative methods of increasing the security and confidence of isolated, vulnerable persons, such as funding a KFOR programme to repair and reinforce the doors of minority homes in Pristina.[44]

One compares the levels of funding and political urgency which drove the war, with the conditions which prevail for post-war Kosovo and is forced to ask whether human rights in Kosovo matter to those in a position to establish and protect them. If human rights there truly mattered, what kinds of initiatives could we expect to see? Consider the unexpected and potentially catastrophic refugee crisis of March 1999 and the alacrity and coherence of the response: if the subsequent political vacuum in Kosovo has merely wrong-footed us – as the refugee crisis did – where is the equivalent dedication to 'winning the peace'? On the other hand, Kosovo has been 'stabilised': although it remains a province of Yugoslavia, it has effectively been separated from Serbia[45] – a condition which its present political turmoil and pervasive abuse of human rights do not threaten. None of the NATO states would say that this is a sufficient political outcome of the war, yet do their actions and omissions in the post-war period suggest anything different?

The current socio-political condition of Kosovo and the faltering efforts of NATO states to address human rights there are not the outcome of a concern for human rights which has lost its political impetus, but of an emergency humanitarianism in which the efforts on behalf of Kosovar Albanian refugees were functionally separate from the viability of human rights in Kosovo, and the Balkans more generally. This kind of detached emergency humanitarianism is hardly new, as our belated and partial efforts in Rwanda and elsewhere make plain. What makes the Kosovo case so worrying is the persistence of Balkans volatility in combination with a hardening of official attitudes toward asylum seekers in Europe and a clear willingness on the part of NATO states to override international law in the interests of perceived national or regional security. With the continuance of minority persecution in Kosovo and the uncertain but ominous trajectory of Balkan politics, another humanitarian disaster remains a clear possibility. But the aftermath of the Kosovo intervention has also opened up an uncertain future for refugee rights as overseen and enacted by UNHCR, as well as the larger legal foundation of an international order which sustains refugee rights and human rights more generally. These are now considered in order.

## HUMANITARIAN DISASTERS: WARNINGS FROM KOSOVO

First, it is plain that the refugee crisis in the Balkans has been rearranged but not addressed. The UN High Commissioner for Refugees visited Kosovo in September 1998 and noted afterwards that 'Kosovo is a political problem, with devastating humanitarian consequences, for which there is only a political solution'. Yet the June 1999 peace agreement between NATO and Serbia is a cessation of hostilities, not a political settlement on which a human rights regime can be established. None would dispute that a force-based order is unlikely to create the conditions for a culture of human rights; nor does it appear remotely likely that one will emerge in the near future. On what diagnosis of the political problem in or 'of' Kosovo could the present situation be said to have provided a solution? It is clear that an international force of 50,000 soldiers will struggle to prevent the level of inter-communal violence which is driving Kosovo toward a mono-ethnic composition, let alone establish the conditions for the enactment of human rights; but what evidence is there that this is a matter of importance commensurate with the bombing of Yugoslavia?

Regionally, tensions have been heightened and total numbers of refugees have not been reduced below pre-war levels:

> UNHCR estimates that ethnic Serbs and Roma newly displaced from Kosovo number 23,500 in Montenegro, and 176,000 in Serbia proper, including 3,257 former refugees from Croatia and Bosnia. This adds to the half million refugees from previous conflicts already in Serbia. Also, the approximately 100,000 ethnic Albanians residing in Serbia proper are reportedly subjected to increasing pressure: at least 4,500 have already fled to Macedonia.[46]

Considered in the narrowest terms of European interest, it is far from plain that the NATO intervention was successful. Despite the scale of voluntary repatriation, Yugoslav asylum applications increased by 60 per cent even as the war was being conducted. And as the flag of humanitarianism flew over the refugee camps, the walls of 'Fortress Europe' were being heightened: 'On August 11, Switzerland, the European country that has taken in most Kosovar refugees, announced that it would repatriate those remaining on its territory.'[47]

Second, the sidelining of UNHCR damages its capacity, both institutionally and operationally. If in the Kosovo case, 'the refugees became too important to leave to UNHCR', this was in part because UNHCR is hard-pressed to honour its statute while responding as it would like – and much of the world expects – to complex emergencies which present it with a daunting range of practical problems and difficult choices, both at field and managerial levels. Critics and donors combine to drive a downward spiral of funding shortages and inconsistent performance – particularly for cases which fail to capture political interests or popular support. Spending on refugees in the Balkans is eleven times greater than for refugees in Africa.[48]

More worryingly, UNHCR's participation in the evacuation of refugees from Kosovo, under circumstances it could neither control nor adequately respond to, poses challenges to UNHCR for the place of protection as part of responding to the larger global refugee crisis while dealing with a variety of pressures, including humanitarian action as a substitute for political engagement:

> Protection seems to be fading rapidly from the refugee agenda. UNHCR's embrace of 'humanitarian action' and the willing endorsement of this move by many states, has compromised the agency's mandate responsibility: it is no longer identified primarily as a protection agency, but primarily as an assistance provider. The identity of the refugee is at yet greater risk of being lost in 'situations' and the new pragmatism, which view the refugee no longer as a woman, man or child in need of protection, but rather as a unit of flight, a unit of displacement, to be contained and thereafter channelled down whatever humanitarian corridor leads to whatever political end.[49]

The fractured and violent Balkans order, the relative prosperity of Western Europe and the political effort now behind containing refugee flight are likely to combine to further marginalise the protection of refugees and the donor-driven capacity of UNHCR to respond in accordance with its mandate.

Third, the violation of international law and the undermining of the United Nations in its primary role of maintaining international peace and security will weaken the law-based order on which human rights depend. The bombing of Yugoslavia was a violation of international law and

NATO's subsequent declaration of its willingness to act in similar fashion should it see fit is deeply troubling, particularly since humanitarian cause can be found for almost any military incursion willed for more directly self-interested purposes. In such cases, human rights can be subsumed within professed humanitarianism and, as we have seen in Kosovo, 'collateral damage' can be extended from the innocent victims of bombing to the unprotected displaced. And if Article 2.4 of the UN Charter can be freely ignored by NATO on a declaration of humanitarian intent, it is open to other states to do likewise as occasion and interests permit. This is not only a profound challenge to the foundation of international order, but also to human rights norms more generally, which are premised on law-based order between as well as within states.

In defence of the NATO bombing, US Deputy Secretary of State Strobe Talbot asserted: 'We must be careful not to subordinate NATO to any other international body or compromise the integrity of its command structure. We will try to act in concert with other organisations, and with respect for their principles and purposes. But the Alliance must reserve the right and the freedom to act when its members, by consensus, deem it necessary.'[50] In view of Western Europe's continuing anxieties about asylum seekers and illegal migrants, Talbot's 'trying to act in concert' should be read as extending not only to UNHCR, but also to the rights of refugees. In other words, in future, adherence to the strictures of international law, including refugee rights, will be conditional. It is highly unlikely that the declaration of 'overwhelming humanitarian necessity' for action undertaken in the name of beleaguered populations or for refugees will take precedence over strategic necessity conceived at a European level.

## CONCLUSION

Beyond Kosovo, the legal, institutional, operational and regional implications of the war, its conduct and aftermath bode ill for human rights and humanitarian action alike. As new interethnic tensions take shape, the region's larger political dynamics have been further agitated by the NATO intervention in Kosovo. Montenegro's support of NATO throughout the war has greatly exacerbated its already tense relations with Serbia. Although the United States has publicly urged the government of Montenegro not to rush into a referendum on independence from Serbia, it has been encouraging its political reforms and greatly increased its aid to the country. While Serbia still endures sanctions, compounded by extensive war damage and further political isolation, every positive reinforcement to Montenegro places further pressure on the regime of President Milosevic. And although the policy of the United States is cautious, the CIA Director recently remarked that 'a showdown will be hard to avoid',[51] while the US Secretary of State has openly called for Milosevic to be removed from power.

Can Western political ends and means be so fashioned as to avoid – and not merely contain – the kind of refugee crisis that could easily be engendered by a 'Balkans endgame'? If another refugee disaster is thought to be the unfortunate but unavoidable price of 'resolving' the larger crisis in the Balkans, we will witness another functional separation of humanitarianism and human rights. And if the outcome mirrors post-intervention Kosovo, a country in which violations of human rights did not cease, but merely changed polarities, the region would then be configured for another generation of systemic abuses of human rights – and an endless stream of refugees.

### NOTES

1. Convention Relating to the Status of Refugees, 28 July 1951.
2. Thomas G. Weiss and Amir Pasic, 'Reinventing UNHCR: Enterprising Humanitarians in the Former Yugoslavia, 1991–1995', *Global Governance*, No.3 (1997), pp.41-57.
3. Patricia Tuitt, 'Rethinking the Refugee Concept', in Frances Nicholson and Patrick Twomey (eds), *Refugee Rights and Realities: Evolving International Concepts and Regimes* (Cambridge: Cambridge University Press, 1999), pp.106–18.
4. UNHCR, *The State of the World's Refugees: A Humanitarian Agenda* (Oxford: Oxford University Press, 1997).
5. Daniel J. Steinbock, 'The Refugee Definition as Law: Issues of Interpretation', in Nicholson and Twomey (note 3), p.20.
6. For example, see Lord Robertson, *Kosovo: An Account of the Crisis* (London: UK Ministry of Defence, 2000).
7. Helena Smith, 'Italy declares emergency over Albanian Refugees', *The Guardian*, 20 Mar. 1997.
8. Ian Traynor, 'Germany's "boat is full"', *The Guardian*, 20 Mar. 1997.
9. '"Mini-Summit" of Five Interior Ministers in Austria: Containing Refugee Influxes', FECL [Fortress Europe Circular Letter], No.55 (August 1998), http://www.fecl.org/circular/5504.htm
10. See UNHCR, 'Background Paper on Refugees and Asylum Seekers from Kosovo' (Geneva: Centre for Documentation and Research, February 1996), http://www.unhcr.ch/refworld/country/cdr/cdrkos.htm; US Department of State, 'Serbia-Montenegro Country Report on Human Rights Practices for 1998' (Washington, DC: Bureau of Democracy, Human Rights and Labour), http://www.state.gov/www/global/human_rights/1998_hrp_report/
11. 'Guiding Principles on Internal Displacement', report on United Nations Commission on Human Rights, 54th Session, 16 Mar.– 24 Apr. 1998, http://www.hri.ca/unifo/unhcr98/annex1.shtml
12. Cited in US Committee for Refugees, 'USCR Special Report: Europe: Reluctant Host to Kosovar Refugees' (Sep. 1998), http://www.refugees.org/news/crisis/Kosovo_e.htm
13. OSCE, *Kosovo/Kosova: As Seen, As Told* (Part III, Chapter 4: 'Introduction: The Violation of Human Rights in Kosovo', and following sections), http://www.osce.org/kosovo/reports/hr/part1/ch4.htm
14. FECL (note 9).

15. See UNHCR, 'EU Common Strategy on Asylum Must Meet Highest Standards of Refugee Protection' (Geneva, 8 Oct. 1999). In the press release, UNHCR also stresses that 'temporary protection must be seen as a complement to, not a substitute for, the protection provided under the 1951 Convention', http://www.unhcr.ch/news/pr/pr991008a.htm

16. Listed in Tord Björk, 'EU Strategy Paper on Asylum and Immigration: Show of "Political Muscle"?' Fortress Europe Circular Letter (9 May 1999), http://www.gsoa.ch/kosovo_nato/199905/19990509.0.html

17. FECL (note 9).

18. Astri Suhrke, Michael Barutciski, Peta Sandison and Rick Garlock, 'The Kosovo Refugee Crisis: An Independent Evaluation of UNHCR's Emergency Preparedness and Response', (EPAU/2000/001, February 2000), http://www.unhcr.ch

19. Cited in Robert Skidelsky, 'NATO's Deadly Legacy from Kosovo', *Financial Times*, 15 Dec. 1999.

20. OSCE (note 13), Part II, Chapter 3: 'The military/security context', http://www.osce.org/kosovo/reports/hr/part 1/ch3.htm

21. Lord Robertson (note 6), p.17.

22. Mark Littman, *Kosovo: Law and Diplomacy* (London: Centre for Policy Studies, 1999), p.17.

23. Cited in *The Observer*, 4 Apr. 1999.

24. Quoted in David Keen, *Refugees: Rationing the Right to Life* (London: Zed Books, 1992), p.30.

25. Carl von Clausewitz, *On War* (London: Penguin Books, 1968), p.109.

26. http://www.nato.int/kosovo/history.htm

27. Author estimate based on Suhrke et al. (note 18), Table 1: 'Cumulative refugee population in Montenegro, Albania and FYR Macedonia, 23 Mar.–9 June 1999', p.117.

28. Ibid., p.14, note 7.

29. The AFOR Mission report is available at http://www.afsouth.nato.int/operations/harbour/

30. Toby Porter, 'Coordination in the Midst of Chaos: the Refugee Crisis in Albania', *Forced Migration Review* No.5, p.4. http://www.fmreview.org/fmro57.htm

31. Suhrke et al. (note 18), p.vi.

32. Gil Loescher, *Beyond Charity: International Cooperation and the Global Refugee Crisis* (Oxford: Oxford University Press, 1993), pp.137–8.

33. Suhrke *et al.*, p.17.

34. See S.Alex Cuncliffe and Michael Pugh, 'UNHCR as Leader in Humanitarian Assistance: A Triumph of Politics Over Law?' and Erin D. Mooney, 'In-Country Protection: Out of Bounds for UNHCR?'in Nicholson and Twomey (note 3), pp.175–99; and 200–19 respectively; Thomas G. Weiss and Amir Pasic (note 2).

35. Amnesty International, 'Former Yugoslav Republic of Macedonia: The Protection of Kosovo Albanian Refugees', Report EUR 65/03/99, May,1999. http://www.amnesty.org/ailib/aipub/EUR/46500399.htm; see also Suhrke et al. (note 18), pp.89–108.

36. Suhrke et al. (note 18), p.115.

37. Ibid., pp.66–7; Toby Porter (note 30), p.4.

38. See Human Rights Watch, 'Kosovo: Focus on Refugees', http://www.hrw.org/hrw/campaigns/kosovo98/flash7.shtml

39. UNHCR, 'UNHCR Begins Organized Repatriation of Kosovar Refugees', UNHCR Press Release, 28 June 1999, http://www.unhcr.ch/news/pr/pr990628.htm; the International Organization for Migration's assisted return to Kosovo statistical update is available at http://www.iom.int/kosovo/iom_activities/Skopje/movements.../mov.ht_break_23_3_2000

40. http://www.osce.org/kosovo/reports/hr/prt2/03-execsum.htm

41. Human Rights Watch, 'Abuses Against Serbs and Roma in the New Kosovo', Vol.11, No.10 (Aug. 1999), http://www.hrw.org/reports/1999/kosov2; see also Mark Lawrence and Annalies Borrel, 'Joint WFP/UNHCR Food Needs Assessment of Minorities in Kosovo, November–December 1999', 5 Feb. 2000.

42. Jarat Chopra, *Peace-Maintenance: The Evolution of International Political Authority* (London: Routledge, 1999).
43. 'UN Raises Alarm After Money Runs Out for Kosovo', Agence France-Presse, 3 Feb. 2000.
44. UNHCR/OSCE, 'Second Assessment of the Situation of Ethnic Minorities in Kosovo' (6 Sep. 1999), <http://www.osce.org/ko[sovo/reports/minorities.htm>
45. 'The NATO Secretary-General, Lord Robertson, warned the Serbian government yesterday to stay out of Kosovo, saying NATO stay in the province as long as was necessary.' 'Kosovo is out of bounds, NATO warns Belgrade', *The Guardian*, 19 Feb. 2000.
46. US Committee for Refugees, 'USCR Special report: Crisis in Kosovo' (7 Sep. 1999), <http://www.refugees.org/news/crisis/kosovo_u090799.htm>
47. Ibid.
48. Matthew J. Gibney, 'Kosovo and beyond: popular and unpopular refugees', *Forced Migration Review* No.5 (Aug. 1999), http://www.fmreview.org/fmr0510.htm
49. Guy S. Goodwin-Gill, 'Refugee Identity and Protection's Fading Prospect', in Nicholson and Twomey (note 3), p.246.
50. Quoted in Bruno Simma, 'NATO's Future "Strategic Concept": From "Out of Area" to "Out of Treaty"?' http://www.ejil.org/journal/Vol10/No1/abl-3.html
51. 'Albright reiterates US support for Montenegro', AFP, 3 Feb. 2000; David Storey, 'Montenegro, citing Serb threat, seeks US aid', Reuters, 2 Feb. 2000; 'US boosts aid to Montenegro as anti-Milosevic drive acelerates', AFP, 31 Jan. 2000.

# 9

# International Humanitarian Law and the Kosovo Crisis

## HILAIRE McCOUBREY

The 1999 Kosovo crisis raises a number of issues of fundamental importance for the development of international law into the twenty-first century. Not unnaturally, attention has largely been focused upon issues of peace enforcement and the working of the UN Security Council in combination with regional arrangements such as NATO,[1] together with the highly controversial issue of the scope, if any, of 'humanitarian intervention' as an exception to article 2(4) of the UN Charter. These questions are explored in other contributions to this collection, but the crisis also raised important questions for international humanitarian law which have received rather less attention, other than in the propagandist claims which are an inevitable, if dangerous, part of the rhetoric of conflict. It must be stressed from the outset that these comments are focused strictly upon international humanitarian law and the lawfulness or otherwise of the tactical conduct of operations rather than upon the lawfulness, or otherwise, of the use of armed force in the resolution of the crisis as such.

Questions arise in this context in relation both to the NATO action and to that of the Serbian forces and the KLA. In relation to the conduct of the Serbian armed forces and the KLA the first and most sensitive question is that of the status of the situation. It was *prima facie* at most a non-international armed conflict occurring within a Serbian province with a dissident majority population. The real question arises, of course, from this latter point. The KLA claims to be in some sense a national liberation army, whereas Serbia denounces them as terrorists and criminals. From the one point of view the situation in Kosovo would have amounted to a non-international, or even an 'internationalised' national liberation, armed conflict governed at some level by the humanitarian laws of armed conflict, while from the other viewpoint it would have been simply a matter of domestic policing and counter-terrorism. Important legal and practical consequences follow from the view taken upon this matter, although it should be emphasised that the practices of community persecution and 'ethnic cleansing' would be unlawful in any event from a general human rights viewpoint.

So far as NATO is concerned, from the *jus in bello* perspective, as from that of the *jus ad bellum*, the major questions arise in relation to the initial air strikes prior to the settlement brokered by President Ahtisaari of Finland and Prime Minister Chernomyrdin of Russia and the deployment of KFOR. Before these questions can usefully be addressed, however, some comment is required upon the general context of the air operations. The air strikes were determined upon after the collapse of the Rambouillet talks. The reason for the collapse of those negotiations is not central to the present analysis, although the issue remains controversial in the context of the *jus ad bellum* and the requirements of the UN Charter. For the present purpose suffice it to say that the NATO position is essentially that the talks collapsed in the face of Serbian refusal to accept external monitoring of the proposed settlement within Kosovo. On behalf of the Belgrade regime it can also be argued that the NATO demand for virtually free movement through the territory of Serbia-Montenegro, which considers itself still, with technical rectitude, to be the Socialist Federal Republic of Yugoslavia,[2] was something which no sovereign state would willingly have accepted. This is undoubtedly true, although it may also be pointed out that, with some appalling exceptions, most other sovereign states have not adopted quasi-genocidal policies of 'ethnic cleansing' in their territories and the absolute concept of sovereignty that such an argument implies is at best outdated. The central issue here is perhaps whether NATO moved precipitately to action in the light of anticipated Russian blockage of any resolution for robust action in the Security Council[3] without considering other possible and more explicitly lawful options. These might have included an attempt to use the 'Uniting for Peace' procedure in the General Assembly, although doubt may be expressed both as to whether a Uniting for Peace resolution can actually authorise use of armed force and, if it could, whether such a resolution could have been adopted within a useful time scale. Another, and perhaps more realistic, option might have been to proceed through the OSCE[4] in a manner which might have anticipated the ultimate settlement brokered by President Ahtisaari and Prime Minister Chernomyrdin.

Be that as it may, the intention of the air strikes was to end the Serbian harassment and 'ethnic cleansing' of the Kosovar Albanians and to force the Serbian government to accept a viable and verifiable settlement in the province. From the beginning there were reasonable doubts about the tactical appropriateness of the air-strike method selected. The harassment and 'ethnic cleansing' was conducted by a combination of the Serbian regular armed forces, the Ministry of the Interior Police and various 'irregular' militias with varying levels of government control and approval. Some of these elements were no doubt vulnerable to air attack, for example through bombing of headquarters buildings, military equipment and the units themselves. Others, and probably most, of them were much less vulnerable to this kind of attack. This was particularly the case for many of the irregular Serbian units operating on the ground in Kosovo and doing so, by definition, in the midst of the Kosovar Albanian population who were supposedly to be protected by the NATO action. The central point is that air power is not generally considered a suitable *sole* means of conducting 'police' enforcement operations. This is not to suggest that air power has no role in such operations; it is rather to make the obvious point that effective policing and/or enforcement ultimately demands a ground commitment with, no doubt, significant air support. The decision to rely solely upon air power in the initial NATO action in the Kosovo crisis seems to have been made upon political rather than military grounds. The leading NATO powers were reluctant to commit ground forces in a combat role because of potential domestic sensitivities, summarised by the somewhat unfairly termed 'CNN factor' – that is to say the traumatic domestic impact of the sight of one's 'own' casualties returning on television news programmes. The point was made manifest at the 1999 Royal British Legion[5] Festival of Remembrance when it was stated that the Kosovo air strikes had been carried out 'without casualties', even though this was hardly the case in Serbia. The same consideration seems to have underpinned the decision to limit the operations to high altitude bombardment. It should in this context be said that neither military logic nor international humanitarian law demands that a commander should do anything other than minimise the risk of casualties in conducting operations. The requirements are rather, respectively, that combat methods should maximise efficacy and be such as to be capable of conduct within the framework of basic legal norms. In both the respects the NATO air strikes raised potentially significant questions.

## HUMANITARIAN NORMS AND THE KLA-SERBIAN CONFLICT

The status of the conflict between the Serbian state and the KLA raises more complex legal questions than might at first be thought and, as in most such situations, the fundamental problem was that of criteria of application. The humanitarian provision for non-international armed conflicts is found at a rather basic level in Common Article 3 of the four 1949 Geneva Conventions, with significant elaboration offered by 1977 Protocol II Additional thereto. The former has customary status whereas the latter as yet does not, although, like 1977 Additional Protocol I, to some degree it merely refines and affirms principles already at least implicit in the earlier provision.[6] Common Article 3 itself refers simply to application, 'in the case of armed conflict not of an international character occurring in the territory of one of the High Contracting Parties'.

For the present purpose this serves to define the question rather than to provide an answer. In contrast with the application of humanitarian provisions in international armed conflicts, a simple criterion founded upon the factual occurrence of hostilities will not suffice, since not only a higher but also a lower threshold of application must be determined. Thus, a confrontation between the police and armed bank robbers may involve literal hostilities but hardly amounts to a 'non-international armed conflict' for the purposes of international humanitarian law,[7] but just where the dividing line lies is much less clear. In this respect 1977 Additional Protocol II affords useful guidance. It provides by article 1(1) that the Protocol does not '[modify] existing conditions of application' and then goes on to specify application in conflicts which are non-international in character and

> take place in the territory of a High Contracting Party between its armed forces and dissident armed forces or other organized armed groups which, under responsible command, exercise such control over a part of the territory as to enable them to carry out sustained and concerted military operations and to implement this Protocol.

It may be remarked in parenthesis that the former Socialist Federal Republic of Yugoslavia was party to both 1977 Additional Protocols, its only reservation relating to non-acquiescence in hostile occupation of Yugoslav territory. Since Serbia-Montenegro claims to be not a successor state to the Federal Republic but to be the legitimate remnant of that state,[8] it may be considered to be precluded from denying that in relevant circumstances it would be bound by the two Protocols.[9]

This said, it is by no means clear that the KLA satisfied the criteria set out in Protocol II, article 1(1). Like many such movements the KLA had, and has, many dimensions, ranging from genuine liberation fighters through terrorists to outright gangsters. There is clearly a structure of hierarchical command and even internal discipline, but there was no effective control of territory and still less any capacity or even evident willingness to apply 1977 Additional Protocol II or even Common Article 3 in such 'operations' as were carried out. It may be added that this impression is strongly reinforced by the KLA's own practice of 'ethnic cleansing', despite the best efforts of KFOR, after the 'liberation' of the territory.

The lower limit of applicability is defined by 1977 Article Protocol II, article 1(2), which provides that 'This Protocol shall not apply to situations of internal disturbances and tensions, such as riots, isolated and sporadic acts of violence and other acts of a similar nature, as not being armed conflicts.' It may reasonably be suggested that the activities of the KLA in Kosovo may have reached beyond this threshold while still not satisfying the essential requirements of article 1(1). That being the case, it would seem that the situation in Kosovo prior to the NATO intervention was not for this purpose a non-international armed conflict to which *jus in bello* norms strictly applied. There remains, however, the further question of the possible impact of claims to national self-determination.

The idea of national self-determination has a considerable pedigree and indeed is to some degree coterminous with the 'modern' concept of the nation-state. Elements of it may be found in the sixteenth-century revolt of the Spanish Netherlands through to the early nineteenth-century Greek War of Independence and the Italian *Risorgimento*. It took on a doctrinal shape, however, only after the First World War when, as a political rather than a legal construct, it was used by the victorious Allies as the conceptual foundations for the dissolution of the Austro-Hungarian and Ottoman empires. This process may, paradoxically, be regarded as the modern source of a number of late twentieth-century security crises, including both the 1990–91 Gulf Conflict and the successive conflicts associated with the dissolution of former Yugoslavia. A legal form was taken on after the Second World War with express recognition in the Preamble to the United Nations Charter. In the UN era it has been moulded almost exclusively by the process of decolonisation, and this has ultimately had a very restrictive impact upon its development. Specifically, in an endeavour to avoid initiating a dangerously destabilising re-division of territories, the UN shaped and limited the process of decolonisation through the *uti possidetis* principle, that is to say, in effect, a concept of liberation within existing colonial boundaries. In areas, like much of sub-Saharan Africa, in which these boundaries were themselves colonial impositions with little relevance to local political structures and traditions, the problem of instability has perhaps been postponed and perpetuated rather than faced in a model which in some cases amounted to little more than a localisation of colonial structures. This in all probability will be one of the serious problems of international law bequeathed by the twentieth to the twenty-first century. More generally, the restrictive twentieth-century UN approach to self-determination confined the concept to the colonial context, curiously in light of the fact that its first modern use, in the post-1918 re-ordering of Europe and the Middle East, was not set in such a context, at least not in that of 'colonialism' as it has been more recently defined. In this sense Kosovo was not a 'colonial' territory, nor was it one which had recently had boundaries outside the Yugoslav state, or specifically, within that state, an existence as a federal entity outside Serbia. This situation illustrates one of the major issues which the international community will have to face in the first half of the twenty-first century. With decolonisation virtually complete, the unsatisfactory condition in which many peoples have been left, both in post-colonial states and, for example in the case of the Kosovar Albanians and the Kurds, in non-colonial territories, is likely to become an increasingly urgent issue from both a security and a human rights viewpoint. In present circumstances, while the Kosovar Albanians might seek either independence or the restoration of the quasi-autonomy which they had enjoyed prior to 1989 as political claims, it is unlikely that they could claim a legal right of national self-determination. It is thus by no means clear that they could be regarded as waging a 'war of national liberation' in their armed resistance to the Belgrade regime. The point is important in the present context since it rules out any claim that the disturbances in Kosovo might have been an 'internationalised' armed conflict within the meaning of article 1(4) of 1977 Additional Protocol I.

If the crisis in Kosovo was not an armed conflict governed by the *jus in bello*, that still did not mean that the brutalities perpetrated against the population were therefore, as Serbia claimed, purely an 'internal' matter. The issue of fundamental human rights violations still arose, as did the questions of 'humanitarian intervention' and, it may be suggested, that of the genuine threat to the peace and security of the sub-region posed by both the refugee crisis and the effects on neighbouring powers, including Albania and the Former Yugoslav Republic of Macedonia (FYROM) and, potentially in the longer term, Greece and even Turkey. This has indeed been suggested elsewhere to have offered a more sound legal and political basis for military intervention in the crisis than some of those that were actually sought to be relied upon.[10]

## HUMANITARIAN NORMS AND THE NATO AIR CAMPAIGN

The NATO air campaign raised rather different questions. The legality or otherwise of the action in itself is a separate issue from that of the application of international humanitarian norms. International humanitarian law is equally applicable to all parties to an armed conflict, irrespective of the causes or balances of rectitude and delict to be found in its origins. The point is important and a means of averting the gross evils of former 'just war' concepts, which Jean Pictet has termed 'the well known and malignant doctrine of the "just war" which ... [was used] to justify the cruelties which abounded in that sanguinary age ... [so that the] worst acts were never crimes, but well deserved penalties ... inflicted on the guilty.'[11]

It may be added in this regard that the revival of 'just war' rhetoric by some of the NATO political leaders was, from this point of view, one of the most disturbing aspects of the Kosovo crisis. Initially, the question again arises of the status of the conflict and the rules applicable. Whatever claims are made in relation to the peace support or enforcement quality of the initial NATO action it manifestly involved the conduct of international hostilities between forces of the NATO Alliance and those of Serbia-Montenegro, or for the present purpose more accurately, those of Serbia. The hostilities were therefore *prima facie* an international armed conflict to which norms of international humanitarian law fully applied, in accordance, *inter alia*, with Article 2 common to the four 1949 Geneva Conventions which refers to application in 'all cases of declared war or any other [international] armed conflict'. It must then be asked whether actual or claimed international peace support or enforcement actions differ from other combat operations in this regard.

This is a somewhat problematic issue so far as 'Blue Helmet' forces, such as UNPROFOR, are concerned.[12] The essential problem is clearly stated by Roberts and Guelff in their comment that

> the United Nations itself is not a party to any international agreements on the laws of war. Moreover, these agreements do not expressly provide for the application of the laws of war to UN forces. However, it is widely held that the laws of war remain directly relevant to such forces.[13]

The present, rather unsatisfactory, situation is defined by an exchange of letters between U Thant and the International Committee of the Red Cross in the 1960s, in which the Secretary-General stated that 'UNO [the United Nations Organisation] insists on its armed forces in the field applying the principles of the 1949 Geneva Conventions as scrupulously as possible'.[14]

The specific reference to the 1949 Geneva Conventions arose, of course, from the particular nature of the exchanges between the UN and the ICRC, but the principle enunciated by U Thant may, however, be taken to apply the norms of the *jus in bello* in general. Ambiguities nonetheless remain. In 1995, in the course of UNPROFOR operations in Bosnia-Hercegovina, some UN military personnel were 'captured' by Bosnian Serb fighters and the question of their entitlement to prisoner-of-war status under 1949 Geneva Convention III in these circumstances arose. The ICRC advised that they were not technically 'prisoners of war' but were entitled nonetheless to equivalent protection while detained.[15] There would obviously be difficulties in envisioning a condition of armed conflict with the United Nations, but the problems of definition and application nonetheless remain. A number of solutions have been advanced, including the 1971 Zagreb Resolution of the Institute of International Law on Conditions of Application of Humanitarian Rules of Armed Conflict to Hostilities in which United Nations Force May be Engaged, and remains at the time of writing an issue under discussion within the UN. Whatever the outcome of these discussions may be, it is clear that other multinational forces engaged in 'enforcement' operations under UN mandate are bound by the norms of international humanitarian law since, whatever their mandate, they are deployed in combat as national forces. This would be even more pointedly the case for forces operating upon more ambiguous legal bases, as in the instance of the initial Kosovo operations carried out by NATO. There was, for example, never any question that international humanitarian law applied to the Coalition in the 1990–91 Gulf Conflict and that captured Iraqi military personnel were entitled to prisoner-of-war status.[16] It may thus be taken that international humanitarian norms applied similarly to the NATO air campaign in 1999.

International humanitarian law is now used as a term embracing the whole of the *jus in bello* rather than merely that part of it associated with the Geneva Conventions and Protocols. Traditionally the *jus in bello* was seen as being divided into 'Hague' and 'Geneva' sectors, named for the respective principal treaty series. The Hague sector was that governing methods and means of warfare, while the Geneva sector made provision for the protection of victims of armed conflict, defined as the wounded, sick and/or shipwrecked, prisoners of war and civilians.[17] There was always a significant degree of overlap between these sectors, not least since both were and are underpinned by a humanitarian imperative for the mitigation of the conduct and effects of hostilities. In relation to the present focus of concern upon aerial bombardment, this was always self-evidently the case since restriction upon targeting is *ex hypothesi* founded upon concern for the potential victims. Since the Second World War, the 'Geneva' provision has been codified in the four 1949 Geneva Conventions supplemented by the two 1977 Additional Protocols.

The Hague sector as it now exists comprises a more diverse body of treaties, of which the oldest of any great significance is the 1868 Declaration of St. Petersburg – an armaments control measure banning small-calibre explosive projectiles. It was followed by the numerous Declarations and Conventions agreed at the 1899 and 1907 Hague Peace Conferences and so on up to and including the Protocols to the UN Conventional Weapons Conventions dealing with laser weapons and landmines agreed in the 1990s. Again, however, the overlap should be emphasised; important provision for the protection of victims of armed conflict, for example in relation to occupied territories, is still found in the Land Warfare Regulations annexed to 1907 Hague Convention IV and, by the same token, the most important modern provisions in relation to targeting and bombardment are found in 1977 Additional Protocol I to the 1949 Geneva Conventions. A significant part of the substance of this law has attained the status of customary international law. This includes the substantive body of the four 1949 Geneva Conventions themselves, the Land Warfare Regulations annexed to 1907 Hague Convention IV, the 1868 Declaration of St. Petersburg, 1907 Hague Convention IV, the 1925 Geneva Gas Protocol and other well-established treaties. Other humanitarian *jus in bello* treaties which have not, or not yet, attained customary status are more problematic, and this is especially the case in the present instance for 1977 Protocol I Additional to the 1949 Geneva Conventions. The Protocol is strictly applicable only as between powers which are each party to it, unlike the 1949 Conventions which, having customary status, are now binding upon all states. The division is not, however, quite so clear cut as this might seem to suggest, since significant elements of the Additional Protocol in some of its most important provisions re-affirm and refine pre-existing basic principles.[18] It may thus fairly be said that the military operations in the Kosovo crisis were governed at a minimum by the established customary norms of international humanitarian law, including those elements of further provision such as 1977 Additional Protocol I which restate existing principles. In its specific references to civilian protection in bombardment, it may strongly be argued that the Protocol is in this way essentially affirmatory rather than innovatory, and it will be so taken in this discussion.

The substantive questions arising from the NATO air operations in the area of international humanitarian law must be treated with some concern in the light of its political and doctrinal context. In some areas, including significant sections of the 'liberal' media, there was a possibly inevitable anti-NATO reaction which eagerly sought and, to their own satisfaction, found illegality in every aspect of the campaign and its conduct. It is not the purpose of this analysis to join or lend support to this predictable chorus, but nor is it possible or acceptable to ignore the fact that a number of serious humanitarian questions did arise from the conduct of the NATO air campaign. The questions are in their nature interlinked but a few broad areas may be separated out for purposes of exposition.

The primary issue was that of targeting – in particular whether the bombardment was adequately discriminatory as between 'military' and 'civilian' targets and indeed whether high-altitude bombardment of this type could in fact be so. Related to this are the questions of target selection – whether television stations, in view of their propagandist role, be considered legitimate targets – and of accidents, in particular the implications of the bombing of the Chinese embassy in Belgrade, if, indeed, this was an accident. The overarching question of political direction of operations and the impact of perhaps undue sensitivities to media 'spin' then arise as serious issues. This concern has potentially serious implications both for the initiation of peace enforcement and other military operations into the twenty-first century and the application of humanitarian norms in any such operations.

## SUBSTANTIVE APPLICATION TO THE NATO CAMPAIGN

If a single fundamental purpose is sought in international humanitarian law it may be found in one of the oldest treaties in this area still in effect, the 1868 Declaration of St. Petersburg which, in its Preamble, states that 'the only legitimate object which States should endeavour to accomplish during war is to weaken the military forces of the enemy'. This was stated in the context of a specific armaments ban,[19] but has come to be recognised as a general norm proscribing the infliction of 'unnecessary suffering'. Both the protection of victims of armed conflict and the restriction of methods and means of warfare are essentially encapsulated in this basic principle. In the present context the 'unnecessary suffering' principle is, in particular, the foundation of rules upon targeting. Restrictions upon legitimate targeting have a considerable pedigree. The Land Warfare Regulations annexed to 1907 Hague Convention IV contains a number of provisions to this effect, some of which have been rather overtaken by subsequent development.[20] However, the requirement of article 27 remains foundational, namely that, in bombardments,

> All necessary steps must be taken to spare, so far as possible, buildings dedicated to religion, art, science, or charitable purposes, historic monuments, hospitals, and places where the sick and wounded are collected, provided they are not being used at the time for military purposes.

Much of its content is also found in both earlier and later humanitarian treaty provisions. Article 25 further forbids the bombardment of settlements, buildings and dwellings that are 'undefended'. Apart from the specific protection of, for example, medical facilities set out presently in 1949 Geneva Conventions I and II, the principle has developed into a restriction of legitimate bombardment to 'military' targets. The 1923 Hague Draft Rules on Aerial Warfare never entered formally into force but were still accepted at the time as a summary of the applicable customary principle and usefully defined the principle in relation to aerial bombardment. They provided by article 24(1) that 'Aerial bombardment is legitimate only when directed at a military objective, that is to say, an object of which the destruction or injury would constitute a distinct military advantage to the belligerent'.

Terror bombardment of civilian populations was expressly forbidden by Article 22. Such bombardment was common practice on the part of both the Axis and the Allies during the Second World War and it is noteworthy that Luftwaffe *blitzkrieg* tactics did not feature in the Nuremberg indictment, largely through fears of the politically damaging effect of a possible *tu quoque* response. The modern position is most effectively summarised by Articles 48 and 51 of 1977 Additional Protocol I to the 1940 Geneva Conventions. Article 48 provides that

> In order to ensure respect for and protection of the civilian population and civilian objects, the Parties to the conflict shall at all times distinguish between the civilian population and combatants and between civilian objects and military objectives and accordingly shall direct their operations only against military objectives.

Article 51 provides that

> (2) The civilian population as such, as well as individual civilians, shall not be the object of attack. Acts or threats of violence the primary purpose of which is to spread terror among the civilian population are prohibited. ...
>
> (4) Indiscriminate attacks are prohibited. Indiscriminate attacks are,
>
> (a) those which are not directed at a specific military objective;
>
> (b) those which employ a method or means of combat which cannot be directed at a specific military objective: or
>
> (c) those which employ a method pr means of combat the effects of which cannot be limited as required by this Protocol.

'Military objectives' are defined by article 52(2) as 'objects which by their nature, location, purpose or use make an effective contribution to military action and whose total or partial destruction, capture or neutralisation, in the circumstances ruling at the time, offers a definite military advantage'.

It will be noted that for this purpose a military objective is not simply a unit or equipment of the armed forces but an object which is substantively contributing or directly relevant to military operations. It is this basic test which must be borne in mind in considering the incidents of the NATO air campaign. The stated immediate aim of the campaign, namely to strike at and disable the Serb units engaged in repression and 'ethnic cleansing' in Kosovo, was perfectly in accordance with the prescription of 'legitimate objects' set out in the Preamble to the 1868 Declaration of St. Petersburg. The problem from the viewpoint of international humanitarian law arises not in the declared objects of the campaign but in the methods by which it was carried out.

*Ex post facto* analyses of the impact of the air campaign have, predictably, varied across a wide spectrum, from official NATO claims of very high levels of accuracy and efficacy to the official Serbian assertion of virtual indiscrimination and slight military effect. The probability is that the campaign was neither so excellently conducted as NATO claims nor so badly performed as Serbia alleges. It is clear that Serbia successfully practised deceptive ruses, for example by attracting NATO attacks to mock armoured units and even roads but also that real damage was inflicted upon the Serbian military and police infrastructure. The real questions for the present purpose arise, however, from certain illustrative specific incidents. Among these the bombing of a bridge with civilian transport upon it, the bombing of a television station and the destruction of the Chinese Embassy in Belgrade were perhaps the most prominent.

The first type of incident is not suggested to have involved a deliberate unlawful attack upon civilians; the situation was rather one of the tragically coincidental presence of civilians upon a target object. A vital communications link may well be a legitimate military objective and the question of civilian casualties in this case is not actually one of targeting but of the proper limits of 'collateral damage'. This rather ugly piece of jargon, which came to prominence, although it did not originate, in the 1990–91 Gulf Conflict, means the accidental infliction of civilian injury or damage in the course of legitimate attack. In such contexts a difficult calculation of military advantage as against possible 'collateral' injury is required. The principle is summarised by the provision of article 57 of 1977 Additional Protocol I to the 1949 Geneva Conventions that:

> (2)(a)  those who plan or decide upon an attack shall, ...
> (iii)  refrain from deciding to launch any attack which may be expected

> to cause incidental loss of life, injury to civilians, damage to civilian objects, or a combination thereof, which would be excessive in relation to the concrete and direct military advantage anticipated.
>
> (b)  an attack shall be cancelled or suspended if it becomes apparent that ... the attack may be expected to cause incidental loss of civilian life, injury to civilians, damage to civilian objects, or a combination thereof, which would be excessive in relation to the concrete and direct military advantage anticipated.

The decision-making process required is self-evidently one of great ethical and practical difficulty and especially so when the pressure of the circumstances under which it will generally be required to operate is considered. The difficulty is exacerbated by the short time-scale of decision-making in the use of modern rapid-reaction weaponry. The point was made painfully obvious by the *Vincennes* incident during the 1980–88 Gulf Conflict. USS *Vincennes* was engaged in protecting American tanker traffic in the Gulf and had been under attack by Iranian Revolutionary Guard units when an aircraft was observed approaching from the Iranian coast. Missiles automatically locked on to the aircraft and the commander was faced with the decision of whether to permit firing to proceed or manually to terminate the firing process. He decided that the aircraft constituted a threat to his ship, the aircraft was shot down and proved to have been an Iranian civil airliner. At the subsequent Court Martial, which found against the commander, substantial criticisms were made of the running of the *Vincennes*, but the difficulties of the required decision-making were nonetheless pointedly illustrated. Had the aircraft not been attacked and proved in fact to be hostile, the commander's position would have been legally no better and practically much worse. In air warfare the time available for decision-making is if anything even less than would generally be the case at sea.

In relation to the Kosovo incident under consideration, the NATO position is essentially that when the civilian vehicle moved onto the bridge as the pilot moved in to attack, there was insufficient time for reconsideration. Much has been made of the fact that the film footage used to demonstrate this point had been speeded up in the normal course of computer analysis and appeared at a subsequent news conference at least at double speed.[21] This, however, is rather beside the point. The attack upon the bridge was in itself entirely legitimate; the presence of the civilian vehicle was a tragic accident and to this the split-second timing of an air attack materially contributed. This appears to have been a case of a tragic but, perhaps, inevitable military accident – a true case of 'collateral injury'.

It was also alleged that on the night of 14–15 May 1999 some 100 Kosovar Albanian refugees were killed in a NATO air raid.[22] This may have been a case of accidental injury, but here there was a strong suspicion, upon the basis of refugee statements, that Serb units had been using Kosovar Albanians as 'human shields', that is to say that their presence was being deployed as an attempt to deflect attack.[23] If this was indeed the case, any responsibility for the resulting injury would have lain with the Serb units themselves, although the general question of the suitability of air power as a sole method of action in this context is again pointedly raised.

The attack upon the Serbian Broadcasting centre and the bombing of the Chinese Embassy raise, respectively, rather different issues. The bombing of the television centre was entirely deliberate and has never been suggested to be otherwise. There was an impression at the time that this was by definition an illegitimate attack upon a non-military objective. The situation was in fact less clear than this, bearing in mind that, as pointed out above, a military objective is one which makes a substantial contribution to military action. Granted that the state-controlled Serbian media played a significant part in sustaining and facilitating the processes of 'ethnic cleansing' in Kosovo, it might properly be seen as being as much part of the machine whose functioning the NATO action was designed to inhibit as the Ministry of the Interior Police. The assumption that this was an independent and objective news reporting and entertainment facility was, at best, naive, but at the same time its direct military relevance was at most secondary. At the present time the attack upon the TV centre must perhaps be viewed as a 'grey area', but one that raises important issues, including, indirectly, those of the possible impact of a form of 'just war' thinking – as will be discussed later.

The bombing and destruction of the Chinese Embassy in Belgrade on the night of 7 May 1999 raises yet more complex and controversial questions. The action was a diplomatic and political disaster, which rendered continued Chinese opposition to NATO or any other robust action in the UN Security Council certain and significantly weakened position of the NATO member-states as against the supporters of Serbia. Exactly how and why the Embassy came to be bombed remains obscure and at the present time, as probably for the foreseeable future, opinion must remain speculative. Entirely understandable Chinese outrage over the bombing, together with inherent antipathy to the NATO action in general, led Beijing to the view that the attack was deliberate and this has found support in some Western analyses. Among the possible bases for such a deliberate attack was the fact of Beijing's support for the Belgrade regime and the possibility that the Embassy might have been passing on useful intelligence. This latter seems highly unlikely, granted that China hardly has access to NATO plans and the conflict itself was taking place in and over Serbian-controlled territory in respect of which Belgrade hardly needed external sources of information. NATO, however, seriously exacerbated suspicions of its actions through its public response, including no less than three mutually incompatible 'explanations' which conveyed a very damaging impression of duplicity. The last of these 'explanations', that the Embassy had been bombed by mistake through use of an out-of-date map, might have been amusing in less grim circumstances. However, it raises the same questions about the quality and interpretation of military intelligence information as did the mistaken bombing of the Amirayah bunker in Baghdad during the 1990–91 Gulf Conflict.[24] A further problem may lie in the apparent belief by NATO in technological infallibility, forgetting or ignoring the fact that the performance of any equipment will be as good, or bad, as its operators and the information upon which they rely. The explanation for this may, as suggested below, lie in a media-shaped agenda which seeks to present a minimum casualty vision of military action which has little basis in reality. Whether or not this is the case, the opinion of an elderly Chinese citizen interviewed in Beijing by BBC Radio[25] in the aftermath of the bombing, that NATO, with all its advanced technology, could hardly have done such a thing by mistake, was both inevitable and understandable. This does not mean, however, that the bombing of the Embassy actually was deliberate. Indeed the entirely predictable political damage caused by the attack would render its having been mounted calculatedly an act of such folly as to be incredible. A neutral embassy, even one 'neutral' on the side of the opposing power, is doubly protected, both as a civilian objective and by diplomatic immunity, although such personnel and buildings are no more immune from genuine 'collateral' injury or damage than other civilian populations or locations. It must also be remembered that an embassy is treated as part of the sovereign territory of state whose diplomats it houses and a deliberate attack upon a neutral embassy could, as China indicated, be considered an act of aggression contrary to article 2(4) of the United Nations Charter. In principle, this could justify a military response in the face of the occurrence of an armed attack under the 'inherent' right of individual and collective self-defence preserved by Article 51 of the United Nations Charter. Such a response would have been extreme and there is no indication that Beijing actually contemplated such action in practice, but the possibility of a China-NATO, and specifically a China-United States, confrontation with incalculable potential was not wholly out of the question. All of these factors suggest that it is more probable that the bombing of the Embassy was a disastrous error rather than a policy decision bordering on insanity. Nonetheless, serious questions are raised by this incident, including, at a minimum, those of the quality and interpretation of available intelligence and the technological mindset of the Alliance. The issue of presentation is, of course, secondary but the role of the media in shaping both military and political agendas may be thought to be of rather greater importance.

## THE POLITICS OF TECHNOLOGY AND PRESENTATION

The 1999 Kosovo crisis was by no means the first armed conflict to be media-influenced. British involvement in the Crimean War owed much to the thundering of *The Times* and the Spanish-American War was in a very real sense brought about by the Hearst newspapers in the United States. The modern impact of the media upon issues of international security has been very variable in quality and effect.[26] This was, in some respects, very pointedly illustrated by events in and in relation to the Kosovo crisis. The presentation of the campaign as a 'humanitarian' intervention rather than a response to a sub-regional security crisis owed much to the desire to gain positive press coverage. The same was even more the case for what amounted to an attempt to present the possibility of a casualty-free, or at least 'own' casualty-free, conflict. This, indeed, was in large part the explanation for the original decision to attempt an entirely air-based campaign and then to restrict the operations to high-altitude bombing. In specific detail this concern manifested itself most clearly in the sometimes rather absurd 'spin-doctoring', of which the attempts to explain away the Chinese Embassy bombing referred to above were perhaps the most obvious example. This, however, was a reflection of a rather deeper problem

There has over the course of recent decades been a strong tendency in NATO, as well as in other militaries, to over-emphasise the potential and capacity of modern technologies. An implication of technological infallibility has been allowed to develop which is, by its nature, ultimately unsustainable. No technology is in fact infallible and none can be relied upon as a substitute for human judgment and responsibility – which are themselves, of course, far from infallible. Where failures either of equipment or the information upon which it is operated occur, the encouragement of such assumptions inevitably generates a presumption of calculated wrongdoing. This was so in relation to the Chinese Embassy bombing. If, as it is suggested, this action was most probably the product of gross error rather than calculation, it would have been better and much less damaging to have admitted this at the outset. In this respect at least Oliver Cromwell's plea to one of his Parliaments to consider that it might be wrong is a counsel which NATO, and the generality of national and international bodies, might also with advantage take heed of in their public explanation for events.


## IMPLICATIONS FOR THE FUTURE

Questions for the future arise from the conduct of all those involved in the various hostilities which occurred in the crisis: the Serb forces and security agencies, the KLA and NATO. So far as the Serb military and security agencies and the KLA were concerned, the issue is essentially a specific example of the general problem of humanitarian protection in non-international armed conflicts.[27] As suggested above, a case may be made out that, as the remnant of the former Socialist Federal Republic of Yugoslavia, Serbia-Montenegro is bound not only by Common Article 3 of the 1949 Geneva Conventions but also by the much more extensive provisions of 1977 Additional Protocol II. Quite clearly neither the Serb units nor the KLA observed any of these humanitarian requirements in the conduct of hostilities in Kosovo prior to the NATO intervention, or, indeed, at any time before the deployment of KFOR.[28] The issue is one of general importance. It is unwise to attempt to predict future patterns of conflict – many of the post-Vietnam presumptions of the later 1970s were swiftly displaced by the experiences of the 1982 Falklands/Malvinas Conflict, the 1980–88 Gulf War, the 1990–91 Gulf Conflict, Somalia, the African Great Lakes crisis and former-Yugoslavia itself – but the continuing and probably increasing incidence of intra-state conflict seems all too likely to be a prominent feature of the first half of the twenty-first century. The question of humanitarian protection in such conflicts is thus one which demands urgent address. Although the substance of the humanitarian provision for non-international armed conflicts is undoubtedly limited in comparison with that made for international hostilities, it clearly forbids the overwhelming proportion of the atrocities actually perpetrated in Kosovo. The problem, in short, is less one of substance than of application. Historically and at present, states have been extremely reluctant to admit that a condition of non-international armed conflict, to which either or both of Common Article 3 of the 1949 Geneva Conventions or 1977 Additional Protocol I applies, exists in their territory. This may in part result from a fear of appearing to concede the legitimacy of armed dissident groups, even though Common Article 3 itself and Article 3(1) of 1977 Additional Protocol II expressly exclude any such implication. Whatever the explanation may be, the record of humanitarian application in intra-state conflicts in the second half of the twentieth century was appalling, and the events in Kosovo were merely a further and horrifying example. The question of international response to such situations lies somewhat beyond the scope of this chapter, although it may be said that in many cases intervention may be justified on the grounds of threats posed to regional or sub-regional security, even without resort to arguments of 'humanitarian intervention'. Whether or not this is thought appropriate or actually done, the development of a permanent international criminal jurisdiction which, judging by the rate of ratification of the 1998 Rome Statute of the International Criminal Court (ICC), may reasonably be expected to become functional at some point between 2001 and 2005, may offer a means of maintenance and enforcement of humanitarian norms in this context. The jurisdiction of the ICC will, by article 3(a)(b)(c) of the Rome Statute, expressly include genocide, crimes against humanity and war crimes. There will in practice be many difficulties in establishing jurisdiction in such cases, not least where the consent to ICC proceedings of a state not party to the Rome Statute would be required by article 12(2) or where a 'sham' investigation or prosecution is carried out by a delinquent state in order to pre-empt any prosecution before the ICC. Notwithstanding these potential difficulties, it may be hoped that a more positive climate of enforcement may come to exist in the twenty-first century than was experienced through much of the second half of the twentieth century.[29] In the meantime Article 8 of the *ad hoc* International Criminal Tribunal for former-Yugoslavia (ICTY) provides that

> The territorial jurisdiction of the International Tribunal shall extend to the *territory of the former Socialist Federal Republic of Yugoslavia*, including its land surface air space and territorial waters. The temporal jurisdiction of the International Tribunal shall extend to a period *beginning on 1 January 1991*.

(The emphases are added.) Although the Kosovo crisis arose after the entry into force of the Statute of the ICTY, there is under the terms of Article 8 every reason to think that war crimes and crimes against humanity committed in or in relation to Kosovo would fall within the jurisdiction of the Tribunal. This would apply to all parties involved in the crisis, including in its later phases NATO. As further evidence of the massacres that took place in the 'ethnic cleansing' in Kosovo emerges, it is possible that ultimately the ICTY represents the last best chance of public exposure and at least a limited degree of just resolution.

So far as the NATO air campaign is concerned, most basic questions arise more in the area of the *jus ad bellum* than that of the *jus in bello*.

They include the extent to which the action was rendered inevitable once the Rambouillet talks had failed, including the question of whether the balance of the blame for that failure attaches to Belgrade or to NATO. It is reasonable to ask, for example, whether the demands for access to Serbian territory[30] might have been abandoned or moderated. It may also be enquired whether a more subtle handing of the Security Council and earlier positive engagement of Russia, possibly through the OSCE, might have brought about the result achieved by the Ahtisaari/Chernomyrdin initiative at an earlier stage with less need for, although not necessarily a total obviation of, robust military action in advance. There are nonetheless major issues concerning the application of the humanitarian *jus in bello* arising from the Kosovo crisis.

The most serious questions in regard to conduct of hostilities arise in relation to the extent to which political direction and media-shaped concerns directed not only the processes which led to the action but also the conduct of the subsequent operations. The point has been made already in relation to the choice of air power as the sole method by which hostilities would be conducted, and the same point may be made also of at least some of the tactical imperatives that were adopted. That the campaign was in general conducted with such professionalism is in itself a tribute to NATO personnel, but the question remains as to whether the methods adopted were wholly appropriate from both political and humanitarian viewpoints. It would be naive to suggest that no robust measures were necessary and even more so to suggest that an opposed ground invasion was a viable early option. The idea that action could ultimately be limited to an aerial campaign was, however, no less unreal. Two major issues emerge from this. In the first place, the decision to deploy military force and the objectives that are set in so doing are and must remain under civilian political direction. However, the means by which these tasks are to be performed should, within the limits of the objectives themselves and the imperatives of the *jus in bello*, be a matter for professional military judgment. Secondly, and at the core of the present argument, those *jus in bello* imperatives cannot lawfully, or ethically, be set aside whatever the basis or intention of a military campaign may be. In this respect the Kosovo operations flagged up certain warning signals.

Among the most significant of these were the operational implications of the arguments of 'humanitarian intervention' which were used as the basis for the action – not, as suggested above, because that was the only possibility but for reasons of presumed public perception. Although such a consequence is not inevitable, operations founded upon such principles skirt dangerously close to ideas of 'just war' with all their inhumanitarian implications. It would be a sad thing indeed if an ethical approach to international relations and security for the twenty-first century were to have the effect of reviving the malign consequences of a much misused doctrine which it was thought had been laid to rest in the carnage of 1914–18. The 1999 Kosovo crisis clearly involved atrocities upon a significant scale. The massacres of Kosovar civilians reflected a clear sense of their humanitarian disentitlement on the part of the Serb security and defence agencies, which may be related to a form of 'just war' mind set. At the same time some of the rhetoric employed by the governments of NATO member states in the course of the crisis also points a warning finger towards a danger of humanitarian regression. The claims of 'humanitarian intervention' upon which the NATO powers chose to found the action[31] seemed in some aspects of the action to revive that confusion of *jus ad bellum* and *jus in bello* norms which was the fatal defect of 'just war' theory from a humanitarian viewpoint. The vitally significant point is that although the *jus ad bellum* and the *jus in bello* are ultimately part of a holistic international response to the problems of security and warfare, they are properly treated as wholly distinct in their operation. The fact, if indeed it was so, that the NATO air strikes were intended as an act of humanitarian intervention in no way compromised the legal protection afforded to population of the territories concerned by international humanitarian law. From the NATO viewpoint, the key question here is not so much the detail of the specific incidents considered above as the choice of aerial bombardment, and specifically of high-level aerial bombardment, as a sole method of conducting hostilities.

There is, of course, no rule of the laws of armed conflict which requires an armed force engaged in hostilities to expose its personnel to unnecessary or avoidable risk for humanitarian or any other reasons. At the same time from, at latest, the conclusion of the 1868 Declaration of St. Petersburg it has been established that, in the succinct words of Article 22 of the Land Warfare Regulations annexed to 1907 Hague Convention IV, 'the right of belligerents to adopt methods and means of injuring the enemy is not unlimited'.

The most worrying aspect of the NATO air campaign from this point of view is the extent to which it was, and could have been, adequately discriminating in its target selection. Collateral injury and damage is an inevitable consequence of almost any bombardment, but the high-level bombing practised by NATO in the 1999 Kosovo crisis did little to minimise the possibility. It is clear that serious mistakes were made, which may or may not have included the politically and humanly disastrous bombing of the Chinese Embassy in Belgrade and it must now be asked whether a differently conducted campaign might have avoided some of these errors. The high-altitude bombing campaign achieved some of its objectives very successfully, but a serious question-mark hangs over the degree of discrimination in targeting which was possible and the extent to which the choice of this as a sole method of waging the campaign was appropriate. This returns the issue to the appropriate balances of political and military input in the devising of such campaigns and concern that humanitarian imperatives should not in any situation become obscured by rhetorical claims of 'humanitarian intervention'.

At the dawn of a new century it would be pleasant to think that the problems of international humanitarian law might, along with armed conflict itself, become matters of historical rather than current concern. Sadly the experience of the Kosovo crisis, on all sides, suggests that many of the old-established problems of international humanitarian law remain all too current and that others, especially as regards non-international conflicts, are manifesting themselves in somewhat varied forms. Of all the issues arising the most worrying is that of the revival of a much abused 'just war' rhetoric. In the thirteenth century St. Thomas Aquinas wrote in his *Summa Theologica*:

> It may happen that the war is declared by the legitimate authority, and for a just cause, and be rendered unlawful through a wicked intention. Hence S. Augustine says[32] the passion for inflicting harm, the cruel thirst for vengeance, an unpacific and relentless spirit ... and such like things, all these are rightly condemned in war.[33]

The cultural, political and legal context was very different from that of the dawn of the twenty-first century; just war thinking as such has at least formally been abandoned, but the implicit dangers nonetheless remain where justification is claimed for any use of force. Some of the attitudes and actions of all parties involved in the 1999 Kosovo crisis suggest that in the implementation and development of international humanitarian law in a new century, especially in connection with claims of humanitarian intervention, the caution uttered by Aquinas in the thirteenth century has a greater modern relevance than one might reasonably have hoped.

NOTES

1. NATO does not consider itself a 'regional organisation' but the UN has adopted a flexible approach to the identification of regional arrangements for this purpose and NATO is clearly willing enough to accept this role in the light of its post-Cold War reorientation. For early discussion, see H. Kelsen, 'Is the North Atlantic Treaty a

Regional Organisation?' *American Journal of International Law*, No.45 (1951), p.162; for consideration of the modern implications see H. McCoubrey and J. Morris, *Regional Peacekeeping in the Post-Cold War Era* (The Hague: Kluwer Law International, 2000), Chapter 4.

2. Undoubtedly Serbia-Montenegro is the remnant of the former Yugoslav State and is entitled to consider itself still to have that name and status. In other respects the claim is paradoxical in so far as the disintegration of the Federal Republic in most of its former territories may be argued to have originated in the policies of greater-Serbian hegemonism adopted by the Milosevic government in an effective abandonment of the carefully structured federalism of the Tito era.

3. A Russian motion in the Security Council to condemn the NATO action as unlawful was defeated 12-3, the PRC and Namibia joining in support. Those opposed included five NATO members and seven non-NATO powers.

4. The Organisation for Security and Co-operation in Europe.

5. The Royal British Legion is a veterans' association which does invaluable work in assisting and supporting the war injured and their families.

6. For discussion see C. Greenwood, 'Customary Law Status of the 1977 Additional Protocols' in A.J.M. Delissen and G.J. Tanja (eds), *Humanitarian Law of Armed Conflict: Challenges Ahead* (The Hague: Martinus Nijhoff, 1991), pp.93–114.

7. For discussion see H. McCoubrey and N.D. White, *International Organizations and Civil Wars* (Aldershot: Dartmouth, 1995), pp.19–23.

8. See note 2.

9. Legally this could be termed an estoppel.

10. See H. McCoubrey, 'Kosovo, NATO and International Law', *International Relations*, Vol.XIV (1999) pp.29–46

11. J. Pictet, *Development and Principles of International Humanitarian Law* (The Hague: Martinus Nijhoff, 1985), pp.13–14

12. For discussion see H. McCoubrey and N.D. White, *The Blue Helmets: Legal Regulation of UN Military Operations* (Aldershot: Dartmouth, 1996), Chapter 8.

13. A. Roberts and R. Guelff (eds), *Documents on the Laws of War*, 2nd ed. (Oxford: Oxford University Press, 1989), p.371.

14. See *International Review of the Red Cross*, January 1962.

15. For discussion of this see McCoubrey and White (note 12), pp.166–9.

16. For discussion see P. Rowe, 'Prisoners of War in the Gulf Area' in P. Rowe (ed.), *The Gulf War 1990–91 in International and English Law* (London: Routledge/Sweet and Maxwell, 1993), pp.188–204.

17. For analysis of the law see H. McCoubrey, *International Humanitarian Law*, 2nd ed. (Aldershot: Ashgate, 1998), also L.C. Green, *The Contemporary Law of Armed Conflict* (Manchester: Manchester University Press, 1993) and F. Kalshoven, *Constraints on the Waging of War*, 2nd ed. (Geneva: International Committee of the Red Cross, 1991).

18. For discussion see C. Greenwood (note 5).

19. The ban is upon small-calibre explosive projectiles.

20. This is, for example, to some degree the case with the Article 26 requirement of advance warning of bombardment wherever possible. This provision looks back to the siege warfare of the Franco-Prussian War rather than to the practical exigencies of modern warfare.

21. This was the subject of argument between the NATO spokesman O'Shea and a BBC presenter on the *Today* programme on 7 January 2000.

22. *The Times* (London), 16 May 1999.

23. The point is made by article 57(1) of 1977 Additional Protocol I. The issue became prominent during the 1990–81 Gulf Conflict, see C. Greenwood, 'Customary International Law and the First Geneva Protocol of 1977 in the Gulf Conflict', in P. Rowe, ed., *op.cit.*, p.63 at p.86

24. See N.D. White and H. McCoubrey, 'International Law and the Use of Force in the Gulf' (1991) *International Relations*, pp. 347-373; also F.J. Hampson, 'Means and Methods of Warfare in the Conflict in the Gulf, in Rowe (note 16), pp.88 and 96-7.

25. BBC Radio 4 *Today* programme, 9 May 1999.
26. See M. Hudson and J. Stanier, *War and the Media* (Stroud: Sutton Publishing, 1997).
27. For extended discussion see H. McCoubrey and N.D. White, *International Organisations and Civil Wars* (Aldershot: Dartmouth, 1995); also L. Moir, 'The Historical Development of the Application of Humanitarian Law in Non-International Armed Conflicts to 1949' *International and Comparative Law Quarterly* No.47 (1998), pp.337–61.
28. The humanitarian norms were not applied thereafter by the Serb forces or the KLA because the conflict had, at least in theory, come to an end.
29. For further discussion see H. McCoubrey, 'War Crimes Jurisdiction and a Permanent International Criminal Court: Advantages and Difficulties', *Journal of Armed Conflict Law*, No.3 (1998), pp.9–26.
30. The claim of Serbia-Montenegro to be the Socialist Federal Republic of Yugoslavia has been acknowledged above, but for the present purpose it is specifically access to Serbian territory which is in question.
31. Although the matter falls outside the immediate scope of this discussion, it is worth pointing out in parenthesis that the Kosovo crisis represented a threat to sub-regional peace and security, not least through the destabilising effect upon neighbouring states of an outpouring of refugees, which might have justified action more clearly within the parameters of Chapter VII of the United Nations Charter. For discussion see H. McCoubrey, 'Kosovo, NATO and International Law', *International Relations*, Vol.XIV (1999), pp. 29-46.
32. *Contra Faustem*, xxii.14.
33. *Summa Theologica* 2a3ae, 40.1, in the English Dominican Translation (New York: Benziger, 1948; London: Sheed and Ward, 5-vol. edition, 1981), Vol.III, p.1354.

# 10

# The Kosovo Indictment of the International Criminal Tribunal for Yugoslavia

## MARC WELLER

On 24 May 1999, the International Criminal Tribunal for the former Yugoslavia (ICTY) made history. It confirmed an indictment against the most senior members of the Yugoslav/Serb leadership, exactly two months after the initiation of hostilities against Yugoslavia by NATO. This action was to have a decisive impact on the prosecution of the conflict, for it signalled that a point of no return had now been crossed. It transformed NATO's use of force from an exercise in coercive diplomacy into an action which approximated an actual 'war' in a more traditional sense. As will be argued below, the Indictment effectively precluded a face-saving peace deal with the Milosevic government in which the use of force was only a minor element of diplomatic choreography. But the Tribunal not only triggered a strategic shift in the armed conflict involving Kosovo. Its confident action also added a remarkable piece to the puzzle of an emerging international constitutional order. The decision to establish the Tribunal in the first place had already significantly challenged three structural principles of the classical international legal order:

- The decision privileged international community interest over the sovereign 'rights' of the state actors involved in the conflict;
- The decision created a supranational institution with objective powers without state consent;
- The decision established a supranational institution with truly independent decision-making authority, ensuring to an extent the primacy of law over considerations of policy.

The actualisation of the powers of the Tribunal in the instance of Kosovo brought home these points with particular force. Before considering these radical changes in the international constitutional order, also against the backdrop of other recent developments, such as the adoption of the Rome Statute for an International Criminal Court, it is necessary briefly to consider the establishment of the Tribunal and contents of the Kosovo Indictment.

## THE INTERNATIONAL TRIBUNAL AND THE KOSOVO INDICTMENT

The creation of the ICTY, much like the establishment of the International Criminal Tribunal for Rwanda which followed, was triggered by extraordinary circumstances. The dramatic nature of these circumstances undoubtedly facilitated the radical and rapid response that was adopted.

### The Establishment of the Tribunal

The ICTY was established in 1993, in the wake of allegations of atrocities committed by military and paramilitary armed forces in the territory of Bosnia and Hercegovina and, previously, in Croatia. These atrocities appeared to be mainly connected with the campaign of 'ethnic cleansing' which had characterised the operations of Yugoslav (JNA/VJ) armed forces and associated Bosnian Serb paramilitary formations and also possibly Croatian militia forces operating in Bosnia and Hercegovina. It is estimated that as a result of these practices, some 250.000 mainly Muslim members of the population of Bosnia and Hercegovina were exterminated and over two million displaced.[1]

The international response to the unfolding tragedy in Bosnia and Hercegovina was hesitant. Under the leadership of the states of the European Union, a policy of non-involvement and containment had been adopted. The rest of Europe was to be isolated from the consequences of the conflict until the parties themselves had had enough of the fighting and had agreed a negotiated peace proposed by the European Union. An ineffective UN presence was maintained in the territory of Bosnia and Hercegovina, to give the illusion of international engagement, while actually serving the project of disengagement and containment. The establishment of the International Criminal Tribunal was driven by similar considerations. The lack of direct intervention to restrain the actors on the ground was to be made up by the distant threat of international accountability.

While the legal drafting body of the United Nations, the International Law Commission, had laboured in vain to establish a Permanent

International Criminal Court virtually since the judgments of Nuremberg and Tokyo had been handed down, the establishment of the Yugoslav Tribunal occurred at a comparatively breathtaking pace. When the conflict in Bosnia and Hercegovina broke out in full force in 1992, the UN Security Council quickly confirmed that all parties were bound by their obligations under international humanitarian law.[2] The Council demanded that breaches of this law had to cease immediately[3] and, when there was no compliance, it requested the UN Secretary-General to establish as a matter of urgency an impartial Commission of Experts to collect evidence of violations and to suggest remedies.[4] In response to an interim report of the Commission, the Council decided on 22 February 1993 on the rapid establishment of an international tribunal for the prosecution of persons responsible for serious violations of international humanitarian law committed in the territory of the former Yugoslavia since 1991.[5] Drawing upon proposals made by several governments and international governmental and non-governmental organisations, the UN Secretary-General's office then produced a draft statute for the Tribunal by 3 May.[6] This proposal was endorsed by the Security Council in Resolution 827 (1993) of 25 May. Contrary to early criticisms, the Tribunal established itself rapidly, compiled indictments and commenced proceedings with considerable vigour.[7]

## Substance of the Indictment

The Indictment put forward by the Chief Prosecutor of the Tribunal, Louise Arbour, on 22 May 1999[8] was directed against five of the most senior leaders of the Federal Republic of Yugoslavia and Serbia: Slobodan Milosevic, President of the Federal Republic of Yugoslavia since 1997; Milan Milutinovic, President of Serbia since 1997; Nikola Sainovic, Deputy Prime Minister of the Federal Republic of Yugoslavia since 1998; Colonel General Dragljub Ojdanic, Chief of the General Staff of the Yugoslav Armed Forces (VJ); and Vlajko Stojiljkovic, Minister of the Interior of Serbia since 1998.

The Tribunal asserted that these individuals had planned, instigated, ordered, committed or otherwise aided the campaign of violence conducted by the forces of the FRY and Serbia in Kosovo. That campaign, it was alleged, consisted of a well-planned and coordinated destruction of property owned by Kosovo Albanian civilians.[9] These civilians had also been systematically harassed, humiliated and degraded through physical and verbal abuses. This campaign of suppression was followed by the unlawful deportation and forcible transfer of hundreds of thousands of Kosovo Albanians from their homes in Kosovo, it was alleged. This policy was supported by increasing attacks on civilian populations, including the widespread shelling of towns and villages, the burning of homes and farms and the systematic seizure and destruction of identity documents and vehicle licences. In addition, killings of Kosovo Albanians had occurred since the launching of NATO's armed operations on 24 March 1999 at numerous locations. The accused were alleged to be linked to these activities by virtue of command responsibility and jointly indicted on three counts of crimes against humanity (deportation, murder, persecutions) and one count of violations of the laws or customs of war (murder).[10]

*Considerations of Process*

The ICTY had asserted its claim to jurisdiction also in relation to Kosovo ever since the outbreak of significant hostilities in the territory, followed by an initial wave of forced displacements early in 1998.[11] However, the Federal Republic of Yugoslavia had consistently denied this claim to jurisdiction. It persisted in this attitude even after the Security Council confirmed the position of the Tribunal in a Chapter VII resolution adopted in November 1998.[12] The failure of Yugoslavia to cooperate was illustrated dramatically when the ICTY Chief Prosecutor was denied access to Kosovo in the wake of the Racak massacre of January 1999 under the full glare of the international media. Needless to say, the Tribunal still had no direct access to Kosovo when it issued its indictment some two months after the massive campaign of displacement of Kosovo Albanians had commenced in March 1999.

In contrast to the work of the Tribunal in relation to Bosnia and Hercegovina, the absence of access to sites of alleged atrocities meant that no forensic evidence could be collected or preserved. No interviews could be conducted in Kosovo itself. Instead, the Tribunal had to rely on external sources in compiling the materials supporting the Indictment, including witness statements obtained by ICTY teams dispatched to the refugee centres in Albania and Macedonia. The Tribunal also received testimony transmitted by NGOs operating in the region, and by some governments. Military intelligence may also have been made available. On this basis, the indictment does refer to some 20 specific incidents of deportations and alleged atrocities.[13] It also features a longer general description of events in Kosovo. It is accompanied by a listing of individuals allegedly killed at specific locations. Overall, the events portrayed in the indictment do appear to support a picture of systematic and grave violations of humanitarian law. Given the confusion surrounding the question of whether or not the Tribunal can consider atrocities in a situation of internal armed conflict to fall under the heading of grave breaches of the Geneva law (Article 2 of the Statute) it is noteworthy that the indictment only alleges 'ordinary' war crimes under Article 3 of the Statute.

The approach of the Tribunal to this case obviously differs markedly to that exhibited in relation to Bosnia and Hercegovina. In the latter case, the Tribunal initially focused on actual perpetrators of specific, individual criminal acts. It did extend its interest also to commanding officers, notably General Ratko Mladic and the political leader of the Srpska entity, Radovan Karadic. However, the leadership of the Federal Republic of Yugoslavia and Serbia, including especially Slobodan Milosevic, was apparently spared, although the Tribunal claims to be investigating further and there were rumours of sealed indictments. Given the magnitude of the suffering inflicted by the Yugoslav armed forces and Serb units on the mainly Muslim population of Bosnia and Hercegovina early in that conflict, and the continued support and control of the local Serb forces by Belgrade, this omission has given rise to an allegation of excessive political prudence on the part of the Tribunal. No such prudence was evident in the case of the Kosovo indictment. Instead of seeking to isolate individual instances of atrocities and to link them to individual perpetrators, the Tribunal instead sought to establish a general pattern of violations. It then simply referred to Article 7 of the Statute, indicating that individual criminal responsibility includes committing, planning, instigating, ordering or aiding and abetting in the planning, preparation or execution of crimes.

The Tribunal did not exhibit a significant degree of evidence in relation to any such activities. No real attempt was made to demonstrate in a specific sense how any of the accused could be tied to the individual instances of atrocities that had been described. Instead, the Tribunal described the official function of the indictees, asserting that the individuals 'had authority or control' over units, commanders and individuals engaged in atrocities by virtue of this function. In this way, the prosecutors appear to have been proceeding from a presumption of responsibility, as opposed to more cautious approaches that would rely on the construction of an actual chain of command relating to the individual acts in question, and the demonstration that specific commands leading to criminal conduct had actually been issued. Given the very widespread and systematic nature of the alleged offences involving a significant part of the official infrastructure of the FRY/Serbia, this approach appears justified. The difference in the Tribunal's approach when compared with its action in relation to the conflict in Bosnia and Hercegovina might perhaps be explained with reference to its external dimension. In contrast, Kosovo was, according to Belgrade, clearly a matter falling exclusively within its own domestic jurisdiction. Hence, no complicating issues of 'international' attribution of the acts of Yugoslav/Serb forces arose and a presumption of command responsibility could be maintained somewhat more easily.

## The Strategic Impact of the Indictment

NATO's air campaign was intended to be conducted in a phased, stepped-up way. It represented a spectacular revival of the escalation theory of the Vietnam era. NATO again attempted to communicate with the leadership of another state through a campaign of carefully graduated steps of violence. It had done so in October 1998, when it had obtained the Holbrooke agreement for the deployment of an international verification mission in Kosovo as a direct result of the threat of the graduated use of force. That threat had been deployed again, in support of the Rambouillet process that sought to pressure the parties into accepting an interim settlement for Kosovo, complete with NATO implementation on the ground.

When NATO launched its first cruise missiles on 24 March 1999, the expectation of the political leadership was that Belgrade would cave in after a few days. President Milosevic would be able to present the prospect of a prolonged air campaign as a fig leaf to his domestic constituents, covering his climb-down when accepting a package not unlike that on offer at Rambouillet itself. However, Belgrade did not play by NATO's rules. Its leadership saw the initiation of conflict not as a handy cover for capitulation to international demands in relation to Kosovo, aiming to restore ethnic Albanian self-governance to the territory. Instead, it provided an excuse to resolve the Kosovo problem once and for all. It commenced an organised and extraordinarily rapid campaign of massive displacement of the ethnic Albanian majority population from the territory. This would deprive the Kosovo Liberation Army (KLA), which had launched significant operations against the Yugoslav infrastructure in Kosovo late in 1997, of a support base. At the same time, the action would shift the demographic composition of the territory, paving the way for an even firmer integration of the territory with Serbia. NATO would be preoccupied with the destabilising consequences of this exodus and its humanitarian implications. Hence, the Alliance had been presented with a classic 'circumventing move' by Belgrade which fell outside NATO's escalatory scheme and could not really be answered within its framework.

While NATO's military leaders had voiced doubts about the possibility of launching a high-tech, zero-casualty air campaign with a view to effectively displacing Serb/Yugoslav control over a territory which it claimed as its historic and religious heartland, politicians could point to the example of Bosnia and Hercegovina. A short, but in their view swift and decisive, NATO air campaign had terminated the armed conflict in that state, they argued. That campaign had not significantly dented the Yugoslav and Bosnian Serb military machine. But it had demonstrated the ability to inflict damage and communicated credible intent to do so, unless Belgrade and its clients in Bosnia and Hercegovina accepted NATO's demands for a settlement of the conflict. The resulting Dayton agreement thus appeared to vindicate the application of coercive diplomacy.

In reality, of course, the Dayton agreement had not frustrated but consolidated Yugoslavia's policy vis-à-vis Bosnia and Hercegovina. While that state continued to exist under the nominal roof of a federal or almost confederal structure, there had been created a self-contained Serb entity adjacent to Serbia proper and connected with it. This Srpska republic exhibited state-like features and was in a position to block, through the new federal structure, any attempt to shape Bosnia and Hercegovina into an effective state of its own. Instead, the Srpska leadership could exercise unchallenged authority in an area which had been purged of non-Serbs and which would not, whatever the protestations of the organised international community, be restored to its previous multi-ethnic character. In essence, Dayton had rewarded the use of force by Belgrade, coupled with a brutal campaign of ethnic cleansing and probable genocide. Moreover, instead of being held to account for this policy, the Milosevic government was rehabilitated. The United States and Western European states now had significant numbers of troops deployed in Bosnia and Hercegovina as part of the SFOR/IFOR peace support operation. Their troops being exposed in a potentially explosive situation, they were placed in a position of dependency in relation to Belgrade. Milosevic was needed to continue to deliver a modicum of stability in the territory.

A similar outcome must have been in Milosevic's mind in relation to Kosovo. NATO would launch its graduated air campaign to little effect against Belgrade's military infrastructure which had been widely dispersed, given the weeks of warning that were available. Yugoslavia/ Serbia would have re-established control over Kosovo, having removed a large portion of the ethnic Albanian population in the process. NATO would cave in to internal political divisions and an increasingly volatile public opinion and would not be able to sustain the use of force indefinitely. The option of the use of force having been exhausted, NATO would have to permit UN mediation to terminate the conflict on Belgrade's terms. That is to say, there would be a confirmation of Yugoslavia's sovereignty in relation to Kosovo, Serbia would remain in political control of the territory and an enfeebled international UN presence would seek to implement a limited autonomy regime within that framework. Only a limited number of refugees would return under those circumstances.

The scale and swiftness of the ethnic cleansing campaign conducted by FRY/Serb forces in Kosovo had jeopardised the chances of success for this strategy. It undermined public opposition to NATO's military action and added to NATO cohesion. The issuing of formal indictments against the top Yugoslav/Serb leadership, however, completely frustrated Belgrade's aims. It was now clear that the allegations of horrendous abuses and of a campaign of systematic ethnic cleansing (but not genocide) in Kosovo were not figments of NATO propaganda. Instead, the allegations had been confirmed by a body which was a creature of the UN Security Council, the international organ exercising primary responsibility in relation to international peace and security. The Tribunal could claim objectivity. And, while human rights organs, also within the context of the UN, had unanimously condemned Yugoslav action in Kosovo, the Tribunal boasted the most specific juridical competence in relation to the matter. Moreover, it had the unique power directly to attach legal consequences to its findings and to seek to enforce them.

President Slobodan Milosevic, the most prominent of the indictees, and his close associates were no longer an indispensable element to a resolution of the Kosovo conflict. Instead, they were to be considered war criminals who might indeed need to be defeated militarily. Given this position, they would find it increasingly difficult to rely on their traditional allies, such as Russia.[14] This prospect contributed to the decision of the Yugoslav leadership to accept the (at least temporary) surrender of Kosovo in the shape of NATO's virtual occupation of the territory, thinly disguised by a UN mandate.[15]

*Community Interest vs. Sovereign Rights*

The strategic impact of the Tribunal's action represents a vindication of international community interest over the traditional doctrine of sovereign rights and non-intervention. These principles obviously define the classical international system and have, until recently, been guarded and preserved by governments. Of course, the new world order conceived at the end of World War Two consecrated universal values that appear to strain the classical system. These were seemingly rendered into positive law in the shape of statutes of *ad hoc* tribunals established in relation to the defeated Axis powers; the UN Charter; supplementary resolutions adopted by the UN General Assembly; and treaties concluded under its aegis. Moreover, international jurisprudence, very much focused on positive law in the inter-war years, appeared to embrace principles of law, such as 'elementary principles of humanity', seemingly based in natural law.[16]

In the shadow of Nazi atrocities and other outrages, the protection of human beings from systematic violation by their government, an occupying power or an enemy force were among these values. However, it very soon emerged that the substance of the values incorporated into the positive legal order was either heavily circumscribed or unhelpfully vague. The definition of genocide, for example, was quite technical and restrictive, to the point of excluding most of the instances of systematic attacks by a government on a defined element of its population which occurred since the coming into force of the Genocide Convention.[17] Crimes against humanity had been introduced into the international legal order in the Nuremberg principles, but their definition was not translated into hard treaty law until 1998. Along with other proposed 'crimes against the peace and security of mankind', this issue was left to linger in the United Nations Law Commission for decades.

Nevertheless, humanitarian core values, although restrictively defined, did at least ripen into hard law over the past half-century in the shape of customary international law. The prohibition of genocide, crimes against humanity, slavery, and grave breaches of the Geneva law on armed conflict have undisputedly become part of general international law – that is to say, these obligations are binding upon all states, whether it can be demonstrated that they have specifically consented to them or not. Moreover, these obligations are also privileged by virtue of enjoying the status of *jus cogens*. Hence, no state can opt out of the obligation to comply. Furthermore, situations brought about by a state in violation of *jus cogens* rules do not enjoy the full protection of the international legal order. Instead, it is accepted that all other states have a legal interest in the matter (the *erga omnes* effect). Slightly more controversially, as these values are the concern of all mankind, it is argued that all states are injured in their rights wherever, whenever and by whatever state a violation of these values is perpetrated.

The *erga omnes* effect of such core values has, however, posed a particular problem. If all states are injured by the violation of these values, either by a state against its own population or in relation to another state, are they also legally entitled to respond? The classical sovereignty-based state system would restrict a broadly-based international community response and only permit action by states which could demonstrate a direct interest in the violation. Now, at this present point of transition from the classical system to an international constitutional order, three avenues of response are emerging. First, the emerging international constitution attaches to some types of violation of *erga omnes* rules genuinely universal international criminal jurisdiction. Hence, all states may enjoy a legal right to exercise criminal justice in relation to the individual perpetrator of the violation through their own municipal courts in general international law. Some crimes that are also established in universal treaties even carry with them a legal obligation for states either to try or extradite suspects or at least to generate the legal basis for such action in their municipal law. However, these treaties do not cover all crimes to which genuine universality attaches. Thus, until the Rome Statute of the International Criminal Court enters into force, crimes against humanity remain defined in general international law, rather than treaty law. There is no general obligation for states to establish the offence in municipal criminal law, or even to try or extradite suspects. This was aptly demonstrated when a forum for trial was sought for Pol Pot after his arrest by the government of Cambodia. His rapid demise upon his arrest disguised the international embarrassment which ensued when it was discovered that only a handful of states had used the fifty-year period since 1945 to establish crimes against humanity in their municipal law.

One might assume that the situation is different at least in relation to all crimes established in universal treaties. But there are important exceptions relating to early international instruments. The Genocide Convention best exemplifies this phenomenon. Instead of establishing genuinely universal jurisdiction, it merely provides for trial before municipal courts 'by a competent tribunal in the territory of which the act was committed'.[18] The Convention also provides for the international administration of criminal jurisdiction through an international penal tribunal that may have jurisdiction with respect to those Contracting Parties which shall have accepted its jurisdiction. Hence, great caution was exhibited when providing for means of actualising the overwhelming international community interest even with respect to genocide.

Second, there has emerged the still controversial concept of crimes of states. This concept has been active in the deliberations of the International Law Commission for several decades in the shape of the famous 'Draft Article 19' of the draft on state responsibility adopted at first reading. International crimes of state do not really seek to attach 'criminal law' consequences to certain conduct of states. Instead, the concept was meant to focus on the consequences for the international community as a whole. All states would be obliged not to recognise the result of a crime of state, not to assist in maintaining that result, and to consult about collective responses. The prospect of the decentralised administration of counter-measures by individual states in relation to *erga omnes* violations and especially international crimes of state has now, however, thrown the deliberations of the International Law Commission into some confusion, even up to the point that it is proposed to drop the term international crimes altogether.

The collective administration of responses to *erga omnes* violations constitutes the third possible type of response. Hitherto, such responses were principally focused on violations touching upon issues of international peace and security according to Article 39 of the United Nations Charter. Since 1990, however, the Security Council has gradually expanded its scope of action under that heading, now including for example violations of humanitarian law, humanitarian emergencies and allegations of terrorism. While this mechanism is being applied selectively, given the realities of the voting procedure in the Council, international collective enforcement powers can now clearly be applied for the vindication of international community interest engaged in these areas. The establishment of the ICTY itself provides a case in point.

Overall, therefore, the ICTY (and the Rwanda Tribunal) confirm the collective international responsibility for fundamental international rule-maintenance. The international legal interest in grave violations of fundamental rules was highlighted, considerations of national sovereignty notwithstanding. The universal right of action in relation to breaches of these rules was also confirmed. The cause of action, utilising a Security Council resolution to establish a true international *ad hoc* tribunal, finally actualised the international community interest in concrete terms, removing the primacy of state jurisdiction and instead locating it in the organs of the emerging international constitutional structure.

### Consent

The establishment of the ICTY, along with the Rwanda Tribunal, through a Chapter VII Security Council resolution, represented an important shift in the way new means of action for the vindication of global community interests, enshrined in fundamental *jus cogens* and *erga omnes* rules, are created. Technically speaking, the Security Council merely generated a subsidiary organ. However, in reality it did far more than that, engaging in quite radical international legislation in the absence of state consent. For, in adopting the Statutes of both Tribunals, it created two bodies exercising new international executive powers. As will be noted below, the Tribunals are endowed with genuine supranational functions, exercised under the heading of 'cooperation and judicial assistance'.[19]

The Council also granted to the Tribunal functions which it does not itself possess. It imposed upon the constituents of the emerging international constitutional order an entirely new structure for the administration of international criminal jurisdiction. True, it has been argued that the Council was careful to limit this jurisdiction to crimes which had previously enjoyed unquestioned genuine universality. However, genuine universality merely means that all states have a sufficient legal interest to exercise jurisdiction in relation to an international crime, wherever committed by a national of whichever state. But the establishment of an international means of exercising such jurisdiction goes a significant step further. After all, it was precisely the unwillingness of states to take that step and to consent to it which had doomed the struggle for an International Criminal Court to failure for nearly half a century. Now, from one moment to the next, this lack of consent was rendered irrelevant by the Council's pronouncement. Moreover, it is not clear that all crimes subject to Tribunal jurisdiction are in fact genuinely universal.[20] Hence, there was not only created a new process-based obligation incumbent upon states, but also a new substantive obligation rendering opposable to them a possibly new claim of genuine universality.

One might also argue that the territorial scope of this jurisdiction was confined to the former Yugoslavia and Rwanda respectively; consequently the impact of the creation of the tribunals was therefore quite limited. Of course, in relation to two states (actually more, given the dissolution of Yugoslavia), the imposition of a new layer of the international administration of justice in the absence of their consent certainly is a radical step. But the Tribunal has objective international personality – its actions are opposable to all states, or at least all UN member states. This applies not only to the issue of judicial assistance. When it was discussed whether the Tribunal should issue indictments against NATO leaders and soldiers in connection with the Kosovo operation, its global reach became rapidly apparent. Suddenly governments, including the United States government which is always strongly opposed to any measures which might expose its soldiers or political leadership to the exercise of jurisdiction by other states or even international bodies, found itself confronted with that very possibility.

## GENUINE SUPRANATIONAL POWERS:
## THE PRIMACY OR LAW OVER POLITICS

It has already been noted that the ICTY enjoys objective powers in relation to the international community as a whole. It also enjoys genuine supranational powers. That is to say, this is one of the very few instances in which an international organ was created which operates entirely outside the control of the constituents of the legal system which it addresses (the states). In fact, short of abolishing the Tribunal through a further Chapter VII resolution, even the Security Council has no role of control or co-decision in the exercise of the judicial function by the Tribunal.[21] Its control only extends to measures it may or may not adopt to enforce the decisions of the Tribunal once the Tribunal has exercised its function. This very fact was of course brought out with particular clarity when the Kosovo indictment was issued. Had such an act been dependent on a previous political or quasi-judicial act, say a decision of the Security Council, it would never have come about.

In this way, the Kosovo indictment powerfully confirms the highly advanced nature of the ICTY. As an international judicial institution, the Tribunal vastly outclasses its 'successor', the International Criminal Court (ICC) which is to be established. As that Court will be based on state consent, its statute admits to significant political control. This control applies especially to the launching of proceedings by the Court. In the case of the ICTY, prosecutors prepare indictments which are then reviewed by a judge of the Tribunal. Proceedings are then conducted exclusively according to judicial considerations. The ICC, on the other hand, can initiate proceedings through its prosecutors, but also on the basis of state application or Security Council action.[22] While this might appear to broaden the scope of ICC activity, it is in fact greatly reduced by the principle of so-called complementarity. Any single state is endowed with the procedural power to remove a case from the ICC. Conceptually the ICC is therefore a very different creature to the ICTY. The former functions until individual states decide to exercise jurisdiction. The latter permits the exercise of jurisdiction of states, but only until it resolves to exercise jurisdiction at the international level. The limited value of the ICC system is easily demonstrated if one imagines that it had been charged with the judicial execution of global community interest in relation to the conflict in Kosovo.

## CONCLUSION:
## THE ACTION OF THE TRIBUNAL IN THE CONTEXT OF THE WIDER DEVELOPMENT OF INTERNATIONAL CRIMINAL JURISDICTION

While the ICTY thus constitutes a more significant contribution to the emerging international constitutional order as far as process and institutional development is concerned, some other advances might also be considered. On the institutional plane, the increasing exercise of quasi-judicial functions by the United Nations Security Council has already been noted. Its expanded jurisdiction now applies beyond the narrow confines of what were classically considered threats to international peace and security. This includes a pattern of practice addressing issues of humanitarian law and related matters that require judicial or quasi-judicial monitoring, the authoritative determination of violations and remedial action.

As the Security Council has in some respects moved into a quasi-judicial role of international rule maintenance, the International Court of Justice (ICJ), the principal judicial organ of the United Nations, has been, somewhat reluctantly, pushed towards a more political profile. It has recently been involved in a number of highly political cases which concern humanitarian and other obligations that attract international criminal jurisdiction. This trend, which begun with the Lockerbie proceedings, has now been carried over into the Yugoslav conflict itself, with two genocide cases pending before the Court brought by Bosnia and Hercegovina and Croatia respectively.[23]

The ICJ has also contributed significantly to the development and understanding of the substantive law to which international criminal jurisdiction attaches, most notably through the Nuclear Weapons Advisory Opinion of 1996.[24] This practice is supported by the increasing body of case-law emanating from the Yugoslav and Rwanda Tribunals, and a recent wave of instances of the administration of international criminal law by municipal courts, including the Pinochet case. That case, while not entirely unambiguous, has clarified to an extent the limited nature of sovereign immunity as a shield from prosecution. And, while poor in institutional terms, the Rome Statute offers considerable advances in relation to substantive law. It significantly expands upon the definition of crimes against humanity in general international law and provides a consolidated description of war crimes.

Overall, therefore, there is a very significant further development of substantive international criminal law attracting universal jurisdiction, indicating the steady growth of the body of rules of international constitutional standing. Correspondingly, the areas of exclusive domestic jurisdiction which can be claimed by states are shrinking further. The sovereign claim of states to exclude international juridical activity in relation to itself or its domestic jurisdiction has been somewhat dented in this context, although more by the two *ad hoc* international criminal tribunals than by the International Criminal Court. This fact has been underscored impressively by the action of the Yugoslav Tribunal in relation to Kosovo.

In this way the Kosovo indictment highlights once again the radical and progressive nature of the decision to establish the ICTY in the first place. This applies to its establishment as a body with objective, genuinely supranational powers without paying regard to the classical structural requirement of state consent. The independent exercise of these powers in the case of Kosovo did have a significant political impact on the prosecution of the conflict. In that sense, the Tribunal also played a strategic role, as its action effectively denied to Belgrade any hope of achieving its principal aims. However, the Tribunal also exercised a strategic role in a wider, more significant sense. Not only did it insist on the application of fundamental principles of humanitarian law in circumstances of 'internal' or mixed armed conflicts, it also clarified, or perhaps advanced, the doctrine of command responsibility in relation to a military and political leadership that launches a systematic and unlawful campaign of violence, but that cannot be tied directly into individual acts of atrocities. In so doing, it consolidated an important element in the substantive law of the emerging international constitution which may have a useful impact on future instances of conflict.[25] This hope is, however, somewhat counterbalanced by some of the other developments relating to the development of international criminal jurisdiction, including ironically the establishment of the International Criminal Court.

## NOTES

1. See Weller, 'Peace-keeping and Peace-enforcement in the Republic of Bosnia and Herzegovina', *Heidelberg Journal of International Law*, No.56 (1996), p.1.
2. Resolution 764 (1992).
3. Resolution 771 (1992).
4. Resolution 780 (1992).
5. Resolution 808 (1993).
6. Report of the Secretary-General pursuant to paragraph 2 of Security Council Resolution 808 (1993), UN Document S/25704, 3 May 1993.
7. See ICTY, *Basic Documents* (1995) and the ICTY *Yearbooks* published from 1995 onwards.
8. The Indictment and all associated materials are reproduced in Weller, *The Kosovo Conflict: The Conduct and Termination of Hostilities and the Renewed Search for a Settlement*, (Cambridge: Documents and Analysis Publishing Ltd., 2000), Chapter 5.
9. Indictment, paras. 34–99.
10. Indictment, para. 100.
11. Prosecutor's Statement Regarding the Tribunal's Jurisdiction over Kosovo, 10 March 1998, and further statements in Weller, *The Crisis in Kosovo 1989–1999* (Cambridge: Documents and Analysis Publishing Ltd., 1999), Chapter 10.
12. Resolution 1207.
13. Indictment, paras 97–98.
14. The strategic impact of the Indictment can perhaps be best measured by the stunned and angry response by Russia.
15. This result was nominally obtained through international mediation involving Finland and Russia. However, in fact Yugoslavia was presented with a non-negotiable catalogue of demands which it had to accept unconditionally. See Security Council Resolution 1244 (1999), Appendices.

16. E.g., Corfu Channel Case, 1949 ICJ 2, 22: 'certain general and well-recognized principles, namely: elementary considerations of humanity, even more exacting in peace than in war'.
17. The most often quoted example concerns the extermination of significant segments of the population of Cambodia by the Pol Pot regime which, technically, falls outside the definition of genocide established in the Convention.
18. Article VI.
19. ICTY Statute, Article 29.
20. Such doubts might arise in relation to war crimes which are not grave breaches. ICTY Statute Article 3.
21. The Council and General Assembly do elect the judges, of course, and the Council appoints the Prosecutor at the suggestion of the Secretary-General. ICTY Statute, Articles 13, 16. The Tribunal is also at times rumoured to exhibit political sensitivity given its dependence on the United Nations organs for its budget.
22. Rome Statute of the International Criminal Court, 37 ILM 999, Articles 13–19 and Part 5, Investigation and Prosecution, Articles 53–61.
23. Yugoslavia has responded with a counter-claim.
24. Legality of the Threat or Use of Nuclear Weapons, 1996 ICJ 226.
25. On the concept of the emerging international constitution see Weller, 'The Reality of the Emerging International Constitutional Order', *Cambridge Review of International Affairs*, No. 10 (1997), p.40.

# PART FOUR:

# Aftermath

# 11
# From Rambouillet to the Kosovo Accords: NATO's War against Serbia and Its Aftermath

## ERIC HERRING

The purpose of war should be to secure a better peace.[1] The question this essay addresses is 'Did NATO's war against Serbia result in a better peace for Kosovo?' 'Better peace' in this context must include better prospects for human rights within and beyond Kosovo. Any answer to this question relies on an assessment of the alternatives to NATO's war and of the conditions which now prevail in Kosovo and the world at large. This article analyses the rejection by Serbia[2] of the Rambouillet Plan[3] and NATO's rejection of Serbia's counter-proposal;[4] the escalation of violence in Kosovo by Serbia following the start of NATO's bombing campaign; the extent to which the deal which ended the war entailed concessions by either side in comparison with Rambouillet; and the situation within and beyond Kosovo since the bombing stopped. The assessment of these issues is organised around an exposition and critique of the pro-war narrative as propounded by NATO and many of the supporters of NATO's war in Kosovo. While one could construct more narratives than just one pro-war and one anti-war, it is useful to structure the main strands of argument regarding the war around this extremely important policy choice.

## THE POLITICS OF RAMBO(UILLET)

The pro-war narrative on the Rambouillet Interim Agreement proposed by the Contact Group (comprising the United States, the United Kingdom, France, Italy and Russia) is that the Contact Group had done everything that it could short of the use of force to get Serbia to accept what was a very reasonable compromise deal, but Serbia rejected it in order to retain a free hand in the ethnic cleansing of Kosovo. The Serbian government had abolished Kosovo's status as an autonomous province of Serbia in 1989. Serbia presented this and its subsequent actions as a defensive reaction to what it portrayed as ethnic cleansing of Serbs from Kosovo by Albanian Kosovar terrorists and attempts by them to achieve full federal status for Kosovo which would allow it to secede and then become part of a Greater Albania. Serbia's absolute minimum negotiating position was no independence for Kosovo.

The anti-war narrative argues that Rambouillet was an offer Yugoslav President Slobodan Milosevic could not have accepted. The Contact Group proposal was effectively a NATO proposal as Russia was in many ways a dissenting voice within the Contact Group.[5] Rambouillet required Serbia to accept a NATO-led 28,000-strong Kosovo Force (KFOR) to oversee the implementation process and be allowed to use force if necessary against any parties violating the agreement (Chapter 5, Article IV.2b). There was no mention of any KFOR accountability to the UN or any other international body. Any non-NATO participation was to be 'subject to the direction and political control of North Atlantic Council (NAC) through the NATO chain of command' (Chapter 7, Article I.1b). That force was to be allowed freedom of movement, access and action throughout Yugoslav territory, air space and waters, not just Kosovo, which was to 'include, but not be limited to, the right of bivouac, manoeuvre, billet, and utilisation of any areas or facilities as required for support, training and operations' (Appendix B, Article 8). Even if there was no practical expectation that NATO would actually venture outside the borders of Kosovo, to require Serbia to accept even in principle such a thing is extraordinary.[6] Without reassurances on the composition, role and political authorisation of the force (including the presence of neutral and Russian forces), KFOR looked to Serbia as if it was simply a transitional guarantor force for Kosovo's independence.

As Rambouillet was merely an interim agreement, the question of what was to follow it was crucial: 'Three years after the entry into force of this Agreement, an international meeting shall be convened to determine a mechanism for a final settlement for Kosovo, on the basis of the will of the people, opinions of relevant authorities, each Party's efforts regarding the implementation of this Agreement, and the Helsinki Final Act' (Chapter 8, Article I.3). US Secretary of State Madeleine Albright apparently gave assurances to the Albanian Kosovar delegation at Rambouillet that the reference to 'the will of the people' meant the will of the people of Kosovo (not Serbia or Yugoslavia) to be expressed in a referendum.[7] The Albanian Kosovar delegation probably signed in the full expectation it was in a no-lose situation – either Serbia would reject the deal, NATO would bomb, and the war of independence would continue; or Serbia would accept the deal and independence would come through a referendum after three years. Milosevic said: 'What they practically attempted to impose in Rambouillet wasn't autonomy but independence.'[8] One might be of the opinion that Serbia, through its brutal violations of human rights, had forfeited its moral right for Kosovo to remain within its borders. On that logic, the KLA has now forfeited its right to an independent Kosovo for the same reason. However, the point here is that the prospect of an independent Kosovo guaranteed Milosevic's rejection of Rambouillet. Ironically, it is likely that the United States did not want Kosovo to become independent. The first draft of the US-sponsored Hill Plan of 1 October 1998 proposed autonomy for Kosovo within Serbia and proposed that this status could be changed only if all parties agreed, which is one of the reasons the unofficial government of Kosovo rejected it.[9] NATO always demanded that the Albanian Kosovar Kosovo Liberation Army (KLA) cease to use force and agree to accept autonomy within Serbia only, and there was a widespread belief that NATO for a long time kept its military threats limited so as not to encourage the KLA.

Attention has been paid by anti-war analysts to the fact that the Serbian National Assembly made a counter-proposal on 23 March, the day before NATO started bombing.[10] This counter-proposal was rejected out of hand by NATO and is ignored or given only a passing mention in pro-war narratives. In this resolution, Serbia condemned the withdrawal of the 2,000 members of the Organisation for Security and Cooperation in Europe (OSCE) Kosovo Verification Mission (KVM) which had been deployed as part of the Holbrooke Plan of October 1998, proposed 'wide-ranging autonomy' for Kosovo within a sovereign Yugoslavia, and rejected 'foreign troops' but stated its willingness to 'examine the character and extent of an international presence in Kosovo' once there had been a political agreement acceptable to all parties. Pro-war analysts could argue that, without a heavily-armed force to guarantee it, the deal would not be worth the paper it was written on in terms of human rights within Kosovo, and the resolution rejected such a force. However, exploration of the potential for compromise, even if improbable, between the Rambouillet plan and Serbian National Assembly resolution involving human rights guarantees and Kosovo's autonomy rather than independence was rejected by NATO in favour of war.

Not only was the United States uninterested in the Serbian counter-proposal, it is likely that the United States wanted and expected Serbia to reject Rambouillet. This is a claim that gets ignored in the pro-war narrative. Former US Secretary of State and National Security Adviser Henry Kissinger has claimed that 'the Rambouillet text ... was a provocation, and excuse to start bombing',[11] and there are reports that Albright told reporters off the record that 'we intentionally set the bar too high for the Serbs to comply. They need some bombing, and that's what they are going to get.'[12] As US President Bill Clinton was consumed by the process of dealing with the impeachment proceedings which were under way against him for lying about his relationship with White House intern Monica Lewinsky, Albright was very much the shaper of US policy, though with Clinton making the final decisions.[13] She believed the situation was similar to the situation in Bosnia in the summer of 1995 and that Milosevic would capitulate very quickly after a few bombs had been dropped. On 13 March, Clinton and most of his advisers agreed with an intelligence report which stated that Milosevic 'would quickly sue for peace after defending his honour'. On 24 March Albright said that the goal was 'achievable in a relatively short period of time'.[14] White House Spokesman Joseph Lockhart made the connection explicit on 24 March when he said 'the President expressed hope that, as in Bosnia, ... a credible threat of force would increase chances for Milosevic to accept a lasting diplomatic solution'.[15] Tony Blinken, Special Adviser to Clinton on the National Security Council, defended this line in April 1999: 'I think that if you look at what happened in Bosnia, there was certainly reason to believe that when faced with NATO airplanes he would quickly calculate that his interests lie in making peace.'[16] The parallel with NATO's bombing of Bosnian Serb nationalists was misleading.[17] Milosevic agreed to the Dayton Peace Agreement over Bosnia-Hercegovina at a time when Bosnian Serb nationalist forces were losing rapidly on the ground to a joint Croatian and Bosnian government offensive. Dayton offered him a chance to avert total defeat and establish a Serb Republic within Bosnia in which the Bosnian Serb nationalists would be able to impose their will and even lay the basis for the partition of Bosnia and the establishment of a Greater Serbia. NATO's bombing alone was not sufficient to secure his acceptance of the Dayton Peace Agreement. In contrast, Serbian forces had the clear upper hand on the ground in Kosovo, and the peace deal on offer would mean the end of Serb minority rule in that province and possibly even the loss of Kosovo, which is much more precious to Serbia in its nationalist ideology and much more important to Milosevic in Serbian coalition politics than any part of Bosnia. Instead of exploring a compromise, NATO started bombing.

## NATO BOMBING: FUEL ON THE FIRE

A key dispute between the pro- and anti-war narratives pertains to the relationship between the commencement of the NATO bombing and the massive escalation of human rights violations by Serbian forces which followed it. I assess this dispute by considering the process of escalation leading up to the bombing, claims regarding Serbian military planning, and the purposes and effects of NATO's bombing campaign.

In the face of extensive discrimination and violent repression by the Yugoslav authorities, the Albanian Kosovars under their unofficially elected leader Ibrahim Rugova had organised non-violent resistance in the 1990s, but this campaign failed to secure political concessions from, or serious international pressure on, the central government.[18] Kosovo had not been on the agenda of the 1995 Dayton peace talks, which was a great political blow to Rugova's non-violent approach. In 1996, some Albanian Kosovars launched violent attacks on Serbian Kosovar civilians and police, and in 1997 the KLA emerged and started claiming responsibility for the attacks on police. The Serbian military response made no attempt to discriminate between the KLA and Albanian Kosovars in general.

While condemning the KLA as terrorists, NATO made increasingly clear military threats against Serbia from spring 1998 onwards. In spring and summer 1998, there was increasing KLA and especially Serbian violence, followed in September 1998 by a significant escalation by Serbian forces. On 13 October 1998, in the Holbrooke Agreement, NATO agreed not to carry out air strikes. In return, Milosevic agreed to return Serbian armed forces in Kosovo to February 1998 levels; accept deployment of the KVM; release and give amnesty to all Albanian Kosovar detainees; and cooperate with the International Criminal Tribunal for former Yugoslavia (ICTY) in its investigations of war crimes in Kosovo. However, the KLA immediately occupied the territory from which the Serbian forces had withdrawn and continued its attacks, and Milosevic resumed his indiscriminate use of force to defeat it. By the end of 1998, the KLA had killed up to 150 Serbian police and perhaps up the same number of Serb civilians, and kidnapped a similar number, while Yugoslav forces had killed 2,000, detained over 1,200 and displaced around 300,000 Albanian Kosovars. On 30 January 1999, the North Atlantic Council stated that 'NATO is ready to take whatever measures are necessary ... to avert a humanitarian catastrophe, by compelling compliance with the demands of the international community'.[19]

Before the bombing, Milosevic was building up his forces in Kosovo. According to Rudolf Scharping, German Minister of Defence, Serbia had a plan called Operation Horseshoe, in which Kosovo would be surrounded on three sides and the Albanian Kosovar population driven through the gap into Albania.[20] Scharping made this claim in April 1999 (that is, while the NATO bombing campaign was still in its early stages).

It is unclear whether Scharping actually had in his possession such a document or whether the German Ministry of Defence deduced such a plan from the Yugoslav pattern of operations.[21] Still in the early stages of the NATO air campaign in April, General Wesley Clark, NATO Supreme Allied Commander in Europe, stated: 'I've never seen those plans in any detail. They've never been shared with me. ... I'm not familiar with any of the details of a plan such as this. But, on the other hand, I'm certainly familiar with the general concept and we received a lot of information about the general concept behind the plan.'[22] If Scharping had the Serbian operational plans, it would have been criminally negligent of him to fail to pass them on to General Clark, whose job it was (at least in some versions of the pro-war narrative) to counter them.

More importantly, the notion of Operation Horseshoe has been used in the pro-war narrative to argue that the ethnic cleansing and human rights violations were about to happen anyway to the same degree and thus that the NATO bombing did nothing to escalate them.[23] This claim can be challenged in a number of ways.[24] First, it has only been asserted that the ferocity of the plan matched the ferocity of Serbia's actions. Releasing the plan (if Germany does possess it) might help, but even then an interpretative effort would be required. Second, preparing forces for a spring offensive is standard military strategy, and would have made sense in view of the concurrent build-up of KLA forces. The Serbian build-up itself cannot prove the existence of intent to carry out comprehensive ethnic cleansing. Third, it is plausible that NATO's escalating threats and demands were an important factor in the military operations Scharping referred to and in determining how fierce the offensive would be. Serbia first had hints of serious US planning for military action against it in summer 1998 and began to plan counter-measures.[25] Plans are implemented in response to circumstances. NATO had shown a willingness in the rest of former Yugoslavia to accept peace deals based on supposed 'facts on the ground', and Serbia may have been intent on creating them as NATO intervention looked more likely. Furthermore, creating a large flow of refugees to inhibit the military operations of an opponent is a common tactic. Fourth, in deciding whether or not to use force, US decision-makers were not being told that Serbia was going to attempt the complete ethnic cleansing of Kosovo regardless of what the United States did. Instead, according to Congressman Porter Goss, Chairman of the House Intelligence Committee, the CIA was warning in early February that NATO air attacks could result in increased ethnic cleansing.[26] General Clark maintains that retaliation against Albanian Kosovar civilians for NATO bombing was 'entirely predictable' and that the Western allies had assumed it would occur.[27] Indeed, in the public debate even before NATO started bombing there was widespread concern about this possibility. It is easy to see how Serbian forces, unable to hit back at NATO directly, would vent their fury against Albanian Kosovars. Accepting the existence and NATO knowledge of Operation Horseshoe as being of the most heinous intent imaginable makes NATO look worse, not better, if NATO started bombing even though it thought the bombing would trigger its full implementation.[28] NATO's claim to concern for human rights is undermined if it knew in advance that a massive refugee flow was about to be produced even if it did not bomb, but made no plans to help those people.

A key element of the pro-war narrative is the argument that NATO could not stand by and do nothing – that there was no alternative to bombing. Aside from the fact that it often does do precisely that, it could have and should have done nothing if 'doing something' would make the prospects for human rights much worse, and that was indeed the opinion of the intelligence community available to NATO. The first thing NATO should have done is seek a compromise, even if it was unlikely. If Milosevic had rejected a compromise, NATO should still have not bombed because of the escalation which it triggered. Furthermore, those who opposed the war argue that it is not their job to get NATO out of the political mess which its approach to human rights (critiqued later in this article) got it into. NATO's official objective was 'to prevent a humanitarian catastrophe', and its chosen means were high-altitude bombing, cruise missiles and economic sanctions. The only way this could have prevented the massacre and expulsion of the Albanian Kosovars would be if Milosevic had capitulated within days. As General Clark said of the NATO bombing: 'It was not designed as a means of blocking Serb ethnic cleansing. It was not designed as a way of waging war against the Serb and MUP [Ministry of the Interior] forces in Kosovo in any way. There was never any intent to do that. That was not the idea.'[29] As the weeks passed, with the humanitarian catastrophe escalating for the peoples of all of Serbia, NATO turned to targeting the military and economic infrastructure of Serbia rather than risk its pilots in lower-level attacks or use ground forces. In the assessment of the United States and Britain, this was the only way that there would be any support from the public and the only way to secure a consensus among NATO's 19 member states. The British government estimates about 10,000 Albanian Kosovars were executed and about 7,000 are thought to have been taken away to Serbia (and are still missing).[30] NATO bombing may have killed between 600 and 1,500 civilians, while Yugoslav sources say about 600 Serbian soldiers and Ministry of the Interior (MUP) troops were killed, mostly by the KLA.[31] Although the pro-war narrative usually attributes all 900,000 displaced persons to Serbia's actions, an unknown proportion of them could have been fleeing anticipated or actual NATO bombing (and in some cases attacks by the KLA).[32] It was not until the beginning of June that a peace deal was secured, by which time Kosovo and much of the rest of Serbia was in ruins.[33]

## HUMAN RIGHTS AND THE PEACE DEAL

The NATO bombing was brought to a halt by the Ahtisaari-Chernomyrdin-Milosevic agreement of 2 June which became known as the Kosovo Accords[34] of 4 June. This agreement was supplemented by the Kosovo Military-Technical Agreement[35] of 9 June between Yugoslavia and NATO and UN Security Council Resolution (SCR) 1244[36] of 10 June. The pro-war narrative is simple: NATO bombed until Serbia capitulated, and thus it was an unambiguous NATO victory. However, there were some elements of compromise.[37] First, although there is one reference to NATO participation and a unified chain of command, all of the documents refer to the force as operating under 'UN auspices' and usually refer in general terms to an 'international security presence' without specifying NATO. Second, the international security force is mentioned only in terms of being present in Kosovo as opposed to having rights throughout Yugoslavia. Third, the preamble of SCR 1244 affirms Yugoslavia's 'sovereignty and territorial integrity'. Paragraph 11(e) refers to 'facilitating a political process designed to determine Kosovo's future status' while it is to be given substantial autonomy in the meantime: Rambouillet is only to be 'taken into account' rather than followed. This leaves open the possibility of extending the three-year deadline and moving some distance from Albright's position that the settlement would involve a referendum within Kosovo. However, it all comes down to how the agreements are implemented in practice. NATO's political clashes with Serbia and Russia and its various statements show that it has the power to impose its interpretation over theirs.[38] How the peace deal is being interpreted and implemented is proving crucial for human rights.

### *Human Rights Violations with Impunity*[39]

In June 1999 Serbian forces were forced to pull out of Kosovo, and the UN Interim Administration Mission in Kosovo (UNMIK) and UN Kosovo Force (KFOR) moved in, as did the armed Albanian Kosovar groups dominated by the KLA. The agreement of 21 June, in which those groups agreed to demilitarise, has not been implemented fully, and the use of small arms, bombs and mortars by Albanian Kosovars is still widespread. There is peace only in the sense that there is no combat between armed groups, and attacks on international agencies are rare. Thousands of non-Albanian Kosovars left Kosovo even before KFOR and the KLA moved in because they feared revenge attacks for participating in human rights abuses and looting or being persecuted simply for not being Albanian Kosovars. The UN High Commissioner for Refugees (UNHCR) estimates that in October 70,000 Serbian Kosovars (out of at least 200,000 before NATO's bombing), 11,000 Roma Kosovars, 20,000 Muslim Slav and Gorani Kosovars and 15,000 Turkish Kosovars remained in Kosovo.[40] Around 300 Serbian Kosovars were killed and a similar number abducted between June and October 1999,[41] and the killings and abductions continue. Even Muslim Slavs have been targeted by some Albanian Kosovars.[42] These human rights abuses are widely portrayed in the Western news media solely in terms of ethnic hatred and revenge by radicalised individual Albanian Kosovars, by groups such as the KLA and very occasionally by Serbian Kosovars. However, the incentives are high to dress up criminal activity by Albanian Kosovars or by gangs from Albania itself as justified ethnic revenge.

Officially, the KLA was disbanded on 20 September, to be replaced by the civilian Kosovo Protection Corps (KPC) with 3,000 active members, 2,000 reservists and ten per cent of its places set aside for non-Albanian Kosovars. It is dominated by former KLA people and in practice the KLA is still functioning: hence I continue to refer to the KLA. Many of those carrying out human rights abuses claim to be from the KLA, and current and former KLA members are reported by Amnesty International to have abused the human rights of Serbian and Romany Kosovars, supposed Romany and Albanian Kosovar collaborators and Albanian Kosovars suspected of mere disloyalty to the KLA.[43] Intimidation and violence is now being carried out in the name of the KPC.[44] Mitrovicë/a,[45] Kosovo's second largest town, is effectively divided, with Serbian Kosovars concentrated in the north and Albanian Kosovars in the south. The KLA is preventing Albanian Kosovars from selling goods to Serbian Kosovars and is preventing Albanian Kosovars from visiting or returning to their homes in the predominantly Serbian Kosovar part of the town. Fearing a violent confrontation, KFOR does not intervene to halt this practice.[46] Hashim Thaçi, Prime Minister of the KLA's provisional government, blames the killings and abductions on 'rogue elements' and has condemned some of them, but has not taken any initiatives to investigate or end these abuses.[47] Obvious worries of what would happen to non-Albanian Kosovars were addressed by NATO Secretary-General Lord George Robertson, who proclaimed that 'NATO will not stand by and see the creation of a single-ethnic Kosovo',[48] but NATO has committed neither the political will nor the resources to prevent it.

## In Spite of it All, Resistance to Ethnic Hatred Continues

For many commentators, multi-ethnic or non-ethnic approaches to human rights are finished in Kosovo. Yet there are many examples of resistance to ethnic hatred if one looks for them, and even the acts of repression are themselves testament to the continuing existence of pockets of resistance. Resistance to mono-ethnicity can be measured in terms of the continuing presence of minority groups such as the substantial Serb minorities in places such as Fushë Kosovë/Kosovo Polje and Gjilan/Gnjilane. Although the Dragash/Gora area has an Albanian Kosovar provisional administration, it has a Gorani Kosovar majority.[49] Seven hundred Serbs had even gone against the tide and returned to the US sector by early November 1999.[50] Possibly some of those who have stayed have done so because they have no money to allow them to leave and nowhere to go. But they are still there in spite of the pressure on them, and their presence provides hope for the future.

There are remarkable examples of those for whom persecution has not been enough to create ethnic hatred within them. After the arrival of NATO, the KLA took away the son of Serbian Kosovar Bozhana Dedic and an unidentified gunman shot and wounded her husband. She finally felt forced to leave the town of Rahovec/Orahovac in central Kosovo. As she left, she nevertheless sympathised with the very people who were driving her out: 'Many wrongs were done to them ... Milosevic is a fascist!'[51] In yet another example of the ways in which the situation does not fit crude ethnic models of the conflict, the convoy of which she was a part was heading for Montenegro because the people on it do not expect to be made welcome in Serbia. The Serbian Orthodox Church has spoken out about the crimes of Serbian forces, but has still come under attack from some Albanian Kosovars. Father Arsinje, a Serbian Orthodox monk in western Kosovo, whose monastery is guarded by KFOR troops, stated that 'we have a strong belief that it will be better ... Maybe it won't be easy but I believe in common sense and the humanity of the Albanians.'[52] On what is often called 'the other side of the ethnic divide', some very brave Albanian Kosovars are speaking out against the KLA. Veton Surroi, the publisher of the newspaper *Koha Ditore*, has condemned attacks on minorities as fascism and a threat to the future of Albanian Kosovars. In response, the KLA's news agency, Kosova Press, openly issued death threats against him and his editor, Baton Haxhiu.[53] According to an Albanian Kosovar woman who survived the war by staying with a Serb friend in Belgrade and who returned to Kosovo after the war, 'Albanians like me, who don't think like a street mob, are in as much danger as the Serbs ... I believe that when this madness settles down, Serbs and Albanians will find a way to live side by side'.[54]

## NATO: Spendthrifts for War, Pennypinchers for Peace

What role have the NATO states played in this desperate struggle to win the peace and secure human rights within Kosovo? UNMIK, which is dominated by NATO-country personnel, is required under SCR 1244, Paragraph 10, to 'provide transitional administration while establishing and overseeing the development of provisional democratic self-governing institutions'. Prior to the holding of OSCE-monitored elections, the KLA's provisional government under Thaçi controlled through unofficial administrations 27 out of 29 communes.[55] The UN lacked the resources to run the communes and relied on these unofficial KLA administrations, which were officially subordinate to UNMIK. These unofficial communal authorities were also very short of resources and relied on collecting unofficial taxes with varying degrees of success, fairness and coercion. According to the International Crisis Group (ICG), a non-governmental organisation, the people are mostly indifferent to these authorities due to their lack of ability to deliver services or are hostile due to actual or perceived KLA involvement in extortion and intimidation. Furthermore, Rugova's Democratic League of Kosovo and others refuse to recognise these communal authorities, and examples of non-Albanian Kosovars serving on authorities for communes with mainly Albanian Kosovar populations are very rare. In the absence of proper security guarantees, Serbian Kosovar leaders have called for ethnic cantons to protect the human rights of Kosovo's remaining non-Albanians: this has been rejected by both UNMIK and Albanian Kosovar representatives as a possible prelude to the partition of Kosovo.

The ICG proposed that, if greater resources are not forthcoming, UNMIK makes the best of a bad job by working with the KLA communal authorities until elections to provide services to all regardless of ethnicity rather than wasting its limited energy on battles for ethnic tokenism in the form of small numbers of minorities serving in communal authorities. Although effective action is better than ineffective tokenism, it needs to be emphasised that the necessary resources are not being provided by NATO to ensure a better peace. Instead, the worst possible elements among the Albanian Kosovars – the KLA – are allowed to run most of Kosovo unofficially, often criminally, and in a way that excludes not only non-Albanian Kosovars but also moderate and non-violent Albanian Kosovars. On 10 October 1999, backed by UN police, the UN administrator successfully expelled the KLA mayor of Suharekë/Suva Reka. This shows that firm action can work, but one-off local actions like this are no substitute for resources and political will coming from the top.

There is a vital need to give people an economic stake in peace and the rule of law, but this is not being done. Of a working-age population of 1,330,000, only about 470,000 are economically active, due to the combined effects of the war, continuing conflict and discrimination. Furthermore, many in work are not being paid, and many unemployed and pensioners are receiving no or reduced benefits.[56] Bernard Kouchner, head of UNMIK, and Kofi Annan, UN Secretary-General, have appealed for more resources to pay the salaries of public officials so that they do not turn the black market or the mafia.[57] UNMIK had a shortfall in its budget of $25 million in 1999 and though Western governments in November 1999 finally got around to pledging $1 billion worth of reconstruction aid, it remains to be seen how much of that money will actually be given. It is dwarfed by the estimated sum of about $30 billion needed for reconstruction in Serbia (including Kosovo) and the $4 billion NATO estimates in spent on its 78-day bombing campaign.[58] Kouchner requested 6,000 police from abroad: 4,700 were promised and only 1,700 have arrived, with little expectation of more.[59]

## NATO Short-term Credibility Bolstered at the Expense of Human Rights

Some pro-war analysts assert that it is self-evident that NATO's motivation was primarily or even purely humanitarian because, it is claimed, NATO had no economic or strategic interests in Kosovo. However, according to US Secretary of Defence William S. Cohen and General Henry H. Shelton, Chairman of the US Joint Chiefs of Staff, NATO had 'three major interests' in going to war in Kosovo: preventing the destabilisation of 'NATO's south-eastern region'; ending repression by Serbia which had produced a refugee flow 'overtaxing bordering nations' infrastructures, and fracturing the NATO alliance'; and responding to Serbian conduct which had 'directly challenged the credibility of NATO'.[60] Cohen and Shelton asserted that 'had NATO not responded ... its own credibility, as well as the credibility of US security commitments throughout the world, would have been called into question'. NATO, and especially the United States, has for a long time been very concerned, even obsessed, about its 'credibility'. It had been making threats for years against Serbia but had not got its way. The United States has also been keen to show that NATO has a post-Cold War role to play, to make use of the decreased constraint provided by the demise of the Soviet Union, to extend NATO's operations outside the NATO area, to establish the acceptability of US-led NATO action without constraints being imposed by the United Nations, and to establish US dominance in interpreting or rejecting international law.[61]

It is easy to believe that NATO decision-makers were sincere in their proclamations of concern for human rights in Kosovo. Sometimes decision-makers lie cynically and self-consciously, but generally people have a great capacity to believe their own words and to believe in their own moral rectitude. However, human rights rhetoric, even when it is sincerely believed by those who employ it, is not enough. After all, claims to be promoting the greater good of humanity have for centuries been a standard concomitant of the most brutal and genocidal of imperialist wars.[62] The question is less about whether or not NATO believed itself to be acting for humanitarian motives than about the nature and desirability of its humanitarianism. It is striking that the humanitarianism of Cohen and Shelton is not one which challenges the notion of sovereignty in the defence of human rights, but which sees the defence of human rights as a means of protecting the sovereignty of the states which are doing the intervening.[63] The anti-war narrative does not demand pure or entirely self-sacrificing motives. It objects to assertions that NATO motives were primarily humanitarian if humanitarianism is defined as putting human rights ahead of state interests. NATO's vision of humanitarianism is state-centric, and therefore will sacrifice or put at risk human rights on a massive scale if it perceives state interests as requiring it. When NATO bombed Serbia to shore up its credibility and show Serbia who is boss, it did so despite intelligence warnings that it would provoke terrible escalation of human rights violations in Kosovo. Hence NATO was guilty of the reckless endangerment of the Kosovars. A favourite supposed trump card used in the pro-war narrative is that we need to listen to the Albanian Kosovars: they wanted NATO to go to war, and they do not regret it even now. However, those who espouse the pro-war narrative suffered from selective hearing. Did Albanian Kosovars want that war – the one in which NATO flew at over 20,000 feet leaving them to be massacred at will by Serbian forces on the ground? Did they want the one after which they are left impoverished, without justice and at the mercy of Thaçi's thugs? Are they listening to Albanian Kosovars like Surroi and Haxhiu who regard non-Albanians as fellow Kosovars?

NATO's promotion of its credibility and state-centric notion of human rights is in trouble even in its own terms when one looks beyond the short term. While there are some within KFOR and the United Nations who are fully committed to protecting what is left of multi-ethnic Kosovo, others in those bodies are of the view that a mono-ethnic Kosovo is the best way forward, to pave the way for what they hope will be a trouble-free referendum on independence in a few years' time. NATO has failed to answer the big question about what it will do if Kosovo votes for independence or unification with Albania. A vote for either option is likely to result in an attack launched by Serbia should the NATO forces withdraw and perhaps even if they do not. Furthermore, an independent Kosovo would be very destabilising: it would lead to increased demands for a Greater Albania through a merger of Albania and Kosovo and through claims on Macedonian and Montenegrin territory inhabited by Albanians. A war between Serbia and Montenegro over the possible independence of the latter would be similarly destabilising. The comprehensive approach needed to stabilise the region and protect human rights is absent.

## Worthy and Unworthy Victims of Human Rights Abuses

The pro-war narrative argues that NATO's humanitarianism should not be questioned just because it helps some but not others – it cannot help everyone. It also assumes that NATO either does nothing or mitigates violations of human rights. The anti-war narrative is superior in having a third category – that NATO may exacerbate human rights abuses, by accident or even design. The most direct comparison available is NATO member-state Turkey, which has also killed thousands, and displaced hundreds of thousands more, to crush both armed and peaceful resistance in a minority group (the Kurds). These are very similar to the figures for the suffering inflicted by Serbia on Kosovo before NATO started bombing. Far from bombing Turkey or imposing an arms embargo, or even just doing nothing, the United States and the rest of NATO (minus Greece of course) has armed it to the teeth and downplayed the repression.

What is it that makes the cases of Kosovo and Turkey different? The anti-war narrative has a systematic explanation: consistency underlies the inconsistency. According to Noam Chomsky, it follows a familiar pattern: 'Serbia is one of those disorderly miscreants that impede the institution of a US-dominated global system, while Turkey is a loyal client state that contributes substantially to that project.'[64] In Chomsky's terms, worthy victims of human rights abuses (such as Albanian Kosovars and Iraqi Kurds after Iraq invaded Kuwait) are those whose suffering is inflicted by an official enemy and thus to be highlighted and portrayed in anguished terms. Unworthy victims (such as Serbian Kosovars, Serbs in the Krajina region of Croatia, Turkish Kurds, Iraqi Kurds before Iraq invaded Kuwait, East Timorese, Lebanese and Palestinians) are those whose suffering is inflicted by a tacit or formal official ally and thus to be de-emphasised or ignored.[65] This approach was exemplified in the actions of William Walker, who, according to Human Rights Watch, as US Ambassador to El Salvador in 1989 played down atrocities by the regime, but, as head of the OSCE's

KVM, played a major role in publicising the massacre of 45 Albanian Kosovars in the village of Racak in spring 1999.[66] Similarly, UNMIK chief Kouchner has argued that the ethnic cleansing of non-Albanian Kosovars which has been taking place since the Serbian withdrawal is different from the ethnic cleansing in Kosovo of Albanian Kosovars because 'all the political leaders in Kosovo say ... that they want to build a Kosovo with all the communities'.[67] However, the rhetoric of the official enemy Milosevic is identical: he has said that 'our approach is multiethnic, multicultural, multireligious and insists on equality of national communities' and 'we make a big difference between the separatist movement in Kosovo and Metohija and the Albanian people that is honest, good'.[68] From their record, I see no reason to believe either the KLA or Milosevic.

*Irresponsible Humanitarianism and the Production of the LocoLocals*

In the pro-war narrative, the discourse of humanitarianism is seen as representing ethico-political progress in comparison with the discourse of national interest, in which action is taken only if it is expected to benefit the nation which the decision-maker rules. However, humanitarianism as developed so far frames humanitarianism and humanitarian intervention in a way which generates irresponsibility at every level. First, it produces an image of loco locals – those immoral others with their ancient ethnic hatreds – who create humanitarian disasters. In this discourse, the societies from which the humanitarians (usually Western ones) come have had at most a marginal role in bringing about these situations. Second, the humanitarians come along and try to manage the dilemma of trying to help without being tricked and manipulated by the devious locals. They are supposedly doing the best they can for human rights in a difficult, even intractable, situation and so they have no choice but to work within the realities on the ground (of commitment to mono-ethnicity) while still trumpeting their own ideals (of commitment to multi-ethnicity). Third, the Western news media generally work within this framing, and they generally framed NATO's war as a worthy enterprise in defence of human rights. Donald Trelford, former editor of *The Observer* and now a Professor of Journalism Studies at the University of Sheffield, complained: 'It is puzzling that so much bad feeling should have developed between the British Government and media when the country's newspapers, on the whole, strongly supported the war and presented Tony Blair as a hawkish hero against his "wobbling alliance partners".'[69] If Trelford is right, on balance the news media served to sell the war to the public rather than maintain the kind of critical distance necessary to hold the government to account and democratic control.

Those in the news media, however critical they try to be, generally work within the state's framing of worthy and unworthy victims of human rights abuses.[70]

The binaries here are temporal and causal (they create the situation, then we intervene), moral (they are morally inferior to us) and spatial (they live there, we live here) with minimal us-them overlap. The discourse of NATO's humanitarianism is an Orientalist or Balkanist one presuming 'our' civilisational superiority.[71] It is a depoliticising discourse which disables criticism by presuming high moral intent as the principal motive of the intervener. In this way, the kind of systematic historical comparisons which help expose the operation of categories of worthy and unworthy victims is sidelined: as David Campbell argues, for humanitarianism to be truly human and not dehumanising, suffering must be put in historical and political context so that the extent of the responsibility of actors claiming humanitarian motives is identified.[72] Irresponsible humanitarianism has permeated NATO policy towards Serbia. NATO has refused to take any responsibility for making negotiations impossible, for triggering the escalation which followed the beginning of its bombing campaign and for failing to prepare to assist the flood of refugees which it fully expected to occur. Now the war is over, it is not meeting its human rights responsibilities under UN SCR 1244 as it is failing to provide physical security and an effective interim civil administration.

NATO likes to think of its perspective on ethnicity and identity as radically different from the ethnic cleansers it claims to oppose.[73] However, they have a great deal in common. They think in terms of identifiable, fixed and distinct groups, and prioritise the ethnic dimension of identity, and the Western notion of self-determination is that nation and state should coincide. Thinking in terms of 'the Serbs' versus 'the Albanians' appears to be natural and commonsensically true, but it is a political construct which has many negative consequences. Reducing all of Kosovo society to 'ten per cent Serb, 90 per cent Albanian' plays into the hands of the ethnic cleansers because such figures give absolutely no weight to those of a mixed ethnic heritage (and the further back through the generations one goes, the more mixed it will be in that supposedly 'pure' Serbs or whoever turn out to be ethnically mixed), or to political differences within the supposed ethnic groups. The notion of multi-ethnic human rights employed in Dayton and the Kosovo peace deal is still an essentialist one of tolerance (suggesting grudging coexistence and putting up with something you neither understand nor like) between fixed and supposedly separate ethnic groups. Typical of this attitude is Chapter 1, Article VII.7 of Rambouillet which states that 'Every person shall have the right freely to choose to be treated or not to be treated as belonging to a national community, and no disadvantage shall result from that choice or from the exercise of the rights connected to that choice.' Yet the main purpose of Article VII is to set out extensive 'additional rights' for national communities and their members both collectively and individually. These are to be additional to the international recognised human rights and fundamental freedoms specified in Article VI. If national communities have additional rights, individuals who do not choose to be identified with a national community must be disadvantaged. Belief in the existence of identifiable, fixed and ethnically distinct groups is a key part of the problem within and far beyond Kosovo. Hence my emphasis on hybridity throughout this article by using the labels 'Serbian Kosovar' and 'Albanian Kosovar' rather than 'Serbian' and 'Albanian', although even these labels do not escape a degree of ethnic reductionism. We need to think in terms of the fluidity and multiple dimensions of identity rather than reinforcing the present ethnic reductionism in which no other axes of identity are acknowledged because it is this reductionism or essentialism that makes ethnic violence possible.

## CONCLUSION

The pro-war narrative, that NATO's actions have resulted in a better peace in terms of human rights within and beyond Kosovo, rests on a series of claims which I have assessed in turn. The first is that the peace deal proposed at Rambouillet by the Contact Group and rejected by Milosevic was a reasonable one. The second is that NATO's war against Serbia and the threats which preceded it did nothing to increase the scale of human rights abuses against the Albanian Kosovars. The third is that the Kosovo Accord which ended the war is essentially the same deal as the one which the Contact Group offered at Rambouillet and represents Milosevic's surrender to NATO's demands. The fourth is that NATO's war against Serbia holds out the prospect of a better peace in Kosovo and elsewhere because it was a victory for the notion of humanitarianism.

My overall argument is that NATO's war did not result in a better peace. First, the Rambouillet peace proposal was unworkable and NATO should have explored compromise instead of going to war. Second, NATO's use of force and its preceding threats made things much worse for Albanian Kosovars by provoking an increase in the human rights violations inflicted on them. NATO anticipated this but used force to bolster its credibility even though it expected this to jeopardise human rights in Kosovo. Third, the peace deal which ended NATO's war against

Serbia involved concessions by NATO, although NATO is managing to a great extent to impose its own interpretation of the outcome. Fourth, NATO's humanitarianism is a deeply flawed and dangerous one which has produced a bad peace in Kosovo in terms of human rights – economic and physical insecurity, crime with impunity, and political structures which reward ethnic mobilisation. Annan has declared that 'we had all the resources for the war, and we should have a similar determination when it comes to rebuilding peace ... we will be knocking on all the doors of the governments who have given us the mandate.'[74] Providing the resources for war but not for peace is only irrational if you assume that this really was a war in which the human rights of the people of Kosovo were the priority. It makes sense if it was a war for NATO credibility at Kosovo's expense, with Kosovar victims of human rights abuses who are deemed worthy to the extent that their suffering can be exploited to portray Serbia as a 'rogue' state,[75] but who will otherwise be left in the lurch with the unworthy victims. I am no automatic opponent of NATO's use of force: I supported the NATO bombing in Bosnia in 1995. If NATO had committed the political will and resources to guaranteeing human rights for all in Kosovo, it could have persuaded many of those who opposed the bombing that it was worthwhile, on balance. Instead, since June 1999 it has presided over human rights violations – almost totally ignored by pro-war analysts – already approaching the scale of those which supposedly triggered its bombing campaign.

A truly humanitarian intervention in Kosovo – that is, one in which the human rights of the people of Kosovo would be the primary concern, in which the specific causes of their suffering were addressed and in which the interveners face up to their many responsibilities – is needed urgently. In Kosovo, it would require economic security to reduce the incentives for crime for material and political gain under an ethnic flag of convenience; physical security so that non-Albanian Kosovars and moderate Albanian Kosovars can stay, organise and speak out; justice to reduce incentives for acts of revenge; and the establishment of a political system which penalises ethnic mobilisation. More generally, it would involve exposing and opposing human rights abuses in equal measure regardless of the perpetrator and not just as a means of securing state sovereignty and discrediting opponents. However, simply recommending a non-ethnic, non-state-centric humanitarianism to NATO is pointless, as NATO embodies and produces ethnic, state-centric politics. Those in academia and the news media who proclaim NATO's war against Serbia and its aftermath to be a triumph for humanitarianism reinforce such politics. The change in NATO policy can only come when the societies within NATO themselves change. In this sense, we need political intervention in NATO as well as in the Balkans.

ACKNOWLEDGEMENTS

I would like to thank Christina Blunt, Ken Booth, Piers Robinson, Richard Shapcott, Jutta Weldes and two anonymous referees for their comments on an earlier draft of this article. Thanks also to Federica Andreoli, Anne Jewell, Polyxeni Leoussi, Dominique Makins, Piers Robinson, Ariadne Sifis and especially Doug Stokes for providing me with much valuable information. The opinions expressed in this article are solely those of the author.

NOTES

1. Michael Howard, *Restraints on War: Studies in the Limitation of Armed Conflict* (Oxford: Oxford University Press, 1979), p.14.
2. The Federal Republic of Yugoslavia (FRY) is composed of the republics of Serbia and Montenegro. Serbia itself includes the province of Vojvodina in the north and Kosovo in the south. Yugoslavia is effectively defunct.
3. *Interim Agreement for Peace and Self-Government in Kosovo* of 23 February 1999: http://www.monde-diplomatique.fr/dossiers/kosovo/rambouillet.html
4. *Main Elements of Self-Governance in Kosovo and Metohija*, 20 Mar. 1999: http://www.serbia-info.com/news/1999-03/20/9890.html; and *Conclusions of Serbian Parliament*, 24 Mar. 1999: http://www.serbia-info.com/news/1999-03/24/10030.html
5. On Russia's role, see Marc Weller, 'The Rambouillet Conference on Kosovo', *International Affairs*, Vol.75, No.2 (1999), pp.212, 227, 229 and 235.
6. Noam Chomsky, *The New Military Humanism: Lessons From Kosovo* (Monroe, ME: Common Courage Press, 1999), p.107.
7. Weller (note 5), pp.232–3, 245.
8. *The Interview of President Milosevic to the American TV Network CBS April 25*, Serbia Info News: http://ww.serbia-info.com/news/1999-04/25/11279.html.
9. Weller (note 5), pp.219–20.
10. Seth Ackerman, *Fairness and Accuracy in Reporting (FAIR) Media Advisory*, 14 May 1999: http://www.fair.org/press-releases/kosovo-solution.html; Chomsky (note 6), pp.108–10.
11. Simon Scott Plummer, 'NATO's War Illegal, Says Lawyer', *The Guardian*, 13 Nov. 1999.
12. Seth Ackerman, 'What Reporters Knew About Kosovo Talks – But Didn't Tell. Was Rambouillet Another Tonkin Gulf?' *FAIR Media Advisory*, 2 June 1999: http://www.lbbs.org/fair_media_advisory.htm.
13. Some have constructed the narrative differently and argued that this was the War of Lewinsky's Dress, namely that Clinton was trying to distract attention from and undermine the impeachment proceedings.
14. Interview in Gavin Hewitt and Tom Mangold, 'The War Room', *Panorama*, BBC1 television, 21 Apr. 1999.
15. White House Press Briefing, 24 Mar. 1999.
16. Interview in Hewitt and Mangold (note 14).
17. See Federica Andreoli, *A Protagonist at the Air-Field, a Ghost at the Castle*, MSc thesis, Department of Politics, University of Bristol, Sept. 1999.
18. See Noel Malcolm, *Kosovo: A Short History* (London: Papermac, 1998), Ch.17; and Julie A. Mertus, *Kosovo: How Myths and Truths Started a War* (London: University of California Press, 1999).
19. Quoted in Weller (note 5), p.223.
20. Interview in Hewitt and Mangold (note 14).

21. Eric Canepa (translation and commentary), 'The Aftermath of the Publication of the German Government Documents', http://www.lbbs.org/ZNETTOPnoanimation.html. See also the German Ministry of Defence website www.bundeswehr.de/kosovo/hufeisen.html.
22. Interview in Hewitt and Mangold (note 14).
23. See, for example, Tony Blair quoted in George Jones, 'Milosevic Will Pay High Price, Says Blair', *The Daily Telegraph*, 23 Mar. 1999.
24. For a more extended critique of this element of the pro-war narrative see Stephen R. Shalom, 'A Just War?' Autumn 1999: http://www.lbbs.org/CrisesCurEvts/a_just_war.htm.
25. Robert Fisk, 'How Fake Guns and Painting the Roads Fooled NATO' and 'Serb Army "Unscathed by NATO"', *The Independent*, 23 June 1999.
26. Interview in Hewitt and Mangold (note 14).
27. Rupert Cornwell, 'Serbs Retaliate With Massacres as NATO Shoots Down Two Jets', *The Independent*, 27 Mar. 1999; Chomsky (note 6), pp.20–21, 36, 81–84.
28. Chomsky (note 6), pp.35–36, 82; Hewitt and Mangold (note 14).
29. Interview in Hewitt and Mangold (note 14).
30. Francis Wheen, 'Death and Denial in Kosovo', *The Guardian*, 3 Nov. 1999.
31. Fisk, 'Serb Army' (note 25).
32. Bob Jiggins, '"Tough on Milosevic and Tough on the Causes of Milosevic": The Manufacture of a Humanitarian Crisis', University of Bradford, June 1999 manuscript, pp.12–17.
33. For an extensive report on human rights abuses in Kosovo between October 1998 and June 1999, see part one of the OSCE report *Kosovo/Kosova: As Seen, As Told*, 6 December 1999: http://www.osce.org/kosovo/reports/hr/htm.index.htm.
34. http://www.newsunlimited.co.uk/Kosovo/Story/0.2763.55664.00.html.
35. http://www.newsunlimited.co.uk/Kosovo/Story/0.2763.57296.00.html.
36. http://www.un.org/Docs/scres/1999/99sc1244.htm.
37. See Phyllis Bennis, 'Differences Between the Ahtisaari-Chernomyrdin Agreement with Milosevic and the Rambouillet Text', 10 June 1999: http://www.lbbs.org/bennissettle.htm; David Peterson 'The Berlin Scenario' and 'What the Documents Really Say About the Occupation of Kosovo', 23 June 1999: http://www.lbbs.org/ZNETTOPnoanimation.html.
38. Chomsky (note 6), pp.117–28; Peterson (note 37).
39. For an extensive report, see Part 2 of the OSCE report (note 33): this covers 14 June to 31 Oct. 1999.
40. International Crisis Group (ICG), *Violence in Kosovo: Who's Killing Whom?* 2 Nov. 1999: http://www.intl-crisis-group.org/projects/sbalkans/reports/kos29rep.htm (no pagination).
41. Amnesty International (AI), *Federal Republic of Yugoslavia. A Broken Circle: "Disappeared" and Abducted in Kosovo Province*, Oct. 1999, AI - Report - EUR 70/106/99: http://www.amnesty.org/ailib/aipub/1999/EUR/47010699.htm (no pagination).
42. 'Janez Kovac' (pseudonym of a Sarajevo journalist), 'Reconciliation in Kosovo Tougher Than in Bosnia', The Institute of War and Peace Reporting (IWPR) Balkan Crisis Report No.88, 29 Oct. 1999: info@iwpr.net.
43. AI (note 41).
44. Steven Erlanger, 'Chaos and Intolerance Now Reign in Kosovo Despite UN's Efforts', *New York Times*, 22 Nov. 1999: http://nytimes.com/library/world/europe/112299kosovo-chaos.html.
45. Where place names in Kosovo are different in Albanian and Serbian, I indicate both versions (Albanian then Serbian), with the exception of Kosova/o where I have adopted the internationally most common version, i.e. Kosovo.
46. Chris Bird, 'Hate-Filled Town Where Hitler Gets a Laugh', *The Guardian*, 13 Oct. 1999.
47. AI (note 41).

48. Quoted in 'Kovac' (note 42).
49. ICG, *Waiting for UNMIK: Local Administration in Kosovo*, 18 Oct. 1999: http://www.intl-crisis-group.org/projects/sbalkans/reports/kos28rep.htm (no pagination).
50. 'Head of UN Mission'.
51. Chris Bird, 'No Sanctuary in Town Ruled by Hate', *The Guardian*, 28 Oct. 1999.
52. Chris Bird, 'Email Chris Bird @ Visokui Decani', *The Guardian*, 29 Nov. 1999.
53. Bird, 'Hate-Filled Town' (note 46). Although Bird's article contained clear examples of resistance to hatred, *The Guardian* chose a headline which portrayed the town as full of hatred.
54. Quoted in 'Kovac' (note 42).
55. This paragraph draws on ICG, *Waiting for UNMIK* (note 49).
56. 'War, Civil Strife and Discriminatory Practices Leave Two-Thirds of Kosovo Unemployed, Says UN Labour Agency Report', 19 Oct. 1999: http://www.un.org/peace/kosovo/news/kosovo2.htm#Anchor23.
57. 'Head of UN Mission in Kosovo Appeals to Security Council for More Funding', 5 Nov. 1999; and 'Secretary-General Tells Security Council More Resources Needed for UN to Administer Kosovo', 12 Oct. 1999: http://www.un.org/peace/kosovo/news/kosovo2.htm#Anchor23.
58. Erlanger (note 44); Richard Norton-Taylor, Peter Capella, 'Bill for Kosovo War Goes Over £30bn', *The Guardian*, 15 Oct. 1999.
59. Reuters, 'UN Mission Chief in Kosovo Pleads for More Police', *The Guardian*, 17 Nov. 1999. See also ICG, *The Policing Gap: Law and Order in the New Kosovo*, 6 August 1999: http://www.intl-crisis-group.org/projects/sbalkans/reports/kos26rep.htm.
60. *Joint Statement on the Kosovo After Action Review, before the Senate Armed Services Committee*, 14 Oct. 1999: http://www.defenselink.mil/news/Oct1999/b10141999_bt478-99.html.
61. Chomsky (note 6), esp. Ch.6. See also Stephen R. Shalom, 'Reflections on NATO and Kosovo', Summer 1999: http://www.zmag.org/chomsky/index.cfm.
62. Chomsky (note 6), esp. pp.74–80.
63. David Campbell, 'Why Fight: Humanitarianism, Principles, and Post-Structuralism', *Millennium: Journal of International Studies*, Vol.28, No.3 (1998), pp.497–521; Nevzat Soguk, *States and Strangers: Refugees and Displacements of Statecraft* (London: University of Minnesota Press, 1999); Peter Nyers, 'Emergency or Emerging Identities? Refugees and Transformations in World Order', *Millennium: Journal of International Studies*, Vol.28, No.1 (1999), pp.1–26.
64. Chomsky (note 6), p.13. See also pp.6–8.
65. Ibid, p.19.
66. Human Rights Watch quoted in ibid, pp.33, 40–48.
67. Quoted in Reuters (note 59).
68. *Interview of President Milosevic* (note 8).
69. Quoted in Michael Evans, 'The Real Battle for War Reporters', *The Times*, 29 Oct. 1999.
70. Edward S. Herman and Noam Chomsky, *Manufacturing Consent: The Political Economy of the Mass Media* (New York: Pantheon Books, 1988), Ch.2.
71. David Campbell, *National Deconstruction: Violence, Identity, and Justice in Bosnia* (London: University of Minnesota Press, 1998), p.90.
72. Campbell, 'Why Fight' (note 63).
73. I am heavily indebted on this point to David Campbell. See especially his *National Deconstruction* (note 71).
74. 'Secretary-General Tells Security Council' (note 57) .
75. See Eric Herring, 'Rogue Rage: Can We Prevent Mass Destruction?' *Journal of Strategic Studies*, Vol.23, No.1 (March 2000), pp.188–212.

# 12
# The Ambiguities of Elections in Kosovo: Democratisation versus Human Rights?

## IAN R. MITCHELL

### BOSNIAN ECHOES?

The citizens of Bosnia are in fact in the middle of a crash course in democratic responsibility...our main goal is eventual withdrawal from a democratic and prosperous region. Any sign of Bosnians, from any quarter, taking responsibility for themselves will be welcomed as evidence that we are at last firmly on that road.[1]

– High Representative to Bosnia Wolfgang Petritsch,
17 September 1999

The establishment of legitimate democratic institutions with accountability to Kosovo's electors, regardless of ethnicity, will be a cornerstone of the project to implement human rights and the rule of law in the province. However, the international community's experience in Bosnia suggests that elections can neither solve difficult security challenges nor necessarily speed the realisation of human and civil rights. On the contrary, election periods invariably bring the underlying conflicts in any society, particularly post-conflict societies, to the surface. The tension between the need to establish democratic legitimacy for self-government, and the recognition that a formal democratic process may not deliver political leadership willing to implement a human rights regime characterises the debate on elections in Kosovo. Given that it is unlikely conditions will exist for 'free and fair' elections in Kosovo, will the act of holding them, and the likely result which will emerge, help or hinder human rights?

Perhaps foreshadowing the dilemmas that face the international community in Kosovo, a senior OSCE official in Bosnia and Hercegovina

(BiH) stated that the creation of sustainable democratic institutions requires 'undemocratic democratisation'.[2] To wit, while the United Nations Security Council Resolution (UNSCR) 1244, the basis for the international protectorate in Kosovo, explicitly provides for self-government, it is vague on the timing and purpose of the formal democratic procedure through which it is to be realised. The key decisions about the details of this democratic step have been left to the United Nations Interim Administration Mission in Kosovo (UNMIK) and one of its supporting partner agencies, the Organization for Security and Cooperation in Europe (OSCE). These key decisions include: who is eligible to vote and in which communities; the timing of the elections; and the question of how the results will be implemented. The 'international community' as used here means the international agencies charged with responsibility for the democratisation process in both Bosnia and Kosovo, and ultimately the body that gives them direction, the UN Security Council.[3]

The criticism of the elections held in BiH, and the democratisation process more generally, provides a framework with which to examine the question of elections in Kosovo. The range of critical analyses can be grouped into three broad schools. Each of them has a different understanding of the purpose of the democratisation project, the role of elections within it and their validity as indicators of the sovereignty of the state in question. I will label these schools 'liberal', 'conservative' and 'autonomist'.[4] The first school argues for greater international intervention to effect democratisation, and marginalises the value of elections held under unfavourable conditions. The International Crisis Group is a key exponent of the 'liberal' view.[5] The conservative school tends to argue that there is little that the international community can do to impose liberal democracy in post-war conditions; in contrast it warns against such imposition as the derogation of sovereignty on the questionable basis of humanitarian intervention. Susan Woodward's work illustrates this privileging of the autonomy of the state.[6] The autonomist school calls for a recognition of the link between ethnic security and democratisation, suggesting that the former must proceed the latter, and failure to recognise the popular expression of ethnic autonomy is a denial of democracy. David Chandler is the prominent, but not the only example of this school.[7] The distinction between the liberal and autonomist schools is the most clear cut; it will be the focus of this essay.

The debate over elections will be assessed from a 'top down' perspective, examining the choices to be made by the international community with responsibility for the development of self-government in

Kosovo. Elections will be taken as the primary focus of the international community's democratisation project, and therefore of this essay. This definition excludes many important factors, most notably the development of civil society. While beyond the scope of this essay, civil society remains a key to the development of a human rights regime and the stability of Kosovo.

This essay will first survey the key themes in the arguments of all three critical schools. Secondly, it will examine the democratisation project in BiH as it affects elections. Finally, it will consider the specific challenges of holding elections in Kosovo and what they may mean for the development of human rights in the province.

### DEMOCRACY VERSUS DEMOCRATISATION

> Democratisation is said to begin when the first set of free and fair elections for national-level office takes place.
>
> – K. Dawisha[8]

The distinction between democracy and democratisation is the key to an understanding of how the schools perceive the relative success or failure of the democratisation projects in Bosnia and Kosovo. The theme of democratisation theory, developed following the end of the Cold War, established it as a 'process' containing a period known as 'transition', and an end-state of 'consolidation'.

> Democratisation as a term describes the overall process of regime change from start to completion ... it therefore embraces both broad processes of what are conventionally referred to in the comparative literature as 'transition' to a liberal or constitutional democracy and its subsequent consolidation. The outcome is a system that should meet certain basic procedural requirements, such as a commitment to regular elections and institutional mechanisms that provide checks on executive power, as well as the guarantee of human rights and emergence of a political culture that is clearly supportive of democratic political life. The principal objective of consolidation is for the risks and uncertainties typical of transition to be gradually reduced to a point where failure in democratisation becomes highly improbable.[9]

Transition is defined as a decisive stage and requires 'above all, negotiating the constitutional settlement and the rules of procedure for political competition, but also dismantling authoritarian agencies and abolishing laws unsuitable for democratic politics'.[10] Consolidation continues the process over a longer period of time involving 'the full rooting of the new democracy, the internalisation of its rules and procedures and the dissemination of democratic values'.[11] Transition in the former Communist states of eastern and south-eastern Europe has taken place in the context of radical economic and social reform, creating new political loyalties and communities, but as often hardening social identification around old or rediscovered loyalties, such as ethnicity.

When democratisation is applied to post-conflict zones which are militarily divided, politically fragmented, ethnically separated and operating under the rule of local warlords rather than the rule of law, it begs the question: who shall correct the rules unsuitable for democratic politics and dismantle authoritarian agencies? In both Bosnia and Kosovo, the international community has assumed this responsibility. Given the concept of democratisation as a process, rather than an end-state, this role, taken to its logical extreme, can extend indefinitely. A state must claim to have consolidated democracy, or more importantly, be judged to have internalised the rules, procedures and values of democracy. Among these values is the promotion of human rights.

## THE MAIN SCHOOLS OF CRITICISM

The leading exponent of the liberal school, both in Bosnia and in Kosovo, is the widely cited International Crisis Group (ICG). Recognising in Bosnia the failure of formal democracy to deliver political regimes which respect the framework of human rights established by the peace agreement, it calls for the international community to take up the role of dismantling impediments to the establishing of liberal democracy. Liberals note, in exasperation, that the political will evident among the international community in the framing of the peace agreement has not been matched by the commitment of the necessary resources for the completion of its aims.[12]

For this school, effective voter choice is not possible without the appropriate conditions for elections. The consistent pattern of electoral support in Bosnia for nationalist parties since 1996 only reflects the near-total domination of the political sphere by nationalist forces, not the people's (assumed) long-term wishes for a liberal democratic regime and the prosperity that this promises.[13]

The ICG, and many others, have stated that Bosnia's elections were held too early, under US pressure.[14] All Bosnia's post war elections have returned nationalist leaders and parties to office. The frustration at not being able to reverse the effects of the war through the first elections led the ICG to comment: 'If one rejects the theory that the very act of voting has a democratising effect on a non-democratic country, then the flawed 1996 general elections in effect turned into a glorified ethnic head count, and proved dangerously counterproductive.'[15]

The failure of the formal democratic process[16] to deliver governments which would recognise, implement and uphold the human rights framework that Dayton provided put at risk the return of refugees and displaced persons to their homes. In this absence of 'democratisation', the liberal school called on the international community to increase the level of its intervention to achieve the aims of the peace agreement.

The conservative criticism of democratisation as practised in Bosnia rejects this prioritisation of the human rights framework at the expense of the political sovereignty of the election's winners. Democratisation, if intended to bring multiethnicity to a country literally and figuratively divided along ethnic lines, is a 'fool's errand' that will end in failure. John Mearsheimer illustrates this attitude: '[Dayton] calls for unifying Bosnia's three hate-filled ethnic groups in a single state. But that goal is infeasible. The Croats and the Serbs want no part of a multiethnic Bosnia – that is why they fought the war in the first place'.[17] To implement policies contrary to this is to risk instability and confusion; worse still, it is irresponsible. The conservative assessment privileges the autonomy of the state over demands for international intervention to assist individuals within the state. For them, a foreign policy aimed at the latter without taking the former into account will fail.[18]

The autonomists share many of the basic preconceptions of the conservative school. They suggest that for the ethnic groups to accept a multicultural political identity, they must first have security for their ethnic community. In Bosnia, the contention, shared with the conservatives, is that the war was fought in support of monoethnic communities. The enforcement of the concept of multiethnicity found in the peace agreement is liable to promote insecurity, and is thereby contrary to a process of reconciliation.

Furthermore, they argue that formal democracy, producing majorities in favour of ethnically exclusive areas, reassures voters of their security and provides the basis for cohering the different communities in a multiethnic state. They reject the liberal contention that voters have not been able to express their real wishes and have not absorbed the culture of democracy necessary to overcome the period of transition. Rather than blame the conditions during elections, or the cultural values of the voters, they suggest that the voters have, in fact, made a rational choice in the circumstances.[19]

The autonomists conclude that the extension of the international regulation of BiH on the basis of the need for continuing democratisation, despite elections deemed by the international community to be 'free and fair', has replaced formal democracy in Bosnia and thereby robbed Bosnians of the capacity for autonomous action. The dynamic of the democratisation process has been to institutionalise fears and insecurities by disempowering Bosnian people and their elected representatives. This notion of disempowerment reappears in the autonomists' assessments of the international community's role in Kosovo. However, the example is made most clearly through an examination of the structure of political responsibility for democratisation in Bosnia.

## BOSNIA: A STALEMATE

Annex 3 of the Dayton Accord stipulates that the Parties agree to 'promote free, fair, and democratic elections and to lay the foundation for representative government and ensure the progressive achievement of democratic goals throughout Bosnia and Hercegovina'.[20] However, the international community has the authority to ensure the implementation of this pledge.

The Office of the High Representative (OHR) is instructed to facilitate the parties' own efforts and to mobilise and, as appropriate, coordinate the activities of the international organisations and agencies involved in the civilian aspects of the peace settlement.[21] The OSCE is the institution responsible for the supervision of elections.[22] This includes the formation of a Provisional Election Commission (PEC), the body responsible for the creation of rules and regulations for the elections, the supervision of the process, and the punishment of any individual or party in violation of the rules. The Chairman of the PEC is the Head of the OSCE Mission to BiH, who holds a deciding, or 'golden', vote, allowing in practice for his complete control of the electoral process.

The initial timeframe for civil implementation of Dayton was set at a fixed period of 12 months.[23] Nine months after the signing of the accord, elections were to provide for representative governments at the state, entity, cantonal and municipal levels. By January 2000, four separate elections had been held on what amounted to a yearly cycle, each seeking to progressively advance and deepen democratisation.

However, this cycle has not established self-sustaining democratic structures. Rather, it has led to two types of government in Bosnia. One has been formally elected through a democratic process, but is collectively unable or unwilling to implement the peace agreement. The other consists of the para-state authorities created by the nationalist parties who continue to dominate the country's political, social and economic life.[24] The latter group, heirs to the Communist Party's levers of social and economic control, have a strategic interest in maintaining the conditions on which their power depends. These include pervasive separation of ethnic communities; fear and insecurity among the general populace; a lack of democratic accountability; breakdown in the rule of law; personalised control over the organs of public order; and the absence of institutions capable of controlling illegal economic activity.[25]

Although political conditions have become more fluid and some of the parties, particularly those in the Republika Srpska, have fragmented or splintered, the dominant nationalist political agenda of separation remains unchanged. It is this lack in the development of political pluralism, or rather the continued influence of the nationalist parties and the corresponding lack of progress in the implementation of Dayton's human rights framework, that fuels calls for increased international powers in Bosnia.[26]

The intention of the Accord was not to create a protectorate, but to offer a 'helping hand', with the clear responsibility for Dayton's implementation resting with the Parties.[27] Critics of the international mandate have proclaimed that it now represents a protectorate, or semi-protectorate, and that the increasingly intrusive role played by the OHR and the OSCE in the conduct of elections is not achieving breakthroughs on substantive issues or contributing to a self-sustaining peace process.[28] The Council of Europe, in which Bosnian political parties uniformly hope for membership as the first step to normalisation in Europe, has stated: 'Since the High Representative is effectively the supreme legislative and executive authority in the country, this means in the final analysis that Bosnia and Hercegovina is not a democracy'.[29]

Despite this role, the High Representative has found that his authority does not translate into actual power.[30] Lacking an enforcement mechanism, such as a loyal constabulary, the OHR is forced to rely on the goodwill and full cooperation of the Parties to implement its decisions, as well as to implement Dayton.[31] It must propagate a political project for which there has never been the willingness among the international community to fully exercise the power that it logically demands. 'Forcing compliance' with the liberal, cosmopolitan components of Dayton is something that the international community seems willing to sanction at the level of the peace conference, but not apply in practice. It remains to be seen whether the same will is available for application in Kosovo.

## SACRIFICING DEMOCRACY FOR HUMAN RIGHTS?

The OSCE's policy decisions in Bosnia illustrate the tension between the international community's electoral objective of a political victory for forces willing to implement the Dayton Accord and the danger of legitimising the power of the nationalist parties. The decisions have affected the status of Bosnian voters, political parties, the rights of citizens to run for office and the shape of local government. Three main examples will be dealt with here: registration of voters, enhancing political pluralism and enforcing mandatory power-sharing arrangements.

Voter registration proved to be the single most contentious issue related to elections in Bosnia. Under Dayton, the vast majority of displaced and refugee voters were accorded a choice as to where they wished to express their political power – either where they had lived prior to the start of the conflict, or where they were presently living.

In the first election under Dayton, citizens had three options: to vote for their previous residence, where they were living presently, or a location where they wished to live in the future. The ICG called this decision and the elections that resulted from it 'an ethnic cleanser's charter'.[32] Liberal opinion, supportive of the Accord's clear-cut emphasis on the right of return, saw this provision as solidifying the results of war and catering to the violent nationalism that now took the form of the dominant political parties. Nationalist parties organised campaigns to intimidate voters to register in those territories that might be vulnerable to loss of political control through displaced or refugee voters. The level of abuse was such that the municipal-level elections, where the political effects were most acute, were postponed three times, eventually being held after a removal of the option to register to vote in a third, future location.[33]

Perceiving the nationalist parties as a block to the development of the BiH state structures, the international community's most important democratisation issue became the growth of pluralist, non-nationalist political parties. The High Representative stated: 'There is a democratic system in the sense that there are democratic elections, but the result of the elections is that they give the advantage to one ethnic group over another. This is only a continuation of war by other means. So in order to develop democratisation, it is necessary to implant more pluralism in the political parties. It is necessary to encourage the development of multiethnic parties'.[34]

The international community sought to achieve this through administrative regulation of the electoral process. By 1998, the OSCE had adopted a policy of funding specifically multiethnic parties, by means of in-kind payments for campaign material production costs. Furthermore, in an effort to curb the continued abuse of the electoral rules and regulations by the nationalist parties, a policy of removal of

candidates from political party lists for infringements by the party, rather
than by the individual, was adopted by the Provisional Election
Commission.[35] Such a high level of engagement drew discreet criticism
even from the OSCE's own election monitoring body, the Office for
Democratic Institutions and Human Rights.[36]

The most direct intervention of the international community into the
realisation of political power from the democratic process was during the
implementation of the 1997 municipal election results. As opposed to the
establishment of municipal governments on the basis of the majority
political parties in the council, representation of minority political parties
in local government was made mandatory throughout BiH. Where
agreement could not, or would not, be reached by the parties involved,
the OSCE and OHR first mediated, and then, where necessary, arbitrated
a binding division of powers. The municipalities were offered incentives
to accept the terms on the basis that aid and reconstruction donors would
not recognise the local government until such time as it had received the
stamp of approval from the PEC.

The implementation of effective municipal government had been
described in 1996 as 'impossible', given the political enmity that existed
between groups.[37] However, there was a clear sense among the leadership
of the international community and the liberal school that failure to
ensure that the political representatives of minority displaced and refugee
voters were able to carry out their functions and represent their
communities in local government would send a signal that the right to
return enshrined in the Dayton Agreement would not be enforced.

The autonomist school, in contrast, emphasises the importance of
public accountability over the right to return. According to Chandler,
'even at city and municipal level there is little accountability to
constituents or autonomy for elected representatives. The international
promotion of multiethnic administrations through sanctions and
dismissals may well reassure neither majorities nor minorities that their
needs will be taken into account in the long term.'[38]

The major step in the BiH democratisation project in 2000 will be the
adoption of the permanent election law. However, the law is subject to
dispute among both opposition and nationalist forces in Bosnia, having
been rejected by the BiH House of Representatives in January 2000.[39]
Prior to the vote, Council of Europe representatives explicitly stated that
the adoption of this key legislation was necessary for Bosnia's eventual
membership in the Council, something supported by all parties.

The refusal of the Parliament to debate the bill came as members of
the liberal school began to lose faith in the pursuit of elections at all.
Suggesting that under the current nationalist control of the political

institutions, 'elections will continue to produce merely the formalities of democracy', one such member has called for the postponement of the local and national elections scheduled to be held in Bosnia in 2000.[40] This line of argument has heightened calls for full protectorate powers, such as are 'enjoyed' by UNMIK in Kosovo. The autonomists question such a manifestation of the democratisation process: when will Bosnia be classed as stable enough to ensure that democratic mandates realised through a formal electoral process are translated into power over events? The liberal response has been to suggest that the extremism and political manipulation of the nationalist parties and their power structures serves only to generate fear and concerns for security, conditions which limit the potential for effective formal democratic processes.

## CONSENSUS AND DIVISION ON KOSOVO

The tension between the liberal and autonomist accounts of democratisation in Bosnia has foreshadowed the extent to which the same issues and questions have been contested in Kosovo. Their ongoing debate has centred around security, the existence of *de facto* (self-appointed) authorities, the need to establish an accurate voter register, the conditions under which effective elections can be held, the timing of the elections and the implementation of the results. However, the issue most fundamental to the resolution of Kosovo's future is not dealt with explicitly under UNSCR 1244.[41] The debate regarding the value and purpose of elections cannot escape the fundamental issue of sovereignty.

UN Special Representative of the Secretary-General Bernard Kouchner has made it clear that he does not have a mandate to create an independent Kosovo.[42] However, the issue of independence will dominate any election that is held. The liberal school has called the issue of unresolved sovereignty UNMIK's 'Achilles Heel'. It suggests that the continuing violence is a product of the uncertainty surrounding the future political situation.[43]

It is on this fundamental issue of sovereignty that autonomists express the greatest concern, linking the international community's growing intervention in Bosnia's policy decisions with ethnic insecurity. Chandler, foreseeing a similar crisis in Kosovo, comments:

> The inevitable consequence of the Kosovo protectorate and the spread of international regulation in the region will be greater insecurity as both Albanian and Serb wishes are ignored. The errors of Bosnia look set to be repeated and ethnic divisions will be cohered. ...The trend towards law-making by international edict makes it impossible for any negotiated

compromise to arise between Serbs, Croats and Muslims [in Bosnia]. In turn, this means that there is little capacity for Bosnian institutions to unify society and overcome divisions. The lesson for Kosovo is that more social autonomy, not less, may be the best path to stability and post-conflict peace building.[44]

The notion of autonomy implicitly accepts the ethnic exclusivism of the dominant nationalist power blocs in Bosnia, sacrificing the possibility of immediate minority refugee return in the name of community security. Applied to Kosovo, this logic would suggest that the current pattern of violence against minorities would eventually force them out or into enclaves, and thereby establish the basis for sustainable, secure communities, albeit cleansed of ethnic diversity. If granting social autonomy means the holding of elections in Kosovo's post-conflict environment, and the creation of a popular government free from 'law-making by international edict', then it seems to suggest little, if any, accountability of the elected government to the international standards of individual human rights which are central to the liberal school's definition of a fully consolidated democracy.

However, what is most interesting about the autonomists' position is what it has in common with the leading light of liberal commentary, the ICG. Under the current UN protectorate, ICG has criticised the UN's failure to draw all Kosovars into a process of consultative government. They deem consultation to be essential to the development of self-governing institutions. Where the ICG differs from Chandler is in the goal it assumes. The end-product of the consultations is intended to reflect the values of a liberal democratic, human-rights-based regime with political 'moderates' in charge. In the liberal model, autonomy based on the results of formal elections is secondary to the success of the democratisation project.[45]

## THE POLICY DILEMMAS FOR THE INTERNATIONAL COMMUNITY

Based on the consensus that improving security in Kosovo requires the international community's acceptance of local authorities who can be held accountable and provide input to the international protectorate, UNMIK has established a system of decision-making involving local politicians. It has drawn into the process the unrecognised 'governments' in Kosovo, two Albanian (one linked to the Democratic League of Kosovo and one to the KLA) and one Serbian.[46] This provides an important alternative to early elections. However, the question of when they must be held remains outstanding.

The decision as to when a vote can be held is restricted by technical issues and bedevilled with political calculation. The act of creating a voter's register illustrates this dilemma. There is the question of the voting rights of former residents of Kosovo – some 500,000 Kosovo Albanians have left the region since 1990 to seek asylum all over Europe, and an estimated 100,000 Kosovo Serbs have left the province in the last two years.[47] There is the same conundrum, as in Bosnia, with the issue of giving internally displaced voters a choice as to where they will vote. Not allowing them a choice will 're-create' for electoral purposes the ethnic distribution as it existed on a fixed date, in 1990 for example. What this does not allow for is whether or not citizens wish to return to an area where they are now a minority. Conversely, allowing the internally displaced voters the choice to vote where they currently reside may cement in place the concentrations of minorities, such as the Serb community in Metrovica. This may be accompanied by the occupation of minority refugees' properties on the assumption that they will never return, nor be allowed to by the local authorities. Also it risks the election of local governments and legislatures 'in exile' to represent displaced minority communities.

From a liberal perspective, conditions for 'effective' elections are already defined in Chapter 3 of the Rambouillet draft.[48] For citizens to enjoy their democratic right to vote, freely and fairly, these conditions must be met:

- Freedom of movement for all citizens;
- Open and free political environment;
- Environment conducive to the return of displaced persons;
- Safe and secure environment that ensures freedom of assembly, association, and expression;
- Electoral legal framework in compliance with commitments [to the OSCE standards];
- Electoral administration representative of the population in terms of national communities and political parties; and
- Free media, effectively accessible to registered political parties and candidates, and available to voters throughout Kosovo.

These are daunting demands. Security in Kosovo remains a major concern. Clearly KFOR will be stretched to its operational limits by the logistical and security support required for the campaign period, the election day itself and the implementation period thereafter. An environment free of intimidation for alternative political parties and independent candidates before the campaign period starts requires an effective police force deployed throughout Kosovo, an effective judiciary with the capacity to enforce remedies, and a media capable of giving candidates equal and fair opportunity and electors an informed choice.

It is very doubtful that elections held in Kosovo in 2000 could meet these standards. However, the ICG 'is convinced that the educational value of working toward elections, even if they are not imminent, can be immense and will inevitably strengthen Kosovar civil society and the hand of the moderates. Most Kosovars agree. People need to learn that democracy is a process.'[49] This falls short of accepting that elections must happen in the near future, but represents a commitment to the principle of holding elections, and to their value for democratisation, and implicitly for the establishment of a human rights regime.

The international community seems to have adopted the notion of democracy as a process. Perhaps in recognition of that, UNMIK has proposed holding local elections first and parliamentary elections at a later date. However, the most persuasive argument for holding local elections first, at least from the point of view of the international community, is the well-founded fear that a duly elected and internationally recognised Kosovo parliament would promptly proclaim complete independence for the province, without even calling for a referendum on the issue.[50] This brings the debate full circle to the unresolved dilemma of the future status of Kosovo.

The scenario of a conflict of priorities between UNMIK and elected governments echoes the problems experienced in Bosnia. Faced with local intransigence on issues of human rights and the rule of law in Kosovo, the international community must decide to support either the democratic mandates of Kosovar politicians or their own project of democratisation.


## CONCLUSION: THE AMBIGUITIES OF ELECTIONS IN KOSOVO

In Kosovo's political environment, the mere fact that elections can be held in 2000 may be taken as an acceptable measure of 'success' for the UN mission, whose official mandate of 12 months expired in June 2000. Although UNMIK's mandate will almost certainly be extended for a further year, it is very doubtful that during that longer period there will be an answer as to whether the democratic process has been institutionalised.

The lesson to be drawn from the political stalemate in Bosnia, despite the repeated cycles of elections, is the importance of integrating the local political forces in Kosovo into a structure of shared responsibility before the elections take place. Local involvement can be seen as a means of increasing levels of political participation, and thereby of responsibility for key facets of the human rights framework: security, freedom of movement and provision of services. It also sharpens the public's awareness of who is accountable for local problems.

Ultimately the debate over elections must be seen in the context of the question of Kosovo's sovereignty. Specifically, whether or not the sovereignty of a polity is secondary to the objectives of the peace agreement. Autonomists remain wary of the liberal understanding of democratisation as a process. They are suspicious that it will provide a justification for delays in the realisation of the post-election social autonomy that they believe is central to negotiation between ethnic groups. However, it is unlikely that this plea for self-government and a reduction of the influence of the international community, though appealing on grounds of its emphasis on self-determination, will 'win' the debate over whether elections are a start-point or an end-point in the gaining of sovereignty. Democratisation, rather than democracy, will be the definitional lens through which Kosovo's elections will be seen.

Will the holding of elections help or hinder the realisation of human rights regime? Such a regime depends on more than the first post-conflict elections would be able to provide, as these elections, if held at all, are sure to be dominated by the issue of independence. Human rights require personal security for citizens and the prospects of a civil society prepared to promote tolerance. They require respect for the rule of law and the accountability to the citizens of those who govern them. The first elections may well solidify ethnic separation, but this, contrary to what the autonomists would suggest, is unlikely to deliver a sense of security for all the ethnic communities of Kosovo.

However, the electoral process, if carried out safely and fairly, can serve as an indicator of the extent to which key democratic and human rights fundamental to the function of a liberal democratic society have been realised. It may be only through the continual engagement in the democratic process that the accountability in government that is essential to the maintenance of human rights will be reinforced. In Kosovo it is essential that the political community, as a whole, take and pass at least this electoral 'test'. A pass mark is unlikely to happen at the first sitting, but that should not halt the efforts to ensure that it can be achieved in the near future.

ACKNOWLEDGEMENTS

I would like to thank Ken Booth, Alex J. Bellamy and Patricia Owens for their comments on a draft of this contribution.

NOTES

1. Petritsch, W., 'The Future of Bosnia Lies with Its People', *The Wall Street Journal Europe*, 17 Sept. 1999.
2. Interview by the author with senior OSCE source, July 1999.
3. In Bosnia the High Representative, officially sanctioned by the United Nations Security Council, reports directly to the Peace Implementation Council (PIC), an *ad hoc* body composed of the states, international organisations and agencies attending the London Peace Implementation conference in December 1995. It is, in effect, the guiding body for policy formation for the governance of BiH. For details on the PIC, see the Office of the High Representative website, http://www.ohr.int/, accessed 21 Nov. 1999.
4. The first two groupings are adapted from D. Chandler, *Bosnia: Faking Democracy after Dayton* (London: Polity, 1999) pp.154–180. This is among the most recent and certainly the most comprehensive treatment of the subject. The importance of his overall critique for understanding the other schools of thought in the Bosnian context is the rationale for a substantial focus on his arguments.
5. ICG maintains a field presence in both Bosnia and Kosovo. For further details see their website at http://www.crisisweb.org/.
6. S. Woodward, 'Should We Think Before We Leap?' *Security Dialogue*, Vol.30, No.3 (Sept. 1999), p.280.
7. Chandler, *Bosnia: Faking Democracy* (note 4), pp.154–180. He is the main, but not the only, member of the school I have labelled 'autonomist'. See also T. Waters, 'The Naked Land: The Dayton Accord, Property Disputes And Bosnia's Real Constitution', *Harvard International Law Journal*, Vol.40, No.2 (Spring 1999), pp.517–93.
8. K. Dawisha, 'Democratisation and Political Participation: Research Concepts and Methodologies', in K. Dawisha and B. Parrot (eds), *Democratisation and Authoritarianism in Post-Communist Societies: Politics, Power and the Struggle for Democracy in South-East Europe* (Cambridge: Cambridge University Press, 1997), p.42, cited in Chandler, *Bosnia: Faking Democracy* (note 4), p.8.
9. G. Pridham and P. Lewis (eds), *Stabilizing Fragile Democracies: Comparing New Party Systems in Southern and Eastern Europe* (London: Routledge, 1996), p.2.
10. Ibid. p.3
11. L. Diamond *et al.* (eds), *Consolidating the Third Wave Democracies* (London: Johns Hopkins University Press, 1997), p.xvii.
12. J. Williams, 'The Ethical Basis of Humanitarian Intervention, the Security Council and Yugoslavia', *International Peacekeeping*, Vol.6, No.2 (Summer 1999), p.19. See also ICG, *Starting from Scratch in Kosovo: The Honeymoon is over*, 10 Dec. 1999, Executive summary, unpaginated, available from http://www.crisisweb.org/, accessed 23 Dec. 1999.
13. Bosnia Daily 1.58 e-mail news service. Available from www.bosnet.org. *Vecernje Novine* – Sarajevo, 6 Dec. 1999. Jacques Paul Klein, UN Special Representative for the Secretary General in BiH, well known for his outspoken views, sums up this position in typical pithy style: 'The problem in the Balkans is not in its people, but its leaders. The leaders of the countries in the Balkans are hard-liners, blinded by nationalism, and they are only interested in keeping their positions.'
14. A. Swardson, 'Bosnia: A Model for Mistakes', *Washington Post*, 28 July 1999.
15. ICG, *Is Dayton Failing? Bosnia Four Years After the Peace Agreement*, 28 Oct. 1999, section on Annex 3: Elections. Available at www.crisisweb.org.
16. ODIHR, *Preliminary Statement of the Coordinator of Election Monitoring*, 14 Sept. 1996. See also *Second Statement of the Coordinator of Election Monitoring*, 17 Sept. 1996. Both these reports, from an agency of the OSCE, express concern for the conditions under which the elections were held, but fail to condemn them as *not* being 'free and fair'. Available at http://www.osce.org/odihr, accessed 11 Jan. 2000.
17. J. Mearsheimer, 'The Only Exit from Bosnia', *New York Times*, 7 Oct. 1997.
18. S. Woodward, 'Should We Think Before We Leap?' *Security Dialogue*, Vol.30, No.3 (September 1999), p.280.
19. X. Bougarel, 'Bosnia and Herzegovina – State and Communitarianism', in D. Dyker

and I. Vejvoda, (eds), *Yugoslavia and After: A Study in Fragmentation, Despair and Rebirth* (London: Longman, 1996). Also cited in Chandler (note 4), p.30.

20. *General Framework Agreement on Peace (GFAP)*, Annex 3, Preamble. Available from http://www.ohr.int/. The General Framework Agreement on Peace (GFAP) was agreed on 21 November 1995 between the Republic of Bosnia and Herzegovina, the Republic of Croatia and the Federal Republic of Yugoslavia (FRY). FRY was authorised to sign on behalf of the Bosnian Serb delegation.

21. GFAP, Annex 10. Available from http://www.ohr.int/gfa/gfa-home.htm.

22. OSCE Mission in BiH website at http://www.oscebih.org./missionoverview/overview-programmes-ele.htm, accessed 7 Dec. 1999: 'The OSCE Mission has had primary responsibility for the organisation and supervision of BiH post-Dayton elections, including national elections in 1996 and 1998, municipal elections in 1997, and special elections in Republika Srpska in 1997. Through the National Election Results Implementation Committee, the Mission has also overseen the implementation of municipal election results, and continues to monitor the work of municipal assemblies throughout BiH.'

23. GFAP, Annex 1-A. The most important part of the deadline concerned the withdrawal of NATO troops within that time period. Available at: http://www.ohr.int/gfa/gfa-home.htm.

24. The nationalist parties have persistently won majorities in all houses of parliament. See *OSCE Office for Democratic Institutions and Human Rights* website for full reports on election monitoring and specific results by race. Available at: http://www.osce. org/odihr/.

25. European Stability Institute, *Reshaping International Priorities in Bosnia and Herzegovina* (1999), p.1, available at http://www.esiweb.org/r01.html, accessed 7 Feb. 2000.

26. ICG, *Is Dayton Failing?* (note 15), Conclusion.

27. ICG, *Kosovo: Let's Learn from Bosnia: Models and Methods of International Administration*, 17 May 1999, unpaginated, accessed 21 July 1999 at http://www.crisis web.org/projects/sbalkans/reports/kos21maina.htm. See also P. Szasz, 'The Protection of Human Rights through the Dayton/Paris Peace Agreement on Bosnia', *American Journal of International Law*, Vol.90, No.2 (April 1996), p.301. Note that the GFAP was signed by the parties, but only witnessed by the international community. They are not governed by the Dayton Agreement *per se*.

28. European Stability Institute, *Reshaping International Priorities in Bosnia and Herzegovina* (1999), p.1, available at http://www.esiweb.org/r01.html, accessed 7 Feb. 2000.

29. Council of Europe Parliamentary Assembly, *Report on the Conformity of the Legal Order of Bosnia and Herzegovina with the Council of Europe Standards*, 7 Jan. 1999, quoted in ibid., p.2.

30. PIC, *Bonn Peace Implementation Conference 1997: 'Bosnian and Herzegovina 1998: Self-sustaining Structures'*, Bonn, 10 Dec., Office of the High Representative, available from: www.ohr.int, accessed 2 Dec. 1999. The High Representative's is the final authority in theatre regarding the interpretation of the Agreement's civilian annexes. He holds the power to enact measures in case of non-compliance by the Parties, specifically to make binding decisions and remove officials and public office holders found to be in violation of legal commitments. See also, ICG, *Is Dayton Failing* (note 26).

31. ICG, *Is Dayton Failing* (note 15).

32. ICG, *Breaking The Mould: Electoral Reform In Bosnia And Herzegovina* (1999), http://www.crisisweb.org.

33. ODIHR Election Observation Mission Reports, *The Elections In Bosnia And Herzegovina, 14 September 1996, Preliminary Statement Of The Co-Ordinator For International Monitoring* and *Bosnia and Herzegovina, Municipal Elections, 13–14 September 1997*. Available at http://www.osceprag.cz/inst/odihr/election, accessed 21 Nov. 1999. The abuse of the voter's choice as to where to vote continued in 1997.

34. Chandler, *Bosnia: Faking Democracy* (note 4) pp.111–12. The PIC Bonn document specifically calls for the international community to help establish new multiethnic parties and help strengthen the existing ones. He cites the Bonn document at the OHR website: http://www.ohr.int/pic98.htm, accessed 1 Dec. 1999.

35. See Election Appeals Sub-Commission, on the OSCE Mission to BiH Website, available at http://www.oscebih.org/easc/eng/easc.htm, accessed 27 Dec. 1999.
36. Office for Democratic Institutions and Human Rights, *Bosnia And Herzegovina Elections 1998, 12–13 September* (1998): 'The environment in which the 1998 elections were held reflects the difficult situation prevailing since the war, including the fact that indicted war criminals remain at large. The special circumstances stemming from this unsettled situation, and the desire to implement the peace agreement, have resulted in the implementation of some extraordinary elements in the process, which would not be acceptable in normal electoral situations. Such measures included striking candidates off party lists for transgressions in which they had no personal role, the absence of an adequate appeals procedure, and providing assistance to parties on the basis of their political programme. In pursuing these and some other policies, there was an increased involvement of the electoral authorities in the political process, leading to a perceived politicisation of the election authorities.' Available at http://www.osce.org/odihr/election/bih4-1.htm, accessed 21 Nov. 1999.
37. Interview by the author with senior OSCE source, July 1999.
38. Chandler, *Faking Democracy* (note 4), p.89.
39. The rejection of the electoral law was denounced in a joint statement by the High Representative and the OSCE Head of Mission as 'irresponsible'. The press statement is available at http://www.oscebih.org/pressreleases/january2000/21-01-press.htm, accessed 22 Jan. 2000.
40. European Stability Initiative, *Elections in 2000: Risks for the Bosnian Peace Process,* 2000, unpaginated. Available from http://www.esiweb.org/background.html, accessed 7 Feb. 2000. The views were expressed in light of the possibilities for positive change among Croat voters in Bosnia following the election of an opposition government in Croatia in January 2000.
41. UN Security Council Resolution 1244. Available from United Nations website http://www.un.org/Docs/scres/1999/99sc1244.htm, accessed 23 Dec. 1999. The international community was given responsibility under United Nations Security Council Resolution 1244, Article 10, 'to establish an international civil presence in Kosovo in order to provide an interim administration for Kosovo under which the people of Kosovo can enjoy substantial autonomy within the Federal Republic of Yugoslavia, and which will provide transitional administration while establishing and overseeing the development of provisional democratic self-governing institutions'. Furthermore, Article 11 makes explicit reference to: 'a) Promoting the establishment, pending a final settlement, of substantial autonomy and self-government in Kosovo, taking full account of Annex 2 and of the Rambouillet accords (S/1999/648)', and '(c) Organising and overseeing the development of provisional institutions for democratic and autonomous self-government pending a political settlement, including the holding of elections'.
42. S. Maliqi, 'Special Report: Chaos and Complexities in Kouchner's Kosovo', *Institute of War and Peace Reporting,* No.107, 14 Jan. 2000. Available at http://www.iwpr.net/index.pl5?archive/bcr/bcr_20000114_2_eng.txt, accessed 21 Jan. 2000.
43. ICG, *Starting from Scratch in Kosovo: The Honeymoon is Over,* 10 Dec. 1999, unpaginated. Available from http;//www.crisisweb.org/projects/sbalkans/reports/kos31rep.htm, accessed 22 Dec. 1999.
44. D. Chandler, 'The Bosnian Protectorate and the Implications for Kosovo', *New Left Review,* No.235 (May–June 1999), p.134.
45. ICG, *Starting from Scratch in Kosovo* (note 43).
46. S. Maliqi (note 42).
47. B. Shala, 'Kosovo Waits For The Vote', *Institute of War and Peace Reporting,* No.96, 26 Nov. 1999. Available at http://www.iwpr.net/index.pl5?archive/bcr/bcr_19991125_1_eng.txt, accessed 21 Jan. 2000.
48. *Rambouillet Agreement: Interim Agreement for Peace and Self-Government in Kosovo,* Chapter 3, Article 1. Available from http://www.state.gov/www/regions/eur/ksvo_rambouillet_text.html, accessed 27 Dec.1999.
49. ICG, *Starting from Scratch in Kosovo* (note 43).
50. B. Shala (note 47).

# 13
# 'Post-Conflict' Kosovo:
# An Anatomy Lesson in the
# Ethics/Politics of Human Rights

## JASMINA HUSANOVIĆ

Time, whose sharp bloodthirsty quill
parts the killed from those who kill,
will pronounce the latter band
as your brand.

– Joseph Brodsky, Bosnia Tune[1]

In the intellectual discourse of the Balkans, 'the anatomy lesson' is a well known and widely used phrase that connotes a type of scholarly exercise that is at the same time a political speech act with strong normative goals.[2] It stands for an anatomical incision into the moral and political heart of complexities that characterise both the ethnonationalist paradigm and the responses to this paradigm. More importantly, it looks towards, even if only discursively, an enactment of the politics of responsibility on revised grounds.

Any analysis that starts from a grass-roots perspective on the societal breakdown in the Balkans demonstrates that the West's promise, being based on the politics of responsibility and the ethics of human rights, was not only inadequate, but also premised on the ideology of victimisation. It is crucial to show that the West's 'new' international politics of human rights is unsustainable with regard to various emancipatory purposes that are presumably at the core of this novel form of 'militaristic humanism'. The events in Kosovo after the NATO intervention demonstrate the dangers lurking behind this emerging, media-facilitated and politically easily utilised ideology of victimisation. With this in mind, the anatomy lesson may now begin.

## THE INSECURITY SITUATION IN KOSOVO: COMMUNITIES OF FEAR

Six months into the operation of rebuilding Kosovar society, two dominant interrelated trends can be discerned: the continuing tide of violence, fear, uncertainty and hence spiralling insecurity; and, second, the continuing exodus and 'enclavisation' of the province's remaining non-Albanians. Such trends threaten to result in the creation of an ethnically homogenous majority of Kosovar Albanian territories and minority, Kosovar non-Albanian, pockets respectively.

According to the United Nations High Commissioner for Refugees (UNHCR), more than 164,000 of the province's minorities (mainly Serb, but also Roma and Gorani) left Kosovo after the arrival of the NATO-led Kosovo Force (KFOR) in June 1999.[3] With regard to the record of violence, the actual war might have stopped, but the average number of killings per week remains at the same level as before the March air strikes.[4] More precisely, the statistics on violence against minorities include the following: 348 murders, 116 kidnappings, 1070 lootings and 1105 cases of arson. These were officially registered and confirmed incidents in four months.[5]

The overall situation regarding ethnic minorities has been characterised by an alarming move away from the prospect of a multiethnic Kosovo. This is observable in four distinct developments which are affirmed even by the international governmental actors in Kosovo in charge of reconstruction, such as OSCE:

> a steady decline in the numbers of ethnic minorities (mainly Serbs and Roma); an increasing tendency towards concentration in mono-ethnic enclaves; continued isolation and restricted freedom of movement; and lack of access to public services – especially education, medical/health care – resulting in efforts to create 'parallel' systems or activities in certain areas.[6]

It would be wrong to imply that it is only Kosovar non-Albanians who are experiencing radical uncertainty. The deep insecurity in Kosovo is a fact of everyday life for all Kosovars regardless of their ethnicity. The range of problems faced include a lack of shelter for tens of thousands of people, no basic services such as heat, electricity and water, no system of civil identification and registration, and while ordinary criminals and war crimes suspects continue to operate in the conditions of effective impunity, there is still no functioning judicial system.[7]

It would be mistaken to assume that the violence inflicted on either an ethnic or purely criminal basis is in any sense irrational or random. Many indicators show that there is a significant degree of systematicity, not just in efforts to destabilise Kosovo but also in the failure to reverse the trends of discrimination, intimidation and violence and to prevent the formation of 'ethnically clean' territories. Contrary to the all-too-easy explanations that call upon the common myths about the Balkans, the task is to point out again and again, in Zizek's words, that 'the moves of every political agent in the former Yugoslavia, reprehensible as they may be, are totally rational within the goals they want to attain – the only exception, the only truly irrational factor in it, is the gaze of the West, babbling about archaic ethnic passions'.[8] In order to explain what might be the forces, agendas and motives behind the further destabilisation of Kosovo, a brief overview of 'who is who' in Kosovo is essential.

## THE POLITICAL STAGE IN FLUX

The political stage in Kosovo has been undergoing profound changes in the last few years, ever since the emergence of the Kosovo Liberation Army (KLA) in the summer of 1996. The degree of unpredictability in the flux of domestic political subjects and forces demanding to be taken seriously has increased since the NATO intervention. This has ultimately led to high levels of confusion, misapprehension and the mismanagement of issues in the attempt to establish a system of governance in the context of the post-intervention political vacuum. With an absence of political, legal and social order, the intricacies of political actors and their networks, the fluidity and changeability of the grass-roots political scene and the appearance of parallel governing bodies have reached a point that might seem bewildering to many. The Kosovars' political stage is at present best understood in relation to three sets of major forces in Kosovo today: the UN, the KLA and two political circles, concentrating respectively around the opposing political figures of Hashim Thaci, the political leader of the KLA, and Ibrahim Rugova, the leader of the Democratic League of Kosovo (LDK).[9] In addition, there is the international military and civilian presence – KFOR and UN Mission in Kosovo (UNMIK), and the OSCE. There are also two governing bodies. The Transitional Council was set up by UNMIK as a local consultative and advisory authority with multi-party multiethnic membership; it has, however, been boycotted both by Rugova's LDK and the Serb representatives.[10] The indigenous body that holds actual executive power is the Provisional Government, formed on 2 April 1999 under Thaci, and hence dominated by the political wing of the KLA. This remains a rather disunited body, inconsistent and permanently reshuffling in internal power struggles.[11] Both the Provisional Government and local *de facto* governments, which sprang up over Kosovo before the UNMIK local administration arrived, operate in parallel to, and more effectively than, the UNMIK-formed bodies. Their mutual relationship is quite complex and often uneasy.[12]

The KLA is viewed as the strongest power grouping in Kosovo today. It is not merely a formerly disorderly army that enjoys the mass support of Kosovar Albanians. It is a political force whose self-declared goal is to become what could be called a populist political party; it has grown into a kind of a national liberation movement with the sole ambition of proclaiming and governing an independent Kosovo. The latter is an attainable aim, given the KLA's organisation, prestige and omnipresence.[13] The substantial body of moderate political forces in Kosovo (the province's trademark during the years of non-violent political resistance against the Belgrade regime) has been largely marginalised and is often threatened with being ushered out of existence.

In the current 'mainstream' domestic political scene, issues of security and multiethnicity are not even close to being priority political goals for the powerful local actors. Virtually all the key activity is directed to the goal of an independent Kosovo, free from Belgrade's control or interference even if that implies creating an all-Albanian Kosovo.[14] Such a goal of independence is not reproachable in itself: it is only when independence becomes synonymous with ethnic homogeneity in its 'pure', 'free-of-the-Other' form that there is a reason for alarm. From the grass-roots point of reference, there seem to be neither viable ethical nor even utilitarian grounds for arguing that Kosovo should remain a part of Serbia. Even the 'historical' grounds in this regard are largely based on nationalist myths. The consequences of such arguments are immense. A crudely designed programme for an independent but all-Albanian Kosovo can only lead to a heightening spiral of insecurity in the region. In this way it is quite likely that the gradual abandonment of the idea of multiethnic Kosovo will backfire in the long term, particularly when threats of both internal destabilisation and regional insecurity are taken into account.

## RADICALISATION AND INSTABILITY

The promise to be realised in Kosovo (and the Balkans in general) is to create and/or sustain stable pluriform and heterogeneous multiethnic communities by replacing the politics of fear with the politics of trust, whereby fear is a result of political and social disintegration, national myths and social pressures and constructs.[15] For this reason the trends of radicalisation of the population along ethnic fault-lines deserve more critical attention. Deradicalisation is probably the first step in building the trust and confidence which constitute the very enzymes for sustainable pluriformity and communal security in sociopolitical locales which have experienced violent ethnonational rifts.[16]

It is therefore necessary to investigate the responsibility for the continuation of violence and increasing destabilisation in Kosovo. A focus solely on the actors in a particular crisis area is undoubtedly insufficient in terms of finding viable remedies in the long run, but it is probably one of the most effective starting-points in any attempt to fight against all the *practices* of domination, exclusion and violence and not simply against the 'bad' actors/individuals/groups. A recent report by the International Crisis Group (ICG) identifies five major sets of forces which might have had a role to play in the continuing destabilisation of the province: radicalised Kosovo Albanians, the KLA, Serbian paramilitaries, criminals from Albania and political rivals in the intra-Kosovar Albanian conflict.[17] With regard to the increased radicalisation of Kosovar Albanians, there are two main reasons behind this trend: the continued imprisonment of an estimated 3,000–7,000 Kosovar Albanians in Serbian prisons accused of undermining the political order, and the high number of Serbs perceived to have committed war crimes who remain at large inside Kosovo.[18] The radicalisation of Kosovar Albanians is a phenomenon which took on violent manifestations of ethnic intolerance rather recently, but particularly, in terms of its *en masse* character, after the NATO intervention. After decades of experiencing unparalleled 'quiet' repression by the Belgrade regime, the level of anger, hatred and vengeance among this population is acted upon in a political security vacuum. This trend has not been countered effectively either by the international community or by the local political leadership.

Considering that the KLA's political goal is an independent Kosovo free from Serbia's control, one logical outcome is a strategy that views an ethnically homogenous Albanian Kosovo as the strongest argument for independence.[19] This could represent the acceptance of a crude ethnonationalist matrix on all issues of political organisation and community. Furthermore, the military wing of the KLA, from the very outset disorderly, is not sufficiently demilitarised. Even if there were to be any nominal support for multiethnicity in the KLA leadership, there is no unified structure and command in its rank and file to guarantee discipline and respect for a multiethnic Kosovo.[20]

With regard to the Serbian paramilitaries, there is more evidence that Serb security forces not only remained in Kosovo but are returning as civilians, particularly in the rich northern parts of Kosovo with a significant Serb population.[21] Future moves by the Belgrade regime will surely stem from a long-term strategy of creating conditions that will make their intervention necessary to protect Serb civilians and eventually to partition Kosovo.[22] This might explain the discouraging of Serb migration from Kosovo, and the instigation of ethnic incidents in and around Serb enclaves in Kosovo. The events in Kosovska Mitrovica in the first few months of 2000 are a case in point. Also, in such a context, criminals from Albania contribute to increasing insecurity and undermine the rule of law by criminal activities which cut across the ethnic divide. However, these Albanian criminal forces are unlikely to undertake any systematic violence. Neither are the political rivals to the Kosovar Albanian political mainstream, in whose interest it is to discredit those political circles that coalesce around the figure of Thaci, likely to stir up a security crisis.[23]

If such dynamics are in the foreground, there are still many moderate forces in Kosovo. They face a difficult time, because they are being threatened for daring to advocate principles of tolerance and multiethnicity. Ordinary citizens are exposed to retribution and are often systematically terrorised by gangs for showing any sign of resistance or non-compliance with the dominant political line of 'independent equals homogenous' Kosovo. For example, the prominent and respectable editor of the most influential Kosovar daily *Koha Ditore*, Veton Surroi, received public death threats for daring to preach ethnic tolerance. It is essential to note that it is not independence for Kosovo *per se* which is a problem; it is the convergence of independence as a political goal and the ethnic-nationalist paradigm.

To summarise: the forces behind the continuing destabilisation of Kosovo reveal that ethnonationalist discourses and practices have not been properly countered by the military intervention and its aftermath, and have certainly not been defeated. Indeed, they remain dominant. However, the achievement of a higher degree of tangible security for the region entails fighting such exclusionary attitudes and practices, and not remaining short-sightedly caught in the internal paradoxes of the new moralism and humanism which operate in the web of crude identity/territory politics.

## AN ALTERNATIVE ON THE MARGINS:
## THE GENESIS OF MODERATE FORCES IN KOSOVO

What one finds now in Kosovar grass-roots can be summarised as follows:

- a disillusioning atmosphere, which by no means indicates the success of some new form of politics in the international arena or an

embodiment of emancipatory policies with regard to the problematic of intervention;
- conundrums of injustice experienced to different extents and for different reasons by all ethnic groups; and
- the radicalisation spiral accompanied by a serious mismanagement of political answers to complex problems.

Yet there is no place for the 'insolubility thesis' here, nor in general when it comes to the intricacies of Balkan dramas. The insolubility thesis in the sense used here stands for the denial of the possibility for overcoming ethnonationalist ideologies and practices and enacting a political and social community in a way that escapes crude politics of identity. There is also no place for simplified remedies through mechanical democracy-building and election procedures that operate within, but do not challenge – and thus perpetuate – the ethnonational matrix. There are suppressed potentialities and resources which attempt to go beyond exclusionary ethnonationalist practices and can be discerned in various moderate forces and practices within Kosovar civil society. They are neither minor nor recent developments, which is why explaining their genesis is essential for the analysis of the radicalisation/deradicalisation and community transformation problematic in Kosovo.

In addition to a variety of minor political parties with moderate programmes which are marginalised and silenced by the strongest power groupings accepting the ethnonationalist ideology, Kosovo still has a vivid civil society. This has been the case in the last ten years. Moreover, during the period of widespread and brutal discrimination against Kosovar Albanians, and in conditions of unparalleled political and civic oppression, the human rights scene in Priština – the informal networks of intellectuals, academics, feminists, students and so on – was impressive in its scope and in the quality of the resulting vision and action.[24] However, this civil society has suffered internal implosions in the most recent and most violent years in Kosovo. Its regeneration and further development are impeded in the context of the radical uncertainty of political, social and everyday life in the post-intervention period. Enhancing such potentials in a systematic and consistent manner is essential for any emancipatory politics, particularly when taking into account the obstacles these people face in a situation of intimidation and retribution in today's Kosovo, with its political, social, economic and judicial vacuums. It still remains to be seen, however, whether the international structures created since June 1999 can mobilise decisive political will in this regard. The record of what the international military and civilian structures in Kosovo have achieved so far leaves a lot to be desired.[25]

The political vision of community transformation beyond ethnonationalist exclusions does not reside only in now rather scattered civil society initiatives. This becomes obvious when one takes into account the fact that such an intense radicalisation of the Kosovar Albanian population is a relatively recent occurrence. More to the point, there is a substantial number in the ordinary population who resist this trend, but fear or are unable for other reasons to channel their resistance and dissatisfaction with the current state of affairs. These 'other reasons' are the struggle of Kosovar citizens to survive in a completely devastated country, where not as much as possible has been done in terms of reconstruction.[26]

The period since 1989 has witnessed the absolute abolition of the cultural and political autonomy of Kosovo within Serbia, and omnipresent discrimination against Kosovar Albanians. However, a sudden, radical and, most importantly, largely spontaneous development took place in the winter and spring of 1990. Kosovar Albanians *en masse* opted for the strategy of non-violence. It was only after this grass-roots change that the Kosovar Albanian elite and Ibrahim Rugova adopted the same approach.[27] This strategy of non-violence characterised years of Kosovar Albanian politics until 1996, when a wave of disillusionment spread through Kosovo. It became obvious after the Dayton Peace Accords that no unified solution was to be advocated on the international scene for the whole region (including Kosovo, which the Kosovar Albanians hoped for),[28] though they had often received promises from Western politicians that the issue of Kosovo would be taken on board at some point. In this atmosphere the KLA emerged and a slow radicalisation of the population, which felt abandoned and utterly powerless against the Serbian regime of repression, began. It is also at this point that the marginalisation of alternative constructions of Kosovar community began.

The non-violent strategy that developed should be seen 'as part of a process through which an identity was being constructed against the Other';[29] it was a reaction to the constructions imposed upon Kosovars by the Serbian elites whereby Kosovar Albanians were vilified and demonised as irredentists, counter-revolutionaries, rapists, thugs and monsters so as to justify the goals and actions instigated by Belgrade. Such a defined oppositional identity served to differentiate oneself and one's group from the oppressors and their myths in *political* rather than essentialist ethnic terms. However, the violence of the period between 1996 and 1999 led to the prevalence of essentialist ethnic identifications by most Kosovars. What is insisted on here, however, is that there is a potential in Kosovo for alternative forms of community and identification, which are necessary for any politics that might go beyond the essentialist ethnonationalist drive. Nevertheless, at the moment and looking at a wider regional security situation, where present-day Serbia is the key axis, such a development can occur only in an independent Kosovo and one with a high degree of international support and investment. Certain borders are still necessary for certain purposes – such as the rule of law in this region – and can be relaxed only in the climate of more trust and confidence. Political identification based on support for non-violence and against oppression among Kosovars presents a small step in that direction, and its legacy in Kosovo's progressive yet largely silent circles, should be utilised and built on for future widespread social and political action.

## THE RECORD OF 'THE INTERNATIONAL COMMUNITY'

In some sense one would expect that the lessons from Bosnia would aid the international community in their performance in Kosovo, in terms of enabling them to take a more proactive stance and more effective strategies for delivering their visionary promises. However, the balance-sheet of the international organisations' achievements in the province so far points to the contrary, regardless of their overwhelming multi-billion-dollar presence. The Kosovar population and local bodies are increasingly frustrated not only by the mismatch between promises and the performance of international actors, but also because Kosovo's indigenous structures are rarely consulted, and are largely excluded from the process of reconstructing Kosovar society.[30] This state of affairs is justified by the lack of political will and low donor input, problems in management and difficulties in logistics, as well as by widespread corruption and internal turf struggles among both leading international organisations and the local leadership.[31] Probably the most important aspects of the international community's involvement, for our purposes here, are the provision of security and democracy-building.

With regard to security, the reports by non-governmental organisations (Amnesty International, ICG) and those by the international agencies in charge of it (UNMIK, OSCE, UNHCR) differ significantly in their assessments. Significantly, the latter reports often turn out to be based on a very narrow understanding of security. For example, in a recent UNHCR/OSCE report one reads that 'creative methods for increasing security, such as reinforcement of doors, installation of emergency calling devices in homes, and the establishment of a hotline between lead agencies and KFOR, are being established by the agencies concerned'.[32] How effective these 'creative' measures can be is merely a rhetorical question when the following is noted: in the sensitive area of Mitrovica, the French KFOR troops 'serve to reinforce the partition' between the Albanian and Serbian parts of the city and claim that problems do not exist; in Gnjilane the American troops hardly venture out from their barracks; and in Orahovac the Russian troops need special permission to leave the barracks because they themselves had greatly exacerbated ethnic tensions there.[33] Similar problems occur with the understaffed UNMIK police force, which is mainly concentrated in the Priština area. Even there, the seven Serbs appointed in the multiethnic Advisory Judicial Commission, the only local judicial body, left because they feared for their safety.[34]

When it comes to democracy-building, the picture is ambiguous. On one side, early elections are insisted on to such an extent that it can almost be seen as the international community's preparation for an exit strategy from Kosovo, or at least as passive observance and transferral of responsibilities. The international community refuses 'to take self-governance by the population of Kosovo as the desired end of every initiative'.[35] Although there are a multitude of ways and opportunities to start a fruitful process of empowerment in Kosovo, based on progressive Kosovar forces, the reluctance to make a mistake by strengthening the 'wrong forces' in Kosovo turns out to be the implementation of the principle of active non-activity, holding back and thereby preserving the *status quo*.

All this appears to be a rather disappointing picture. It becomes less surprising if treating Kosovars as 'errant children in want of firm parenting'[36] is understood as a remnant of, or a logical follow-up to, the ideology of victimisation. Rather than working actively on the deradicalisation of Kosovo and the building of security for the region based on a more in-depth analysis of the overall social and political situation, the international community is actually behaving and acting as an accomplice in the perpetuation of ethnonationalist logic. This pseudo-*perpetuum mobile* of ethnonationalism breeds on insecurity, and is enhanced by ineffectiveness in countering and reversing it, but it can be stopped. Communities of mistrust, hostility and fear are not a historical inevitability in the Balkans, but systematic and powerful political constructs. As such, alternative forms of political practice can still replace them.

## TOWARDS COMMUNITIES OF INTEREST, TRUST AND CONFIDENCE

It is quite apparent that the issue of securing human rights in destabilised and rifted communities caught in the matrix of ethnonationalism is inextricable from larger issues of security and political community in general. Any anatomy lesson that deals both with the internal paradoxes of the politics of intervention and its grass-roots manifestations reveals some often superficial and flawed responses to the crisis (which, on the other side, points to the need for a genuinely emancipatory practice). In the case of ethnonationalist problematics, such an emancipatory practice implies a certain form of deradicalisation, or rather a move from communities of fear towards communities of interest, trust and confidence. The practice of democracy and what is often simultaneously defined as human rights is possible in a meaningful way only in an environment where the principles of civic political association occupy more significant ground than the dominant ideology of a rigid identity/territory nexus. Regardless of official proclamations, support for a more civic option that fights against the practices of the politics of identity (and not within its constraints) is the only way out of the region's insecurity riddles. It is rather idealistic to expect decisively orchestrated political action in this direction in the Balkans considering the record of the last decade in this respect. However, that is not to say that one should not take into account specific proposals and issues that have the aim of achieving long-term security for south-eastern Europe. The Stability Pact for South Eastern Europe represents a promising (though yet to be realised) step in a civic-based, regional security-oriented direction.

In his book *The Warrior's Honour*, Michael Ignatieff talks about the coexistence of the political and the personal plane of consciousness, whereby myths struggle with experience and the fit between the individual and the collective, personal and national. Identity is always imperfect.[37] The importance of this search for a story of 'how communities of fear are created out of communities of interest', which connects the 'collapse of state power and the rise of nationalist paranoia down at the human level', cannot be overestimated.[38] If radicalisation trends are to be reversed and transformed into deradicalising societal and political movements, there has to be a complementary search and struggle for both a story and a practice of how communities of security are created out of communities of fear/insecurity. What this necessitates is a permanent rearticulation and the exercise of our critical faculties, whereby various forms of exclusionary practices are continuously resisted and hopefully defeated. If the dialectics of group-formation and static identification with a group is ultimately a sacrifice of these critical faculties, then any search for trust and confidence as the basis for more just multiethnic communities has to be critically sensitive to, and *responsible for*, complex issues of inclusion and exclusion. It is a gradual and slow process. At the moment this presents a daunting task, even in Bosnia where there have been historical, cultural and sociological experiences of a more inclusive practice of community in terms of ethnic and/or religious differences. Unlike Bosnia, in the case of Kosovo, where there has been very little genuinely shared political, social, cultural or civic experience between different ethnic groups in the last decades, the issues are even more perplexing. The domino effect of ethnonationalist ideologies and praxis in the Balkans should not be much of a surprise. However, there are both moral resources for 'doing' political community in Kosovo in more inclusive terms, as well as social forces and practices that embody or might embody this goal. It remains to be seen whether any significant success in this respect can be expected in isolation without tackling the wider regional context.

It is not the Kosovars' insistence on independence which is the crux of the problem here, nor their own 'group' radicalisation. The problem is the pertinence and the perpetuation of the politics of identity in its most violent form – ethnonationalism, thanks to both the dominant actors in the region and the West's actions or non-actions. The problem is that the territory of the Balkans is pluriform and heteronomous and can be altered only through violence, genocide, exodus and enclavisation. Any attempt to work on democratisation, human rights and social justice in a context of ideology and politics, which ultimately deny this grass-roots lived experience, will suffer internal implosion. For example, formal democratisation, through its insistence on procedures, cements the *status quo*. This occurs either through the 'territorial' results of genocide, whereby war criminals roam free and refugees cannot go home, or through the fact that power and resources enjoyed by semi-legal anti-democratic nationalist groupings are doubly legitimised. Even those very liberal actions by the international community, for example supporting local civil society, are superficial both in content and outcomes when judged against the overall context, and the supposed goal of working towards just pluriform secure communities. These approaches are often of an administrative-bureaucratic nature, without long-term vision and strong enough commitment, piecemeal in their ambition to the point of crippling the purpose of civil society, apologetic or hypocritical in front of what has to be resisted (namely, ethnonationalist logic). This is because on one side the liberal response by the international community works with and actively perpetuates the very logic it claims to be attempting to subvert by complementary 'make-up' gestures in the direction of civil society. Or is it rather that the 'international community' itself does not yet have an answer to how pluriformity and heteronomy can be accommodated in viable, less exclusionary and more just forms of political organisation and community? If this is so, then Slavoj Zizek's words offer a provocative yet lucid insight:

In former Yugoslavia, we are lost not because of our primitive dreams and myths preventing us from speaking the enlightened language of Europe, but because we pay in flesh the price for being the stuff the Other's dreams are made of. ... Far from being the other of Europe, former Yugoslavia was rather Europe itself in its Otherness, the screen onto which Europe projected its own repressed reverse.[39]

Europe's 'repressed reverse' expresses itself through the techniques of power and knowledge which aim at containing dangerous manifestations of pluriformity and heteronomy, as something 'outside'. These categories are often boxed in the category of the 'irrational' (rationality being linked to uniformity, autonomy, consistency, objectivity, and other concepts that supposedly characterise the European 'self'). If such logic does sum up most of the Western response so far, then the Balkans is still the ultimate test in the politics of responsibility. This 'new' responsibility refers to the process of dealing with pluriformity and heteronomy in a more inclusive and just manner, whereby 'self' and 'other', 'inside' and 'outside', are not viewed as separate social and political entities of thought and action. Multiethnicity as a principle of political organisation requires radical rethinking of some basic concepts of our ethics and politics.

Where does this responsibility come from and what forms should it take? What perhaps springs to mind first is that the assertion that geography is one's destiny is rarely as convincing and as profoundly experienced as it is in the Balkans. Is there a responsibility that comes from territory? Experiencing the practical consequences of this question is surprisingly enlightening with regard to identifying one's place and duty as an intellectual who is engaged in a continuous process of making and acting upon ethico-political choices and decisions. Indeed, with this (as with any) territory comes a certain dynamic of ethical responsibility from which there is no retreat[40] – even more so, perhaps, because of the 'standard' logic of political thinking and practice that surrounds the Balkans as a 'privileged site of phantasmic investments'[41] both from within and from outside the very area in question.

What follows from this brief anatomical incision into the moral and political heart of a few of the key complexities behind the current appalling security situation in Kosovo can be summarised as follows. Six months after the NATO intervention, any grass-roots perspective on the outcomes of the latest Western pursuit of the politics of intervention reveals that the long-awaited honeymoon between the ethics and politics of human rights in the international arena never actually materialised. One of the reasons behind such a state of affairs, resulting from this latest interventionist embodiment of the new post-Cold War moralism, may be that there has never been a decisive and adequate ethico-political promise with regard to what is to be done in the new Balkan hotspot. At most, any detectable hint of a serious promise was without fail an almost naive sound-bite informed by the ideology of victimisation, which in itself can never result in the genuinely emancipatory political actions so necessary in the Balkans. Therefore, the dangers immanent in the politics of delivering security, peace and human rights, which is underpinned by this ideology of victimisation, have to be assessed and successfully struggled against with respect to Kosovo. The outline of the current security situation in the province seems to be pointing towards a complete failure of the whole operation (including the trends of furthering radicalisation, violence, insecurity and disenchantment within the Kosovar population, as well as incompetencies when it comes to reversing these trends). The issues of human rights and security have to be rethought and dealt with from a perspective that is sensitive to the grass-roots problematics of highly destabilised and divided communities. It becomes apparent that, in dealing with the 'everydayness' of Kosovo, it is all too possible to remain caught in present phantasms of abstract and empty political categories, whereby the liberal West makes it appear that it is sorting out yet another Balkan 'eruption of ethnic passions'.[42] The question remains whether there is a way out of this impasse.

## THE IDEOLOGY OF VICTIMISATION VERSUS THE POLITICS OF RESPONSIBILITY: TOWARDS POST-PESSIMISM?

The politics of intervention is always in an important sense the politics of a promise, whose ethico-political nature opens up undoubtedly one of the most daunting questions in the discourse and practice of international politics today. In this respect, one faces a conundrum when attempting to answer a seemingly simple question: what was the ethico-political promise behind the NATO intervention in Kosovo? It can hardly be disputed that the West's action was experienced and understood as a promise to those who suffered violence and on whose behalf the West decided to intervene, and it was acted upon as though it was a matter of delivering that promise unreservedly. When observed superficially, a logical conclusion seems to be that the promise entailed simply putting an end to the horror lived by Kosovar Albanians, a goal which required an orchestrated mobilisation of popular support for a decisive military action in the name of the human rights of an ethnic group. However, such a simplified articulation of the ethico-political promise about the ten-year long Balkan turmoil can hardly stand any test of criticism. The current insecurity situation in Kosovo, where violence and exclusions of an ethnonational character pertain, shows that the goal has not been achieved.

It has long been clear to many civic-oriented participants in the Balkans that depoliticised appeals to human rights cannot bring long-term solutions to this region. And yet what one faces during the whole Kosovo episode is a subtle construction of an 'ideal subject-victim': this is not a political subject with a clear agenda, but a powerless victim of local circumstances, stripped of political identity and political goals, and left with only bare suffering at its human core – all of which renders any proper political assessment of it obsolete and almost inappropriate.[42] Therefore, it was to be expected that the final consequence of this approach would be the articulation and implementation of inadequate and inefficient political action to remedy the problem. As soon as the international military and civilian organisations entered the territory of Kosovo in June 1999 to build a political community and public order from scratch, the flawed black-and-white image that underlined the constructed politics of militaristic humanism began to crack immediately and irrevocably. Political subjects and political agendas could no longer be ushered out of existence, marginalised or depoliticised, and the issues to be dealt with, such as how to build a 'community of security or interest out of a community of fear', could no longer fit into the neat and abstract categories and patterns of protecting the human rights of powerless victims. The political stage that emerged after the summer of 1999 was not at all uncommon in the Balkan context. To any observer of the events there, it was obvious that violence was continuing, this time mainly, but not solely, against non-Albanian Kosovar populations, and that the notion of a humanistic multicultural society appeared more and more to be a far cry from reality. Indeed, the ideology of victimisation reveals its full internal paradox when a grass-roots perspective is given to an anatomical incision into the region's ethical and political matters. In other words, new avenues of analysis and action seem to be opened when the crux of the issue – how to build a meaningful community of trust for all its citizens in a particular locale – is contextualised.

Therefore, the spiral of ethnonationalist conflict, mistrust, fear, antagonism and violence that has been witnessed in Kosovo since the summer of 1999 is unquestionably alarming, but it is neither perplexing nor surprising. As Slavoj Zizek notes, the ideology of victimisation entails the axiom 'the Other to be protected is good insofar as it remains a victim', and when it no longer behaves in accordance with such a role, 'it all of a sudden magically turns into a terrorist, fundamentalist, drug-trafficking Other'.[43] Does this mean that ordinary Kosovar Albanians, now violating the human rights of the non-Albanian population, are suddenly the 'bad guys'? Or is it rather that the politics of intervention that is based on the new moralism and ideology of victimisation actually often ensures, though in a somewhat peculiar sense, that victims 'remain victims, inhabitants of a devastated country with a passive population'; that they are not to be effectively encouraged to become an active political force in reconstructing society on an alternative basis to the dominant matrix of political life in Kosovo and larger area in the last few decades?[44] The grass-roots record in Kosovo now indicates that the encouragement of alternatives and empowerment are not the key notions underpinning what is going on – it is rather hesitation, reluctance and passivity. So, when the record of achievement in Kosovo since the war ended is assessed, a gloomy picture that affirms the contentions above indicates a fundamental rearticulation of ethico-political goals and practice is essential in the Balkans; for it is impossible to cut off Kosovo from the larger context of regional insecurity.[45] There is an urgent need, a duty, to postulate the politics of responsibility in this and other conflict areas *not against a group of people or a state* that violates human rights on ethno-nationalist grounds, *but against all concrete practices of exclusion, nationalism, racism, colonialism and patriarchalism.*[46] Only in this vein can what are described as the 'insoluble paradoxes' of a Kosovo, or a Dayton-like Bosnia and so on, be effectively tackled so that the very 'insolubility thesis' becomes revealed as yet another myth that perpetuates the logic and exclusionary politics of identity. The *conditio sine qua non* of resolving such situations today is surely a clearer set and more robust political promises and responsibilities that fight effectively against the discourses and practices of the ethnonationalist paradigm and flesh out concrete political agendas, forces and means for such purposes. This entails much more than merely intervening under the umbrella of the ideology of victimisation, and superfluous administrative-bureaucratic liberal responses to crises. It entails the enactment of the art of the possible that stems from the ethos and political practice of responsibility with genuine grass-roots sensibilities.

Instead of being imprisoned by regressive myths, why not start, for instance, by abandoning the pervading sceptical aloofness or simple unoriginality and lack of commitment when faced with the challenging aporias of politics? Why not begin by adopting something of the attitude and commitment which is embodied in a multiethnic Kosovar youth NGO which calls itself 'Post-Pessimists'. Then, perhaps, the ethics/politics of human rights might enter the stage beyond not only illusory optimisms but also unjustifiable and unsustainable pessimisms in thought and action. After all, to paraphrase Marx, liberations are historical, not simply mental, acts.

## ACKNOWLEDGEMENTS

I would like to thank Ken Booth, Patricia Owens, Ian Mitchell and Alex J. Bellamy for their most valuable and thoughtful criticisms of the first draft of this article. I would also like to express my deep gratitude to Professor Rusmir Mahmutćehajić, the staff of the International Forum Bosnia, and Rishi Ruparellia for their unreserved support during the time of writing up the first draft.

## NOTES

1. R. Ali and L. Lifschultz (eds.), *Why Bosnia? Writings on the Balkan War* (CT: The Pamphleteer's Press, 1993), p.339.
2. This is particularly so since the famous 1970s debate between Danilo Kis, a novelist from Novi Sad, and the Belgrade literary circles. For the purposes of this article I both paraphrase and recall the ethical imperative epitomised in the famous response by Danilo Kis, 'The Anatomy Lesson', to the 1970s nationalist attack on his novel *A Tomb for Boris Davidovich*. See D. Kis, *Homo Poeticus: Essays and Interviews* (Manchester: Carcanet Press, 1996) for an introduction to the debate.
3. See the report by Human Rights Watch, 'Federal Republic of Yugoslavia: Abuses Against Serbs and Roma in the New Kosovo', *Human Rights Watch*, Vol.11, No.10 (D) (August 1999), http://www.hrw.org/hrw/reports/1999/kosov2/, p.1.
4. ICG Report, 'Violence in Kosovo: Who's Killing Whom?', 2 Nov. 1999 (amended version), http://www.intl-crisis-group.org/, p.1.
5. UNHCR/OSCE Report, 'Overview of the Situation of Ethnic Minorities in Kosovo', 3 Nov. 1999, http://www.osce.org/kosovo/reports/minorities_1103.htm, footnote 4.
6. Ibid., paragraph 4.
7. ICG Report, 'Starting from Scratch in Kosovo: The Honeymoon Is Over', http://www.intl-crisis-group.org/, pp.1-2.
8. S. Zizek, 'Caught in Another's Dream in Bosnia', in Ali and Lifschultz (note 1), p.239.
9. ICG report, 'Who's Who in Kosovo', 31 Aug. 1999, http://www.intl-crisis-group.org/, pp.1–2.
10. Ibid., p.5.
11. Ibid., p.6.
12. Ibid., p.6. See also ICG Report,'Waiting for UNMIK: Local Administration in Kosovo', 18 Oct. 1999, http://www.intl-crisis-group.org/, p.3.
13. ICG Report (note 9), p.2.
14. Ibid., p.3.
15. By pluriform and heterogeneous communities I mean the communities which do not have a uniform and autonomous substance, and cannot be reduced to or forced into exclusive and crude self/other oppositions between 'collectivities' that constitute them.
16. On the trust and confidence debate see A.B. Seligman, 'Pouzdanje i pitanje civilnog drustva' ['Trust and the Question of Civil Society'], *Forum Bosnae*, Vol.3–4 (1999), pp.34–44; and R. Mahmutcehajic, 'Bosansko pitanje u svijetu' ['Bosnian Question on the World'], *Forum Bosnae*, Vol.3–4 (1999), pp.73–97.
17. ICG report (note 4), pp.2–6.
18. Ibid., p.2.
19. Ibid., p.4.
20. Ibid., p.3.
21. Ibid., p.4., also various NATO press conferences (see http://www.un.org/kosovo/, for press briefs).
22. Ibid. p.5.
23. Ibid., pp.6–8.
24. I base these views on my own professional experience in the civil society sector in the former Yugoslavia which enabled me to meet and work with various NGOs and institutions in the region.

25. See ICG Report (note 7) for a devastating account of the international community's performance in Kosovo so far.
26. See various OSCE, HRW and UNHCR reports quoted in notes above.
27. S. Maliqi, 'The Albanians of Kosovo: Self-Determination Through Nonviolence', in Ali and Lifschultz (note 1), pp.331–2.
28. Noel Malcolm, *Kosovo: A Short History* (London: Macmillan, 1998), pp.353–5.
29. S. Maliqi (note 27), p.332.
30. ICG report (note 7), p.2.
31. Ibid., p.2.
32. UNHCR/OSCE Report (note 5), p.6.
33. ICG report (note 7), p.3.
34. UNMIK Report, *UNMIK's Four Pillars: The First Six Months*, December 1999, http://www.un.org./kosovo/pages/kosovo_quanda.htm, p.2.
35. ICG report (note 7), p.6.
36. Ibid., p.6.
37. M. Ignatieff, *The Warrior's Honour: Ethnic War and the Modern Conscience* (London: Vintage, 1998), pp.37–8.
38. Ibid., p.39.
39. S. Zizek (note 8), p.238.
40. See reflections by Susan Sontag in her 'Introduction' to D. Kis, *Homo Poeticus* (note 2), p.viii.
41. S. Zizek, (note 8), p.238.
42. Ibid., p.238.
43. For a more in-depth commentary on this paradox, see S. Zizek, 'Attempts to Escape the Logic of Capitalism', *London Review of Books*, 28 Oct. 1999, p.7.
44. Ibid., p.7.
45. Ibid., p.7.
46. For example, see a collection of up-to-date reports on the south Balkans and Kosovo by the International Crisis Group (ICG), http://www.intl-crisis-group.org/.
47. S. Zizek (note 43), p.7.

# PART FIVE:

# Forum
Is Humanitarian War a Contradiction in Terms?

# A Qualified Defence of the Use of Force for 'Humanitarian' Reasons

## CHRIS BROWN

'Humanitarian war' is not, as this Forum invites us to consider, a contradiction in terms, but it is a very unwelcome turn of phrase. The term is usually taken to convey the idea of fighting a war for humanitarian *reasons*, but the inevitable connotation is that war *itself* could be, in certain circumstances, conducted in a humanitarian manner. But, although there are those in the West who have indeed talked of 'humanising' war, all recent experience suggests that this is not possible. However much is made of avoiding 'collateral damage' and delivering 'surgical strikes' with 'precision-guided' ordnance, war involves killing and hurting people, whether deliberately or by mistake (and there always are mistakes). Moreover, unless the fighting is confined to an uninhabited island, 'people' in this context will always include the innocent as well as soldiers (many of whom are, themselves, likely to be 'innocent' in any non-technical sense of the term). Bomb a bridge or a power station today and a child will go hungry tomorrow; the same logic, incidentally, applies to economic sanctions – there is no magic way of damaging a country or a regime that does not involve hurting the people who live there. The people of Iraq would be glad to be provide chapter and verse. In short, whatever the means of exercising force employed, war is not a humane activity, and, it should be said, it is only the comfortable citizens of the post-industrial world who need to be reminded of this very uncomfortable fact.

But does this mean that it is never right for states to employ military force in response to gross violations of human dignity? The answer has to be No. War is never going to be humane, but conventional thought in the West has always argued, rightly, that there are some circumstances in which a resort to force is a legitimate response to manifest injustice. Specifically, force employed proportionally to the offence, with the intention of righting a wrong, with reasonable prospects of success, under proper authority and with care being taken, as far as possible, to protect the innocent can be the right response to injustice. Before asking whether these conditions were actually met in Kosovo in the spring of 1999, it may be helpful to assess the strength of this position in general terms by comparing it with two-and-a-half common alternatives.

The first alternative is that military force should only be employed by states in defence of the 'national interest' which for these purposes is defined restrictively in terms of the material interests of the state/people in question; in crude shorthand this is 'realism' – Michael Mandelbaum has been perhaps the most eloquent of its recent defenders in the Kosovo context.[1] Although realism sometimes promotes prudence in international affairs, which in general is no bad thing, it rests on premises which are unacceptable. Realists assume that there is a qualitative difference between the obligations we owe fellow-citizens and those we owe to non-citizens, such that force might sometimes be used to defend the interests of the former but never those of the latter, even in circumstances where they are suffering grievous wrong. However, while there are good reasons for thinking that it is right to pay special attention to the interests of our fellow citizens, there is no good reason to make the gap between 'us' and 'everyone else' as wide as this. Putting the same point differently, realists assume that it is possible to have a substantially materialist account of 'our' interests, which would exclude in principle non-material factors such as the values we wish to see promoted in the world. But there are no material interests in this sense of the term (although there may be material factors which contribute to our account of who we are and what we believe). In short, the desire to live in a world in which gross violations of human dignity do not take place, and a willingness to help to bring this about, is as legitimate a basis for 'national interest' as the defence of national borders or state sovereignty.

The second alternative to the position espoused in this essay is that of the pacifist who believes that the sanctity of life entails that there are no circumstances in which the use of force could ever be justified – Tolstoy, Ghandi, perhaps Jesus are referents here. It is difficult to respond to this position. Although cast in absolute terms, it actually appears to rest on an – implausibly dogmatic – consequentialist argument; that is to say, pacifism makes practical sense if, and only if, it is believed that the costs associated with the use of force will always and necessarily outweigh whatever benefits it brings. Alternatively, it might be thought that reasoning in this way is irrelevant because God simply will not allow evil to prevail – will, as it were, sanctify the innocent victims of violence. As a card-carrying atheist I obviously cannot make anything of this argument; in any event, most Christians actually seem to prefer to reason along the lines of 'God helping those who help themselves'.

There are very few absolutist pacifists around today, but rather more writers who fall into the 'half' category noted above, which is composed of those who believe that there are no circumstances in which force can be justified *when it is employed by the United States and its allies* – one might term this mind-set 'Pilgerism' after its most ubiquitous proponent.[2] The default Pilgerist position is that the US/West should be condemned for *inaction* in the face of global injustice, but, when force actually *is* used, on the face of it for humanitarian reasons, Pilgerism holds that, contrary to appearances, the motives of such action must necessarily be construed as narrowly self-serving, designed at all times to promote the interests of world capitalism and the American Empire. The general line here is illustrated by John Pilger's recent explanation of how UN Peacekeeping in East Timor is actually designed to help Indonesia (and 'world capital') retain control over the territory after independence, an explanation, it has to be said, that appears not to have convinced either the Indonesian government or people or, more to the point, the East Timorese themselves who seem, unaccountably, to have welcomed these new UN oppressors.[3]

There is, of course, more to Pilgerism than simple rancour. The US is the leading military and economic power in the world today, which means it has the largest stake in preserving the current global system which, in turn, often involves preserving manifest inequalities and injustices. US foreign policy has on occasion involved support for, indeed the establishment of, repressive regimes, and the (inevitably) selective nature of US condemnations of human rights abuses leaves an unpleasant taste, amplified by the moralising rhetoric to which US leaders are prone. But although the past record of a state is not irrelevant to a judgment of its current motivations, neither can it substitute for an open, unprejudiced examination of the circumstances of particular cases. Nor is it sensible to fly in the face of common sense and stretch one's intellectual integrity to breaking point in order to demonstrate that whatever the US is doing *must* be evil. The characteristic Pilgerist depiction of the US as some kind of satanic force in global politics is an unworthy, infantile response to the complexities of contemporary international relations.

To summarise, the conventional notion that there are some circumstances where the use of force is appropriate, morally and politically, is eminently defensible. Were these circumstances present in Kosovo in the spring of 1999? This can be broken down into several clusters of discrete questions – only provisional and tentative answers are offered here, but the questions themselves are, I think, the right ones.

First, and simplest, was the Yugoslav government grossly violating the human dignity and rights of the majority community in Kosovo? Yes. The forceful deportation of the Kosovo Albanians was probably speeded-up by NATO's bombing campaign, but the record of the Yugoslav government since the suspension by Milosevic of Kosovan autonomy in 1989, and in particular the state terrorism of 1998 and early 1999, could not be justified as part of a campaign against KLA guerrillas (their existence itself a response to earlier oppression), and can only be seen as a prelude to the ethnic cleansing of the province.

Second, was force the 'last resort' (i.e., were there no effective non-violent methods of intervening), and was the basic intention of NATO that of responding to the wrong being done to the Kosovo Albanians (as opposed to promoting some other, less worthy, goals)? Provisionally, yes and yes. Again, the record of the last decade suggests that non-military pressures (e.g., unarmed observers or economic sanctions) are ineffective ways of dealing with the Yugoslav regime. Milosevic's position relies now on the Serbian nationalism he has done so much to create (or revitalise), and in Bosnia and elsewhere he has proved unwilling to respond to non-military pressures when doing so would compromise that support. Attempts to demonstrate that the Rambouillet Accords were deliberately sabotaged by the United States to provoke a war rely on a number of myths (e.g., the alleged secrecy of the accords, actually available on the Internet from day one) and misunderstandings, deliberate or otherwise (the economic provisions designed to protect Kosovo from Yugoslav sanctions being seen as part of a neo-liberal plot). No-one has yet produced a convincing reason why the US would deliberately seek to become involved in a war with Yugoslavia (unless, of course, one takes the Pilgerist line that since the US is a satanic force, *any* reason is convincing, however implausible). Once the war was on, not losing it certainly became a NATO interest – but that is a different point.

Third, was NATO the right body to respond to the situation emerging in Kosovo? This is a difficult question. Those who argue that only the UN is able to legitimise this kind of action will say no, but are then obliged to tell some sort of story about what should be done in circumstances where the UN is prevented from acting in the face of manifest injustice by the veto of a permanent member (as obviously would have been the case on this occasion). Others will argue that UN approval *as such* cannot alone determine what is the right response to suffering and injustice, although it may contribute to the formation of such a determination, as does, on this occasion, the approval of the overwhelming majority of

European states – the neighbours of Yugoslavia and Kosovo – for NATO action.

Finally, was the force employed by NATO proportional to the offence? Were the rights of non-combatants respected? And, was there, at the outset, a reasonable prospect that the action would be successful in the sense of decreasing the amount of the suffering to which it was a response? Here things are much less clear-cut and there is reason to think that Nato behaved with considerable irresponsibility. The action seems to have been initiated on the implausible assumption that a mere demonstration of force would be sufficient to bring Milosevic into line. When it became clear that this was not the case and that mass deportations were taking place, NATO, after a period of indecision, settled on a mixed strategy involving: arming and legitimising the KLA (with inevitable consequences in terms of the future politics of Kosovo); strategic bombing of the infrastructure of Serbia with a view to increasing the general pain level for the Serbian people; the threat of a ground offensive; and hopes that diplomatic moves – and the first two strategies – would make the third one unnecessary. Although Nato made every effort to avoid civilian casualties (we know this because there would have been far more had this *not* been the case), the inevitable errors and accidents that did take place were certainly added to by the political requirement that the lives of NATO airmen should not be put at risk – a political requirement, it should be noted, insisted upon by the very same people who also are the first to condemn the accidents which it generates, thus illustrating the confusion of benevolent 'humanitarians' in the face of the realities of warfare.

In the event, for reasons which are still unclear, NATO managed to occupy Kosovo without a ground war, but the situation they have inherited will be a source of intractable problems for years to come; in effect NATO has taken over responsibility for a ruined province with an understandably vengeful majority population bent on taking out their anger on those of the minority who remain; with the distinct possibility that the aftermath of its 'success' will involve the destabilisation of Montenegro and Macedonia, and the certainty that all the other countries of the region are looking to it, and the EU, to meet the cost of clearing up the mess.

So 'a perfect failure', as Mandelbaum would have it, the humanitarian intentions of the action betrayed by its political ineptitude? Even if this were the case, it says nothing about the general principle involved – except that it is always a good idea to act intelligently whatever your goals might be – but, in any event, the judgement is too harsh. It is, of course, easy to re-run the events of the last ten years in such a way as to produce a better outcome. Had the West instituted a sustained programme of material support for civil society in both Kosovo and Serbia ten years ago, and had Nato shown a willingness to use the necessary force to prevent aggression and humanitarian disasters whoever was responsible – whether it be Serb violence against Slovenia and Croatia, the ethnic cleansing of the Krajina by the Croatian government or the rape of Bosnia by Croats and Serbs – then things would have looked very different last spring. The Albanian majority in Kosovo would have felt secure from persecution (and would have been deterred from persecuting the minority in their turn) and the Serbs would have had to find some way of asserting the symbolic significance to them of Kosovo without expelling peoples whose forefathers had lived in the province for centuries. But this sort of hypothetical, counterfactual history is of little practical use. The leaders of the West had to decide what to do in the here and now, not what they or their predecessors ought to have done over the previous decade. Whatever reservations there might be about the actual policy followed, to have simply walked away after the failure of Rambouillet and allowed the steady destruction of the Kosovo Albanian community to continue would have led to a far worse outcome, materially and morally, than the mess that actually resulted. This was not a humanitarian war – no war ever is – but, in the end, the use of force to prevent, then redress, a great wrong was, taking all things into consideration, the right – and humanitarian – response to a difficult situation.

ACKOWLEDGEMENTS

Thanks for comments on an earlier draft to the editor and Christopher Coker, Tim Dunne, Christopher Hill, Andrew Linklater, Andrew Mason, Terry Nardin and Paul Taylor, none of whom are responsible for the conclusions reached here.

NOTES

1. See Michael Mandelbaum, 'A Perfect Failure' *Foreign Affairs*, No.78 (1999), pp.2–8.
2. See John Pilger, *Hidden Agendas* (New York: Vintage, 1997) and numerous interventions in the *Guardian* over the last year (e.g., on Kosovo, 'Morality, don't make me laugh', Guardian, 20 Apr. 1999; 'Acts of Murder', *Guardian*, 18 May 1999). Noam Chomsky provides the intellectual basis for Pilgerism – see his *The New Military Humanism* (London: Pluto, 1999) specifically on Kosovo; other practising Pilgerists might include Edward Said ('It's time the world stood up to the American bully', *Observer*, 11 Apr. 1999) and Tariq Ali ('Dogs of War', *Guardian*, 26 May 1999).
3. John Pilger 'Under the influence: the real reason for the United Nations' role in East Timor is to maintain Indonesian control', *Guardian*, 21 Sept. 1999.

# Can There be Such a Thing as a Just War?

## MELANIE McDONAGH

Yes, but we don't call it that. The expression is too absolute for the temper of the age, and you should use it with discretion. Like the words 'ethical foreign policy', which are so ruthlessly sent up by old cynics like the former foreign secretary Lord Carrington, the expression invites a hail of bitterly sarcastic letters to the *Guardian*. The common preference of British government during the Kosovo campaign was for the expression 'humanitarian intervention'. Justice means to give each his due. Humanitarianism, which is usually linked to the word 'aid', suggests that we are trying to make the world a better place, which is at once more pleasing and less austere to contemporary sensibilities. George Robertson, as Defence Secretary, endlessly repeated during the conflict that the Allies' intention was to ensure the return of the Albanian refugees to their homes. It was an impeccably humanitarian aspiration, hardly ever linked by its champions to the bald little noun 'war'.

Yet the Kosovo conflict was a war, despite the technical reasons why war was not declared on Yugoslavia. And it was just. Fighting against organized ethnic violence is a just cause. The systematic dispossession of hundreds of thousands of Albanian citizens in Kosovo by the forces of the Yugoslav state from August 1998 was a grim and unacceptable action by a government against its own citizens. The trajectory of Belgrade-sponsored violence that was established from the summer of 1998, and continued under the very noses of the international monitors from the OSCE in October, could be seen to have only one possible end – the ethnic cleansing of the greater part of the Albanian population from Kosovo. The pace and brutality of the project was unquestionably quickened and intensified by the NATO action in March, but the notion, which I have heard advanced everywhere from the House of Commons to the *Spectator* magazine, that the bombing initiated the ethnic cleansing, is a result of what Catholics used to call culpable ignorance. Although in some cases, the technical theological expression, invincible ignorance, would do equally well. What made us go to war? Last year we had a European state – Yugoslavia – which was engaging in systematic terror against an ethnic group – the Albanians – who were in 9:1 majority in a province where the government has long aimed for ethnic hegemony for another group: its own, the Serbs. The consequences were not only catastrophic for the Albanians; the creation of great numbers of refugees could only be destabilising for a fragile region – especially for neighbouring Macedonia. There were, therefore, good pragmatic reasons as well as moral ones for interfering – as Russia and China would no doubt put it – in the liberty of a state to terrorise its own citizens. Misha Glenny, in his widely-reviewed new book, *The Balkans*, begins with a sustained assault on the British Prime Minister for his statement to the House of Commons that Kosovo was 'on the doorstep of Europe', which the author, bizarrely, interprets as an attempt by Mr Blair to distance Kosovo from Europe. The thrust of that statement was exactly the opposite: Kososvo is under the very noses of the states of the European Union; it was not a far-away country – it was Europe's problem. During the war in Bosnia, Germany played host to no fewer than half a million refugees from ethnic cleansing and war. We are our brother's keeper, if for no better reason than that he may have the bad taste to demand asylum from us when he is expelled from his home.

But it would be odd to suggest that it was solely the actions of the Serbian leader last year that brought on, and justified, the NATO bombing. Of course this was true in the short term. But any understanding of our collective response to the situation in Kosovo must take account of the context of what went before, notably in Bosnia. How anyone could have examined the actions of Belgrade in Kosovo except as part of the continuum of the wars in former Yugoslavia in which the regime of Slobodan Milosevic was the first mover is beyond me. I know what happened during the war in Bosnia because I went there during the war as a journalist more times than I can count but the reality of that war is, or should be, common knowledge. Even among the Nelson Mandelas and the Jimmy Carters, who waxed so very indignant about the NATO action. Yet the massacre at Srebrenica (deaths: *circa* 8,000) seemed to have had less effect on them than the bombing of the Chinese Embassy in Belgrade (deaths: three).

And what should be branded into our collective consciousness is the fact that for three months from May 1992, the Bosnian Serb Army, controlled from Belgrade, with the arms and backing of the Yugoslav Army, cleansed by murder and expulsion no less than 70 per cent of the territory of Bosnia-Hercegovina. The other aggressor in the Bosnian war was the Croatian government, but its part in the dismemberment of Bosnia followed and was made possible by Serbian action. Thus, when the same Belgrade government which had precipitated and indirectly executed the mass ethnic cleansing in one state of former Yugoslavia begins the same process in another unit of the former Federation (Kosovo was an autonomous region), we justifiably expect the worst for the Albanians. We had been here before. Incidentally, the course of the war in Bosnia does rather give the lie to the notion that the Belgrade regime is only driven to mass murder and dispossession when it is inflamed by NATO interference: the cleansing of the greater part of Bosnia of its non-Serb population took place without any action on our part whatever. More's the pity.

Indeed when I stood at the crossing point at Morina, between Yugoslavia and Albania, on Good Friday last year, and heard the stories of the Albanian refugees who walked across the border carrying blankets and suitcases and babies, what struck me most was the sickening sense of déjà vu. The names of the paramilitaries who did the killing were just the same as in Bosnia – Arkan's people, and Seselj's – and the stories of local Serbs acting in concert with the paramilitaries from outside. There was the same synchronised action by the army, the police, the irregulars, the local Serbs. I had heard all this before, in 1992, when I spoke to the refugees in Travnik from the Prijedor region of north-west Bosnia, where some of the worst ethnic cleansing had happened. Actually, the cleansing in Kosovo was relatively efficient, and most of the refugees pushed from the territory quickly, rather than kept in camps where torture was practised. The cleansing of Kosovo, dreadful as it was, was far less terrible than that of northern and Eastern Bosnia.

But, this time, the Albanian refugees spilling over the border were greeted by a phalanx of reporters. You didn't get that to the same extent after the Bosnian camps in Omarska and Keratherm were opened in 1992. At Morina, the chief crossing-point for the refugees, the first thing that the poor people walking across the border saw was the CNN crew standing on the grass verge and the ITN man talking to camera; indeed I saw one old couple walk hand in hand from Kosovo into exile in Albania with a German cameraman walking backwards in front of them, filming into their faces. When another old man collapsed in exhaustion, a photographer muscled his relatives out of the way to take pictures.

Justice was not done in Bosnia, though its claim to outside help was, as a sovereign state, greater than Kosovo, partly because there were no cameras when and where it mattered to put the case for intervention as forcibly as in Kosovo. We could not, however, be immune to the human suffering of the Kosovars because there was no escaping those images, at least of the survivors once they crossed to safety. I know what you're thinking – how vulgar it is for our sense of justice to be driven by television. All I can say is that it's a pity that CNN weren't in Srebrenica and Rwanda as well. But the limitations of the media coverage are only now apparent. There has been a sustained attempt by pundits like John Laughland and John Pilger, to name only two in the British press, to deny the extent of the murders during the cleansing in Kosovo, even though fewer than a third of the suspected grave sites have been investigated by the International War Crimes Tribunal, and over two thousand bodies have been exhumed to date. It really does look as though unless there is television coverage, preferably in the presence of the BBC's John Simpson, of an actual massacre, or else television coverage of the exhumation of the corpses, with DNA corroboration of identity, there will always be found people to deny that the killings took place or else were monstrously exaggerated. The word of scores of survivors and witnesses, given quite independently of each other, is not enough. The lesson that a prudent government will take from the reaction to the war is that if you are going to commit mass murder of an ethnic group, it is well worth taking pains to dispose of the bodies. How fortunate it was that the Yugoslav forces had a week's notice to prepare for their withdrawal.

When I was in Klina, in Kosovo, in June, I met a boy of 17 who had bullet wounds which I saw, in his shoulder and leg; he said that he had been part of a group of perhaps a hundred men from a nearby village, who were taken from their refugee convoy, and shot in batches of ten – he had survived because the other bodies had fallen on top of him and he had pretended to be dead. He had told the same story, over and over again; the details of the story had never changed. Yet those hundred bodies have not been found; are we then to deny that anything happened?

Indeed, the extent of the revisionism on the war is causing me to doubt the evidence of my own eyes and ears. The well-known journalist, Robert Fisk, wrote a letter attacking an article of mine in the *Irish Times* in which he asserted that the Serbs who did the killings and cleansing in Kosovo were from outside the province – he knew, because he saw the paramilitaries withdrawing from Kosovo personally. Not only did I speak to innumerable Kosovars from different parts of the province who asserted that their Serbian neighbours had collaborated with the militias, I actually have a Serbian friend from Pristina, who, as a conscript in the Yugoslav Army, took part in the ethnic cleansing of the Has area.

Before leaving the revisionists who deny the justice of the war, let me turn to the feminist writer, Germaine Greer, who, in a speech in Westminster Hall denounced the bombing and asked rhetorically: 'Those Albanians on whose behalf we're meant to be acting – has anyone asked them what they want?' I did. After talking to scores of refugees – particularly women – I can say two things quite categorically. Not one of them was not supportive of the bombing. And not one of them said that the bombing had forced them from their home, as opposed to men with masks and guns, and tanks, and knives.

But to return to the context of the Kosovo war, I am not trying to suggest that there can be an exact equation between Kosovo and Bosnia. Kosovo was a federal unit of the old Yugoslavia – and when the federation was dissolved it had a good claim to self-determination like the other federal units. It did not, however, have Bosnia's long history as a self-governing political entity with historic borders. But knowing what we did about the ends and means of Mr Milosevic from the previous wars, it would have been unthinkable to have left the Kosovars to their fate at his hands. It still is.

One of the old criteria for a just war was that every other means should be exhausted first before resorting to force. And while this holds good for the Allies, it does too for the Albanians. The Kosovo Albanians did not lightly resort to armed terrorism to break free of the embrace of the Yugoslav state. They made a remarkable practical effort at conflict prevention – though this is normally a matter for interminable international conferences in expensive hotels.

I first visited Kosovo in 1992 – the cliché of the war, right from the start, was that the war started here, and that it would finish there. (Actually, the cliche may be wrong – it may finish in Montenegro.) Then, the Albanians were running a parallel state. Nearly all of them had been sacked from state employment after 1991, following the withdrawal of Kosovo's autonomy by Belgrade. Albanian schools and university system had been closed down; beatings were commonplace; Albanian language papers had been closed. And the response of the LDK, under its leader, Ibrahim Rugova, had been the Gandhiesque strategy of passive resistance. He stubbornly demanded independence for Kosovo, preferably as an international protectorate, and spent much of his time giving interviews to Scandinavian peace groups, in the hopes of bringing Kosovo to international attention. As a policy, it failed. Kosovo hardly made it to the small print of the Dayton Agreement in 1995, which effectively partitioned Bosnia. Ibrahim Rugova's policy of attempting to internationalise the Kosovo problem looked like a joke. I interviewed a prominent LDK politician, Fehmet Agani, at that time and he was worried that the young people would be radicalised by the failure of passive resistance. How right he was; it was in 1996/97 that the KLA came to the fore, brought into being not by the radical policies of its leadership, but by the perceived failure of the alternatives. Kosovo only came to the serious attention of politicians here when the Yugoslav Army responded to KLA actions by attacks on Albanian civilians and villages. As a postscript I might remark that Fehmet Agani, perhaps the best of the Kosovar moderates, was shot by the Serbs earlier this year. If gangland politics are so evident in the Kosovo Albanian community now, it might perhaps occur to their critics to acknowledge that the systematic killing of Albanian professionals and politicians during the ethnic cleansing – something which many refugees mentioned to me – had something to do with it, as indeed, did the efforts of the Belgrade regime since 1990 to suppress the education system of the Albanians and harass their teachers. It would be wrong to conclude an argument that the war in Kosovo was just without reference to the dreadful ethnic attacks on Serbian civilians by Albanians since June, when KFOR entered Kosovo. Hundreds of Serbs and Gypsies have been murdered. Indeed, in June last year, my friends and I helped to ferry vans full of terrified elderly Serbs from Urosevac to Kosovo Polje. As one of them said, the Serbs who had done the bad things had fled; it was the innocent who were suffering. One couple told me that they were beaten not only by an Albanian neighbour, but by an Albanian from across the border: the participation of the Albanian mafia in the expulsion and killing of innocent Serbs is an ugly reality. But the context for these deaths – though not an excuse – is the initial ethnic cleansing of the Albanians. It would also have helped if the Serbs of Kosovo, as a community, had acknowledged publicly what had happened to the Albanians and had apologised. It would also have helped if the *de facto* governor of Kosovo, Bernard Kouchner, had been given the 6,000 international police he had asked for, rather than only 1,700 of them.

Indeed, the question in my mind is not whether there is such a thing as a just war. This one was. What I want to know is, can there be such a thing as a just peace? And the jury is out on that one.

# The 1999 Kosovo War through a South African Lens

## JOHN STREMLAU

South Africa was a distant bystander to the terrible tragedy in Yugoslavia. But the images of ethnic cleansing and the North Atlantic Treaty Organisation (NATO) bombing were hard to ignore. Publicly, the Department of Foreign Affairs called consistently for a political solution and remained critical of NATO bombing without the benefit of a United Nations (UN) mandate. Privately, officials conceded that the human rights atrocities perpetrated by Serbian forces against the Kosovar Albanian majority in Kosovo had left the Western democracies with few alternatives when the 78-day bombing campaign began in early March 1999 and ended with Serbian President Slobodan Milosevic's effective surrender on 3 June. Once the war ended, the UN moved in to establish its authority as the *de facto* government of Kosovo. Since then, governments everywhere have been reassessing the implications of this extraordinary intervention.

### BOMBING FOR HUMAN RIGHTS?

The war, it should be remembered, began with deadly miscalculations, both by NATO and Milosevic, which created in the tiny Yugoslav province Europe's worst humanitarian crisis in 50 years. The Western powers initially assumed that the bombing campaign would be short-lived, much like the one used in 1995 that forced Milosevic to agree to negotiate the Dayton accords and produced the uneasy NATO-enforced peace in Bosnia, which still prevails. But Kosovo, unlike Bosnia, is still a Yugoslav province and contains some of the most sacred historic and religious sites of the Serbian people. So when the bombing of Kosovo began, it not only stiffened Serbian resistance; worse, it accelerated Milosevic's brutal campaign for the forced removal of virtually all of the two million Kosovar Albanians who comprised 90 per cent of the province's pre-war population. Vivid television images beamed into living rooms across Europe and America reinforced the resolve of the 19 NATO members to sustain their unprecedented military intervention and eventually to extend the bombing to targets across the whole of Serbia.

But contrary to the impressions that global television networks and other US-dominated media conveyed to South Africa, this was not a reprise of the 1991 US-led Gulf War. CNN images of nightly high-tech bombing raids and familiar Pentagon briefings belied a fundamentally different purpose in using military force. Wars, the strategist Karl von Clausewitz declared, have a grammar but no logic. Although the military grammar of the two campaigns looked the same on TV, the goals were not. Reversing Iraqi aggression against another state is more acceptable under international law, and enjoyed a formal UN mandate. Redressing the human rights abuses against Kosovar Albanians remains a problematic political challenge. After 11 weeks of NATO bombing the Kosovars returned, but most of the 180,000 Serbs in Kosovo at the beginning of the 1999 sought refuge elsewhere.

This example cannot please South Africa and other young democracies that are valiantly striving to overcome their own peculiar histories of ethnic, racial and religious divisions. Initial impressions may be worse than the longer-term effects, but in the development of a post-Cold War global order, the intervention in Serbia may prove to be a turning point. Historians should scrutinise this action by the Western powers as a possible indicator of the shape of things to come.

NATO's intervention in Yugoslavia was not for conquest or to gain material advantage. It reflected a new and spreading post-Cold War doctrine that holds leaders accountable for extreme abuses of domestic power. South Africa, which once was the target of unprecedented foreign intervention – albeit non-military – for the crimes of apartheid, now promotes human rights and good governance as the basis for an African Renaissance. After Kosovo the Western powers may be somewhat more willing to back South African initiatives to prevent and resolve the sectarian conflicts in Africa that also result from massive human rights violations and generate many more refugees than the Balkan conflicts have.

The effort to redress human rights abuses in Kosovo was also significant, as primarily, a regional experiment. European governments and publics were more directly and extensively engaged in the design, execution and in dealing with the consequences of the Kosovo operation than was the case in the Gulf War. The US, in effect, provided external allied assistance. Moreover, throughout the air campaign there was virtually no European peace movement, in contrast with the protests over the Gulf War and earlier US-led military interventions, especially during the Vietnam War in the 1960s. This surprising European consensus may have reflected the lingering effects of the Nazi holocaust. But whatever the reasons, the Kosovo humanitarian intervention marked a hinge point in European history.

There can be no doubt that it was the NATO bombing, and not diplomacy, that forced the capitulation of Yugoslav dictator Slobodan Milosevic and the withdrawal of what was left of his 40,000 troops in Kosovo. Military strategists who argued that bombing alone would not work were wrong. Bill Clinton, Tony Blair and other NATO politicians, who have never known combat, envisioned winning without losing any of their own forces, and they persisted until 25,000 bombing sorties against a Yugoslav territory barely five times the size of Kruger Park achieved the objective without any NATO combat deaths.

This successful show of force also runs counter to a cherished South African claim that all conflicts can and must be solved by peaceful means, despite Pretoria's own recourse to military means to control a dangerous situation in Lesotho.

The problems which the Europeans felt compelled to address are the same ones that threaten regional peace and prosperity around the world. They reflect the mismatch of states and nations that since 1989 have led to more than four million deaths – primarily those of civilians – caught in the deadly crossfire of conflicts resulting from intra-state (usually inter-ethnic) conflict. The causes in the former Yugoslavia are not unlike those that have resulted in a proliferation of deadly conflicts in Africa. These have been summarised by Laurie Nathan of the Centre for Conflict Resolution in Cape Town as: authoritarian rule, the exclusion of minority groups from governance, economic and other inequities and a state that lacks the capacity to manage political and social conflict.

When South African leaders appeal to Europe and the US to assist African-led efforts to deal with the problems of ethnic conflict, they should note these similarities and the importance of not allowing double standards to undercut the promise of mutually beneficial North-South cooperation. Also, they should remind donors continually of the huge disparity in foreign assistance fund allocations. Resources are being poured into reconstructing Kosovo and, once Milosevic is gone, will go to Serbia. Estimates for reconstructing Yugoslavia run as high as a trillion rand. This could end up further undercutting development in Africa as scarce donor funds are diverted to the Balkans.

## STRATEGIC IMPLICATIONS?

Alarmists who feared Kosovo would trigger another Cold War were wrong. Russia threw in its lot with the West, much as it did in Bosnia, and played a critical role in helping to end the conflict. NATO-Russian cooperation surely serves the interests of African countries, many of whom are still recovering from the effects of the first Cold War. Fears of unrestrained American power also seem exaggerated. In 1992 the US threatened Milosevic with military action if he used force against the Kosovar Albanians. But Washington repeatedly failed to take action, because Clinton could not act alone without destroying NATO, affronting Russia, and risking another threat of impeachment at home. Although the Kosovo intervention was not initially as broad-based as that in Bosnia, it too eventually became a NATO, Russian and UN peace operation.

However, Pretoria and other UN supporters rightly view NATO's military action as undercutting the UN's authority to protect small states from the powerful ones. While the Kosovo war was fought without a UN mandate, several 12-to-3 votes were taken by the Security Council that were cited by NATO as evidence of broad international support for their action against Milosevic. And since the end of hostilities the prominent role given to the UN in Kosovo should reassure those who feared the UN might be permanently marginalised. The UN has asserted its authority under Kosovo UN administrator Bernard Kouchner, who has set up a transitional council and already is planning for April 2000 province-wide elections. With the UN playing a much larger role in overseeing civilian welfare and the reconstruction of Kosovo than it did in Bosnia, this should strengthen Kofi Annan's hand in pressing for greater resources to begin to redress the West's double standard in spending billions to promote human security in Europe while allowing as bad or worse atrocities to persist in Africa.

Despite the cycle of ethnic conflict in Kosovo, and the difficulties the UN will have in persuading a significant number of the more than 160,000 Serbs who fled as NATO entered the province and the Kosovar Albanians returned to go back, the defeat of Slobodan Milosevic is a long-term defeat for ethnic nationalism. Commitments by NATO and others to continue to respect Yugoslav sovereignty over Kosovo may seem a cruel fiction in light of the evident hatred Kosovar Albanians harbour for their Serb persecutors. In August 1999 barely 20,000 Serbs remained in the province. Yet there is a spreading international consensus, which lies behind NATO's decision to continue to treat Kosovo as part of Yugoslavia, that without political frameworks to manage cultural diversity no decent society is possible. No one can deny that intolerance is intense in the Balkans, much as it was in South Africa a decade ago. At the same time, South Africa also demonstrates that no forced separation of people is inevitable; or that no ethnic divisions cannot with goodwill be overcome.

## LESSONS FOR SOUTH AFRICA

Above all, the tragedy of Kosovo is a sharp reminder to South Africa of the evils of ethnic factionalism and the need to honour forever President Mandela's pledge that human rights will be the guiding light of the nation's foreign and domestic policies.

Second, too easily overlooked is the simple fact that leaders matter. Ten years ago South Africa, not only Yugoslavia, appeared on the brink of terrible civil strife. People in both countries were embittered by long histories of foreign domination and racial, ethnic and religious tensions that were made worse by deepening economic distress and inequities. Leaders of these troubled nations faced very tough choices. Milosevic decided to consolidate his political base by an appeal to ethnic nationalism. Mandela chose the path of national reconciliation, inclusion and constitutional democracy. Neither man's choice was inevitable, but the results were stunningly different. Today South Africa is thriving and Yugoslavia is in ruins.

A third lesson has to do with the failure to take preventive action, which in this case would have required a credible threat of force to restrain Milosevic. How regional organisations and the UN can be better equipped to take effective preventive action when a crisis is brewing within a sovereign state – in this case Yugoslavia – is one of the toughest and most vital issues of the post Cold-War era. Kosovo is another terrible reminder of the urgent need for the international community to reach a new consensus about how to balance better the two competing principles of international order: respect for the inviolability of borders and the rights to self-determination. All this is an obvious challenge that South Africa cannot ignore, given that most deadly conflicts in Africa erupt within countries, before drawing in others.

No one can say the world was not warned of Milosevic's intentions. In 1989 he went to Kosovo in a blaze of publicity to celebrate the six-hundredth anniversary of a heroic Serbian defeat by invading Turks and his promise to reassert Serbian hegemony was an early warning to the world. During the escalating ethnic conflict that followed, ways could have been found to prevent the catastrophe that was unfolding. But in the aftermath of the Cold War the major Western powers – most notably the

US – have been unable or unwilling to achieve political consensus domestically, among themselves, and with the rest of the UN, on how to deal with a growing list of deadly domestic and regional conflicts. One exception was the decision to reverse the 1990 Iraqi invasion of Kuwait. Toward less strategically important conflicts in Somalia, Rwanda, Congo, West Africa, the Caucasus and the Balkans their actions have more often been cautious, confused and contradictory.

Milosevic's aggressive actions in the early 1990s, including the wanton shelling of the historic Croatian city of Dubrovnik, went largely unchallenged. US President George Bush was gearing up his re-election campaign, had just won the Gulf War, and took the position that Yugoslavia was a European problem. As then Secretary of State James Baker quipped to an aide, 'We don't have a dog in that fight.' The European democracies were divided, and faced constituencies with various historic and ethnic ties to different communities in the six Yugoslav republics. When the two richest, Croatia and Slovenia, sought self-determination in 1991 from the threat of Serbian domination, Croatia's traditional ally Germany quickly granted recognition and persuaded the rest of the EU to follow suit, thus also fuelling Serbian paranoia and aggression. On Christmas Eve 1992, in reaction to rising repression in Kosovo, Secretary of State Lawrence Eagleburger dispatched the acting US ambassador in Belgrade to see Milosevic to deliver the following brief pointed message: In the event of conflict in Kosovo caused by Serbian action, the US will be prepared to employ military force against Serbians in Kosovo and Serbia proper. This effort to prevent greater deadly conflict suffered from two fatal weaknesses. The threat was not backed by the resolve of the US to act if necessary, nor did it have the authority and legitimacy of a UN mandate.

The US, as a democracy, is usually slow to go to war unless it faces a clear and imminent danger, as when Japan bombed Pearl Harbor on 7 December 1941. Building domestic consensus to put resources and people at risk is never easy, especially when the threat is seen as distant and indirect. Building a multilateral consensus for possible military action is a much more daunting political task. When countries do muster the will to use collective military force, it is usually too late for prevention and – as in Kosovo – the medicine may appear worse than the disease. As South African democracy takes root it too faces the need to build domestic and foreign support.

Another lesson that South Africans can draw from the Balkan crisis is the inherent limitations of the UN when confronted by a major crisis within one of its member states. The UN and its Security Council badly need reform and its biggest debtor, the US, must pay its bills. But even under the best of circumstances the UN is likely to be too bound by traditional concepts of sovereignty to help prevent the severe abuses of power that are generating millions of refugees and causing regional instability across the globe, including much of Africa. The alternative points to the growing importance of finding regional solutions for regional problems.

Of course, the UN must play a role in developing and legitimising the norms, institutions, and political will required to promote peace with justice in and among sovereign states. But it has become a huge conglomeration of 185 members, with widely different interests and governments that tolerate varying degrees of domestic dissent. A global consensus on when human rights abuse is a sufficient threat to international peace to merit intervention is at present a political impossibility. For the foreseeable future, the most promising experiments in multilateral peace operations are likely to remain at the regional level, perhaps with the backing of like-minded outside powers and preferably with the blessing of the UN. These realities will place special burdens on regional leaders such as South Africa. One such burden will be to decide when, where, how and with whom to use military force to prevent and resolve conflicts within and between neighbours.

Finally, in the aftermath of Kosovo – and the more recent crisis in East Timor – South Africa should not be bashful in holding up their domestic political achievements as an example to others. As Nelson Mandela declared in his farewell address to Parliament: 'It is a measure of our success as a nation that an international community that inspired hope in us, in turn itself finds hope in how we overcame the divisions of centuries by reaching out to one another.' It is a shame Mandela could not have taught this simple lesson to Milosevic.

# No Good Deed Shall Go Unpunished

## COLIN S. GRAY

'Humanitarian war' has no future. If NATO's assault on Serbia over Kosovo in 1999 was the first case in history of this oxymoronic phenomenon, it is likely also to be the last. Kosovo 1999 did not herald a Brave New World, a world wherein those who would do evil against their own citizens tremble in anticipation of action by a terribly precise swift sword wielded by the likes of such unmilitary Soldiers of Virtue as a Tony Blair and a Bill Clinton (not to mention such doughty Warriors for The Right as a Robin Cook, a Madeleine Albright and even a Claire Short). Instead, Kosovo 1999 illustrates yet again why the tenets and lore of (neo-) classical realism deserve their authority. This is not a matter of opinion. The world, and world politics – meaning we humans with our (in)humanity – works as it does in ways and for reasons easily accessible to empirical enquiry. Much as hope is not a strategy, so good – at least sincere, if necessarily culturally bound – intentions cannot provide a sound basis for navigation in foreign policy. I must hasten to add that hope and good intentions are inherently attractive and praiseworthy. The problem arises when the necessity for their presence is confused with a sufficiency of guidance for policy.

We neo-classical realists can have difficulty explaining the ethics of realism, or the realism and reality of our ethics, to people of other persuasions. To minimise misunderstanding I must state with the utmost clarity that I believe that we humans are moral beings incapable of *not* making moral judgments, and there is an important moral dimension to foreign policy and strategy. Neo-classical realists are, however, strategists in the most essential of senses. That is to say, we think consequentially rather than deontologically (at least as a general rule); we reason from end to end, rather than strictly about value in particular ends considered out of consequential historical contexts. We favour doing what we regard as good, because we regard it as good, but only if the cost is very low. Even more do we favour doing no harm, save in the context where the doing of harm is a genuinely regrettable necessity if some much greater good is to be secured.

Classical realism should be equated neither with the Athenian dictum expressed in the Melian Dialogue nor with the nightmarish vision expounded by Thomas Hobbes. Nonetheless, it is always well to remember the temptation to abuse unmatched power, as well as the potential for political affairs to stumble towards the edge of chaos. In order to lift the veil a little on the ethics, perhaps ethic, of classical realism, as they bear upon humanitarian war, or wars of humanitarian intervention, I will advance a commentary keyed to five complementary and somewhat overlapping arguments.

First, *people – including people like us – are selfish*. Both Islamic warriors committed to *Jihad*, and Christian warriors on papally-blessed crusades, expected to be rewarded for the risks they undertook for their right conduct. Much as a defence consultant can prosper financially while serving the higher good of national and even international security, so crusaders in all periods and of all ideological/religious flavours, behave selfishly. Of course, we are all capable of selfless acts. But our domain of interest here is social, not physical, science. Theory, 'law' or lore, for social science, looks for most-case validity, not ironclad predictability. If a single apple detached from a tree declines to fall to the ground, then Sir Isaac Newton's reputation is in trouble. In contrast, some altruistic examples of human behaviour do not imperil motivational theory keyed to rewards, tangible and intangible. Eternal life, medals or hard cash, the details do not matter. If the case for individual human selfishness is very strong, no matter how sanctified the rewards at issue, how much stronger still is the case for the actuality of selfish regard when we turn to consider the collective behaviour by polities which we term policy? Security communities never act solely because of the moral judgment that a particular course is *right*. Even aside from the non-trivial point that polities are not moral persons, deontology cannot serve unaided as a guide to action. The rightness or otherwise of a mission can tell us nothing in particular about its feasibility.

Matters for decision in foreign policy require the posing and answering of three questions: (1) What is going on out there? (2) What does it mean for us? (i.e., do we care, and if so, how much do we care?) (3) What, if anything, can we do to affect the course of events? In other words, policy decision needs to rest upon an understanding of events and assessment of the level of our interest in those events (classical national interest analysis), and then, if our interest is judged substantial, in a cold calculation of what difference we might be able to make.

Second, *selfishness 'works' for the general benefit because, as the eternal canon of classical realism affirms, prudence is the golden rule in statecraft.* It is not useful, by any exercise in ethical assay, for polities to pursue close variants of *Moralpolitik*. One need not subscribe to much of the post-modernist world view in order to know that policy motivation is rarely captured in its entirety by authoritative contemporary explanation. The fact of the matter is that in foreign policy, as in so much else, culture rules ethics. Rarely, if ever, do policy-makers perceive a range of options, only one of which has the 'morally healthy, low-evil' label on it. In practice, policy-makers reasoning consequentially are likely to find every option more or less morally ambiguous. Fortunately for their mental well-being, they are certain to be able to persuade themselves that expedient behaviour is right enough behaviour. Situational ethics are wonderfully convenient. The determined ethicist thus has at least two major existential difficulties with which to deal. First, both the general and the specific notions of right conduct in foreign policy always are coloured, and typically are driven, by the culture(s) of the community in question. Second, encultured policy-makers must make their decisions for policy action or inaction in historical situations commanded by appreciations, accurate or otherwise, of consequences.

When we (neo-)classical realists reaffirm the authority of prudence for statecraft, we do not imply that a particular course of action easily can be flagged as 'the prudent choice'. Nonetheless, we do insist that prudent behaviour has to mean behaviour selected by consequentialist reasoning. To behave prudently is to behave according to the strategic logic of means and ends, and that logic as a general rule does not allow for a morality of absolute ends. By way of illustration, NATO does not intervene in Chechnya, because it would be grossly imprudent for it to do so. The mafia would-be polity of Chechnya may well be judged by us to have the balance of right on its side, but so what? Recall that long traditional just-war doctrine requires not only that war, if waged, should be waged as a last resort, for a right intent and by a lawful authority. That wise and prudent doctrine also requires that war be waged with a good prospect of success, and that its proportionate and discriminate conduct should not do more harm than good (whatever the strength of the original right intent).

Third, *just behaviour does not succeed because it is just.* Because culture leads ethics, justice is an uncertain trumpet calling for action in world politics. It may well be true that the sword of righteousness is sharp. Unfortunately, any and every belligerent polity whose domestic character and/or foreign policy appears to us to be the expression of a criminal enterprise, is likely to believe that God, Allah, History or whatever is on its side. Wars can be well waged on behalf of morally appalling (to us) policy visions. History is not a morality tale. Good and evil universally submit to local definition. As a particularly encultured (neo-)classical realist, I do not assert a moral relativism. I am not at all confused about the deeds that I deem evil, and that I would like to oppose – for strong preference, oppose effectively. However, I do not confuse my clear notion of good and evil, even my clear notion of what those ideas ought to mean in policy practice for all polities, with the actual and permanent facts of ethical diversity.

Fourth, *we cannot bomb our way to Heaven on Earth – not even discriminately with GPS assistance.* The realist canon, properly read, adjures us to do no more harm than we need do *en route*, indeed endlessly *en route*, as we seek perennially and prudently to live in peace with tolerable security. It is the height of classical realist ambition to shape the global political context so that the prospects for such peace with security (understood broadly, which is to say including considerations of justice and economic well-being and so forth) are maximised for a generation. It is reasonable and therefore practicable to aspire to shape and manage a particular condition of 'order' for perhaps 20 years (i.e., a 'generation'). Much beyond 20 years and the possibilities for historical contingency to produce huge, and apparently chaotic, non-linear dynamic outcomes, overwhelm sensible aspiration for policy.

Man's inhumanity to Man, certainly the propensity for that, is endemic in our very humanity itself. Beyond the inconvenient and troubling point that my good cause is certain to be someone else's bad cause, a policy commitment to the enforcement of the right in world politics would be a foolish commitment to endless combat. An 'ethical foreign policy' of absolute ends, if more than moralistic flatulence, would be one that could contemplate as a regrettable necessity what an American soldier famously once said of a dilemma in Vietnam: 'We had to destroy the village in order to save it'. No matter how sincere the moral impulse to act consequent upon the recognition of evil, that impulse must fail the real, indeed the realism, test in world affairs – it directs policy that cannot work. The evil deeds that our (in)humanity allows, or encourages, us humans to commit is not akin to a disease that can be eradicated. We may stamp on a thug here, and pull teeth from a rogue there, but an ethical foreign policy worthy of the name is simply Mission Impossible. For that reason it is foolish and unarguably imprudent.

Fifth, *because we are in the realm of social, rather than physical, science, some arguable exceptions are allowed to the general lore of 'realistic' statecraft.* Classical realists, unlike neo-realists, accommodate a richly complex tapestry of influences upon the course of international history. As polities act to protect their reputation and prestige, so also might they act in genuine expression of moral outrage. I must admit that I cannot find an example of a decision to fight motivated wholly by moral impulse, but I am willing to concede the possibility. All governments, democratic and authoritarian, are bound to be sensitive to domestically articulated demands for foreign action, whether those demands are rooted in ethical or material considerations or, more likely, both. Just as even the most self-serving of state policies can be dressed up in moralistic rhetoric, so every truly ethical issue in foreign policy is certain to lend itself to skilled explanation in terms of the national interest. For example, although we can argue that for NATO Kosovo 1999 was history's first plausible example of strictly humanitarian war, it should not be imagined that the more traditional issues of statecraft were entirely absent.

We classical realists – certainly this classical realist – insist upon a consequentialist ethics which includes prudence as a policy guide. No matter how heinous the 'bad guys', we oppose collective suicide, and we are against manifest futility masquerading as responsible policy and strategy. However, some actual, unfolding or plausibly impending crimes are so awful, whether or not they are judged likely to have consequences intolerable for our idea of a tolerable 'world order', that they should be prevented if possible, at least arrested under way, or, *faute de mieux*, be magnets for a powerfully retributive justice. These sentiments are not a repudiation of the lore of realism in world politics. Rather are they recognition that general rules in human affairs must allow for occasional exceptions. Moral outrage is not a sound basis for policy, but periodically it is so insistent that prudent policy-makers must bow to its demands. In so bowing, they should behave strategically, which is to say with a careful regard to balancing means with (in this case very largely morally defined) ends.

A pragmatic problem with *Moralpolitik* is that it is characteristically unyielding to suggestions for compromise. When policy success is morally defined, the stakes in conflict become absolute. If we permit, let alone dignify by treaty, even some fraction of behaviour we have proclaimed morally intolerable, our entire policy is compromised. A pervasive difficulty with the idea, let alone the attempted practice, of humanitarian war is that it suggests no candidate-reliable test for the level and kind of inhumanity that should trigger corrective action. A further problem is the one standard in principle to all would-be exercises in collective security. Specifically, for reasons of culture and geopolitics our moral outrage will be felt very variably across different security communities. Finally, a council of prudence advises that history suggests the *general* wisdom in allowing local atrocities and their consequences to be treated locally on terms and to outcomes that are locally sustainable. That is *general* wisdom only. As noted, there will be occasional exceptions. The lore of prudent statecraft, however, warns that polity Boy Scouts acting in world politics with pure hearts and sophisticated weapons are more likely to do harm than good.

# Air Power and the Liberal Politics of War

## TARAK BARKAWI

The war in Kosovo was shaped by the contemporary character of Western society and politics, together productive of a distinctively liberal contradiction at the core of NATO's campaign. While the war was legitimated in terms of humanitarian necessity, seemingly requiring an immediate and forceful response, the Western powers committed only to a slowly escalating air campaign. To be sure, many liberal commentators called for greater use of force.[1] But political leadership for the most part did not seek to mobilise the public for a potentially costly and protracted war, calculating that neither their electoral nor their strategic interests justified it. It was therefore necessary to wage a 'humanitarian war' in which Western casualties would be few. Air power supplied the solution. When coupled with precision guided munitions, it had the additional advantage of largely avoiding civilian casualties, further facilitating humanitarian justifications for the campaign.

The difficulty with this solution was that it made Allied strategy incoherent, placing severe constraints on NATO's ability to achieve its objectives. Allied strategy was incoherent in another more significant sense as well. Liberal justifications for a 'humanitarian war' over Kosovo construct an inherently problematic link between military means and humanitarian ends. Below, the ways in which the liberal politics of war shaped and constrained the nature of NATO operations are considered, following which the humanitarian legitimation for the war is critiqued.

The use of air power alone to stop Serbian military and paramilitary operations in Kosovo in the absence of a land campaign or the threat of one presented insoluble strategic dilemmas. Air power cannot occupy ground, nor can it provide direct control over territory and population.

It is for this reason that, during the bombing campaign, the Serbs were able to conduct their ethnic cleansing operations with near impunity. The OSCE monitors had been withdrawn and there were no NATO ground forces present to obstruct the Serbs. The immediate effect of the bombing, then, was to worsen exponentially the crisis facing the Kosovars. Throughout the war, Serb forces used the bombing as an excuse to conduct massacres, often claiming the victims were due to NATO air action.

While air power cannot control territory or stop ethnic cleansing, it can destroy structures and military equipment and kill people. Strategies of air power seek to degrade civilian infrastructure and military capabilities to the point where the enemy is unwilling or unable to carry on the war. The initiative can pass to the recipient of the air strikes, as it is the leadership of the bombed country which decides how much punishment to take before seeking peace terms.

Beyond these general limitations in the use of air power alone, the liberal politics of war created further constraints for NATO operations, namely the insistence that there were to be few or no casualties suffered by Allied forces. Pilots were directed to fly above 15,000 feet in order to reduce their exposure to Serbian anti-aircraft fire. This limited their ability to detect and destroy Serb forces in Kosovo. The camouflage, decoys and other techniques used by the Serbian forces to foil NATO strikes were all the more effective.[2] In general, ground forces, as long as they do not have to concentrate to fight other ground forces, can ride out air bombardment relatively easily, no matter how severe. They will take some casualties, to be sure. But they can be dispersed and dug in, munitions and other supplies can be hidden, while NATO aircraft hit empty barracks and supply depots. Indeed, a long-term guerrilla war waged from mountain bases was part of the doctrine of the Yugoslav army.

Being unable to halt ethnic cleansing operations directly, or even seriously to damage the forces carrying them out, NATO turned to the bombardment of Serbian political and military infrastructure in an effort to convince Milosevic to capitulate. But here NATO encountered another constraint. While Serbian ethnic cleansing and crimes against humanity had to be stopped, in doing so as few Serbian and Kosovan civilians as possible were to be killed. In air staff jargon, there was to be no collateral damage. Much evidence so far suggests the strikes were indeed very precise, hitting their intended targets with few civilian casualties – even, it seems, in the case of the Chinese Embassy.[3] These limitations on the killing of Serbian civilians muted the impact of the bombing. Even legitimate targets had to be hit in such a way as to reduce casualties. NATO often had to be content with bombing empty government buildings in the dead of night. The restrictive rules of engagement meant that many missions were cancelled and more resources used in hitting targets than necessary. None of this seemed to alter the traditional effect of bombing on civilian populations, which is to increase solidarity with and support for their political leadership. NATO ran the risk that it would run out of office buildings and factories to bomb, while Milosevic remained in power, his forces in Kosovo, and his population rallied behind him, in shared rage at the West's attack on tiny Serbia.

One can see the contradiction in the liberal politics of war at work. The insistence that there be no Allied casualties meant that the strategy adopted could not actually stop or even seriously impinge upon the ability of the Serbs to conduct ethnic cleansing operations in Kosovo, the ostensible purpose for which NATO went to war in the first place. The insistence that there be as few civilian casualties as possible meant that the strategy of bombarding Serbian political and military infrastructure was limited in its effectiveness to achieve the ends of the campaign, even while causing significant damage. The West was neither willing to risk the lives of its own soldiers nor to bear the burden of shedding others' blood, a burden the waging of war necessarily entails.

In the end, Milosevic chose to pull out of Kosovo. It is impossible to know exactly why he did so; perhaps it was the withdrawal of Russian diplomatic support. It is clear that he did not have to do so. His armed forces were still largely intact and in good order, as was demonstrated when they pulled out from Kosovo. He could have all too easily called NATO's bluff, forcing it to continue the bombing of Serbia or risk a ground invasion of Kosovo. For Nato, either course of action would have skewered it upon the contradictions of the liberal politics of war, as either Serbian civilians or NATO soldiers would have had ultimately to die in number in order to achieve victory. Advocates of the use of air power alone for 'humanitarian' or other purposes should not draw as much satisfaction from the outcome of Operation Allied Force as they have done. Indeed the apparent result has been the creation of a unitary ethnic protectorate in Kosovo, one for Albanian Kosovars rather than Serbs. This was not the avowed purpose for which NATO waged war.

That NATO achieved 'victory' in terms of forcing Milosevic to pull out of Kosovo, but not in terms of its wider political objectives, leads to the question of the humanitarian legitimation for the war in Kosovo. All strategy seeks to make a link between military means and political, that is to say evaluative, ends, and can be critiqued for the validity and logical consistency of this link.[4] Taking seriously the humanitarian justification for the war in Kosovo does not mean that humanitarian motives were the only reason, much less the explanation, for NATO's campaign. However, in the current era, Western military action is legitimated in humanitarian terms. Such legitimation constrains and shapes the exercise of military power, both as to the initiation and manner of its use. Identifying contradictions in the ideology of humanitarian war can determine the ways in which it both obscures and enables the operation of a set of power relations.

'Humanitarianism' is an extraordinarily powerful tool of legitimation. It is very difficult to oppose something justified in such terms. Yet, as Carl Schmitt reminded us some time ago, there is no actual political entity which corresponds to 'humanity', rather only those which seek to speak in the name of it. In identifying oneself as 'humanitarian,' one correspondingly strips one's enemies of *their* humanity, thereby sanctioning extreme violence against them.[5] Accordingly, the notion of 'humanitarian war' constitutes the West as 'humane intervener' and the objects of intervention as 'inhuman barbarians'. This identity construction does not reflect either the historical or contemporary nature of relations between the West and those countries in which humanitarian crises occur. It diverts attention to the question of relative levels of 'civilisation' and the practices, as well as abuses, of 'civility'. As a consequence, it obscures the implication of Western societies in creating the conditions in which the humanitarian crises of recent years have arisen. While liberal opinion debates whether or not to intervene 'humanely', it is forgotten for how long the West has sought to exacerbate the inequalities of power and wealth in the world. Western powers have played and do play a major role in creating the social, economic and political conditions conducive to violent conflict and human suffering.[6] The neo-liberal economic response to the collapse of Communism was a significant factor in the break-up of Yugoslavia and consequent rise of radical nationalist political movements.[7] In obscuring these relations with tropes of civilisation and barbarism, the language of 'humanitarianism' works to legitimate global hierarchies of power and inequality. The West's own inhumanity is ignored, as is the civility of the 'barbarians' and the complexities of their contexts and conflicts. Indeed, Africa, where the West bears tremendous responsibility for its historical and ongoing plundering and exploitation, is seen through the lens of the ideology of 'humanitarian intervention' as the very seat of 'barbarism'.

Rather than a humanitarianism that faces squarely the consequences of Western wealth and power for the rest of the planet, the notion of 'humanitarian war' offers an irresistible and exciting morality tale in which Western militaries are figured as the sword of justice. Air power plays a crucial role in sheltering this tale from the ambiguities of war. Precision-guided munitions give apparent credence to the idea that one can wage a war in which the 'innocent' are spared and only 'villains' killed, while the technological superiority of Western air forces ensures that they are largely safe from enemy action. Politicians can promise their citizens that good is being done in faraway lands but that there will be no body bags. Liberal opinion leaders can claim that the ethical fog of war is illuminated in sharp contrasts of good and evil, right and wrong. Indeed, the word 'war' is hardly mentioned at all, but rather euphemisms of Orwellian proportions, such as 'humanitarian intervention' or 'peace enforcement.'

While the utility of 'humanitarian war' in obscuring power relations and diverting attention is crucial to its role of legitimation, there is also a disjuncture in the manner in which it links military means to ethical purposes. At the end of the twentieth century, to arrive at the idea that 'humanity' might be served through the aerial bombardment or invasion of Serbia says much about the naïveté of the liberal encounter with war, the processes war sets in train, and the diabolical ethical dilemmas it involves for those seeking to achieve good with violence. Advocates of the use of force for 'humanitarian' purposes have the best of intentions and are convinced that their wars are of some 'new' type, rendering 'old' thinking about war irrelevant.[8] They forget that many a Western expeditionary force sent out to crush 'barbarism' and bring 'progress' achieved something quite other. The moral paradoxes of war are inescapable, stemming as they do from the perennial problems of the relationship between politics and violence.[9] The character and outcome of military operations resist easy harmony with moral purposes. It is in the nature of war to undermine or even reverse the ends sought. A war fought for the principle of multiethnic tolerance produces a unitary ethnic protectorate. The Kosovar population, brutalised and radicalised by the Serb assault, now seeks to 'cleanse' and murder the remaining Kosovar Serbs. They, like so many who experience war first hand, have been remade in war's own image. Quite understandably, they have little time for pious notions of multiethnic democracy and liberal tolerance of difference. Wartime violence, like all violence, has a strong tendency to beget further violence. It is difficult to imagine Kosovo rejoining Serbia or surviving as an independent state. Rather, NATO's campaign may well end up being one step in the struggle for greater Albania, one which could ignite a major conflagration in future involving at a minimum Macedonia, Albania and Serbia.

It is incumbent upon us to think clearly about the political and ethical issues involved in using violence in the name of 'humanity.' There are many evils in the world, many villains who bring them about, and much suffering. Invariably, constructions of the villains against whom the West chooses to wage righteous war are far more revealing of the West than of its enemies' irredeemable otherness. The fact remains that while justifying its war in terms of a response to Serb 'barbarism' and 'crimes against humanity', the West wanted its moral crusade on the cheap. It was unwilling to bear war's necessary ethical trade-offs, in this case the killing of civilians. It was unwilling also to offer up the lives of its soldiers.[10] So the response to the crisis in Kosovo was aerial bombardment from a safe height. Certainly there were many liberal pundits who argued, from an even safer distance, that ground troops should have been committed. If in future they remain convinced that this or that eruption of 'barbarism' demands that war be waged in the name of 'humanity', they may consider finding the courage of their convictions and making a choice that was in fact available to them in Kosovo. They could have joined the KLA, just as many in the old Left set off to join the International Brigade of the Spanish Republican Army.[11] The experience of the ambiguities and horrors of war up close and personal may well cure them of their enthusiasm for 'peace enforcement'.

ACKNOWLEDGEMENTS

Thanks to Ken Booth, Shane Brighton, Susan Carruthers, Colin McInnes and Mark Laffey for assistance in writing this paper.

NOTES

1. See for example Daniel Goldhagen, 'German Lessons', *Guardian*, 29 Apr. 1999, in which he argues for the invasion and occupation of Yugoslavia, not just Kosovo.
2. See Tim Ripley, 'Kosovo: A Bomb Damage Assessment', *Jane's Intelligence Review*, Vol.11, No.9 (1 Sept. 1999).
3. Ibid. The Chinese Embassy was acting as a rebroadcast station from Belgrade to the Serb forces in Kosovo, Serbian communications having been cut by NATO strikes. See John Sweeney *et al.*, 'Why America Bombed the Chinese Embassy', *The Observer*, 28 Nov. 1999.
4. Tarak Barkawi, 'Strategy as a Vocation: Weber, Morgenthau and Modern Strategic Studies', *Review of International Studies*, Vol.24, No.2 (1998).
5. Carl Schmitt, *The Concept of the Political* (Chicago, IL: University of Chicago Press, 1996), pp.54–5.
6. Peter Gowan, 'The NATO Powers and the Balkan Tragedy', *New Left Review*, No.234 (1999), p.103.
7. Robin Blackburn, 'The Break-up of Yugoslavia and the Fate of Bosnia', *New Left Review*, No.199 (1993), pp.102–3; Michel Chossudovsky, *The Globalization of Poverty: Impacts of IMF and World Bank Reforms* (London: Zed Books, 1999); Susan L. Woodward, *Balkan Tragedy: Chaos and Dissolution after the Cold War* (Washington, DC: Brookings Institution, 1995).
8. See Mary Kaldor, *New and Old Wars: Organized Violence in a Global Era* (Cambridge: Polity Press, 1999). A close reading of this text shows that what the author has in mind

is not so 'new' as she thinks. The argument, for example, that UNPROFOR should have used more force in Bosnia to push humanitarian aide through (chapter 3) means that significant forces would have had to be deployed, as the few armoured personnel carriers escorting convoys were inherently vulnerable to superior Serb forces. But deploying significant forces, and waging war in pursuit of 'cosmpolitan' aims, would amount precisely to the kind of 'old' war Kaldor claims is extinct: large scale, conventional fighting between regular forces each under the command of political leaderships pursuing ideological goals.

9. See Max Weber, 'Politics as a Vocation', in H.H. Gerth and C. Wright Mills (eds), *From Max Weber: Essays in Sociology* (New York: Oxford University Press, 1946), pp.77–128.

10. Indeed, often the West cannot be asked to make even lesser sacrifices. The commitment of Dutch troops to the safe areas in Bosnia was initially very popular among the Dutch public and politicians, as it seemed that Holland was 'doing something' in the face of humanitarian emergency. However, as the Serbs restricted the supplies delivered to the Dutch battalion in Srebrenica, there was a chorus of complaints from the soldiers (professional volunteers), their families and politicians regarding the lack of *amenities*, such as fresh food and hot water, with one father writing to the Ministry of Defence complaining that his daughter could not take a hot shower. See Jan Willem Honig and Norbert Both, *Srebrenica: Record of a War Crime* (London: Penguin Books, 1996), pp.118–37.

11. See Tariq Ali, 'Springtime for NATO', *New Left Review*, No.234 (1999), p.69.

# Ten Flaws of Just Wars

## KEN BOOTH

The ancient doctrine of the Just War is the ancestor of the very contemporary notion of 'humanitarian war'. NATO's military campaign against Serbia in 1999 was justified on ethical grounds, not traditional national interests. This essay is a critique of the rationale of Just War/humanitarian war, and of its accompanying political/strategic mindset. I will argue that the Just War tradition/doctrine is supposed to restrain war, but that it has not, cannot and will not do so; in practice it only makes things worse by legitimising and honouring war. In particular, the construction a universal human rights culture – one of the foundations for global human security – will be delayed rather than advanced by militarised humanitarianism.

*1. Just Wars justify escalation.* Over the centuries, the idea of Just War was developed to establish restraint in an area of politics in which rules tend to be weakest. War is seen as the ultimate cockpit of necessity, and 'necessity knows no law'. But instead of becoming a force for restraint, Just War thinking has often served to excuse or provoke excess.

By the twentieth century, the combination of Westphalian statism, rampant nationalism, military-technological innovation and industrial gigantism had produced the potential for absolute war. There seemed no end to the escalation ladder. During the Cold War a strategic posture threatening nuclear holocaust was dubbed the 'just deterrent'. Donald A. Wells, writing in the late 1960s against the background of a recent Total War and an increasingly violent 'Limited War' in Vietnam in the foreground, argued that states justify inflicting any horror upon an enemy as long as they claim their cause is just.[1] Because a just cause demands unconditional commitment, the desire for justice and the injunction to respect proportionality are necessarily in tension. The former pushes towards extremes, the latter towards restraint. In an ideological age, and with the options opened up by technology, the ancient doctrine of restraint became a modern justification for totality. A.J.P. Taylor noted this many years ago when he commented that in the nineteenth century Bismarck had fought necessary wars and killed thousands, whereas in the twentieth century we had fought just wars and killed millions. If one's cause is 'just' it seems any level of escalation can be justified, even nuclear armageddon.

When governments persuade themselves they are fighting a Just War, and try to propagandise their populations accordingly, escalation is inevitable unless the enemy quickly collapses. The danger-signals were there in 1999 when NATO's leaders discovered that the war would not be over in the few days they had predicted. The tension between just cause and proportionality kicked in immediately. Once NATO had so publicly declared its hand for the refugees, what price justice? Had Milosevic kept his forces in the field for longer, one wonders just how far NATO would have escalated. Short of accepting a humiliating climbdown, or a massive escalation using ground forces, NATO could only intensify the bombing and expand the target list. Moreover, the decisive strategic bombardment of Serbia would have become an absolute imperative had NATO deployed ground forces, in order to reduce NATO casualties. Then, had body bags been flown home, in dozens, or hundreds, one wonders what would have represented 'proportionality' in Serbian blood. Just Wars can be used to justify anything. In, around and over Kosovo through the summer of 1999, the combination of militant moralism and democratic desperation was potentially deadly.

*2. Just Wars degrade their proponents, as well as destroy their opponents.*
Just Wars are dangerous for the targeted enemy and the inevitable victims of collateral damage, but they also degrade the society that convinces itself that it is fighting for Right against Evil. This was particularly evident in Britain in 1999 where Blair's government was loud with Just War rhetoric.

British public debate about the war was diminished by its government's crusading. Parliament was sidelined, and domestic critics pilloried. Democracy was a war aim, but was discouraged among the allies. 'The Serbs' were demonised. Milosevic's vicious ethnic cleansing was inflated to be the ultimate crime of 'genocide'. Mindless comparisons were made between Milosevic's Kosovo and the Nazi Holocaust. Innocent Serbs were killed, not intentionally but predictably, as a result of the decision to fight a zero-casualty campaign; and all the blame for what happened was shifted to the dictator in Belgrade.

Some in the West during the war suspected that manipulation had replaced reporting, and they questioned the 'truth' of the situation as stated by leaders or official spokespersons or uncritical reporters following press conferences. But critical judgment in society generally tends to disappear once the bugle blows. Governments encourage it. In a highly symbolic event, following an attack, in error, by NATO warplanes on a refugee convoy, the response from Downing Street was to send its *spinmeister* to Brussels to ensure better media presentation. NATO was determined to win not only in the air over Kosovo, but also over the air-waves more generally.

Historically, Just Wars have involved societies being willing to die for a cause, and not simply kill for one. Kosovo represented a change, and to many it was chilling. Whatever humanitarian war does to the enemy, we should also think of how it degrades us – just like nuclear strategy or torture. In the Kosovo campaign our armed forces were asked to perform not the traditional heroic role of the warrior, or even of the policeman, but rather the cold and heartless trade of the executioner.

3. *Just Wars are just war.* The idea of the Just War is beguiling, because it ennobles the profession of violence, and offers a set of conditions that seem to suggest rational control and restraint. However, its defining conditions – 'just cause', 'right intention', 'proportionality' and the rest – have been criticised for as long as the tradition, and rightly so. In practice they have been broadened, ignored, misused and manipulated.

*Just cause* is very subjective, including the application of 'self defence', widely seen as its only authentic case. *Right intention* is equally problematic. A decision-maker's reasons may well not be the causes for action, so how are we to know? What constitutes *legitimate authority* is a matter of political preference rather than legal nicety. *Last resort* sounds a sensible guide to policy, but how can anybody ever know whether more effort might work, while in some strategic circumstances a first strike might be thought to constitute a 'last' resort? The idea of a *formal declaration* of war has become increasingly anachronistic, while *reasonable hope* is vague. War is a condition of uncertainty, in which even the most expert can disagree in advance about the prospects, and in which events have a habit of fooling everybody. Finally, *proportionality* sounds more helpful than it is, in an activity in which changing circumstances, vital interests and group emotion defy ethical arithmetic.

NATO's campaign against Serbia illustrates some of these problems. The issue of 'just cause' was controversial, as the war was clearly not for self-defence, while many believed the campaign to be a breach of international law, regardless of claims about 'legitimacy' – another term of politics rather than principle. 'Right intention' was disputed by those who believed that behind the rhetoric of humanitarianism lay traditional state interests, especially the US desire to impose its authority on NATO and hence European affairs. The selectivity of the West's intervention was seen by critics as a justification for suspecting a masking of reasons and causes. As is expected these days, war was not declared. Was it a last resort? Proponents say 'yes' and point to Belgrade's intransigence, but critics point to the virtual ultimatum delivered at Rambouillet, and argue that NATO was looking for a rationalisation for war, not a way of avoiding one. Just War conditions provide a cover which allows power to do what power can do. If this is true, the Just War is best seen as a continuation of war by other rhetoric.

4. *Just Wars encourage bad strategy.* Political leaders with Just War mindsets are rarely professional specialists in violence. In Just Wars, strategy is therefore handed to amateurs, and this was the case in 1999. The campaign was characterised by strategic mishandling on the part of the political leadership, rather than military incompetence. Misjudged wars can be fought competently.

When a politician 'wants' war, mistakes are bound to occur. This is especially the case – to recall Tennyson – if someone believes that their strength is as the strength of ten because their heart is pure. The desire to celebrate NATO's fiftieth anniversary in style almost certainly affected the timing of the war, but by the time they struck they could not protect the refugees; they could only try to punish the ethnic cleansers, and thereby imperil the refugees further. It was a short war, but long on politico-strategic blunders. Long-range air strikes could not achieve the initial objective declared by NATO. The will of the opponent was seriously underestimated, while confidence in NATO's capability was exaggerated. Cruise-missile humanitarianism and bombing from a safe height could not stop the brutality being carried out against the Albanian Kosovars on the ground, and almost certainly exacerbated it. The early and public ruling out of the ground force option was naïve. Strategic miscalculations were compounded by diplomatic errors, notably the offending of the Russians, the failure to secure UN support, and the problems with China following the bombing of its Belgrade Embassy.

To place NATO's 'victory' into context, it is instructive to compare the relative strengths of the two belligerents: the collective GNPs of the NATO allies with that of Serbia, and the respective orders-of-battle of the combatants. When Milosevic (still in power) felt compelled to withdraw his forces (still largely intact) from the field of battle into the national heartland (for the moment), it followed one of the most one-sided military contests in history. On the one side the most economically and militarily powerful alliance ever, and on the other a small nation with no capability to strike back militarily. They had only the defenceless Albanians to lash out against. A Just War encourages bad strategy by elevating amateur strategists. A zero-casualty victory, however, naturally discourages criticism.

*5. Just Wars feed self-righteousness*. Because the politicians leading NATO believed they were engaged in a just struggle against the demon Milosevic, they developed a pious certainty of righteousness and an evident absence of guilt about what they did. Neither of these traits is conducive to true humanitarian politics. The best of the 'West' is not represented by the hubris of humanitarian imperialism, expressing itself as claim to be universal judge, jury and executioner.

First, at the politico-military level the NATO allies claimed 'legitimacy' in acting militarily in what some regarded as the internal problems of another country. This polarised world politics. The action was widely seen as illegal, and failed to get unambiguous Security Council endorsement. NATO thereby dealt a blow to the authority and future of the UN. This precedent can now be used by every regional hegemon. It is worth recalling that in the 1930s the League of Nations began to collapse when great powers disregarded its authority.

NATO's unilateralist posture had other negative consequences. It increased a West-versus-the-Rest polarisation, encouraging the former to feel superior, fighting for civilised values, while the latter was made to feel both inferior and threatened. Only the United States can project military power across the globe, and in recent years has zeroed in its missiles and bombs at a growing list of countries. The Pentagon talks of 'full-spectrum dominance 2010' and the Secretary of State, Madeleine Albright, argues that Americans stand taller than the rest – 'that is why we can see further'. This mixture of self-righteousness and technological hubris represents a real and growing threat to those not identified as the White House's friends from the South. Potential targets will look towards their defences, including, perhaps, the building of primitive weapons of mass destruction.

Second, at the tactical level (not to mention their role in the macro-situation) self-righteousness led Western leaders to avoid accepting responsibility for some events in the war. What happened was blamed on others. War is always a deadly business and casualties are its first truth. Technical mistakes and bad luck are one thing when contemplating death and injury to those with some claim to be 'innocent', but in Kosovo (and Serbia) some of these casualties were directly and predictably the result of the Blair/Clinton priority of overseeing a UK/US casualty-free war. The deaths of refugees from friendly fire – and of innocent Serbs from that which was less friendly if not intentionally deadly – cannot simply be explained away as one of the unavoidable 'frictions' of war. It was a direct result of NATO strategy, and any attempt to argue differently is casuistic spin. To fail to take responsibility for one's actions is not a good foundation for humanitarian politics. Neither is hypocrisy. And here there was much, from the gap between the sympathy expressed towards the Kosovar refugees and the increasing lack of sympathy in Britain towards asylum-seekers, and the selectivity of the international community's humanitarian interventions.

Third, at a psychological level, self righteousness begets self-righteousness. Predictably, cruise-missile humanitarianism could not protect those being killed and terrorised by the Serb forces and paramilitaries on the ground. The opposite was the case; the bombing created circumstances in which they could carry out their ethnic cleansing with yet greater ferocity. NATO was not responsible for the Milosevic campaign of ethnic cleansing in 1999, but its strategy did create the cover of war for the ethnic cleansers, and for inflaming the latter's desire to extract revenge against the defenceless Albanians they despised – victims who, unlike NATO's warplanes, were accessible. NATO's moralising and missiles also had the effect of pushing the Serbian population behind a leader whose unpopularity had grown in the space opened up by peace following Dayton.

As piety grows and guilt diminishes, there is an ethic cleansing of the conscience; this may be the prelude to worse. Instead of taking responsibility for innocent casualties, for the increased terror inflicted on the Kosovar Albanians, for the damage done to the region's economy, and for the failure to prevent the ethnic cleansing of the Kosovar Serbs – all the direct result of NATO's strategy – the blame was shifted to the offending demon in Belgrade. NATO did have choices. When self-righteousness expands, and blame is denied, the important still small voice of conscience is silenced – a necessary element in any true humanitarian politics.

6. *Just Wars promote militarisation.* If guilt was silenced during the war, it had grown in Western minds during the preceding years: for not acting decisively in Bosnia (and Rwanda), for allowing the massacre at Srebrenica, and for ignoring the developing Kosovo tragedy. Furthermore, it was surely not an accident that NATO's most militant

leaders, Clinton and Blair, felt they had something to prove. In earlier incarnations, the former was an anti-Vietnam war rebel and the latter a member of CND. On military matters therefore, neither wanted to be outflanked in toughness. In addition, when it comes to 'duties beyond borders' centre-left politicians always have stronger interventionary instincts than their counterparts on the right. All in all, Kosovo was an opportunity for feel-good punishment. It was the militarisation of guilt.

Militarised humanitarianism causes a number of problems. First, the valorisation of military action flies in the face of humanitarianism, which requires the erosion of the legitimacy of using military force. Second, the more force is seen to be successful, the more it is likely to be used. The instrument will shape the will to use it. Third, high-tech, zero-casualty wars, fought for just causes are a godsend to arms manufacturers: just profit. Finally, the new humanitarian militarism has promoted a changed attitude among some sections of society, in which imperialism, strategy, and warriors are being reinvented for the twenty-first century. We are seeing the rise of post-modern Midases of militarism: everything they touch turns to 'new'. But there is more that is old than new in war, including the soundest lessons of all: military force is always a blunt tool, often used in error, and best left only to 'supreme emergencies'.

Militant humanitarianism risks leading Western societies down the dangerous path of ennobling the use of military force. Humanitarian warriors are providing good copy for recruiting advertisements.

*7. Just War thinking distracts attention from human security.* As it intensified through the 1990s, the Kosovo tragedy revealed that the Anglo-American special relationship did not give priority to human security. There were rhetorical flourishes, but little in the flourishing of resources. Old thinking, once again, was caught out in Kosovo. It showed that human rights are a critical security issue, and that when they are being massively violated, trouble usually follows. The same will be true now the war has ended, unless appropriate resources are devoted to peace-building.

Kosovo for a decade at least had been a humanitarian disaster waiting to happen. Security via conflict prevention was notable by its absence. Specialists on the region tried to draw attention to the dangers, but Western policy-makers avoided the issue(s), at Dayton and on other occasions. Meanwhile, the non-violent approach represented by Rugova gave way to the terrorist tactics of the KLA, which ultimately provoked the desired overreaction on the part of Belgrade, and the recruitment of the NATO air force. It is not now possible to know whether conflict prevention measures would have worked, only that opportunities were missed. Because we know the end of the story, it is tempting to assume that it had to be, but we know from other situations that different choices can result in different outcomes. South Africa, for example, radically shifted its internal political arrangements without the long-feared interracial blood bath. Political crossroads are inevitable, whereas conflict is only inevitable if the key decision-makers approach cross-roads with the wrong road-maps, and so turn in fateful directions.

Having overlooked human security before March 1999, the signs subsequently have not been encouraging. Typically, the stabilisation plan for the Balkans came far too late, when the air war was taking place, and at a much higher cost than would have been the case before the region was 'degraded' by NATO air power. It was predictable that it would take a long time before there could be a satisfactory security situation, and this remains the case today, with a mono-ethnic Kosovo likely to become independent, tension on the ground, approximately as many displaced persons in Serbia as in Kosovo's neighbours a year earlier, and Serbia joining the region's economic basket-cases. Military victory is easier than human security, especially when, as some predicted, the allies have chosen not to give the same attention and resources to the reconstruction of the Balkans as they gave to the air campaign. Other issues now demand attention, resources are squeezed, and supplying reinforced doors for improving the human security of frightened Serbian Kosovars still in the province does not have the priority that supplying bombs to coerce Milosevic had a year earlier.

*8. Just Wars stimulate self-delusion.* Self-delusion occurs when a decision-making group deceives itself about what is happening. Self-delusion is part of the pathology of 'groupthink'; this was evident among NATO leaders in terms of both ends (*jus ad bellum*) and means (*jus in bello*).

The allies claimed that they stood on the moral high ground. This was self-deception because their action was both selective and illegal. The former is particularly significant here, being an issue of ethics, not law: one surely cannot claim the moral high ground if one's moral reach is selective. Note here humanitarian disasters where the West also had good cause to act, and reasonable capabilities, but did not. Western governments do not 'do something' if there are serious costs, be they commercial (Indonesia/East Timor) or strategic (Turkey/the Kurds). The West's knee-jerk defence of selectivity asserts: 'Because you cannot do good everywhere does not mean that you should not do good somewhere'. This is a consequentialist defence of a *particular* action, not a principled defence of *one's sense of moral duty*. It merely says that on a particular occasion one acted *in accordance with* humanitarian objectives; not that as a matter of principle one acts *out of respect* for them.

Second, when it comes to *jus in bello*, we should not be deceived by surface impressions. The allies did try to fight according to the laws of war, not least because it might be politically beneficial in terms of the attitudes of wavering watchers. But it does not follow that the ends are just, because the means attempt to be. We are mistaken if we think that because we are fighting carefully, with discrimination, that we therefore have justice on our side. Furthermore, fighting with discrimination is easier when one has all the technical and economic resources, and strategic advantages; when the enemy cannot fight back; when one has no soldiers fighting and dying in the front line; and when one's civilians are not under attack. This is the war-fighting of the 'culture of contentment', whose beneficiaries invariably mistake virtue for good luck.

Hypocrisy and the lack of commitment among the G9 to building a global Just Peace contradicts the story our governments tell themselves, and us, about their humanitarian sensibilities and moral imaginations. The lives of the world's poor tell a different story. Just War is another deception.

*9. Just Wars perpetuate human wrongs.* The claim to be motivated by humanitarian impulses, I believe, necessarily implies a commitment to a universalist perspective. Humanitarianism has to be universalist, though there may be contingent reasons why action is not taken in particular cases. Power differentials, for example, might be overwhelming. When governments do not act when human rights are being massively abused, we accept that national interests are determining; I think there is good reason to think the same when they selectively do act and claim that humanitarian motives are decisive. If there were selfish reasons why the West did not act during the genocides in East Timor and Rwanda, then is it not reasonable to look for selfish motives when the West does intervene, as in Kosovo?

Just War thinking is yet another example of the way Western elites connive in perpetuating human wrongs by always privileging the victims of politics over the victims of economics. In this way the humanitarian war over Kosovo again revealed a selective moral imagination. If saving the lives of threatened people was their aim, then the rich governments of NATO could have saved far more by shifting resources away from military spending and the victims of Milosevic's politics, towards the south and the victims of Western-dominated economics. But while fighting a Just War burnishes the self-image, redistribution is a threat.

The willingness to engage in a Just War shows a concern for political victims (albeit selective) which the Washington Consensus does not reveal for economic victims. Cruise-missile humanitarianism is a psychological and material distraction from doing more to alleviate what is still the biggest division between people(s), that between the haves and have-nots.

The NATO allies could have helped others, elsewhere, but they did not. The bottom line is that if governments are not passably consistent when confronted by humanitarian disasters, their claim to be humanitarian crusaders in any circumstances is compromised. This selective morality is another version of ethic cleansing.

*10. Just Wars legitimise war.* NATO chose not to call its armed conflict with Milosevic's regime a 'war' for a mixture of propaganda and legalistic reasons, but by any sensible definition it was a war, albeit a particularly one-sided encounter. Words matter, but so does matter: a war by any other name hurts as much.

The fundamental flaw, left to the last, is that at the heart of the Just War tradition is the idea of war in some circumstances being 'just'. Following Kant, I want to argue that all wars should be regarded as wrong, though particular wars can be regarded as necessary or excusable.[2] Kant hated war, but believed that a pacifist position was unrealistic in the world of states then existing and in the 'self-incurred immaturity' of human society. But he did not believe this situation need last forever. War for him was not an inevitable feature of human life; it was a choice. Consequently he rejected those theories of international relations – such as the doctrine of Just War or the Grotian international society position – that accepted war as a fatal necessity. War will remain central to human history, he argued, as long as we keep choosing it. We could choose for it to be different, based on common reason, and develop a set of global social relations in which the conditions of civil society operate. Until this new stage has been reached, Kant believed that war might sometimes be necessary, but should never be legitimised.

Whatever else it did, NATO's campaign has helped keep alive the idea of the legitimacy of war. Indeed, the casualty-free victory (for NATO) probably enhanced the acceptability of such wars as an instrument of politics. On ethical grounds, I believe that outsiders have a duty to respond to massive violations of human rights; they should 'do something', but undertaking actions that legitimise war is not one of them. The refugees could have been cared for. The resources spent on military missions could have been used to improve the prospects for human security generally. Asylum-seekers to the West and the needy elsewhere could have been treated more humanely. Diplomacy could

324 *The Kosovo Tragedy*

have engaged with creating a security community in south-eastern Europe. The verdict of the UN could have been respected. For Kant, choices about war should be made in relation to his belief that creating a world-wide legal order should be at the basis for actions; NATO did not choose the unambiguously legal route. A Just War was not fought against the apartheid South African state, and need not have been in the Balkans. The construction of a human rights culture globally requires outsiders to do something in the face of human disasters, but it does not require making war.

It is a mistake to describe any war as just. Reviving the Just War tradition for the twenty-first century, as in seeking to use its criteria to assess a war, represents the legitimisation of a practice the world needs to marginalise. The presumption should always be against war, both in general and in particular, though as an instrument of politics it cannot yet be ruled out. War can be necessary or excusable; it is such when it is fought clearly in self-defence or with the endorsement of the UN Security Council. This is not perfect, but it the best that can be done at this stage of world society. To do other is to continue to legitimise war, and all that goes with it, at all levels of human society: from nuclear strategies that threaten environmental and human catastrophe, through the opportunity costs created by militarised economies, to the daily realities of domestic violence perpetuated by macho images of man-the-warrior.

NOTES

1. Donald A. Wells, 'How Much Can the "Just War" Justify?', *Journal of Philosophy*, Vol.66 (23), December 1969, pp.819–29. On the 'just deterrent', see Rev. Richard Harries (ed.), *What Hope in an Armed World?* (London: Pickering and Inglis, 1982) p.108, and his 'In search of a just deterrent', *The Times*, 1 Mar. 1984.
2. See Howard Williams and Ken Booth, 'Kant: Theorist beyond Limits', pp.71–98 in Ian Clark and Iver B. Neumann (eds), *Classical Theories of International Relations* (London: Macmillan, 1996).

# 'Humanitarian Wars', Realist Geopolitics and Genocidal Practices: 'Saving the Kosovars'

## RICHARD FALK

### GEOPOLITICS AFTER THE COLD WAR

The Cold War was generally interpreted as an encounter between nuclear superpowers that led opposed alliances and sustained their respective identities by reference to antagonistic ideologies. Such an image of the global setting lent support to the argument that international politics could be best understood from a perspective of bipolarity. Since the end of the Cold War a decade ago, and the collapse of the Soviet Union two years later, it is more difficult to find an illuminating image to capture the essence of world order. The two main claimants have been 'globalization' and 'unipolarity'. Neither image helps us grasp the changing role of the sovereign state nor the preoccupation during the 1990s with intra-state violence and conflict, a class of instances that Mary Kaldor has helpfully dubbed 'new wars'.

Partly these concerns reflect a perceived threat to world order that derives from unexpected sources in recent years. The main challenges are associated with the dynamics of 'the weak state' unable to sustain order within its territorial boundaries rather than with the traditional focus of international relations, the expansionist machinations of 'the strong state'. These latter concerns seem increasingly anachronistic.

It is also necessary to take account of an array of normative issues (moral and legal) that have been foregrounded by the socialist collapse. The West, and the United States in particular, had relied on its supposed normative superiority to mobilise support at home and abroad during the Cold War, especially throughout the 1980s endgame. By associating the Soviet 'other' with 'the evil empire' it was inevitable that Americans would project themselves as 'the virtuous empire'. Not only was this surge of Manicheanism congenial with the preferred modality of the binary way that the Western mind works, but it lent itself to justifying recourse to violence in a variety of international situations, as well as to promoting capitalism as the wave of the future *à la* Fukuyama. This sense of a Lockean self came to shape the identity of many Americans, providing the foundation for their persisting activism in a world that now lacked the geopolitical convenience of a strategic enemy. The most ardent warriors of the Cold War era are continuing to spend most of their waking hours searching for a new enemy worthy of geopolitcal stature. In sequence, first Japan, then Islam, international terrorism and 'the rogue states', and most recently China have each been trotted out before the public as worthy adversaries. Fortunately, the casting has not been able to produce a credible enemy, at least not yet. In the absence of an enemy, the case on behalf of international force poses a political and conceptual challenge for liberals and realists alike.

At this point this central geopolitical puzzle remains unsolved: how to validate the projection of American military power in the aftermath of the Cold War. What is worth fighting for in such a world? The Gulf War provided a partial response: it is worth fighting for oil, nonproliferation, and the stability of the Middle East, and further, it is possible to translate military superiority into political outcomes (the reversal of the Iraqi conquest of Kuwait, and the elimination of Iraq as a regional threat) at a minimal cost in casualties. But Saddam Hussein's aggression was an anomaly for the 1990s, an *international* war of expansion that seriously threatened major interests of regional and global actors. Such a luxury was unlikely to recur soon!

The emergent challenge associated with the breakdown of domestic public order of weak states could not often validate an international response by invoking traditional realist justifications. Something else was needed. Into such a strategic vacuum entered a range of humanitarian concerns, some genuine, others suspect. The process got started in the form of 'humanitarian peacekeeping' under United Nations auspices, backed by a Security Council consensus. Somalia came first, then Bosnia. Both ended in failure, as did the 1994 non-response to large-scale genocide in Rwanda. What went wrong? Whatever the auspices, interventionary undertakings with political objectives are likely to be confronted by violent resistance if perceived by indigenous political factions to be helping their domestic adversary. In other words, in Somalia what started out in 1991 as a humanitarian operation to overcome famine, disease and chaos became in its second phase an effort to establish political order in a partisan manner, and this immediately engendered indigenous violent resistance to the UN presence.

In Bosnia, the humanitarian mission was situated in the midst of an ethnic cleansing campaign of atrocity that could not simultaneously be both impartial as to the conflict and effective in protecting the civilian targets of abuse. The failure of the UN presence to protect Bosnian civilians even at the 'safe haven' of Srebrenica has now been acknowledged in a detailed UN report. It was not only the complicity of the UN with the agents of humanitarian catastrophe, but it was the unwillingness of the members of the Security Council to provide the UN with the resources required to carry out its assigned mission. There was both a failure of political will and a consensus between the permanent members that was so thin that it could be maintained only so long as it was kept ineffectual in relation to the play of forces at work.

In Rwanda, coming a year after the backlash in Somalia, the humanitarian urgency prompted only the most minimal response at a time when even a relatively minor effort might have saved hundreds of thousands of lives. There was ample warning of the Hutu plan to commit mass genocide, and good reason to believe that a timely UN augmented response could have made a difference. Again, the UN failure reflected the refusal of the major states, especially the United States in this instance, to take the risks of engagement in Rwanda. The memory of the breakdown of the Somalia undertaking was too fresh in Washington to risk some sort of repetition in Rwanda where no strategic interests existed.

There are several factors present. The global media as actor, calling selective attention to humanitarian catastrophes in a manner that either highlighted or backgrounded a given situation, influenced the behaviour of key governments. Further, the unipolar structure of world order, especially with respect to the logistics of long-distance diplomacy, has meant that the outlook of the US Government had a decisive influence on what was undertaken, and how. And finally, the espousal of international human rights and democracy as major global agenda items meant that the idea of territorial sovereignty, so central to Westphalian notions of statecraft and written into the UN Charter, were being significantly eroded. Part of the social contract between the UN and its member states was that state/society relations were not subject to UN intervention unless the Security Council concluded that the situation posed a serious threat to *international* peace and security. Such a development made it *conceptually* more difficult for governments to defend the position that severe violations of the basic rights of their own citizenry were only of domestic concern. But it also raised understandable anxieties on the part of countries that were sensitive to the colonial legacy and were suspicious about the genuineness of humanitarian claims as being post-colonial pretexts for renewed Western intervention in their internal affairs. Such suspicions were accentuated by the manner in which the United States exerted an overbearing influence in the Security Council, as manifested especially in the Gulf War setting. The domestic jurisdiction limitation on the UN role in peace and security provided a major source of protection and reassurance for countries without a right of veto, an important reassurance given that most members could not expect consistent participation in, or even access to, Security Council proceedings.

There are some further structural reasons to be wary of an endorsement of humanitarian intervention well-depicted years ago in John Vincent's now classic study of the doctrine and practice of intervention as a dimension of Westphalian statecraft.[1] In brief, Vincent emphasises the absence of impartial sources of assessment in relation to the facts in issue that leads to self-serving interpretations. It might also be stressed that governments cannot be trusted with respect to their public justifications for recourse to international force, tending to stress moral motivations and to conceal their more selfish strategic goals. Such mistrust is reinforced by the extensive efforts of intervening governments to envelop their decisional processes in secrecy. This pertains particularly to hegemonic democracies that habitually disguise any self-seeking and imperialist motives for international action behind a veil of benevolence. Such a pattern of consideration is most relevant to an assessment of American-led humanitarian diplomacy, as the United States Government depends on strong public approval for its overseas military undertakings that are not clearly associated with conventional national interests. These considerations exert pressure on American leaders to base humanitarian initiatives on a convincing line of moral justification, especially when there is no longer a strategic adversary on the scene. At the same time, as we shall note in relation to Kosovo, the moralising imperative in the absence of strategic threat does not seem sufficiently compelling to justify the sacrifice of young American lives.

In the lead-up to Kosovo, then, there are a series of developments that culminated in recourse to the first 'humanitarian war'. To begin with, the perceived failure of UN humanitarian peacekeeping in relation to Somalia, Bosnia and Rwanda encouraged a search for a more effective approach to humanitarian catastrophe. Further, the acknowledgment of moral guilt by leading governments in relation to these severe instances of ethnic strife in the early 1990s, especially in the setting of former Yugoslavia, made it politically unacceptable to wait on the sidelines while a new tragedy unfolded in Kosovo. This consideration was strengthened by the extremely dirty hands of the West resulting from its earlier willingness to strike a Faustian Bargain with Milosevic as a helpful means of finding the diplomatic solution to the Bosnian War at Dayton in 1995. Such factors were given additional weight due to the American disillusionment with the United Nations that expressed itself as hostility toward the organisation by the conservative majority in the US Congress. And finally, there was a widespread sense that European unity in the 1990s could not survive a second round of ethnic cleansing within its geographic domain, which overlapped with the complementary concerns that US involvement in Europe and the viability of NATO depended upon quickly finding a new *raison d'être*.

The mention of such contextual factors is not tantamount to asserting the impossibility of humanitarian war in general, or even to discount the relevance of humanitarian concerns in shaping the international response to Serb atrocities and state terror in Kosovo during the months prior to the NATO campaign of 1999. What is being suggested, however, is the importance of not too readily accepting a humanitarian rationale for war. Paul Ricoeur's recommendation of 'an ethic of suspicion' seems especially appropriate whenever the powerful proclaim that a major use of international force is 'a humanitarian war'.

## SCEPTICISM ABOUT HUMANITARIAN CLAIMS IN KOSOVO

There are further reasons to be sceptical in relation to the actuality of the NATO response aside from the generic difficulties associated with accepting the authenticity of a humanitarian rationale for this particular war:

*The pre-war diplomacy.* One of the most important efforts of international law is to restrict uses of force to defensive modes or under UN auspices. Here, there was neither, allegedly because the Security Council was blocked by the prospect of Russian and Chinese vetoes. Under such circumstances, the claim to prevent genocide or to stop the commission of crimes against humanity is the essential basis for the legitimacy of the operation. But recourse to war even under these exceptional circumstances can only be treated as a permissible departure from normal restraints on the use of force if a maximal effort was made to achieve a diplomatic solution. The NATO countries contend that the combination of the efforts at Rambouillet and the shuttle diplomacy of Richard Holbrooke exhausted all reasonable efforts to reach an acceptable political settlement of the dispute. Critics, however, are not convinced. They wonder why the terms offered Belgrade at Rambouillet seemed so rigidly insistent on highlighting the NATO role, which could only be understood as a slap in the face of Yugoslav sovereignty. They wonder even more why the diplomacy to end the war brought to the fore more acceptable negotiators in the persons of Chernomyrdin and Ahtisaari. They wonder further why the Russians were allowed such a dominant role in the post-war peacekeeping, and why the role of NATO was virtually eclipsed by assigning the formal and fundamental post-conflict responsibility to the United Nations. It would seem that had the search for a peaceful settlement been undertaken in good faith this pattern of pre-war and post-war diplomacy would have been reversed! Without access to internal diplomatic communications and the real objectives of the main players it will be impossible to gain a conclusive view as to whether the pre-war diplomacy presupposed that a NATO bluff was enough to avert war, or that it was believed no concessions were necessary because even if the bluff did not work, Belgrade would give in after a few days of bombing. It seems likely that Milosevic, too, may have been bluffing, counting on the lack of political will and unity on the NATO side to persist, at worst, beyond a few days of bombing.

If appraised by Ricoeur's criterion, it seems impossible to conclude that NATO upheld its burden of persuasion. It is not plausible, given the available evidence, to conclude that recourse to war by NATO without a UN mandate was primarily motivated by humanitarian concerns for the Kosovars

*Conduct of the NATO War.* The exclusive reliance on air power to achieve 'victory' in a war concerning arrangements internal to a sovereign state was a novelty in the long history of warfare. The justification for such an approach was premised almost exclusively on the basis that there was insufficient political support in NATO countries for any reliance on ground troops or on strategies that could result in extensive casualties. In deference to these considerations, NATO waged a high altitude air campaign consisting of some 13,000 sorties that produced considerable 'collateral' civilian damage in Serbia and Kosovo. The civilian infrastructure in former Yugoslavia was targeted directly after the initial target list composed of military sites was exhausted after the first few days of bombing without achieving the expected response in Belgrade.

Such tactics raise further doubts about the claim of a humanitarian war. First of all, to shift the risks of casualties to the side that is being assisted, tarnishes at the very least the humanitarian dimension of the undertaking. Such an impression is strengthened by the total absence of battle casualties on the NATO side, and the estimated death of some 2,000 Kosovar and Serb civilians. Secondly, the political pressures to avoid casualties does not exempt the tactics chosen from legal and moral scrutiny. At most, it suggests that liberal democracies, given their current political culture, are unwilling to accept the costs of conducting a humanitarian war in a humanitarian manner. Further, to the extent that the tactics relied upon were in violation of the laws of war, which claim to set *minimum* guidelines for warfare to avoid excessive damage and superfluous suffering, there is a further erosion of the humanitarian pretension. Thirdly, the targeting of the civilian infrastructure of former Yugoslavia raises additional humanitarian concerns.

It does seem correct to take note of an accelerating pattern of Serb atrocities prior to the war, and the recourse to a policy of ethnic cleansing almost immediately upon the onset of the bombing campaign. The pre-war atrocities are probably best regarded at this point as expressions of state terror led by Belgrade as part of its effort to defeat the KLA insurgency rather than as a distinct plan for ethnic cleansing. The fact that the NATO bombing appeared to trigger a systematic plan guided from Belgrade to expel and terrorise the Albanian population of Kosovo as a whole does not by itself establish that the war was justified on humanitarian grounds. It also does not support the view, that even if the war was initially justified, this justification was later nullified by the Serbian reaction that appeared to worsen, at least temporarily, the humanitarian catastrophe befalling the Albanians. The relevant test concerns the real motivations and the extent to which the Serb response was or should have been anticipated. If the massive Serb terror came as a surprise, then it does not bear on the evaluation of the interventionary decision, but if foretold, then it would add further doubts to those who question the humanitarian character of the war.

*Concerns after the War.* In support of the humanitarian claim it is important to take note of the degree to which the Kosovars greeted the NATO-constituted peacekeeping forces as liberators, as well as the rapidity with which a large proportion of the refugees returned to Kosovo despite its devastated conditions.

But it is also necessary to admit the relevance of Albanian crimes of vengeance directed at the Serb and Roma minorities in Kosovo despite the KFOR occupying peacekeeping force and the United Nation UNMIK mission designed to administer the process of restoring normalcy to Kosovo. Since the international administration of Kosovo commenced, a large proportion of the Serb population has evidently felt obliged to flee from Kosovo altogether or to retreat from their homes to the northern part of the province in which there is more protection. In effect, the goals of a multiethnic Kosovo have been superseded by the post-war

The Kosovo Tragedy

predominance of the KLA and the Albanian population, and their thinly disguised intention to turn this transitional period into a process that results in total political independence for an Albanian Kosovo. The KLA goal is to avoid either the emergence of a *de facto* UN protectorate in Kosovo or the reintegration of Kosovo into the Federal Republic of Yugoslavia.


## CONCLUSION

It would be premature at this point to reach definitive conclusions about the Kosovo experience. At the same time, certain preliminary assessments can be made on the basis of what is known. In this spirit, it does not seem responsible to regard the NATO campaign as 'a humanitarian war'. The intervention did appear to terminate one instance of humanitarian catastrophe, although it seems to have given rise to a second, lesser comparable catastrophe directed at the Serbs and Roma minorities in Kosovo. To be genuinely justifiable as a humanitarian exception to the UN system governing the use of force, there needed to be a more diligent effort on the NATO side to act in good faith within the limits of international law, as well as a more convincing effort to choose war only after all reasonable diplomatic possibilities had been exhausted. Beyond this, the conduct of the war by NATO and by maintaining sanctions against Yugoslavia, the post-war diplomacy seemed punitive toward the Serbian civilian population. It was also incapable of fulfilling the proclaimed NATO/UN goals of securing a multiethnic Kosovo that remains within Serbia, although with a renewal of its autonomous status.

At the same time, a drift toward growing Serb state terror and genocide was disrupted by the intervention. No territorial or resource ambitions could be attributed to the NATO side, thereby strengthening the humanitarian claims. The Kosovar refugees 'voted' impressively in favour of the humanitarian interpretation when they returned massively and voluntarily, exhibiting fulsome gratitude to the international peacekeepers. The United Nations, while never endorsing the intervention, held back from censuring the intervention, and has even appeared to ratify the outcome by agreeing to play such a pivotal role in the post-war administration of Kosovo. Further, the willingness to respond in Kosovo definitely helped build political support for a UN humanitarian peacekeeping mission undertaken immediately thereafter for the sake of the people of East Timor.

Account should also be taken of the fact that the Kosovo intervention placed the Christian West on the side of the Albanian Muslim community and in opposition to the Christian Serbs. Such an alignment is an important refutation, at least in relation to this conflict, of Samuel Huntington's thesis that bloody conflicts in the contemporary world almost inevitably will exhibit 'a clash of civilizations'. From what has been argued above, such an alignment does not by itself establish humanitarian character of the NATO action, and is quite consistent with either a geopolitical explanation or with an analysis that suggests that the political and ideological realities in the leading NATO countries precluded a genuine humanitarian undertaking.

What seems to emerge is a complex mixed message. The prevailing ideas and the dominant actors on the global stage are not capable of humanitarian warfare if there is any perceived prospect that they might incur serious human costs in so doing. For these reasons, to the extent that genuine humanitarian considerations are involved, as they were in relation to Kosovo, any action taken is likely to be either under-funded and insufficient, or will rely on forms of interventionary violence that are themselves illegal, and anti-humanitarian. In contrast, interventions that are reinforced by sufficient political will and appropriate resources are likely to be only nominally 'humanitarian', and are better understood by reference to the strategic interests that are at stake even if these are officially downplayed or denied as the basis of action.

The precedent of a NATO war without prior Security Council authorisation has already had troublesome ramifications. The Russians, in waging their brutal war against Chechnya, have repeatedly invoked the NATO precedent, contending with a shred of plausibility that using force within one's own sovereign territory is less damaging to world order than the unilateralism of NATO's war against a foreign country. Of course, there is a crucial difference. NATO was reacting to widely reported crimes against humanity and state terror, if not ethnic cleansing. Moscow is engaged in a war of annihilation to frustrate the aspirations of the people of Chechnya to achieve political independence and self-determination in the face of a long reign of abusive rule, and only inauthentically basing its action on claims of counter-terror.

As of the year 2000, it seems structurally impossible to envision 'humanitarian wars' in the future. What is ideologically likely, and structurally possible, are humanitarian initiatives pursued as a result of transnational social pressures, abetted by global media attention. It is also reasonable to anticipate 'geopolitical interventionary wars' that are validated by reference to humanitarian concerns. Such is the prospect in a world where the normative agenda is receiving growing prominence, but the role of power is still predominantly determined by the self-help character of a state-centric world in which security policy is shaped by realist sensibilities. Such sensibilities remain ill at ease with humanitarian claims, despite recent rhetorical pretensions to the contrary, except possibly when searching for public policy justifications.

## NOTE

1. R.J. Vincent, *Nonintervention in International Order* (Princeton, NJ: Princeton University Press, 1974).

# PART SIX:

# Documents

# United Nations Convention on the Prevention and Punishment of the Crime of Genocide

Approved and proposed for signature and accession by General Assembly Resolution 260 (III) A of 9 December 1948.

Entry into force: 12 January 1951, in accordance with article XIII

The Contracting Parties,

Having considered the declaration made by the General Assembly of the United Nations in its resolution 96 (I) dated 11 December 1946 that genocide is a crime under international law, contrary to the spirit and aims of the United Nations and condemned by the civilized world;

Recognizing that at all periods of history genocide has inflicted great losses on humanity; and

Being convinced that, in order to liberate mankind from such an odious scourge, international co-operation is required;

Hereby agree as hereinafter provided.

### Article 1
The Contracting Parties confirm that genocide, whether committed in time of peace or in time of war, is a crime under international law which they undertake to prevent and to punish.

### Article 2
In the present Convention, genocide means any of the following acts committed with intent to destroy, in whole or in part, a national, ethnical, racial or religious group, as such:
(a) Killing members of the group;
(b) Causing serious bodily or mental harm to members of the group;
(c) Deliberately inflicting on the group conditions of life calculated to bring about its physical destruction in whole or in part;
(d) Imposing measures intended to prevent births within the group;
(e) Forcibly transferring children of the group to another group.

**Article 3**

The following acts shall be punishable:

(a) Genocide;

(b) Conspiracy to commit genocide;

(c) Direct and public incitement to commit genocide;

(d) Attempt to commit genocide;

(e) Complicity in genocide.

**Article 4**

Persons committing genocide or any of the other acts enumerated in Article 3 shall be punished, whether they are constitutionally responsible rulers, public officials or private individuals.

**Article 5**

The Contracting Parties undertake to enact, in accordance with their respective Constitutions, the necessary legislation to give effect to the provisions of the present Convention and, in particular, to provide effective penalties for persons guilty of genocide or any of the other acts enumerated in Article 3.

**Article 6**

Persons charged with genocide or any of the other acts enumerated in Article 3 shall be tried by a competent tribunal of the State in the territory of which the act was committed, or by such international penal tribunal as may have jurisdiction with respect to those Contracting Parties which shall have accepted its jurisdiction.

**Article 7**

Genocide and the other acts enumerated in Article 3 shall not be considered as political crimes for the purpose of extradition.

The Contracting Parties pledge themselves in such cases to grant extradition in accordance with their laws and treaties in force.

**Article 8**

Any Contracting Party may call upon the competent organs of the United Nations to take such action under the Charter of the United Nations as they consider appropriate for the prevention and suppression of acts of genocide or any of the other acts enumerated in Article 3.

**Article 9**

Disputes between the Contracting Parties relating to the interpretation, application or fulfilment of the present Convention, including those relating to the responsibility of a State for genocide or any of the other acts enumerated in Article 3, shall be submitted to the International Court of Justice at the request of any of the parties to the dispute.

## Article 10
The present Convention, of which the Chinese, English, French, Russian and Spanish texts are equally authentic, shall bear the date of 9 December 1948.

## Article 11
The present Convention shall be open until 31 December 1949 for signature on behalf of any Member of the United Nations and of any non-member State to which an invitation to sign has been addressed by the General Assembly.

The present Convention shall be ratified, and the instruments of ratification shall be deposited with the Secretary-General of the United Nations.

After 1 January 1950, the present Convention may be acceded to on behalf of any
   Member of the United Nations and of any non-member State which has received an invitation as aforesaid.

Instruments of accession shall be deposited with the Secretary-General of the United Nations.

## Article 12
Any Contracting Party may at any time, by notification addressed to the Secretary-General of the United Nations, extend the application of the present Convention to all or any of the territories for the conduct of whose foreign relations that Contracting Party is responsible.

## Article 13
On the day when the first twenty instruments of ratification or accession have been deposited, the Secretary-General shall draw up a proces-verbal and transmit a copy of it to each Member of the United Nations and to each of the non-member States contemplated in Article 11.

The present Convention shall come into force on the ninetieth day following the date of deposit of the twentieth instrument of ratification or accession.

Any ratification or accession effected subsequent to the latter date shall become effective on the ninetieth day following the deposit of the instrument of ratification or accession.

## Article 14
The present Convention shall remain in effect for a period of ten years as from the date of its coming into force.

It shall thereafter remain in force for successive periods of five years for such Contracting Parties as have not denounced it at least six months before the expiration of the current period.

Denunciation shall be effected by a written notification addressed to the Secretary-General of the United Nations.

## Article 15
If, as a result of denunciations, the number of Parties to the present Convention

should become less than sixteen, the Convention shall cease to be in force as from the date on which the last of these denunciations shall become effective.

**Article 16**

A request for the revision of the present Convention may be made at any time by any Contracting Party by means of a notification in writing addressed to the Secretary-General.

The General Assembly shall decide upon the steps, if any, to be taken in respect of such request.

**Article 17**

The Secretary-General of the United Nations shall notify all Members of the United Nations and the non-member States contemplated in Article 11 of the following:

(a) Signatures, ratifications and accessions received in accordance with Article 11;

(b) Notifications received in accordance with Article 12;

(c) The date upon which the present Convention comes into force in accordance with Article 13;

(d) Denunciations received in accordance with Article 14;

(e) The abrogation of the Convention in accordance with Article 15;

(f) Notifications received in accordance with Article 16.

**Article 18**

The original of the present Convention shall be deposited in the archives of the United Nations.

A certified copy of the Convention shall be transmitted to all Members of the United Nations and to the non-member States contemplated in Article 11.

**Article 19**

The present Convention shall be registered by the Secretary-General of the United Nations on the date of its coming into force.

Excerpted from http://www.unhchr.ch/html/menu3/b/p_genoci.htm

# Resolution 1160 (1998)

Adopted by the Security Council at its 3868th meeting, on 31 March 1998

The Security Council,

Noting with appreciation the statements of the Foreign Ministers of France, Germany, Italy, the Russian Federation, the United Kingdom of Great Britain and Northern Ireland and the United States of America (the Contact Group) of 9 and 25 March 1998 (S/1998/223 and S/1998/272), including the proposal on a comprehensive arms embargo on the Federal Republic of Yugoslavia, including Kosovo,

Welcoming the decision of the Special Session of the Permanent Council of the Organization for Security and Cooperation in Europe (OSCE) of 11 March 1998 (S/1998/246),

Condemning the use of excessive force by Serbian police forces against civilians and peaceful demonstrators in Kosovo, as well as all acts of terrorism by the Kosovo Liberation Army or any other group or individual and all external support for terrorist activity in Kosovo, including finance, arms and training,

Noting the declaration of 18 March 1998 by the President of the Republic of Serbia on the political process in Kosovo and Metohija (S/1998/250),

Noting also the clear commitment of senior representatives of the Kosovar Albanian community to non-violence,

Noting that there has been some progress in implementing the actions indicated in the Contact Group statement of 9 March 1998, but stressing that further progress is required,

Affirming the commitment of all Member States to the sovereignty and territorial integrity of the Federal Republic of Yugoslavia,

Acting under Chapter VII of the Charter of the United Nations,

1. Calls upon the Federal Republic of Yugoslavia immediately to take the further necessary steps to achieve a political solution to the issue of Kosovo through dialogue and to implement the actions indicated in the Contact Group statements of 9 and 25 March 1998;

2. Calls also upon the Kosovar Albanian leadership to condemn all terrorist action, and emphasizes that all elements in the Kosovar Albanian community should pursue their goals by peaceful means only;

3. Underlines that the way to defeat violence and terrorism in Kosovo is for the authorities in Belgrade to offer the Kosovar Albanian community a genuine political process;

4. Calls upon the authorities in Belgrade and the leadership of the Kosovar Albanian community urgently to enter without preconditions into a meaningful dialogue on political status issues, and notes the readiness of the Contact Group to facilitate such a dialogue;

5. Agrees, without prejudging the outcome of that dialogue, with the proposal in the Contact Group statements of 9 and 25 March 1998 that the principles for a solution of the Kosovo problem should be based on the territorial integrity of the Federal Republic of Yugoslavia and should be in accordance with OSCE standards, including those set out in the Helsinki Final Act of the Conference on Security and Cooperation in Europe of 1975, and the Charter of the United Nations, and that such a solution must also take into account the rights of the Kosovar Albanians and all who live in Kosovo, and expresses its support for an enhanced status for Kosovo which would include a substantially greater degree of autonomy and meaningful self-administration;

6. Welcomes the signature on 23 March 1998 of an agreement on measures to implement the 1996 Education Agreement, calls upon all parties to ensure that its implementation proceeds smoothly and without delay according to the agreed timetable and expresses its readiness to consider measures if either party blocks implementation;

7. Expresses its support for the efforts of the OSCE for a peaceful resolution of the crisis in Kosovo, including through the Personal Representative of the Chairman-in-Office for the Federal Republic of Yugoslavia, who is also the Special Representative of the European Union, and the return of the OSCE long-term missions;

8. Decides that all States shall, for the purposes of fostering peace and stability in Kosovo, prevent the sale or supply to the Federal Republic of Yugoslavia, including Kosovo, by their nationals or from their territories or using their flag vessels and aircraft, of arms and related matériel of all types, such as weapons and ammunition, military vehicles and equipment and spare parts for the aforementioned, and shall prevent arming and training for terrorist activities there;

9. Decides to establish, in accordance with rule 28 of its provisional rules of procedure, a committee of the Security Council, consisting of all the members of the Council, to undertake the following tasks and to report on its work to the Council with its observations and recommendations:

(a) to seek from all States information regarding the action taken by them concerning the effective implementation of the prohibitions imposed by this resolution;

(b) to consider any information brought to its attention by any State concerning violations of the prohibitions imposed by this resolution and to recommend appropriate measures in response thereto;

(c) to make periodic reports to the Security Council on information submitted to it regarding alleged violations of the prohibitions imposed by this resolution;

(d) to promulgate such guidelines as may be necessary to facilitate the implementation of the prohibitions imposed by this resolution;

(e) to examine the reports submitted pursuant to paragraph 12 below;

10. Calls upon all States and all international and regional organizations to act strictly in conformity with this resolution, notwithstanding the existence of any rights granted or obligations conferred or imposed by any international agreement or of any contract entered into or any license or permit granted prior to the entry into force of the prohibitions imposed by this resolution, and stresses in this context the importance of continuing implementation of the Agreement on Subregional Arms Control signed in Florence on 14 June 1996;

11. Requests the Secretary-General to provide all necessary assistance to the committee established by paragraph 9 above and to make the necessary arrangements in the Secretariat for this purpose;

12. Requests States to report to the committee established by paragraph 9 above within 30 days of adoption of this resolution on the steps they have taken to give effect to the prohibitions imposed by this resolution;

13. Invites the OSCE to keep the Secretary-General informed on the situation in Kosovo and on measures taken by that organization in this regard;

14. Requests the Secretary-General to keep the Council regularly informed and to report on the situation in Kosovo and the implementation of this resolution no later than 30 days following the adoption of this resolution and every 30 days thereafter;

15. Further requests that the Secretary-General, in consultation with appropriate regional organizations, include in his first report recommendations for the establishment of a comprehensive regime to monitor the implementation of the prohibitions imposed by this resolution, and calls upon all States, in particular neighbouring States, to extend full cooperation in this regard;

16. Decides to review the situation on the basis of the reports of the Secretary-General, which will take into account the assessments of, inter alia, the Contact Group, the OSCE and the European Union, and decides also to reconsider the

prohibitions imposed by this resolution, including action to terminate them, following receipt of the assessment of the Secretary-General that the Government of the Federal Republic of Yugoslavia, cooperating in a constructive manner with the Contact Group, have:

(a) begun a substantive dialogue in accordance with paragraph 4 above, including the participation of an outside representative or representatives, unless any failure to do so is not because of the position of the Federal Republic of Yugoslavia or Serbian authorities;

(b) withdrawn the special police units and ceased action by the security forces affecting the civilian population;

(c) allowed access to Kosovo by humanitarian organizations as well as representatives of Contact Group and other embassies;

(d) accepted a mission by the Personal Representative of the OSCE Chairman-in-Office for the Federal Republic of Yugoslavia that would include a new and specific mandate for addressing the problems in Kosovo, as well as the return of the OSCE long-term missions;

(e) facilitated a mission to Kosovo by the United Nations High Commissioner for Human Rights;

17. Urges the Office of the Prosecutor of the International Tribunal established pursuant to resolution 827 (1993) of 25 May 1993 to begin gathering information related to the violence in Kosovo that may fall within its jurisdiction, and notes that the authorities of the Federal Republic of Yugoslavia have an obligation to cooperate with the Tribunal and that the Contact Group countries will make available to the Tribunal substantiated relevant information in their possession;

18. Affirms that concrete progress to resolve the serious political and human rights issues in Kosovo will improve the international position of the Federal Republic of Yugoslavia and prospects for normalization of its international relationships and full participation in international institutions;

19. Emphasizes that failure to make constructive progress towards the peaceful resolution of the situation in Kosovo will lead to the consideration of additional measures;

20. Decides to remain seized of the matter.

Excerpted from http://www.un.org/Docs/scres/1998/sres1160.htm

# Resolution 1199 (1998)

Adopted by the Security Council at its 3930th meeting on 23 September 1998

The Security Council,

Recalling its resolution 1160 (1998) of 31 March 1998,

Having considered the reports of the Secretary-General pursuant to that resolution, and in particular his report of 4 September 1998 (S/1998/834 and Add.1),

Noting with appreciation the statement of the Foreign Ministers of France, Germany, Italy, the Russian Federation, the United Kingdom of Great Britain and Northern Ireland and the United States of America (the Contact Group) of 12 June 1998 at the conclusion of the Contact Group's meeting with the Foreign Ministers of Canada and Japan (S/1998/567, annex), and the further statement of the Contact Group made in Bonn on 8 July 1998 (S/1998/657),

Noting also with appreciation the joint statement by the Presidents of the Russian Federation and the Federal Republic of Yugoslavia of 16 June 1998 (S/1998/526),

Noting further the communication by the Prosecutor of the International Tribunal for the Former Yugoslavia to the Contact Group on 7 July 1998, expressing the view that the situation in Kosovo represents an armed conflict within the terms of the mandate of the Tribunal,

Gravely concerned at the recent intense fighting in Kosovo and in particular the excessive and indiscriminate use of force by Serbian security forces and the Yugoslav Army which have resulted in numerous civilian casualties and, according to the estimate of the Secretary-General, the displacement of over 230,000 persons from their homes,

Deeply concerned by the flow of refugees into northern Albania, Bosnia and Herzegovina and other European countries as a result of the use of force in Kosovo, as well as by the increasing numbers of displaced persons within Kosovo, and other parts of the Federal Republic of Yugoslavia, up to 50,000 of whom the United Nations High Commissioner for Refugees has estimated are without shelter and other basic necessities,

Reaffirming the right of all refugees and displaced persons to return to their homes in safety, and underlining the responsibility of the Federal Republic of Yugoslavia for creating the conditions which allow them to do so,

Condemning all acts of violence by any party, as well as terrorism in pursuit of political goals by any group or individual, and all external support for such activities in Kosovo, including the supply of arms and training for terrorist activities in Kosovo and expressing concern at the reports of continuing violations of the prohibitions imposed by resolution 1160 (1998),

Deeply concerned by the rapid deterioration in the humanitarian situation throughout Kosovo, alarmed at the impending humanitarian catastrophe as described in the report of the Secretary-General, and emphasizing the need to prevent this from happening,

Deeply concerned also by reports of increasing violations of human rights and of international humanitarian law, and emphasizing the need to ensure that the rights of all inhabitants of Kosovo are respected,

Reaffirming the objectives of resolution 1160 (1998), in which the Council expressed support for a peaceful resolution of the Kosovo problem which would include an enhanced status for Kosovo, a substantially greater degree of autonomy, and meaningful self-administration,

Reaffirming also the commitment of all Member States to the sovereignty and territorial integrity of the Federal Republic of Yugoslavia,

Affirming that the deterioration of the situation in Kosovo, Federal Republic of Yugoslavia, constitutes a threat to peace and security in the region,

Acting under Chapter VII of the Charter of the United Nations,

1. Demands that all parties, groups and individuals immediately cease hostilities and maintain a ceasefire in Kosovo, Federal Republic of Yugoslavia, which would enhance the prospects for a meaningful dialogue between the authorities of the Federal Republic of Yugoslavia and the Kosovo Albanian leadership and reduce the risks of a humanitarian catastrophe;

2. Demands also that the authorities of the Federal Republic of Yugoslavia and the Kosovo Albanian leadership take immediate steps to improve the humanitarian situation and to avert the impending humanitarian catastrophe;

3. Calls upon the authorities in the Federal Republic of Yugoslavia and the Kosovo Albanian leadership to enter immediately into a meaningful dialogue without preconditions and with international involvement, and to a clear timetable, leading to an end of the crisis and to a negotiated political solution to the issue of Kosovo, and welcomes the current efforts aimed at facilitating such a dialogue;

4. Demands further that the Federal Republic of Yugoslavia, in addition to the measures called for under resolution 1160 (1998), implement immediately the following concrete measures towards achieving a political solution to the situation in Kosovo as contained in the Contact Group statement of 12 June 1998:
(a) cease all action by the security forces affecting the civilian population and order the withdrawal of security units used for civilian repression;
(b) enable effective and continuous international monitoring in Kosovo by the European Community Monitoring Mission and diplomatic missions accredited to the Federal Republic of Yugoslavia, including access and complete freedom

of movement of such monitors to, from and within Kosovo unimpeded by government authorities, and expeditious issuance of appropriate travel documents to international personnel contributing to the monitoring;

(c) facilitate, in agreement with the UNHCR and the International Committee of the Red Cross (ICRC), the safe return of refugees and displaced persons to their homes and allow free and unimpeded access for humanitarian organizations and supplies to Kosovo;

(d) make rapid progress to a clear timetable, in the dialogue referred to in paragraph 3 with the Kosovo Albanian community called for in resolution 1160 (1998), with the aim of agreeing confidence-building measures and finding a political solution to the problems of Kosovo;

5. Notes, in this connection, the commitments of the President of the Federal Republic of Yugoslavia, in his joint statement with the President of the Russian Federation of 16 June 1998:

(a) to resolve existing problems by political means on the basis of equality for all citizens and ethnic communities in Kosovo;

(b) not to carry out any repressive actions against the peaceful population;

(c) to provide full freedom of movement for and ensure that there will be no restrictions on representatives of foreign States and international institutions accredited to the Federal Republic of Yugoslavia monitoring the situation in Kosovo;

(d) to ensure full and unimpeded access for humanitarian organizations, the ICRC and the UNHCR, and delivery of humanitarian supplies;

(e) to facilitate the unimpeded return of refugees and displaced persons under programmes agreed with the UNHCR and the ICRC, providing State aid for the reconstruction of destroyed homes,

(f) and calls for the full implementation of these commitments;

6. Insists that the Kosovo Albanian leadership condemn all terrorist action, and emphasizes that all elements in the Kosovo Albanian community should pursue their goals by peaceful means only;

7. Recalls the obligations of all States to implement fully the prohibitions imposed by resolution 1160 (1998);

8. Endorses the steps taken to establish effective international monitoring of the situation in Kosovo, and in this connection welcomes the establishment of the Kosovo Diplomatic Observer Mission;

9. Urges States and international organizations represented in the Federal Republic of Yugoslavia to make available personnel to fulfil the responsibility of carrying out effective and continuous international monitoring in Kosovo until the objectives of this resolution and those of resolution 1160 (1998) are achieved;

10. Reminds the Federal Republic of Yugoslavia that it has the primary responsibility for the security of all diplomatic personnel accredited to the Federal Republic of Yugoslavia as well as the safety and security of all international and non-governmental humanitarian personnel in the Federal Republic of Yugoslavia and calls upon the authorities of the Federal Republic of Yugoslavia and all others concerned in the Federal Republic of Yugoslavia to take all appropriate steps to ensure that monitoring personnel performing functions under this resolution are not subject to the threat or use of force or interference of any kind;

11. Requests States to pursue all means consistent with their domestic legislation and relevant international law to prevent funds collected on their territory being used to contravene resolution 1160 (1998);

12. Calls upon Member States and others concerned to provide adequate resources for humanitarian assistance in the region and to respond promptly and generously to the United Nations Consolidated Inter-Agency Appeal for Humanitarian Assistance Related to the Kosovo Crisis;

13. Calls upon the authorities of the Federal Republic of Yugoslavia, the leaders of the Kosovo Albanian community and all others concerned to cooperate fully with the Prosecutor of the International Tribunal for the Former Yugoslavia in the investigation of possible violations within the jurisdiction of the Tribunal;

14. Underlines also the need for the authorities of the Federal Republic of Yugoslavia to bring to justice those members of the security forces who have been involved in the mistreatment of civilians and the deliberate destruction of property;

15. Requests the Secretary-General to provide regular reports to the Council as necessary on his assessment of compliance with this resolution by the authorities of the Federal Republic of Yugoslavia and all elements in the Kosovo Albanian community, including through his regular reports on compliance with resolution 1160 (1998);

16. Decides, should the concrete measures demanded in this resolution and resolution 1160 (1998) not be taken, to consider further action and additional measures to maintain or restore peace and stability in the region;

17. Decides to remain seized of the matter.

Excerpted from http://www.un.org/Docs/scres/1998/sres1199.htm

# Interim Agreement for Peace and Self-government in Kosovo

## 23 February 1999

[Edited to contain Amendment and Comprehensive Assessment, Framework Principles, Confidence-Building Measures, Principles of Democratic Self-Government in Kosovo, Human Rights and Fundamental Freedoms, National Communities, Conduct and Supervision of Elections, Conditions for Elections, Economic Issues, Institutions Implementation Mission, Other Forces, Operations and Authority of the KFOR, Status of Multi-National Military, Implementation Force, Amendment, Comprehensive Assessment, and Final Clauses]

### Article I: Amendment and Comprehensive Assessment

The Parties to the present Agreement,

Convinced of the need for a peaceful and political solution in Kosovo as a prerequisite for stability and democracy,

Determined to establish a peaceful environment in Kosovo,

Reaffirming their commitment to the Purposes and Principles of the United Nations, as well as to OSCE principles, including the Helsinki Final Act and theCharter of Paris for a new Europe,

Recalling the commitment of the international community to the sovereignty and territorial integrity of the Federal Republic of Yugoslavia,

Recalling the basic elements/principles adopted by the Contact Group at its ministerial meeting in London on 29 January 1999,

Recognizing the need for democratic self-government in Kosovo, including full participation of the members of all national communities in political decision-making,

Desiring to ensure the protection of the human rights of all persons in Kosovo, as well as the rights of the members of all national communities,

Recognizing the ongoing contribution of the OSCE to peace and stability in Kosovo,

Noting that the present Agreement has been concluded under the auspices of the members of the Contact Group and the European Union and undertaking with respect to these members and the European Union to abide by this Agreement,

Aware that full respect for the present Agreement will be central for the development of relations with European institutions,

Have agreed as follows:

FRAMEWORK

**Article I: Principles**
1. All citizens in Kosovo shall enjoy, without discrimination, the equal rights and freedoms set forth in this Agreement.

2. National communities and their members shall have additional rights specified in Chapter 1. Kosovo, Federal, and Republic authorities shall not interfere with the exercise of these additional rights. The national communities shall be legally equal as specified herein, and shall not use their additional rights to endanger the rights of other national communities or the rights of citizens, the sovereignty and territorial integrity of the Federal Republic of Yugoslavia, or the functioning of representative democratic government in Kosovo.

3. All authorities in Kosovo shall fully respect human rights, democracy, and the equality of citizens and national communities.

4. Citizens in Kosovo shall have the right to democratic self-government through legislative, executive, judicial, and other institutions established in accordance with this Agreement. They shall have the opportunity to be represented in all institutions in Kosovo. The right to democratic self-government shall include the right to participate in free and fair elections.

5. Every person in Kosovo may have access to international institutions for the protection of their rights in accordance with the procedures of such institutions.

6. The Parties accept that they will act only within their powers and responsibilities in Kosovo as specified by this Agreement. Acts outside those powers and responsibilities shall be null and void. Kosovo shall have all rights and powers set forth herein, including in particular as specified in the Constitution at Chapter 1. This Agreement shall prevail over any other legal provisions of the Parties and shall be directly applicable. The Parties shall harmonize their governing practices and documents with this Agreement.

7. The Parties agree to cooperate fully with all international organizations working in Kosovo on the implementation of this Agreement.

**Article II: Confidence-Building Measures**
*End of Use of Force*
1. Use of force in Kosovo shall cease immediately. In accordance with this Agreement, alleged violations of the cease-fire shall be reported to international observers and shall not be used to justify use of force in response.

2. The status of police and security forces in Kosovo, including withdrawal of forces, shall be governed by the terms of this Agreement. Paramilitary and irregular forces in Kosovo are incompatible with the terms of this Agreement.

*Return*
3. The Parties recognize that all persons have the right to return to their homes. Appropriate authorities shall take all measures necessary to facilitate the safe return of persons, including issuing necessary documents. All persons shall have the right to reoccupy their real property, assert their occupancy rights in state-owned property, and recover their other property and personal possessions. The Parties shall take all measures necessary to readmit returning persons to Kosovo.

4. The Parties shall cooperate fully with all efforts by the United Nations High Commissioner for Refugees, (UNHCR) and other international and non-governmental organizations concerning the repatriation and return of persons, including those organizations, monitoring of the treatment of persons following their return.

*Access for International Assistance*
5. There shall be no impediments to the normal flow of goods into Kosovo, including materials for the reconstruction of homes and structures. The Federal Republic of Yugoslavia shall not require visas, customs, or licensing for persons or things for the Implementation Mission (IM), the UNHCR, and other international organizations, as well as for non- governmental organizations working in Kosovo as determined by the Chief of the Implementation Mission (CIM).

6. All staff, whether national or international, working with international or non-governmental organizations including with the Yugoslav Red Cross, shall be allowed unrestricted access to the Kosovo population for purposes of international assistance. All persons in Kosovo shall similarly have safe, unhindered, and direct access to the staff of such organizations.

*Other Issues*
7. Federal organs shall not take any decisions that have a differential, disproportionate, injurious, or discriminatory effect on Kosovo. Such decisions, if any, shall be void with regard to Kosovo.

8. Martial law shall not be declared in Kosovo.

9. The Parties shall immediately comply with all requests for support from the implementation Mission (IM). The IM shall have its own broadcast frequencies for radio and television programming in Kosovo. The Federal Republic of Yugoslavia shall provide all necessary facilities, including frequencies for radio

communications, to all humanitarian organizations responsible for delivering aid in Kosovo.

## Detention of Combatants and Justice Issues

10. All abducted persons or other persons held without charge shall be released. The Parties shall also release and transfer in accordance with this Agreement all persons held in connection with the conflict. The Parties shall cooperate fully with the International Committee of the Red Cross (ICRC) to facilitate its work in accordance with its mandate, including ensuring full access to all such persons, irrespective of their status, wherever they might be held, for visits in accordance with the ICRC's standard operating procedures.

11. The Parties shall provide information, through tracing mechanisms of the ICRC, to families of all persons who are unaccounted for. The Parties shall cooperate fully with the ICRC and the International Commission on Missing Persons in their efforts to determine the identity, whereabouts, and fate of those unaccounted for.

12. Each Party:
(a) shall not prosecute anyone for crimes related to the conflict in Kosovo, except for persons accused of having committed serious violations of international humanitarian law. In order to facilitate transparency, the Parties shall grant access to foreign experts (including forensics experts) along with state investigators;
(b) shall grant a general amnesty for all persons already convicted of committing politically motivated crimes related to the conflict in Kosovo. This amnesty shall not apply to those properly convicted of committing serious violations of international humanitarian law at a fair and open trial conducted pursuant to international standards.

13. All Parties shall comply with their obligation to cooperate in the investigation and prosecution of serious violations of international humanitarian law.
(a) As required by United Nations Security Council resolution 827 (1993) and subsequent resolutions, the Parties shall fully cooperate with the International Criminal Tribunal for the Former Yugoslavia in its investigations and prosecutions, including complying with its requests for assistance and its orders.
(b) The Parties shall also allow complete, unimpeded, and unfettered access to international experts – including forensics experts and investigators – to investigate allegations of serious violations of international humanitarian law.

CHAPTER 1
CONSTITUTION

## Article I: Principles of Democratic Self-Government in Kosovo

1. Kosovo shall govern itself democratically through the legislative, executive, judicial, and other organs and institutions specified herein. Organs and

institutions of Kosovo shall exercise their authorities consistent with the terms of this Agreement.

2. All authorities in Kosovo shall fully respect human rights, democracy, and the equality of citizens and national communities.

3. The Federal Republic of Yugoslavia has competence in Kosovo over the following areas, except as specified elsewhere in this Agreement:
(a) territorial integrity,
(b) maintaining a common market within the Federal Republic of Yugoslavia, which power shall be exercised in a manner that does not discriminate against Kosovo,
(c) monetary policy,
(d) defense,
(e) foreign policy,
(f) customs services,
(g) federal taxation,
(h) federal elections, and
(i) other areas specified in this Agreement.

4. The Republic of Serbia shall have competence in Kosovo as specified in this Agreement, including in relation to Republic elections.

5. Citizens in Kosovo-may continue to participate in areas in which the Federal Republic of Yugoslavia and the Republic of Serbia have competence through their representation in relevant institutions, without prejudice to the exercise of competence by Kosovo authorities set forth in this Agreement.

6. With respect to Kosovo:
(a) There shall be no changes to the borders of Kosovo;
(b) Deployment and use of police and security forces shall be governed by Chapters 2 and 7 of this Agreement; and
(c) Kosovo shall have authority to conduct foreign relations within its areas of responsibility equivalent to the power provided to Republics under Article 7 of the Constitution of the Federal Republic of Yugoslavia.

### Article VI: Human Rights and Fundamental Freedoms
1. All authorities in Kosovo shall ensure internationally recognized human rights and fundamental freedoms.

2. The rights and freedoms set forth in the European Convention for the Protection of Human Rights and Fundamental Freedoms and its Protocols shall apply directly in Kosovo. Other internationally recognized human rights instruments enacted into law by the Kosovo Assembly shall also apply. These rights and freedoms shall have priority over all other law.

3. All courts, agencies, governmental institutions, and other public institutions of Kosovo or operating in relation to Kosovo shall conform to these human rights and fundamental freedoms.

**Article VII: National Communities**
1. National communities and their members shall have additional rights as set forth below in order to preserve and express their national, cultural, religious, and linguistic identities in accordance with international standards and the Helsinki Final Act. Such rights shall be exercised in conformity with human rights and fundamental freedoms.

2. Each national community may elect, through democratic means and in a manner consistent with the principles of Chapter 3 of this Agreement, institutions to administer its affairs in Kosovo.

3. The national communities shall be subject to the laws applicable in Kosovo, provided that any act or decision concerning national communities must be non-discriminatory. The Assembly shall decide upon a procedure for resolving disputes between national communities.

4. The additional rights of the national communities, acting through their democratically elected institutions, are to:
(a) preserve and protect their national, cultural, religious, and linguistic identities, including by:
  (i)   inscribing local names of towns and villages, of squares and streets, and of other topographic names in the language and alphabet of the national community in addition to signs in Albanian and Serbian, consistent with decisions about style made by the communal institutions;
  (ii)  providing information in the language and alphabet of the national community;
  (iii) providing for education and establishing educational institutions, in particular for schooling in their own language and alphabet and in national culture and history, for which relevant authorities will provide financial assistance; curricula shall reflect a spirit of tolerance between national communities and respect for the rights of members of all national communities in accordance with international standards;
  (iv)  enjoying unhindered contacts with representatives of their respective national communities, within the Federal Republic of Yugoslavia and abroad;
  (v)   using and displaying national symbols, including symbols of the Federal Republic of Yugoslavia and the Republic of Serbia;
  (vi)  protecting national traditions on family law by, if the community decides, arranging rules in the field of inheritance; family and matrimonial relations; tutorship; and adoption;

(vii)  the preservation of sites of religious, historical, or cultural importance to the national community in cooperation with other authorities;

(viii)  implementing public health and social services on a non-discriminatory basis as to citizens and national communities;

(ix)  operating religious institutions in cooperation with religious authorities; and

(x)  participating in regional and international non-governmental organizations in accordance with procedures of these organizations;

(b)  be guaranteed access to, and representation in, public broadcast media, including provisions for separate programming in relevant languages under the direction of those nominated by the respective national community on a fair and equitable basis; and

(c)  finance their activities by collecting contributions the national communities may decide to levy on members of their own communities.

5. Members of national communities shall also be individually guaranteed:

(a) the right to enjoy unhindered contacts with members of their respective national communities elsewhere in the Federal Republic of Yugoslavia and abroad;

(b) equal access to employment in public services at all levels;

(c) the right to use their languages and alphabets;

(d) the right to use and display national community symbols;

(e) the right to participate in democratic institutions that will determine the national community's exercise of the collective rights set forth in this Article; and

(f) the right to establish cultural and religious associations, for which relevant authorities will provide financial assistance.

6. Each national community and, where appropriate, their members acting individually may exercise these additional rights through Federal institutions and institutions of the Republics, in accordance with the procedures of those institutions and without prejudice to the ability of Kosovo institutions to carry out their responsibilities.

7. Every person shall have the right freely to choose to be treated or not to be treated as belonging to a national community, and no disadvantage shall result from that choice or from the exercise of the rights connected to that choice.

CHAPTER 3
CONDUCT AND SUPERVISION OF ELECTIONS

**Article I: Conditions for Elections**
1. The Parties shall ensure that conditions exist for the organization of free and fair elections, which include but are not limited to:

(a) freedom of movement for all citizens;
(b) an open and free political environment;
(c) an environment conducive to the return of displaced persons;
(d) a safe and secure environment that ensures freedom of assembly, association, and expression;
(e) an electoral legal framework of rules and regulations complying with OSCE commitments, which will be implemented by a Central Election Commission, as set forth in Article III, which is representative of the population of Kosovo in terms of national communities and political parties; and
(f) free media, effectively accessible to registered political parties and candidates, and available to voters throughout Kosovo.

2. The Parties request the OSCE to certify when elections will he effective under current conditions in Kosovo, and to provide assistance to the Parties to create conditions for free and fair elections.

CHAPTER 4A
ECONOMIC ISSUES

Article I
1. The economy of Kosovo shall function in accordance with free market principles.

CHAPTER 5
IMPLEMENTATION I

Article I: Institutions Implementation Mission
1. The Parties invite the OSCE, in cooperation with the European Union, to constitute an Implementation Mission in Kosovo. All responsibilities and powers previously vested in the Kosovo Verification Mission and its Head by prior agreements shall be continued in the Implementation Mission and its Chief.

Article V: Other Forces
1. The actions of Forces in Kosovo other than KFOR, VJ, MUP, or local police forces provided for in Chapter 2 (hereinafter referred to as 'Other Forces') shall be in accordance with this Article. Upon EIF, all Other Forces in Kosovo must immediately observe the provisions of Article I, paragraph 2, Article II, paragraph 1, and Article III and in addition refrain from all hostile intent, military training and formations, organization of demonstrations, and any movement in either direction or smuggling across international borders or the boundary between Kosovo and other parts of the FRY. Furthermore, upon EIF, all Other Forces in Kosovo must publicly commit themselves to demilitarize on terms to be determined by COMKFOR, renounce violence, guarantee security of international personnel, and respect the international borders of the FRY and all terms of this Chapter.

2. Except as approved by COMKFOR, from K-Day, all other Forces in Kosovo must not carry weapons:

## CHAPTER 7
## IMPLEMENTATION II

### Article VIII: Operations and Authority of the KFOR

1. Consistent with the general obligations of Article I, the Parties understand and agree that the KFOR will deploy and operate without hindrance and with the authority to take all necessary action to help ensure compliance with this Chapter.

2. The Parties understand and agree that the KFOR shall have the right:
(a) to monitor and help ensure compliance by all Parties with this Chapter and to respond promptly to any violations and restore compliance, using military force if required. This includes necessary action to:
  (i)  enforce VJ and MUP reductions;
  (ii) enforce demilitarization of Other Forces;
  (iii) enforce restrictions on all VJ, MUP and Other Forces' activities, movement and training in Kosovo;
(b) to establish liaison arrangements with IM, and support IM as appropriate;
(c) to establish liaison arrangements with local Kosovo authorities, with Other Forces, and with FRY and Serbian civil and military authorities;
(d) to observe, monitor, and inspect any and all facilities or activities in Kosovo, including within the Border Zone, that the COMKFOR believes has or may have military capability, or are or may be associated with the employment of military or police capabilities, or are otherwise relevant to compliance with this Chapter;
(e) to require the Parties to mark and clear minefields and obstacles and to monitor their performance;
(f) to require the Parties to participate in the Joint Military Commission and its subordinate military commissions as described in Article XI.

3. The Parties understand and agree that the KFOR shall have the right to fulfill its supporting tasks, within the limits of its assigned principal tasks, its capabilities, and available resources, and as directed by the NAC, which include the following:
(a) to help create secure conditions for the conduct by others of other tasks associated with this Agreement, including free and fair elections;
(b) to assist the movement of organizations in the accomplishment of humanitarian missions;
(c) to assist international agencies in fulfilling their responsibilities in Kosovo;
(d) to observe and prevent interference with the movement of civilian populations, refugees, and displaced persons, and to respond appropriately to deliberate threat to life and person.

4. The Parties understand and agree that further directives from the NAC may establish additional duties and responsibilities for the KFOR in implementing this Chapter.

5. KFOR operations shall be governed by the following provisions:

(a) KFOR and its personnel shall have the legal status, rights, and obligations specified in Appendix 13 to this Chapter;

(b) The KFOR shall have the right to use all necessary means to ensure its full ability to communicate and shall have the right to the unrestricted use of the entire electromagnetic spectrum. In implementing this right, the KFOR shall make reasonable efforts to coordinate with the appropriate authorities of the Parties;

(c) The KFOR shall have the right to control and regulate surface traffic throughout Kosovo including the movement of the Forces of the Parties. All military training activities and movements in Kosovo must be authorized in advance by COMKFOR;

(d) The KFOR shall have complete and unimpeded freedom of movement by ground, air, and water into and throughout Kosovo. It shall in Kosovo have the right to bivouac, maneuver, billet, and utilize any areas or facilities to carry out its responsibilities as required for its support, training, and operations, with such advance notice as may be practicable. Neither the KFOR nor any of its personnel shall be liable for any damages to public or private property that they may cause in the course of duties related to the implementation of this Chapter. Roadblocks, checkpoints, or other impediments to KFOR freedom of movement shall constitute a breach of this Chapter and the violating Party shall be subject to military action by the KFOR, including the use of necessary force to ensure compliance with this Chapter.

## APPENDICES

**Appendix B: Status of Multi-National Military Implementation Force**

1. For the purposes of this Appendix, the following expressions shall have the meanings hereunder assigned to them:

(a) 'NATO' means the North Atlantic Treaty Organization (NATO), its subsidiary bodies, its military Headquarters, the NATO-led KFOR, and any elements/units forming any part of KFOR or supporting KFOR, whether or not they are from a NATO member country and whether or not they are under NATO or national command and control, when acting in furtherance of this Agreement.

(b) 'Authorities in the FRY' means appropriate authorities, whether Federal, Republic, Kosovo or other.

(c) 'NATO personnel' means the military, civilian, and contractor personnel assigned or attached to or employed by NATO, including the military, civilian, and contractor personnel from non-NATO states participating in the Operation, with the exception of personnel locally hired.

(d) 'the Operation' means the support, implementation, preparation, and participation by NATO and NATO personnel in furtherance of this Chapter.

(e) 'Military Headquarters' means any entity, whatever its denomination, consisting of or constituted in part by NATO military personnel established in order to fulfill the Operation.

(f) 'Authorities' means the appropriate responsible individual, agency, or organization of the Parties.

(g) 'Contractor personnel' means the technical experts or functional specialists whose services are required by NATO and who are in the territory of the FRY exclusively to serve NATO either in an advisory capacity in technical matters, or for the setting up, operation, or maintenance of equipment, unless they are:

(1) nationals of the FRY; or

(2) persons ordinarily resident in the FRY.

(h) 'Official use' means any use of goods purchased, or of the services received and intended for the performance of any function as required by the operation of the Headquarters.

(i) 'Facilities' means all buildings, structures, premises, and land required for conducting the operational, training, and administrative activities by NATO for the Operation as well as for accommodation-of NATO personnel.

2. Without prejudice to their privileges and immunities under this Appendix, all NATO personnel shall respect the laws applicable in the FRY, whether Federal, Republic, Kosovo, or other, insofar as compliance with those laws is compatible with the entrusted tasks/mandate and shall refrain from activities not compatible with the nature of the Operation.

3. The Parties recognize the need for expeditious departure and entry procedures for NATO personnel. Such personnel shall be exempt from passport and visa regulations and the registration requirements applicable to aliens. At all entry and exit points to/from the FRY, NATO personnel shall be permitted to enter/exit the FRY on production of a national identification (ID) card. NATO personnel shall carry identification which they may be requested to produce for the authorities in the FRY, but operations, training, and movement shall not be allowed to be impeded or delayed by such requests.

4. NATO military personnel shall normally wear uniforms, and NATO personnel may possess and carry arms if authorized to do so by their orders. The Parties shall accept as valid, without tax or fee, drivers, licenses and permits issued to NATO personnel by their respective national authorities.

5. NATO shall be permitted to display the NATO flag and/or national flags of its constituent national elements/units on any NATO uniform, means of transport, or facility.

(a) NATO shall be immune from all legal process, whether civil, administrative, or criminal.

(b) NATO personnel, under all circumstances and at all times, shall be immune from the Parties, jurisdiction in respect of any civil, administrative, criminal, or disciplinary offenses which may be committed by them in the FRY. The Parties shall assist States participating in the operation in the exercise of their jurisdiction over their own nationals.

(c) Notwithstanding the above, and with the NATO Commander's express agreement in each case, the authorities in the FRY may exceptionally exercise jurisdiction in such matters, but only in respect of Contractor personnel who are not subject to the jurisdiction of their nation of citizenship.

7. NATO personnel shall be immune from any form of arrest, investigation, or detention by the authorities in the FRY. NATO personnel erroneously arrested or detained shall immediately be turned over to NATO authorities.

8. NATO personnel shall enjoy, together with their vehicles, vessels, aircraft, and equipment, free and unrestricted passage and unimpeded access throughout the FRY including associated airspace and territorial waters. This shall include, but not be limited to, the right of bivouac, maneuver, billet, and utilization of any areas or facilities as required for support, training, and operations.

9. NATO shall be exempt from duties, taxes, and other charges and inspections and custom regulations including providing inventories or other routine customs documentation, for personnel, vehicles, vessels, aircraft, equipment, supplies, and provisions entering, exiting, or transiting the territory of the FRY in support of the Operation.

10. The authorities in the FRY shall facilitate, on a priority basis and with all appropriate means, all movement of personnel, vehicles, vessels, aircraft, equipment, or supplies, through or in the airspace, ports, airports, or roads used. No charges may be assessed against NATO for air navigation, landing, or takeoff of aircraft, whether government-owned or chartered. Similarly, no duties, dues, tolls or charges may be assessed against NATO ships, whether government-owned or chartered, for the mere entry and exit of ports. Vehicles, vessels, and aircraft used in support of the operation shall not be subject to licensing or registration requirements, nor commercial insurance.

11. NATO is granted the use of airports, roads, rails, and ports without payment of fees, duties, dues, tolls, or charges occasioned by mere use. NATO shall not, however, claim exemption from reasonable charges for specific services requested and received, but perations/movement and access shall not be allowed to be impeded pending payment for such services.

12. NATO personnel shall be exempt from taxation by the Parties on the salaries and emoluments received from NATO and on any income received from outside the FRY.

13. NATO personnel and their tangible moveable property imported into, acquired in, or exported from the FRY shall be exempt from all duties, taxes, and other charges and inspections and custom regulations.

14. NATO shall be allowed to import and to export, free of duty, taxes and other charges, such equipment, provisions, and supplies as NATO shall require for the operation, provided such goods are for the official use of NATO or for sale to NATO personnel. Goods sold shall be solely for the use of NATO personnel and not transferable to unauthorized persons.

15. The Parties recognize that the use of communications channels is necessary for the Operation. NATO shall be allowed to operate its own internal mail services. The Parties shall, upon simple request, grant all telecommunications services, including broadcast services, needed for the Operation, as determined by NATO. This shall include the right to utilize such means and services as required to assure full ability to communicate, and the right to use all of the electromagnetic spectrum for this purpose, free of cost. In implementing this right, NATO shall make every reasonable effort to coordinate with and take into account the needs and requirements of appropriate authorities in the FRY.

16. The Parties shall provide, free of cost, such public facilities as NATO shall require to prepare for and execute the Operation. The Parties shall assist NATO in obtaining, at the lowest rate, the necessary utilities, such as electricity, water, gas and other resources, as NATO shall require for the Operation.

17. NATO and NATO personnel shall be immune from claims of any sort which arise out of activities in pursuance of the operation; however, NATO will entertain claims on an ex gratia basis.

18. NATO shall be allowed to contract directly for the acquisition of goods, services, and construction from any source within and outside the FRY. Such contracts, goods, services, and construction shall not be subject to the payment of duties, taxes, or other charges. NATO may also carry out construction works with their own personnel.

19. Commercial undertakings operating in the FRY only in the service of NATO shall be exempt from local laws and regulations with respect to the terms and conditions of their employment and licensing and registration of employees, businesses, and corporations.

20. NATO may hire local personnel who on an individual basis shall remain subject to local laws and regulations with the exception of labor/employment laws. However, local personnel hired by NATO shall:
(a) be immune from legal process in respect of words spoken or written and all acts performed by them in their official capacity;

(b) be immune from national services and/or national military service obligations;

(c) be subject only to employment terms and conditions established by NATO; and

(d) be exempt from taxation on the salaries and emoluments paid to them by NATO.

21. In carrying out its authorities under this Chapter, NATO is authorized to detain individuals and, as quickly as possible, turn them over to appropriate officials.

22. NATO may, in the conduct of the Operation, have need to make improvements or modifications to certain infrastructure in the FRY, such as roads, bridges, tunnels, buildings, and utility systems. Any such improvements or modifications of a non-temporary nature shall become part of and in the same ownership as that infrastructure. Temporary improvements or modifications may be removed at the discretion of the NATO Commander, and the infrastructure returned to as near its original condition as possible, fair wear and tear excepted.

23. Failing any prior settlement, disputes with the regard to the interpretation or application of this Appendix shall be settled between NATO and the appropriate authorities in the FRY.

24. Supplementary arrangements with any of the Parties may be concluded to facilitate any details connected with the Operation.

25. The provisions of this Appendix shall remain in force until completion of the Operation or as the Parties and NATO otherwise agree.

CHAPTER 8
AMENDMENT, COMPREHENSIVE ASSESSMENT, AND FINAL CLAUSES

**Article I: Amendment and Comprehensive Assessment**
3. Three years after the entry into force of this Agreement, an international meeting shall be convened to determine a mechanism for a final settlement for Kosovo, on the basis of the will of the people, opinions of relevant authorities, each Party's efforts regarding the implementation of this Agreement, and the Helsinki Final Act, and to undertake a comprehensive assessment of the implementation of this Agreement and to consider proposals by any Party for additional measures.

Excerpted from http://www.balkanaction.org

# Proposal of the Parliament of Serbia for Self-governance in Kosovo and Metohija

Main elements of self-governance in Kosovo and Metohija
20 March 1999

## I: PRINCIPLES OF SELF-GOVERNANCE

1. Respecting the multi-ethnic content of Kosovo and Metohija, the self-governance is based on the citizen home-rule in Kosovo and Metohija and on the home-rule of the national communities.

2. Respecting the sovereignty and territorial integrity of the Federal Republic of Yugoslavia and of the Republic of Serbia, the self-governance is based on the wide authorization and rights of the organs and of the national communities in Kosovo and Metohija alongside with the authorization and rights of the federal organs and of the organs of the Republic of Serbia in Kosovo and Metohija.

3. The self-governance in Kosovo and Metohija is to be carried out through the Assembly, legislative, judicial and other organs and through institution of Kosovo and Metohija. Therefore, the names and authorization of those organs shall respect the sovereignty, territorial integrity and constitution of the Federal Republic of Yugoslavia and of the Republic of Serbia.

4. Respecting the legitimate efforts of every national community in Kosovo and Metohija to express and protect its interests, the self-governance in Kosovo and Metohija is based on the equality of all national communities and on the impossibility of imposing some interests of one community to others.

Elements of the self-governance in Kosovo and Metohija represent the basis for the Basic Act, which shall establish the status of Kosovo and Metohija within the Republic of Serbia.

Excerpted from http://www.serbia-info.com/news/1999-03/20/9890.html

# Military-Technical Agreement

9 June 1999 between the International Security Force ('KFOR') and the Governments of the Federal Republic of Yugoslavia and the Republic of Serbia

[Edited to contain General Obligations, Cessation of Hostilities, International security force ('KFOR') operations, Undertaking of demilitarisation and transformation by the UCK, and Cross-Border activity]

**Article I: General Obligations**
1. The Parties to this Agreement reaffirm the document presented by President Ahtisaari to President Milosevic and approved by the Serb Parliament and the Federal Government on June 3, 1999, to include deployment in Kosovo under UN auspices of effective international civil and security presences. The Parties further note that the UN Security Council is prepared to adopt a resolution, which has been introduced, regarding these presences.

2. The State Governmental authorities of the Federal Republic of Yugoslavia and the Republic of Serbia understand and agree that the international security force ('KFOR') will deploy following the adoption of the UNSCR referred to in paragraph 1 and operate without hindrance within Kosovo and with the authority to take all necessary action to establish and maintain a secure environment for all citizens of Kosovo and otherwise carry out its mission. They further agree to comply with all of the obligations of this Agreement and to facilitate the deployment and operation of this force.

3. The purposes of these obligations are as follows:
(a) To establish a durable cessation of hostilities, under no circumstances shall any Forces of the FRY and the Republic of Serbia enter into, reenter, or remain within the territory of Kosovo or the Ground Safety Zone (GSZ) and the Air Safety Zone (ASZ) described in paragraph 3. Article I without the prior express consent of the international security force ('KFOR') commander. Local police will be allowed to remain in the GSZ.
The above paragraph is without prejudice to the agreed return of FRY and Serbian personnel which will be the subject of a subsequent separate agreement as provided for in paragraph 6 of the document mentioned in paragraph 1 of this Article.
(b) To provide for the support and authorization of the international security force ('KFOR') and in particular to authorize the international security force ('KFOR') to take such actions as are required, including the use of necessary force, to ensure compliance with this Agreement and protection of the international security force ('KFOR'), and to contribute to a secure

environment for the international civil implementation presence, and other international organisations, agencies, and non-governmental organisations (details in Appendix B).

## Article II: Cessation of Hostilities

1. The FRY Forces shall immediately, upon entry into force (EIF) of this Agreement, refrain from committing any hostile or provocative acts of any type against any person in Kosovo and will order armed forces to cease all such activities. They shall not encourage, organise or support hostile or provocative demonstrations.

Phased Withdrawal of FRY Forces (ground): The FRY agrees to a phased withdrawal of all FRY Forces from Kosovo to locations in Serbia outside Kosovo. FRY Forces will mark and clear minefields, booby traps and obstacles. As they withdraw, FRY Forces will clear all lines of communication by removing all mines, demolitions, booby traps, obstacles and charges. They will also mark all sides of all minefields. International security forces' ('KFOR') entry and deployment into Kosovo will be synchronized. The phased withdrawal of FRY Forces from Kosovo will be in accordance with the sequence outlined below:

## B: International security force ('KFOR') operations

1. Consistent with the general obligations of the Military Technical Agreement, the State Governmental authorities of the FRY and the Republic of Serbia understand and agree that the international security force ('KFOR') will deploy and operate without hindrance within Kosovo and with the authority to take all necessary action to establish and maintain a secure environment for all citizens of Kosovo.

2. The international security force ('KFOR') commander shall have the authority, without interference or permission, to do all that he judges necessary and proper, including the use of military force, to protect the international security force ('KFOR'), the international civil implementation presence, and to carry out the responsibilities inherent in this Military Technical Agreement and the Peace Settlement which it supports.

3. The international security force ('KFOR') nor any of its personnel or staff shall be liable for any damages to public or private property that they may cause in the course of duties related to the implementation of this Agreement. The parties will agree a Status of Forces Agreement (SOFA) as soon as possible.

4. The international security force ('KFOR') shall have the right:
(a) To monitor and ensure compliance with this Agreement and to respond promptly to any violations and restore compliance, using military force if required. This includes necessary actions to:
  (i)  Enforce withdrawals of FRY forces.
  (ii) Enforce compliance following the return of selected FRY personnel to Kosovo

    (iii) Provide assistance to other international entities involved in the implementation or otherwise authorised by the UNSC.

(b)    To establish liaison arrangements with local Kosovo authorities, and with FRY/Serbian civil and military authorities.

(c)    To observe, monitor and inspect any and all facilities or activities in Kosovo that the international security force ('KFOR') commander believes has or may have military or police capability, or may be associated with the employment of military or police capabilities, or are otherwise relevant to compliance with this Agreement.

5. Notwithstanding any other provision of this Agreement, the Parties understand and agree that the international security force ('KFOR') commander has the right and is authorised to compel the removal, withdrawal, or relocation of specific Forces and weapons, and to order the cessation of any activities whenever the international security force ('KFOR') commander determines a potential threat to either the international security force ('KFOR') or its mission, or to another Party. Forces failing to redeploy, withdraw, relocate, or to cease threatening or potentially threatening activities following such a demand by the international security force ('KFOR') shall be subject to military action by the international security force ('KFOR'), including the use of necessary force, to ensure compliance.

*Note:*
1. Turkey recognises the Republic of Macedonia with its constitutional name.

### Undertaking of demilitarisation and transformation by the UCK

1. This Undertaking provides for a ceasefire by the UCK, their disengagement from the zones of conflict, subsequent demilitarisation and reintegration into civil society. In accordance with the terms of UNSCR 1244 and taking account of the obligations agreed to at Rambouillet and the public commitments mady by the Kosovar Albanian Rambouillet delegation.

2. The UCK undertake to renounce the use of force to comply with the directions of the Commander of the international security force in Kosovo (COMKFOR), and where applicable the bead of the interim civil administration for Kosovo, and to resolve peacefully any questions relating to the implementation of this undertaking.

3. The UCK agree that the International Security Presence (KFOR) and the international civil presence will continue to deploy and operate without hindrance within Kosovo and that KFOR has the authority to take all necessary action to establish and maintain a secure environment for all citizens of Kosovo and otherwise carry out its mission.

# Documents

4. The UCK agrees to comply with all of the obligations of this Undertaking and to ensure that with immediate effect all UCK forces in Kosovo and in neighbouring countries will observe the provisions of this Undertaking, will refrain from all hostile or provocative acts, hostile intent and freeze military movement in either direction across International borders or the boundary between Kosovo and other parts of the FRY, or any other actions inconsistent with the spirit of UNSCR 1244. The UCK in Kosovo agree to commit themselves publicly to demilitarise in accordance with paragraphs 22 and 23, refrain from activities which jeopardise the safety of international governmental and non-governmental personnel including KFOR, and to facilitate the deployment and operation of KFOR.

5. The purposes of this Undertaking are as follows:
(a) To establish a durable cessation of hostilities.
(b) To provide for the support and authorisation of the KFOR and in particular to authorise the KFOR to take such actions as are required, including the use of necessary force in accordance with KFOR's rules of engagement, to ensure compliance with this Undertaking and protection of the KFOR, and to contribute to a secure environment for the international civil implementation presence, and other international organisations, agencies, and non-governmental organisations and the civil populace.

6. The actions of the UCK shall be in accordance with this Undertaking. The KFOR commander in consultation, where appropriate, with the interim civil administrator will be the final authority regarding the interpretation of this Undertaking and the security aspects of the peace settlement it supports. His determinations will be binding on all parties and persons.

**Cessation of Hostilities**
8. With immediate effect on signature the UCK agrees to comply with this Undertaking and with the directions of COMKFOR. Any forces which fall to comply with this Undertaking or with the directions of COMKFOR will be liable to military action as deemed appropriate by COMKFOR.

9. With immediate effect on signature of this Undertaking all hostile acts by the UCK will cease. The UCK Chief of General Staff undertakes to issue clear and precise instructions to all units and personnel under his command, to ensure contact with the FRY force is avoided and to comply fully with the arrangements for bringing this Undertaking into effect. He will make announcements immediately following final signature of this Undertaking, which will be broadcast regularly through all appropriate channels to assist in ensuring that instructions to maintain this Undertaking reach all the forces under his command and are understood by the public in general.

10. The UCK undertakes and agrees in particular:

(a) To cease the firing of all weapons and use of explosive devices.

(b) Not to place any mines, barriers or checkpoints, nor maintain any observation posts or protective obstacles.

(c) The destruction of buildings, facilities or structures is not permitted. It shall not engage in any military, security, or training related activities, including ground or air defence operations, in or over Kosovo or GSZ, without the prior express approval of COMKFOR.

(d) Not to attack, detain or intimidate any civilians in Kosovo, nor shall they attack, confiscate or violate the property of civilians in Kosovo.

11. The UCK agrees not to conduct any reprisals, counter-attacks, or any unilateral actions in response to violations of the UNSCR 1244 and other extant agreements relating to Kosovo. This in no way denies the right of self-defence.

12. The UCK agrees not to interfere with those FRY personnel that return to Kosovo to conduct specific tasks as authorised and directed by COMKFOR.

14. Within 4 days of signature of this Undertaking :

   a. The UCK will close all fighting positions, entrenchments, and checkpoints on roads, and mark their minefields and booby traps.

   b. The UCK Chief of General Staff shall report in writing completion of the above requirement to COMKFOR and continue to provide weekly detailed written status reports until demilitarisation, as detailed in the following paragraphs, is complete.

## Cross-Border Activity

15. With immediate effect the UCK will cease the movement of armed bodies into neighbouring countries. All movement of armed bodies into Kosovo will be subject to the prior approval of COMKFOR.

# Resolution 1244 (1999)

Adopted by the Security Council at its 4011th meeting, on 10 June 1999

The Security Council,

Bearing in mind the purposes and principles of the Charter of the United Nations, and the primary responsibility of the Security Council for the maintenance of international peace and security,

Recalling its resolutions 1160 (1998) of 31 March 1998, 1199 (1998) of 23 September 1998, 1203 (1998) of 24 October 1998 and 1239 (1999) of 14 May 1999,

Regretting that there has not been full compliance with the requirements of these resolutions,

Determined to resolve the grave humanitarian situation in Kosovo, Federal Republic of Yugoslavia, and to provide for the safe and free return of all refugees and displaced persons to their homes,

Condemning all acts of violence against the Kosovo population as well as all terrorist acts by any party,

Recalling the statement made by the Secretary-General on 9 April 1999, expressing concern at the humanitarian tragedy taking place in Kosovo,

Reaffirming the right of all refugees and displaced persons to return to their homes in safety,

Recalling the jurisdiction and the mandate of the International Tribunal for the Former Yugoslavia,

Welcoming the general principles on a political solution to the Kosovo crisis adopted on 6 May 1999 (S/1999/516, annex 1 to this resolution) and welcoming also the acceptance by the Federal Republic of Yugoslavia of the principles set forth in points 1 to 9 of the paper presented in Belgrade on 2 June 1999 (S/1999/649, annex 2 to this resolution), and the Federal Republic of Yugoslavia's agreement to that paper,

Reaffirming the commitment of all Member States to the sovereignty and territorial integrity of the Federal Republic of Yugoslavia and the other States of the region, as set out in the Helsinki Final Act and annex 2,

Reaffirming the call in previous resolutions for substantial autonomy and meaningful self-administration for Kosovo,

Determining that the situation in the region continues to constitute a threat to international peace and security,

Determined to ensure the safety and security of international personnel and the implementation by all concerned of their responsibilities under the present resolution, and acting for these purposes under Chapter VII of the Charter of the United Nations,

1. Decides that a political solution to the Kosovo crisis shall be based on the general principles in annex 1 and as further elaborated in the principles and other required elements in annex 2;

2. Welcomes the acceptance by the Federal Republic of Yugoslavia of the principles and other required elements referred to in paragraph 1 above, and demands the full cooperation of the Federal Republic of Yugoslavia in their rapid implementation;

3. Demands in particular that the Federal Republic of Yugoslavia put an immediate and verifiable end to violence and repression in Kosovo, and begin and complete verifiable phased withdrawal from Kosovo of all military, police and paramilitary forces according to a rapid timetable, with which the deployment of the international security presence in Kosovo will be synchronized;

4. Confirms that after the withdrawal an agreed number of Yugoslav and Serb military and police personnel will be permitted to return to Kosovo to perform the functions in accordance with annex 2;

5. Decides on the deployment in Kosovo, under United Nations auspices, of international civil and security presences, with appropriate equipment and personnel as required, and welcomes the agreement of the Federal Republic of Yugoslavia to such presences;

6. Requests the Secretary-General to appoint, in consultation with the Security Council, a Special Representative to control the implementation of the international civil presence, and further requests the Secretary-General to instruct his Special Representative to coordinate closely with the international security presence to ensure that both presences operate towards the same goals and in a mutually supportive manner;

7. Authorizes Member States and relevant international organizations to establish the international security presence in Kosovo as set out in point 4 of annex 2 with all necessary means to fulfil its responsibilities under paragraph 9 below;

8. Affirms the need for the rapid early deployment of effective international civil and security presences to Kosovo, and demands that the parties cooperate fully in their deployment;

9. Decides that the responsibilities of the international security presence to be deployed and acting in Kosovo will include:

(a) Deterring renewed hostilities, maintaining and where necessary enforcing a ceasefire, and ensuring the withdrawal and preventing the return into Kosovo of Federal and Republic military, police and paramilitary forces, except as provided in point 6 of annex 2;

(b) Demilitarizing the Kosovo Liberation Army (KLA) and other armed Kosovo Albanian groups as required in paragraph 15 below;

(c) Establishing a secure environment in which refugees and displaced persons can return home in safety, the international civil presence can operate, a transitional administration can be established, and humanitarian aid can be delivered;

(d) Ensuring public safety and order until the international civil presence can take responsibility for this task;

(e) Supervising demining until the international civil presence can, as appropriate, take over responsibility for this task;

(f) Supporting, as appropriate, and coordinating closely with the work of the international civil presence;

(g) Conducting border monitoring duties as required;

(h) Ensuring the protection and freedom of movement of itself, the international civil presence, and other international organizations;

10. Authorizes the Secretary-General, with the assistance of relevant international organizations, to establish an international civil presence in Kosovo in order to provide an interim administration for Kosovo under which the people of Kosovo can enjoy substantial autonomy within the Federal Republic of Yugoslavia, and which will provide transitional administration while establishing and overseeing the development of provisional democratic self-governing institutions to ensure conditions for a peaceful and normal life for all inhabitants of Kosovo;

11. Decides that the main responsibilities of the international civil presence will include:

(a) Promoting the establishment, pending a final settlement, of substantial autonomy and self-government in Kosovo, taking full account of annex 2 and of the Rambouillet accords (S/1999/648);

(b) Performing basic civilian administrative functions where and as long as required;

(c) Organizing and overseeing the development of provisional institutions for democratic and autonomous self-government pending a political settlement, including the holding of elections;

(d) Transferring, as these institutions are established, its administrative responsibilities while overseeing and supporting the consolidation of Kosovo's local provisional institutions and other peace-building activities;

(e) Facilitating a political process designed to determine Kosovo's future status, taking into account the Rambouillet accords (S/1999/648);

(f) In a final stage, overseeing the transfer of authority from Kosovo's provisional institutions to institutions established under a political settlement;

(g) Supporting the reconstruction of key infrastructure and other economic reconstruction;

(h) Supporting, in coordination with international humanitarian organizations, humanitarian and disaster relief aid;

(i) Maintaining civil law and order, including establishing local police forces and meanwhile through the deployment of international police personnel to serve in Kosovo;

(j) Protecting and promoting human rights;

(k) Assuring the safe and unimpeded return of all refugees and displaced persons to their homes in Kosovo;

12. Emphasizes the need for coordinated humanitarian relief operations, and for the Federal Republic of Yugoslavia to allow unimpeded access to Kosovo by humanitarian aid organizations and to cooperate with such organizations so as to ensure the fast and effective delivery of international aid;

13. Encourages all Member States and international organizations to contribute to economic and social reconstruction as well as to the safe return of refugees and displaced persons, and emphasizes in this context the importance of convening an international donors' conference, particularly for the purposes set out in paragraph 11 (g) above, at the earliest possible date;

14. Demands full cooperation by all concerned, including the international security presence, with the International Tribunal for the Former Yugoslavia;

15. Demands that the KLA and other armed Kosovo Albanian groups end immediately all offensive actions and comply with the requirements for demilitarization as laid down by the head of the international security presence in consultation with the Special Representative of the Secretary-General;

16. Decides that the prohibitions imposed by paragraph 8 of resolution 1160 (1998) shall not apply to arms and related matériel for the use of the international civil and security presences;

17. Welcomes the work in hand in the European Union and other international organizations to develop a comprehensive approach to the economic development and stabilization of the region affected by the Kosovo crisis, including the implementation of a Stability Pact for South Eastern Europe with broad international participation in order to further the promotion of democracy, economic prosperity, stability and regional cooperation;

18. Demands that all States in the region cooperate fully in the implementation of all aspects of this resolution;

19. Decides that the international civil and security presences are established for an initial period of 12 months, to continue thereafter unless the Security Council decides otherwise;

20. Requests the Secretary-General to report to the Council at regular intervals on the implementation of this resolution, including reports from the leaderships of the international civil and security presences, the first reports to be submitted within 30 days of the adoption of this resolution;

21. Decides to remain actively seized of the matter.

**Annex 1: Statement by the Chairman on the conclusion of the meeting of the G-8 Foreign Ministers held at the Petersberg Centre on 6 May 1999**
The G-8 Foreign Ministers adopted the following general principles on the political solution to the Kosovo crisis:

Immediate and verifiable end of violence and repression in Kosovo;

Withdrawal from Kosovo of military, police and paramilitary forces;

Deployment in Kosovo of effective international civil and security presences, endorsed and adopted by the United Nations, capable of guaranteeing the achievement of the common objectives;

Establishment of an interim administration for Kosovo to be decided by the Security Council of the United Nations to ensure conditions for a peaceful and normal life for all inhabitants in Kosovo;

The safe and free return of all refugees and displaced persons and unimpeded access to Kosovo by humanitarian aid organizations;

A political process towards the establishment of an interim political framework agreement providing for a substantial self-government for Kosovo, taking full account of the Rambouillet accords and the principles of sovereignty and territorial integrity of the Federal Republic of Yugoslavia and the other countries of the region, and the demilitarization of the KLA;

Comprehensive approach to the economic development and stabilization of the crisis region.

**Annex 2**
Agreement should be reached on the following principles to move towards a resolution of the Kosovo crisis:
1. An immediate and verifiable end of violence and repression in Kosovo.

2. Verifiable withdrawal from Kosovo of all military, police and paramilitary forces according to a rapid timetable.

3. Deployment in Kosovo under United Nations auspices of effective international civil and security presences, acting as may be decided under Chapter VII of the Charter, capable of guaranteeing the achievement of common objectives.

4. The international security presence with substantial North Atlantic Treaty Organization participation must be deployed under unified command and control and authorized to establish a safe environment for all people in Kosovo and to facilitate the safe return to their homes of all displaced persons and refugees.

5. Establishment of an interim administration for Kosovo as a part of the international civil presence under which the people of Kosovo can enjoy substantial autonomy within the Federal Republic of Yugoslavia, to be decided by the Security Council of the United Nations. The interim administration to provide transitional administration while establishing and overseeing the development of provisional democratic self-governing institutions to ensure conditions for a peaceful and normal life for all inhabitants in Kosovo.

6. After withdrawal, an agreed number of Yugoslav and Serbian personnel will be permitted to return to perform the following functions:
Liaison with the international civil mission and the international security presence;
Marking/clearing minefields;
Maintaining a presence at Serb patrimonial sites;
Maintaining a presence at key border crossings.

7. Safe and free return of all refugees and displaced persons under the supervision of the Office of the United Nations High Commissioner for Refugees and unimpeded access to Kosovo by humanitarian aid organizations.

8. A political process towards the establishment of an interim political framework agreement providing for substantial self-government for Kosovo, taking full account of the Rambouillet accords and the principles of sovereignty and territorial integrity of the Federal Republic of Yugoslavia and the other countries of the region, and the demilitarization of UCK. Negotiations between the parties for a settlement should not delay or disrupt the establishment of democratic self-governing institutions.

9. A comprehensive approach to the economic development and stabilization of the crisis region. This will include the implementation of a stability pact for South-Eastern Europe with broad international participation in order to further promotion of democracy, economic prosperity, stability and regional cooperation.

10. Suspension of military activity will require acceptance of the principles set forth above in addition to agreement to other, previously identified, required elements, which are specified in the note below.1 A military-technical agreement will then be rapidly concluded that would, among other things, specify additional modalities, including the roles and functions of Yugoslav/Serb personnel in Kosovo:

*Withdrawal*
Procedures for withdrawals, including the phased, detailed schedule and delineation of a buffer area in Serbia beyond which forces will be withdrawn;

*Returning personnel*
Equipment associated with returning personnel;

Terms of reference for their functional responsibilities;

Timetable for their return;

Delineation of their geographical areas of operation;

Rules governing their relationship to the international security presence and the international civil mission.

*Notes:*
1 Other required elements:

A rapid and precise timetable for withdrawals, meaning, e.g., seven days to complete withdrawal and air defence weapons withdrawn outside a 25-kilometre mutual safety zone within 48 hours;

Return of personnel for the four functions specified above will be under the supervision of the international security presence and will be limited to a small agreed number (hundreds, not thousands);

Suspension of military activity will occur after the beginning of verifiable withdrawals;

The discussion and achievement of a military-technical agreement shall not extend the previously determined time for completion of withdrawals.

Excerpted from http://www.un.org/Docs/scres/1999/99sc1244.htm

# Notes on Contributors

Tarak Barkawi is lecturer in Strategic Studies in the Department of International Politics, University of Wales, Aberystwyth, specialising in the international dimensions of political and military sociology.

Alex J. Bellamy is lecturer in Defence Studies for King's College London Defence Studies Department, at the Joint Services Command and Staff College. His research focuses on the history and politics of the Balkans.

Ken Booth is E.H. Carr Professor of International Politics and Head of Department in the Department of International Politics, University of Wales, Aberystwyth.

Chris Brown is Professor of International Relations at the London School of Economics. He is a former Chair of the British International Studies Association.

Tim Dunne is Senior Lecturer in the Department of International Politics, University of Wales, Aberystwyth. He is Associate Editor of the *Review of International Studies*.

Richard Falk is Albert G. Milbank Professor of International Law and Practice at Princeton University. He is one of the original members of the World Order Models Project.

Colin S. Gray is Professor of International Politics and Strategic Studies at Reading University. His previous posts include President of the National Institute for Public Policy, Washington DC, and Professor of International Politics and Director of the Centre for Security Studies at the University of Hull.

**Marianne Hanson** is Senior Lecturer in the Department of Government, University of Queensland, Brisbane, Australia, specialising in the area of international security.

**Eric Herring** is lecturer in the Department of Politics, University of Bristol, specialising in international politics and security studies.

**Jasmina Husanović** has worked for national and international non-governmental organisations in Bosnia, and been active in Bosnian civil society initiatives since 1992. She is presently a research student in the Department of International Politics, University of Wales, Aberystwyth.

**Caroline Kennedy-Pipe** is Reader in Politics at the University of Durham. She is editor of *Civil Wars*, and specialises in Cold War history and international relations.

**Daniela Kroslak** is a research student in the Department of International Politics, University of Wales, Aberystwyth, working on the role of external actors in cases of genocide, especially Rwanda in 1994.

**Hilaire McCoubrey** was a Professor in the University of Hull Law School, and Director of the University's Centre for International Defence Law Studies. He was a member of various bodies concerned with international humanitarian war and the laws of armed conflict.

**Melanie McDonagh** is an Irish journalist based in London who has visited the former Yugoslavia many times. She writes for a number of papers including the *Evening Standard*.

**Ian R. Mitchell** is a former Political Advisor and Director of Implementation in the OSCE Mission to Bosnia and Herzegovina (1996–98). He is now writing a PhD in the Department of International Politics, University of Wales, Aberystwyth.

**Penny Stanley** is a former journalist who wrote a PhD on British press representations of mass rape in the Balkans; she is interested in the media and women's issues, especially women's human rights, and is currently a director of an organisation in the voluntary sector.

**John Stremlau** is Head of the Department of International Relations at the University of Witwatersrand, Johannesburg, South Africa. Previously he was an officer of the Rockefeller Foundation and Deputy Director of the Policy Planning Staff in the US State Department, and served in Bosnia.

**William G. Walker,** a US foreign service officer, was Ambassador to El Salvador (1988–92), the US Transitional Administrator in Eastern Slavonia (1997–98), and Head of the OSCE's Kosovo Verification Mission (1998–99).

**Carrie Booth Walling** is Program Coordinator for Women for Women International in Washington DC, where she manages a sponsorship programme for women in Bosnia, Kosovo, Rwanda, Nigeria and Bangladesh.

**Marc Weller** is Assistant Director of Studies, Centre of International Studies, University of Cambridge, and Director, European Centre for Minority Issues, Flensberg, Germany.

**Nicholas J. Wheeler** is Senior Lecturer in the Department of International Politics at the University of Wales, Aberystwyth, specialising in humanitarian intervention, human rights, and international security.

**Jim Whitman** lectures in the Department of Peace Studies, Bradford University. He is co-editor of the *Journal of Humanitarian Assistance*, and general editor of the Macmillan *Global Issues* series.

# Index

Abbot, Diane, 154
Aborigine societies, 31, 34, 51
Acadians, 51
Africa, 179, 296, 301, 310;
    ethnic conflict in, 297–8;
    holocaust, 38;
    Renaissance, 296;
    Southern, 19;
    West, 300
Agani, Fehmet, 293, 294
Ahtisaari, Martti, 185, 202, 232, 330
air power, 186, 307, 311, 321
Albania, 5, 36, 78, 80, 109, 122, 135,
    169, 171, 172, 173, 189, 210, 237,
    291;
    AFOR, 172;
    Ghegs;
    'Greater', 4, 226, 238, 311; 114;
    language, 107, 114
Albanian University, 107
Albright, Madeline, 226, 228, 302, 318
Alexander the Great, 48
Allen, Beverly, 74
Amnesty International, 107, 110, 117,
    118, 119, 120, 121, 233, 271
Ancient-hatreds thesis, 7
Annan Kofi, 60, 159, 236, 242
apartheid, 296
Aquinas, St. Thomas, 204
Arabs, 54
Arbour, Louise, 209
Arkan, 291
Armenia, 48, 51, 52
Arsinje, Father, 234
Assyria, 50

asylum seekers, 15, 167–70, 178, 319,
    323
asylum states, 166
Auschwitz, 32, 43
Aust, Anthony, 153
Australia, 31, 34, 51
Austria, 38, 56, 167, 168, 168, 174
Austro-Hungarian Empire, 188
Azerbaijan, 48
Aztecs, 34

Babar, Alamgir, 38
Badinter Arbitration Commission, 119
Baker, James, 300
Balkans, ix, x, 4, 6, 7, 8, 10, 11, 15, 20,
    21, 72, 88, 91, 94, 127, 132, 161, 164,
    179, 181, 240, 243, 263, 265, 266,
    269, 273, 274, 275, 276, 277, 278,
    296, 297, 299;
    geo-strategic environment, 101;
    War (1912–13), 106
Bangledesh, 71
Basher, N., 68
Bauman, Zygmunt, 27
Belarus, 129, 152
Belgium, 69
Belgrade Centre Against Sexual Violence,
    79
Bengal, 72
Berlin Wall, ix, 2
Beqaj, Behlull, 115
Biberaj, Elez, 116
biological warfare, 3
Bismarck, 315
Blace Incident, 173, 174

Blair, Tony, 9, 153, 238, 290, 297, 302, 315, 320
Blinken, Tony, 228
Bosnia and Hercegovina, ix, 1, 3, 13, 19, 28, 47, 60, 61, 74, 75, 76, 78, 81, 87, 88, 93, 99, 100, 112, 116, 117, 136; 137, 146, 167, 174, 178, 191, 208, 209, 210, 213, 220, 228, 242, 246, 247, 273, 174, 286, 290, 291, 292, 295, 298, 326, 327, 328;
  Bosnian-Croats, 93, 98;
  Bosnian-Serb army (VRS), 93;
  Council of Ministers, 96;
  democracy in, 247–55;
  Entity Armed Forces, 90;
  House of Representatives, 254;
  Inter-Entity boundary line, 88;
  Inter-Entity Legal Commission, 90;
  International Police Task Force (IPTF), 90;
  mass rape in, 72–6;
  Muslim-Croat Federation in, 88;
  Muslims, 33, 98, 255;
  Parliamentary Assembly, 96;
  Provisional Election Commission (PEC), 251, 254;
  Serbs, 33, 62, 98, 100, 203, 255;
  war in, 72, 329;
  Zone of Separation, 88
Brazil, 157
Britain, 2, 9, 35, 51, 52, 78, 133, 147, 149, 153, 156, 170, 225, 231, 289, 315, 319;
  House of Commons, 119, 153, 190;
  Kosovo Diplomatic Observer Mission (UKKDOM), 132;
  special relationship with U.S., 320
British Broadcasting Corporation (BBC), 198, 292
Brodsky, Joseph, 263
Brown, Chris, 159
Brownlie, Ian, 151
Brownmiller, Susan, 68
Bulgaria, 54
Bull, Hedley, 150, 151, 159, 160
Bullough, Vern, 68
Burundi, 47
Bush, George, 300

Cambodia, 29, 31, 35, 42, 52, 159, 177, 216
Campaign for Nuclear Disarmament (CND), 320
Campbell, David, 240
Canada, 51, 153, 155, 156
Carter, Jimmy, 290

Central Intelligence Agency (CIA), 181, 230
Chalk, Frank, 32, 33, 35
Chandler, David, 97, 247, 254, 255, 256
Charney, Israel, 31, 32
Chechnya, 3, 304, 333
Chemical warfare, 38
Chernomyrdin, Victor, 185, 202, 232, 330
China, 152, 156, 158, 160, 161, 326
Chinese Embassy in Belgrade, bombing of, 33, 193, 195, 197–8, 203, 290, 308, 317
Chomsky, Noam, 238
Churchill, Winston, 53
Civil rights, 60, 137
Civil society, 22, 160, 258, 259, 269, 270, 274
Clark, General Wesley, 128, 230, 231
Clausewitz, Carl Von, 171
Clinton, William, 2, 9, 37, 228, 297, 298, 302, 319, 320
CNN, 22, 186, 291, 296
Cohen, William, 236, 237
Cold War, 4, 14, 7, 47, 147, 149, 158, 161, 248, 296, 299, 314, 325, 326
Collateral damage, 283, 330;
  civilian casualties, 307, 308
Contact Group, 133, 225, 226, 241
Cook, Robin, 35, 132, 154, 302
Council of Europe, 254
Crimea, 54
Crimean War, 199
Croatia, 61, 73, 74, 75, 81, 87, 88, 106, 112, 116, 128, 136, 178, 208, 220, 238, 250, 256, 288, 291, 300
Cromwell, Oliver, 200
Cubrilovic, Vasa, 115, 116, 121
Curzon, Lord, 52
Cyrillic, Serbian, 114, 115
Czechoslovakia, 31

Danish Institute of International Affairs, 151, 152
Dawisha, Karen, 248
Dayton Peace Agreement (DPA), 8, 12, 13, 62, 87–101, 116, 117, 119, 127, 213, 228, 229, 240, 250, 251, 253, 254, 270, 278, 295, 319, 320;
  civil/military divide, 94–5
Dedic, Bozhana, 234
Demaci, Adem, 109
democracy, 9, 17, 56, 98, 99, 264, 272, 295, 300, 311, 328;
  versus democratization, 248–9
Dresden, 33
Dublin Convention, 168

Eagleburger, Lawrence, 300
East Pakistan, 159
East Timor, 3, 42, 47, 54, 238, 321, 322, 332
Economic sanctions, 160
El Salvador, 238
*Erga omnes*, 215–16, 217
Ethnic cleansing, ix, 1, 10, 11, 12, 13, 36,
    41, 47–64, 99, 120, 137, 174, 186,
    240, 253, 264, 319, 327;
    conflict, 137–8, 297;
    'hatreds', 7;
    polities, 9, 242;
    resistance to, 234–6
Europe, x, 9, 27, 38, 53, 133, 137, 149,
    177, 179, 189, 275, 287, 290, 295,
    296, 317;
    East, 20;
    South-East, 10, 20, 137, 249;
    West, 10, 15, 164, 167, 169, 170, 175,
    179, 189, 275, 287, 290, 295, 296,
    317
European Council on Refugees and Exiles,
    168
European Union (EU), ix, 3, 73, 87, 96,
    129, 158, 167, 172, 208, 290, 300;
    Kosovo Diplomatic Observer Mission
    (EUKOM), 132

Falklands/Malvinas Conflict (1982), 200
Fascism, 111
Federal Republic of Yugoslavia (FRY), 3, 4,
    27, 36, 62, 118, 121, 128, 132, 152,
    185, 209, 210;
    armed forces, 16
Fein, Helen, 78, 269
Finland, 185
Finnemore, Martha, 147
Fisk, Robert, 292
Fortress Europe, 167–70
France, 10, 69, 71, 133, 149, 225;
    Kosovo Diplomatic Observer Mission
    (KDOM), 132
Franck, Thomas, 151

G9, 322
Gabon, 157
Gambia, 157
General Framework Agreement for Peace
    in Bosnia and Hercegovina (GFAP), 87;
    *see Dayton Peace Agreement*
Geneva Convention, 53, 72, 165, 187,
    190, 191, 194, 200
Genocide, ix, 1, 10, 11, 12, 27–43, 50,
    62, 63, 105, 120, 138, 215, 315;
    Convention, 11, 27, 28, 30, 35, 39, 40,
    41, 105, 215, 216, 337–40;

expansionist view of, 11, 27, 32, 41;
    restrictionist view of, 11, 27, 41;
    UN definition of, 33, 35
Germany, 10, 27, 31, 32, 33, 43, 48, 52,
    53, 54, 56, 71, 132, 133, 158, 167,
    230, 296, 300
Ghandism, 5, 119, 293
Glenny, Misha, 6, 7, 75, 290
Gold, Dore, 38
Gorani Kosovars, 233, 264
Goss, Porter, 230
Great Powers, 6
Greece, 52, 54, 58, 174
Greek War of Independence, 188
Greer, Germaine, 293
Grotius, Hugo, 149, 323
*Guardian, The*, 289
Guelff, R., 190
Gulf Conflict (1980–88), 196, 200
Gulf War (1990–91), 191, 195, 198, 200,
    296, 297, 300, 326, 328
Gurr, Ted, 33

Hague Convention, 192, 193, 203
Hague Tribunal, 72, 77, 78, 81, 93
Haiti, 19, 29, 72, 172
Hannum, Hurst, 34
Harff, Barbara, 32, 33
Hawk, Davidm 34
Haxhui, Baton, 234, 237
Hayden, Robert, 62
Higgins, Rosalyn, 148, 150
Hill, Christopher, 129, 130, 132, 139,
    227
Hiroshima, 33
Hitler, Adolf, 31, 34, 35, 42, 52, 53
Hoffman, Stanley, 113
Holbrooke, Richard, 127, 128, 130, 134,
    212, 227, 329;
    talks with Milosovic, 128, 134, 138
Holocaust, 11, 27, 31, 32, 42, 52, 53, 315
Homosexuals, 53
Hostages, 165
Hoxha, Enver, 109
Human Rights;
    abuses, 17, 62, 63, 78, 136;
    culture, 11;
Human Rights Law (HRL), 165;
    implementation, 12, 71, 81, 130, 131;
    verification, 130;
    versus democratization, 246–59;
    versus humanitarianism, 164–88
Human Rights Watch, 91, 105, 118, 119,
    120, 176, 238
Humanitarian war, ix, 2, 5, 14, 18, 145,
    147, 148, 150, 151, 159, 161, 199,

204, 242, 263, 269, 277, 283–8, 289, 303, 314, 316, 320, 328;
liberal justification for, 307, 309;
unilateral, 147, 160, 161
Humanitarianism, 15, 17, 175, 186–93, 239, 240, 241, 287, 289, 310
Huntington, Samuel, 333
Hussein, Saddam, 326
Hutus, 327

Ignatieff, Michael, 99, 273
Implementation Force for Bosnia (IFOR), 88, 89, 94, 95, 213
India, 152, 157, 159, 160;
intervention in East Pakistan (1971), 150
Indonesia, 321
Intellectuals, 269
Internally Displaced Persons (IDPs), 87, 91, 168, 169
International community, 9, 92, 96, 98, 128, 130–31, 136, 157, 166, 173, 207, 229, 246, 247, 252, 253, 258, 259, 267, 271–2, 274, 319
International Court of Justice (ICJ), 148, 149, 151, 154, 220
International Criminal Court (ICC), 16, 201, 208, 209, 216, 218, 219, 220, 221
International Criminal Tribunal for the former Yugoslavia (ICTY), 39, 90, 93, 201, 207–21, 229, 292;
Kosovo Indictment, 16, 17
International Crisis Group (ICG), 94, 96, 97, 235, 247, 249, 253, 256, 267, 271
International Humanitarian Law, 165, 184–204, 210
International Law, 12, 15, 16, 36, 40, 60, 77, 81, 146, 152, 155, 165, 177, 296;
Commission, 217;
customary, 146, 148, 150
International Monetary Fund (IMF), 8
International Relations/Politics, 21, 42
International society of states, 11, 150, 160, 323;
pluralist view of, 14, 150;
solidarist view of, 14, 150
International system, 59, 214
Iranian Revolutionary Guard, 196
Iraq, 54, 56, 153, 154, 155, 171, 191, 283, 196;
and Kurds, 238
Ireland, 20, 38
*Irish Times, The*, 292
Islam, 50, 303, 326;
Western perceptions of, 75
Israel, 20, 38;

conflict with Palestinians, 32
Italy, 71, 133, 158, 167, 174, 188, 225
ITN, 291
Iztetbegovic, Alija, 112

Japan, 33, 70, 300, 326
Jashari, Adem, 120, 121
Jashari, Nazim, 121
Jevtic, Atanesije, 111
Jews, 27, 31, 35, 43, 52
Jonassohn, Kurt, 32, 33, 35
*Jus ad bellum*, 185, 201, 203, 321
*Jus cogens*, 149, 215, 217
*Jus in bello*, 165, 184, 188, 191, 201, 202, 203, 321, 322
Just War, 16, 17, 190, 202, 203, 314–24

Kaldor, Mary, 325
Kambanda, Jean, 38
Kant, Immanuel, 323, 324
Kanther, Manfred, 168
Karadzic, Radovan, 39, 93, 211
Kennet, Lord, 154
Kissinger, Henry, 227
*Koha Ditore*, 115, 234, 268
Kohl, Christine von, 110
Kosovo;
Accords, 17, 232, 241;
Albanianization of, 107;
Battle of (1389), 69;
Communist Party of, 107, 113;
Democratic Party of (LDK), 122, 235, 256, 293;
economy, 108, 112, 116–17, 119;
Executive Council of the Province, 113;
health care system, 117;
judicial system, 264, 269;
KFOR, 4, 176, 177, 185, 188, 200, 226, 232, 234, 257, 264, 270, 272, 331;
meaning of, 20–23;
Military Technical Agreement on, 232, 364–8;
Protection Corps (KPC), 233;
Provisional Government, 265;
Socialist Autonomous Province of, 113;
Transitional Council, 265
Kosovo Liberation Army/*Ushtria Climitare e Kosoves* (KLA/UCK), 8, 16, 37, 62, 78, 105, 118, 119, 120, 122, 128, 132, 134, 137, 168, 170, 184, 186, 187, 188, 200, 212, 227, 229, 232, 265, 234, 235, 239, 265, 267, 270, 294, 312, 320, 332
Kosovo Verification Mission (KVM), 13, 14, 127, 129, 130, 168, 169, 227, 238
Kosovar Albanians, 4, 7, 8, 13, 18, 36, 41,

59, 61, 78, 81, 100, 105, 106, 107, 108, 109, 11-, 11, 115, 116, 117, 118, 120, 121, 122, 161, 167, 168, 169, 170, 171, 173, 175, 177, 185, 186, 189, 197, 209, 226, 229, 230, 231, 233, 242, 235, 237, 239, 257, 266, 270, 276, 286, 296, 298, 319, 331, 332
Kosovar Serbs, 4, 110, 114, 116, 135, 233, 235, 241, 242, 257, 291, 298, 331
Kouchner, Bernard, 176, 236, 239, 255, 294, 298
Kuper, Leo, 30, 32, 33, 34, 35
Kurds, 54, 63, 159, 166, 171, 238, 321
Kuwait, 238, 326

Lake, David, 57, 58
Laughland, John, 292
League of Nations, 52, 53, 318
Lebanon, 238
Lemkin, Raphael, 27, 28, 29, 40
Levi, Primo, 43
Lewinsky, Monica, 228
Libal, Wolfgang, 110
Liberal;
  democracy, 56, 249;
  imperialism, 4;
  politics of war, 309
Lockerbie Proceedings, 220

Macedonia, 36, 135, 171, 172, 173, 174, 178, 189, 210, 238, 287, 290, 311
Malaysia, 156, 158
Malcolm, Noel, 111
Mandela, Nelson, 290, 299, 310
Mandelbaum, Michael, 284, 287
Mann, Michael, 56
Maori, 51
Martinovic, Djordje, 111, 112
Marx, Karl, 278
Matsui, General Iwane, 70
McDougal, Myers, 148
Mearsheimer, John, 250
Media, 192, 199–200, 210, 233, 239, 240, 242, 296, 333
Mertus, Julie, 109, 110
Middle East, 189, 326
Milner, Lord, 31
Milosovic, Slobodan, 1, 3, 5, 7, 8, 11, 16, 17, 27, 35, 39, 40, 48, 58, 60, 61, 78, 110, 112–18, 122, 130, 131, 134, 136, 139, 140, 149, 156, 161, 170, 171, 181, 212, 213, 226, 227, 231, 234, 239, 286, 290, 295, 297, 298, 300, 301, 308, 309, 315, 317, 329, 330;
  indictment of, 207, 209, 211
Milutinovic, Milan, 209

Mladic, Ratko, 39, 93, 211
Montenegro, 3, 78, 105, 112, 113, 171, 178, 180, 187, 230, 287
*Moralpolitik*, 19
Morocco, 71
Mundo, Fernando del, 105
Muslims, 8, 71, 75, 76, 81, 156, 176, 255
My Lai massacre, 32

Nagorno-Karabakh, 48
Naminia, 152, 156
Nanking International Relief Committee, 70
Nathan, Laurie, 297
Nationalists, 58, 71, 107, 109, 253, 272, 298, 314
Nazis, 28, 38, 48, 52, 215, 315
Near East, 68
Netherlands, The, 153, 155
Nettleton, Clive, 171
New Zealand, 51
Newton, Sir Isaac, 303
Niarchos, Catherine, 72
Nicaragua, 149, 154
Nietzsche, Friedrich, 67
Nolte, Ernst, 32
Non-Governmental Organizations (NGOs), 129, 130, 135, 139, 160, 210, 278
Non-intervention principles, 30
North Atlantic Council (NAC), 171, 226, 229
North Atlantic Treaty Organization (NATO), 3, 5, 9, 17, 63, 78, 87, 93, 94, 121, 133, 137, 151, 153, 155, 167, 178, 180, 184, 234, 242, 263, 287, 295, 296, 304, 306, 315, 316, 329, 332;
  anti-NATO reaction, 192, 237, 238, 293;
  bombing campaign against FRY, ix, 1, 2, 4, 15, 19, 27, 61, 62, 100, 145, 156, 158, 161, 164, 168, 170, 171, 175, 186, 188, 189–99, 213, 225, 241, 275, 289, 302, 307–12, 333;
  legitimacy of bombing, 14, 145–62
Northern Ireland, 10
Norway, 135
Nuremberg Charter, 53, 215
Nuremberg War Crimes Tribunal, 70, 71, 209
Nushi, Pajazit, 110

*Observer, The*, 239
Office of the High Representative (OHR), 87, 92, 94, 95, 96, 97, 98, 251, 252, 254

Ojdanic, Dragljub, 209
Omarska Camp, 74, 77
Open Broadcasting Network, 90
Operation Allied Force, 309
Operation Horseshoe, 121, 229, 230
Opinio juris, 149, 150, 154, 155, 156, 162
Organization for Security and Co-operation in Europe (OSCE), 13, 80, 87, 90, 96, 127–40, 168, 170, 176, 177, 227, 238, 246, 247, 251, 252, 253, 254, 265, 271, 289, 308;
Office for Democratic Institutions and Human Rights (ODIHR), 129;
Permanent Council, 128
Organization of Islamic States, 158
Orthodox Christians, 51
Orwell, George, 20
Ottoman Empire, 112, 149, 188
Ottoman Turks, 51, 106
Owen David, 119, 122

Pakistan, 38, 71, 72
Palestinians, 20, 32, 63, 238
Patton, General, 67
Peace-enforcement, 184
Peace Implementation Council (PIC), 132
Peacekeeping, 80, 127, 128, 285, 328
Pentagon, 296, 318
Petritsch, Ambassador, 130, 132, 139
Pictet, Jean, 190
Pilger, John, 285, 286, 292
Pol Pot, 31, 42, 52, 150, 216
Poland, 28, 53
Police violence, 108–12, 117, 119
Political Science, 42
Poplasen, Kikola, 92
Post-pessimists, 18, 276–8
Potsdam Protocols, 53
Pristina Economic Institute, 116
Propaganda, 73, 171, 193
Proposal of the Parliament of Serbia for Self-Governance in Kosovo, 363
Prostitution, 81
Protestants, 51
Public opinion, 160

Racak massacre, 121, 134, 139, 140, 210
Rambouillet Accords, 17, 121, 139, 169, 185, 202, 212, 225–8, 232, 240, 241, 257, 286, 288, 317, 329
Rankovic, Aleksander, 106, 109
Rape;
    camps, 121;
    as genocide, 40, 74;
    history of, 67–71;

of Nanking, 70;
punishing, 76–8
in war, 1, 10, 12, 68, 76, 79, 110, 111, 270;
realism, 20, 284
    Neo-classical realism, 19, 302–36
refugees, 9, 15, 18, 52, 62, 79, 100, 132, 164, 167–81, 197, 214, 291;
    legal definition, 164–5;
    NATO intervention, 170–72, 230–31;
    UN Convention on, 165
Reisman, Michael, 148
Republika Srpska, 88, 90, 91, 96, 252
Ricoeur, Paul, 329, 330
Rilindja, 115, 116
Roberts, Adam, 2, 190
Robertson, George, 35, 72, 76, 170, 233, 289
Rodley, Nigel, 151
Rogue states, 242
Romani, 42, 53, 118, 176, 178, 233, 264, 294
Rome Statute, 208, 216, 220
Romulus, King, 68
Roosevelt, Franklin, D., 53
Rosenberg, Tina, 20
Rothschild, Donald, 57, 58
Royal British Legion, 186
Rugova, Ibrahim, 5, 8, 114, 119, 120, 122, 134, 235, 265, 270, 293, 320
Rule of law, 9
Rummel, R.J., 42, 55, 56
Russia, 48, 51, 129, 133, 145, 149, 152, 156, 157, 158, 160, 161, 185, 202, 214, 225, 226, 232, 272, 290, 298, 333;
    Kosovo Diplomatic Observer Mission (KDOM), 132
Rwanda, 16, 28, 37, 54, 63, 145, 161, 177, 218, 292, 319, 322, 328;
    Criminal Court, 39;
    genocide, 30, 31, 38, 145, 171, 326, 327;
    International Criminal Tribunal, 40, 217, 220
Ryan, Cornelius, 70

Safe havens, 327
Sainovic, Nikola, 209
Santayana, George, 42
Sartre, Jean-Paul, 31
Scandinavia, 293
Scharping, Rudolf, 229, 230
Schnegen Agreement, 176
Scotland, 69
Serbia, 1, 3, 16, 56, 74, 75, 87, 105, 113, 122, 176, 178, 180, 186, 189, 190, 195, 229, 236, 250, 266, 267, 288, 302, 311, 315;

Communist Party, 108;
'cultural revolution', 110;
'Greater', 106, 228;
Ministry of Interior (MUP), 105, 117, 120, 121, 137, 231;
National Assembly, 227;
nationalism, 5, 60, 77, 81, 112, 115, 286;
Parliament, 115;
relations with Albania, 107;
Serbo-Croat language, 107
Shawcross, Sir Hartley, 40
Shelton, Henry, 236, 237
Short, Claire, 302
Sikkink, Kathryn, 147
Simpson, John, 292
Singleton, Fred, 108
Slavery, 215
Somalia, 19, 80, 146, 200, 326, 327, 328
South Africa, 10, 31, 320, 324;
lessons from, 295–301
Soviet Union, 2,9, 35, 48, 54, 56, 70, 71, 236, 325
Spain, 34, 174
*Spectator, The*, 290
Spotlight, 120
Stability Pact for South-East Europe, 273
Stabilization Force (SFOR), 88, 93, 94, 213
Stalin, Joseph, 53
Stambolic, Ivan, 112
Steinbock, Daniel, 166
Stojiljkovic, Vlajko, 209
Stolenberg, Theodore, 119
Surgical strikes, 283
Surroi, Veton, 115, 234, 237, 268
Switzerland, 37, 179
Symons, Baroness, 154

Tadic, Dusko, 77
Talbot, Strobe, 180
*Tanjug*, 109
Tanzania, 39, 159;
intervention in Uganda (1979), 150
Tatz, Colin, 32, 41, 42
Taylor, A.J.P., 315
Terrorism, 137, 184
Teson, Fernando, 148
Thaci, Hashim, 233, 237, 265, 268
Thant U, 190
Thomas, Robert, 112
*Times, The*, 199
Tito, Josip, 8, 106, 107, 108, 110
Tokyo War Crimes Trials, 70, 209
Totalitarian regimes, 55, 56
Treaty of Lausanne, 52

Trelford, Donald, 239
Trotsky, Leon, 106
Tudjman, Franjo, 112
Turkey, 51, 52, 63, 149, 176, 238;
Kurds, 238, 321;
language, 107

Uganda, 159
Ukraine, 38, 54, 106, 129
United Nations (UN); 3, 15, 37, 60, 74, 89, 87, 96, 100, 101,117, 167, 176, 179, 190, 208, 213, 214, 218, 226, 236, 256, 285, 286, 295, 310, 324, 328, 332;
Chapter VII of Charter, 145, 146, 148, 154, 156, 161;
Charter, 55, 58, 59, 145, 147, 148, 152, 155, 158, 161, 180, 184, 185, 188, 198, 217, 327;
Children's Fund (UNICEF), 117;
Commission of Experts, 48, 73;
Economic and Social Council (ECOSOC), 29, 72;
General Assembly, 29, 30, 38, 145, 148, 158, 159, 160, 161, 185, 214;
High Commissioner for Refugees (UNHCR), 15, 80, 105, 121, 135, 165, 166, 172–5, 177, 178, 179, 233, 247, 254, 271;
Interim Administration Mission in Kosovo (UNMIK), 176, 232, 235, 236, 239, 247, 255, 258, 265, 266, 271, 272;
International Police Task Force (IPTF), 94;
Law Commission, 215;
Protection Force (UNPROFOR), 190;
Security Council, 16, 48, 54, 76, 100, 127, 145, 148, 152, 155, 158, 159, 160, 173, 184, 185, 197, 202, 209, 214, 219, 220, 247, 300, 318, 324, 326, 327, 328, 329, 333;
Security Council Resolution (SCR)
SCR 1199, 153, 345–8;
SCR 1244, 232, 255;
SCR 1203, 153
United States, 3, 9, 28, 32, 42, 56, 88, 95–6, 127, 129, 133, 155, 174, 213, 218, 225, 226, 231, 238, 249, 285, 286, 296, 298, 300, 305, 318, 319, 325, 327, 328;
Congress, 95, 329;
Kosovo Diplomatic Observer Mission (USKDOM), 132
Uniting for Peace Resolution, 158, 185
Universal Declaration of Human Rights, 55, 59, 72, 165

University of Pristina, 107, 109, 114
*Uti possi dentis*, 188

Vietnam, 159;
    intervention in Cambodia (1979), 29, 50;
    War, 9, 20, 32, 305, 314
Vitora, Francisco de, 67
Vllasi, Azem, 113
Vojvodina, 112, 113

Walker, William, 238
Washington Consensus, 323
Weber, Max, 34
Weeks, J., 68
Wells, Donald, 314
West, The, 236, 265, 274, 283, 288, 316, 317, 320, 321, 325, 328;
    imperialism, 100;
    interventionism, 100
Western journalists, 28, 35, 78;
    *see media*
Westerndorp, Carlos, 97
Westphalian international system, 314, 327
White, Nigel, 156, 158

Wiesel, Elie, 42
Woodward, Susan, 95, 247
World Bank, 173
World Heath Organization, 117
World War I, 69, 80, 106, 188, 203
World War II, 10, 28, 42, 48, 53, 67, 70, 71, 106, 111, 137, 166, 188, 191, 194, 214

Yel'chenko, Volodymyr, 38
Youngs, Tim, 119
Yugoslavia, 6, 8, 16, 19, 38, 59, 76, 92, 108, 112, 167, 171, 173, 200, 286, 287, 328; 1974
    Constitution, 13, 106–8, 113, 122;
    Armed Forces, 61, 105, 119, 120, 121, 170, 209, 291, 292, 307, 308;
    Communist Party, 106, 139, 310;
    disintegration of, 7, 58, 137;
    League of Communists (LCY), 109;
    *see Federal Republic of Yugoslavia, Serbia*
Yugoslav Airlines, 168

Zagji, Gazmed, 107
Zizek, Slavoj, 265, 274, 277